Beyond Sectarianism

Beyond Sectarianism

Ambiguity, Hermeneutics, and the Formations
of Religious Identity in Islam

Tehseen Thaver

PENN

UNIVERSITY OF PENNSYLVANIA PRESS

PHILADELPHIA

Published by
University of Pennsylvania Press
Philadelphia, Pennsylvania 19104-4112
www.pennpress.org

Printed in the United States of America on acid-free paper
10 9 8 7 6 5 4 3 2 1

Hardcover ISBN: 978-1-5128-2594-7
eBook ISBN: 978-1-5128-2595-4

A catalogue record for this book is available
from the Library of Congress.

The support of my parents, Gulnoor and Ayaz Thaver, opened the door to innumerable possibilities. It is to them that I dedicate this book.

CONTENTS

NOTE ON STYLE

To facilitate the accessibility of this book beyond specialist audiences I have not included any diacritical marks except ' for *'ayn* and ' for *hamza*. All dates follow the Gregorian solar calendar.

LIST OF FIGURES

Introduction

Thinking the Question of Imami Exegesis

In the introduction to an unfinished text later titled *The Specialties of the Imams* (*Khasa'is al-A'imma*), the renowned late tenth- early eleventh-century religious scholar, poet, and historian al-Sharif al-Radi (d. 1015) writes: "the Imamate is my normative anchor, and the knot and site of my faith (*al-Imama madhhabi wa 'alayha 'aqdi wa mu'taqadi*).[1] This is an unambiguous statement in which an eleventh-century figure categorically identifies himself as an Imami Shi'i.[2] But what, exactly, did declarations of affiliation with the Imami Shi'i entail and represent at this time? How should scholars writing about religious identity today interpret and understand a declaration of this sort from a period so far removed from our own? How, for example, did al-Radi's sense of belonging to a particular religious group in tenth-century Baghdad play out in his scholarship and in his intellectual life? This book takes up these broad conceptual questions in an attempt to achieve the more specific task of complicating dominant understandings of the relationship between sectarian identity and Qur'an exegesis, or *tafsir*. I do so through a close reading of an instructive and fascinating yet less explored literary exegesis of the Qur'an: al-Sharif al-Radi's *Hermeneutical Realities in [Uncovering] the Ambiguities of Revelation*, (*Haqa'iq al-Tawil fi Mutashabih al-Tanzil*),[3] hereafter called *Haqa'iq*.[4]

Before I introduce further this text, its author, and the key questions and goals of this book, a brief word on a vexing conundrum that hovers over the study of any exegetical enterprise undertaken by a scholar connected to the Imami Shi'i tradition: the authority to interpret the Qur'an lies exclusively with the Imams or successors of Prophet Muhammad from his noble family, the last of whom, according to Twelver Shi'i doctrine, went into occultation in the tenth century. Hence, although in a state of hiding, the twelfth Imam is still regarded as the authoritative guide for the community. Where, then, after the Twelve Imams, is the normative authority of Qur'an commentaries composed by Shi'i scholars derived from? Put differently, given the flourishing tradition of Shi'i scholars like al-Radi penning commentaries on the Qur'an up until current times, with what reasoning or justification do they transgress the very limits of interpretive authority that they themselves have erected by valorizing the Twelve Imams as the exclusive interpreters of the Qur'an? In what religious capacity do Shi'i exegetes after the Twelve Imams present their oral and written interpretations of the Qur'an?

As I began my research on this project, it became apparent quite early that approaching "Twelver Shi'i Qur'an hermeneutics" as an interpretive method that corresponds to clearly defined Shi'i "beliefs," is a relatively recent formulation that reflects a particular normative ideal of what the category "Shi'i" signifies. It belongs to a discourse that regards Shi'i identity as a predetermined, predictable, unchanging entity that, under all circumstances, privileges the same historical and theological narratives. To invoke Twelver Shi'i hermeneutics is to thus ascribe to these texts a commonality on the basis of their author's sectarian affiliation, and to presuppose that the foremost determinant for their hermeneutical choices is that of sectarian orientation. This position is both conceptually and historically untenable. As religion scholar Adam Gaiser has helpfully argued in his recent critique of the category of sectarianism in the study of Islam:

> Turning to the ways that early Muslims conceptualized the religious subgroups in their midst, it is noteworthy that they tend not to use binary, tertiary, or relational terminology ("church-sect-cult" or "sect-denomination"), but rather to abstract the main groups using a singular concept. Thus, the terms *firqa/firaq*, *nihla/nihal*, *madhhab/madhahib*, and later *ta'ifa/tawa'if*, tend to evenly designate Shi'ites, Kharijites, Murji'ites, Mu'tazilites, as well as those later known under the rubric of Sunnis.[5]

To Gaiser's observation about the incongruity of the category of sectarianism in early Islam one can gainfully fold historian Ussama Makdisi's broader methodological caution about this category:

> Sunni, Shi'i, Maronite, Jewish, Armenian or Orthodox Christian identifications are not etched uniformly into the fabric of the past

and present. They are historical designations whose meanings have changed and whose salience has ebbed and flowed. At any given moment, communal identities may appear to be entirely genuine and palpable. They may be positive or negative, open-minded or insular. These identities, nevertheless, are not recovered from some container of the past that preserves an unadulterated sense of self and other. They are, instead, produced over and over again in different forms and for different reasons. They manifest only after having been riven by innumerable schisms and after having undergone repeated redefinitions throughout their long histories.[6]

Returning to the question of Shi'i Qur'an exegesis: in 2009, as part of my doctoral work, I was pursuing and seeking to understand what I earlier described as the conundrum of "Twelver Shi'i exegesis" during a research trip to Qom, Iran, one of the main centers of Twelver Shi'i learning in the world today. I asked students and scholars how they explained the thriving tradition of Imami exegesis in the absence of the Imams. The most frequent response I received to this question was that in Shi'i commentaries of the Qur'an composed after the period of the twelve appointed successors, the presence of these designated successors is ensured through the inclusion of their collected sayings and teachings. So, essentially, their response to the question of how Shi'i exegesis could continue after the twelve successors of Prophet Muhammad can be summarized as follows: the invocation and mobilization of the sayings and teachings of the Twelve Imams in the Qur'an commentaries of later exegetes confirmed the legitimacy and authority of their works. This response is telling. It illustrates how the doctrinal demand for Imami authority determines current Twelver Shi'i scholars' conceptions and articulations of the common thread that ties "Imami exegesis" together. According to these students and scholars, faithful adherence to Imami authority is not forsaken in the absence of the Imams but rather confirmed and revitalized through a hermeneutical structure that relies exclusively on their teachings. This portrayal of Imami exegesis as tradition-centered or as exclusively derived from Imami sayings is but one account of the Imami exegetical tradition. It is channeled by the concerted effort to carve an explicitly Shi'i exegetical paradigm that draws on the authority of the Imams and that could thus be distinguished along sectarian lines. But what are some other interpretive styles and normative commitments, irreducible to and not primarily animated by sectarian concerns alone, that have populated Shi'i exegetical works? This is a key question of this book.[7]

I returned to Qom some years later and, in this setting, my selection of al-Radi's Qur'an commentary for a research topic of "Twelver Shi'i exegesis" was met with disapproval. I was repeatedly advised that a better choice for my research was the work of his brother, al-Sharif al-Murtada (d. 1044); this reasoning was based on the fact that it is al-Murtada's formulations of Shi'i theological arguments that persist in centers of Twelver Shi'i learning until today. What became clear to me through these conversations was that al-Radi's Qur'an commentary is not part of the existing textual canon of Imami exegesis. While his work is not outright rejected as falling outside the fold, it is certainly not considered representative of what is understood to constitute a distinct "Twelver Shi'i hermeneutic." My objective in writing this book is not to offer a corrective by arguing for the inclusion of al-Radi's Qur'an commentary in a prescribed canon of Shi'i exegesis. Rather, I wish to highlight and offer conceptual alternatives to precisely any canonical notion of Shi'i exegesis informed primarily by a commitment to predetermined sectarian convictions. More on this point soon.

To be fair, a sectarian-driven approach to Imami exegesis is not only found among adherents within the tradition today. Rather, it is perhaps echoed in even more explicit terms in Euro-American scholarship about Shi'i exegesis, from early Orientalist writings up until the present day. What I mean by a sectarian-driven approach is this: an approach that assumes and reinforces modern sectarian binaries and assumptions in the very kinds of questions it asks of premodern actors and texts. To again quote Makdisi:

> "Sectarianism," indeed, is not simply a reflection of significant frac-
> tures in a religiously diverse society. It is also a language, an accusa-
> tion, a judgment, an imagination, and an ideological fiction that has
> been deployed by both Middle Eastern and Western nations, com-
> munities, and individuals to create modern political and ideological
> frameworks within which supposedly innate sectarian problems can
> be contained, if not overcome.[8]

In the specific context of this book, what I mean by a sectarian-driven approach to the study of Qur'an exegesis is the assumption that the exegesis and hermeneutics of scholars identified as Shi'i are exclusively the products of distinct and trademark Shi'i theological commitments and outlooks. As scholar of Islam Devin Stewart puts it in his important study, *Islamic Legal Orthodoxy: Twelver Shiite Responses to the Sunni Legal System*:

The tendency to view Shiite history and thought as a logical projection or unambiguous derivation of the theory of the imamate has shaped the study of many aspects of Shiite Islam. It has often prevented or impeded the examination of Shiite topics from other angles, despite the tremendous change in the organization of the Shiite community which occurred after the Occultation.[9]

To be clear, I draw on and am indebted to some excellent scholarship on Shi'i Qur'an commentaries, but I nonetheless find problematic the persistence of a pervasive assumption in this field that posits a neat correspondence between the sectarian identity of exegetes and their hermeneutical sensibilities. The primary concern in several Western scholarly examinations of Shi'i exegesis consists of identifying what characterizes or makes the work distinctly Shi'i.[10] So, for instance, it is often assumed that a Shi'i scholar's exegetical work must fit a certain template of what a Shi'i Qur'an commentary should look like and what it must focus on, which inevitably is assumed to be a focus on signature Shi'i doctrines, such as an emphasis on the sacrality of the Prophet's family, an anti-Sunni polemical orientation,[11] or the preponderance of a characteristically Shi'i hermeneutic, captivated by the hidden or inner meanings of the text.[12]

This book questions a sectarian-driven approach to the study of the Shi'i Qur'an commentary tradition and seeks to offer alternate theorizations and modes of inquiry. It performs this task through a close reading of al-Sharif al-Radi's Qur'an commentary, the *Haqa'iq*, a text the key features of which I will describe in considerable detail, momentarily. It is my contention that a narrow sectarian-driven approach to the study of Shi'i Qur'an commentary traditions, one that assumes perfect correspondence between sectarian identity and hermeneutics, leaves much to be explored in the vast corpus of literature that currently comes under the classification of Twelver Shi'i exegesis. The crux of the intervention I make is to present alternate readings of Muslim exegetical traditions that disrupt the imposition of a modern division of life into sectarian binaries onto a premodern world and archive that did not operate according to the logic of such sectarian divisions. My argument is not to undermine the presence and, indeed, the critical role of Imami sayings (*hadith*) in several Qur'an commentaries authored by Shi'i scholars. Moreover, certainly, several exegetical works authored by Shi'i scholars do adopt and assert an explicitly Shi'i theological position. At the same time, however, privileging such seemingly sectarian hermeneutical preferences as the most worthy aspect of discussion in Shi'i Qur'an commentaries is problematic.

While sectarian interests might be a part of Shiʻi exegetical projects, their problem spaces are not exhausted by such interests.

Through a close reading of the text, context, and key theoretical concerns showcased in al-Sharif al-Radi's Qurʾan commentary, this book makes three major arguments that are situated at the intersection of the fields of religious studies, Islamic studies, Qurʾanic studies, Shiʻi studies, and the study of Arabic language and literature. First, as I will elaborate in much further detail over the course of this introduction, modern sectarian assumptions and categorizations are often unsuitable for and are frustrated by the exegetical operations and horizons of a tenth-century figure like al-Radi. Second, al-Radi's literary Qurʾan commentary, which articulated a theory of language as a reflection of ontological reality, drew from and contributed to an emerging canon of the Arabic language constituted by the Qurʾan, pre-Islamic Arabic poetry, and the everyday speech of Arabs. And third, even as his Qurʾan commentary was informed by a confluence of multiple intellectual currents in tenth century Baghdad covering a wide range of the Muslim Humanities, the relationship of his exegesis to concurrent literary, theological, and legal traditions was too dynamic, nonlinear, and subtle to be conceptualized as a relationship of influence or absorption. The six chapters of this book that I describe in the latter half of this introduction present and try to establish these arguments by combining careful readings of al-Radi's commentary and connected texts with detailed discussions of the broader historiographic and theoretical stakes of this project. Thus, this book aims to both provide an in-depth examination of the exegetical contribution of an immensely profitable yet less studied Muslim scholar, al-Sharif al-Radi, and to rethink prominent categories of analysis like "Shiʻi Qurʾan exegesis," while offering novel and hopefully productive avenues for future research. I want to begin by elaborating the idea of sectarian-driven approaches to the study of Qurʾan exegesis and some of the major problems associated with it.

Conceptual and Historiographical Intervention:
Reframing Religious Identity

In addition to the narrowing effect on a scholar's identity, a presumed correspondence of sect and hermeneutics also presents other problems. Let me highlight three problems most relevant to the concerns of the study of "Shiʻi exegesis." First is the problem of anachronism involved in viewing the premodern world through the prism of resoundingly modern and, indeed, liberal Protestant categories like sect that replicate the colonial world religions paradigm by presuming an already agreed upon orthodoxy from which individual sects may then differ.[13] Put differently, a sectarian-driven approach to the examination of Qur'anic exegesis holds far-reaching implications for how we access the very question of religious identity in the present. The idea that sectarian identity and interpretive horizons must correspond reinforces and perpetuates a modern understanding of identity as accountable and responsible to a particular narration of its memory. It is precisely such a modern competitive imaginary of religious identity, at peace with the empiricist mechanisms and powers of the modern state, that haunts the memory of the categories "Sunni" and "Shi'i" today. Conceptually, at the heart of the term Sunni-Shi'i conflict is a conception of history as a linear unfolding of an innate antagonism between two communities with separate, distinct, and competing memory traces. And an approach toward the study of Qur'an exegesis that privileges sectarian identity as the underlying determinant of an exegete's hermeneutical choices reproduces such a competitive understanding of religious identity. Certainly, the point here is not that the Sunni-Shi'i divide is a modern invention. However, positing a relationship of neat correspondence between hermeneutics and sectarian identity is clearly indebted to a modern conception of religious identity as distinct, divisible, and readily sequestered from competing religious identities.[14]

In this book, I examine Shi'i identity as an ongoing moral argument that is invested with and divested of particular meanings and orientations in specific moments of authoritative discourse and debates. Seen this way, one would approach Shi'ism as an "embodied argument," made possible and visible in particular historical conjunctures of authoritative debates, discord, disagreement, and dissent.[15] I want to be clear that, with this argument, I do not deny the heuristic value or the existence of a Shi'i identity. This is evident from my own use of this term in this book. However, I do hold that what it stands for cannot be canonized into a predictable and predetermined entity, even if we are bound by terminology to refer to it by this name.

Turning to the second problem: a concept like "Shi'i exegesis" and, in a connected vein, sectarian framings that inform questions like "What does a Shi'i Qur'an commentary look like?" reinforce and normalize the minoritized status of the Shi'i tradition by uncritically replicating a question-and-answer space[16] governed by and grounded in majoritarian sensibilities. After all, it is not a coincidence that while so much of the field of Shi'i Qur'an commentaries is oriented by the force of questions like "What are the characteristic features of a Shiʿi Qurʾan commentary?" that same question is rarely asked or would sound rather odd if posed in the context of Sunni Qurʾan commentaries.

Third, and perhaps most importantly, the major problem with the imposition of predetermined categories and questions inflected by modern assumptions and desires is that they foreclose a range of questions and possibilities that one can explore and bring into view by closely navigating the internal logics of a discursive tradition—in this case, the tradition of premodern Shiʿi exegesis. That is precisely what I try to do, by asking and addressing a different set of questions that might deepen our understanding of the texts, contexts, and conceptual possibilities marking the terrain of early and medieval Muslim exegetical traditions.

Productive Ambiguities: Language, Revelation, and Hermeneutics

Beyond Sectarianism argues for and illustrates the importance of broadening our analytical horizons in the study of Twelver Shiʿi exegesis. By examining and highlighting moments in al-Radi's Qurʾan commentary, the *Haqaʾiq*, that might poach the normative stability of binary frameworks of religious identity, this book attempts to mobilize a discursive artifact from early Islam to open new avenues for approaching religious identity and understanding the tradition of Qurʾanic exegesis.

Al-Radi's commentary is a literary exegesis of the Qurʾan. In it, the trope of "ambiguity" functions as the principle interpretive device. Al-Radi identifies the Qurʾan's "ambiguous verses" (*mutashabihat*) as those verses deemed to contain theological, linguistic, and other difficulties that require the extensive exertion of hermeneutical energies. Today, "*mutashabih*" is typically translated into English as "ambiguous" or "ambiguity" (as I also have).[17] For al-Radi, as for many of his contemporaries in early Islam, the term *mutashabih* encompassed a panoply of meanings and cognate categories including uncertain, obscure, difficult to understand (*mushkil*), strange (*gharib*), figurative (*majaz*),[18] homonymous (*mushtarak*), polysemous, similar (*mushabbih*), or requiring guided explanation. When I translate *mutashabih* as ambiguous for heuristic purposes, it is this family of concepts and meanings that I intend with the articulation of this category, with some of its modalities more punctuated than others at particular instances. I will return to the question of how al-Radi understood the concept of *mutashabih* at different moments over the course of this book.

The category of *mutashabih* verses around which al-Radi frames his discussion is a Qur'anic term, derived from a verse equally familiar and contested: verse 3:7. For centuries, this verse has been the starting point for scholarly discussions on the question of interpretive and thus religious authority. The verse describes scripture as a composition of two kinds of verses: the *muhkam* (definite, clear) and the *mutashabih* (ambiguous). It reads:

> It is He who revealed to you the scripture, part of which is definite [*muhkam*] verses; these are the mother of the book. Other (verses) are ambiguous [*mutashabih*]. Those with deviation in their hearts are the ones who follow the ambiguous parts of it, desiring seduction and desiring its interpretation. But none knows its interpretation except God and those who are rooted in knowledge. They say, "We believe in it, all is from our Lord." But only those who understand take notice.[19]

According to this verse, the *muhkam* verses are distinguished from the *mutashabih* verses due to their definite quality, a point that is further reinforced by their being named the "mother of the book." Critical to note here is that the actual task of determining which of the Qur'an's verses fall under the category of clear or ambiguous was ultimately left to the individual interpreter.

In al-Radi's commentary on the ambiguous verses, not only does he take authoritative positions on which verses are ambiguous and why, but, more importantly, he uses literary arguments to uncover their meanings. This is a crucial point because, by turning to literary arguments as authoritative proof for his interpretations, al-Radi departs from the main sources relied upon by previous generations of Shi'i exegetes. Prior to al-Radi, Shi'i exegetes had primarily invoked the authoritative tradition of sayings of the Prophet and the twelve appointed successors from his family.[20] This meant that the intended meaning and application of any given verse was determined by identifying explicatory statements made by the Prophet or by his twelve appointed successors. Such a tradition-centered approach to exegesis during the early years of Shi'i scholarship speaks to a moment when the Imams as authoritative leaders of the community were still living among the people (the twelfth and final Imam's occultation is said to have occurred in 941). However, under the unprecedented circumstances of the second half of the tenth century, whereby the Imam was no longer among the people, Twelver Shi'i scholars found themselves in a radically altered intellectual and political terrain.[21] It was at this critical juncture in Twelver Shi'i thought that a figure like al-Radi composed a Qur'an commentary in which *language* became the most authoritative and indispensable tool used to disentangle and resolve the literary and theological conundrums that populate the Qur'an.

As I will show in Chapter 2, al-Radi's hermeneutical choices reflect an intellectual training and career informed by a moment of tremendous epistemological cross-pollination between multiple scholarly traditions in early Islam. Yet, in recent Euro-American scholarship, al-Radi's writings continue to be approached through a framework that privileges his Shi'i identity as the primary determinant of his thought.[22] By focusing primarily on his relationship to a preexisting template of Shi'i exegesis, such an approach narrows the set of questions we bring to works composed by Shi'i scholars such as al-Sharif al-Radi.

Interrupting such a sectarian-driven approach to the examination of Qur'anic exegesis, I show that al-Radi's Qur'an commentary represents an instructive site through which to explore the variety of ways in which religious identity informed the interpretive frameworks of scholars during the Buyid period[23]—a moment marked by striking intellectual porosity, when religious thinkers, litterateurs, and rulers alike participated to create a rich and lively milieu of scholarly discourse, debate, and exchange. Accordingly, far from adopting rigid methods that conform to fixed sectarian templates, al-Radi strategically mobilized the literary trope of Qur'anic ambiguity for remarkably varied hermeneutical and political projects.

Here, I should anticipate and respond to a possible objection that one might raise. This will also allow me to further elaborate the texture of my intervention into the academic study of religion. One may object that al-Radi's case represents an idiosyncrasy that cannot bring into question the otherwise predictable correspondence between sectarian leanings and hermeneutical choices in the Shi'i exegetical tradition. To frame this possible objection as a question: Is al-Radi's case not simply an anomaly and idiosyncrasy that radically departs from an otherwise strictly sectarian commentarial tradition? I would counterargue that such objections would miss the central thrust of my argument. My point is not a historicist argument for replacing one narrative of Shi'i hermeneutics (one that privileges sectarian identity) with another that entirely dismisses the importance of that identity. No doubt al-Radi was a Shi'i scholar who enthusiastically identified with and shared Shi'i doctrinal commitments. My point is not to undermine the significance of al-Radi's identity as a Shi'i scholar. Rather, my point is that his exegetical horizons, the sorts of questions his exegesis enables us to ask, or the sorts of conceptual dividends one can draw from an analysis of his exegesis cannot be subsumed or even dominated by his sectarian identity. Regardless of whether one should consider a major figure like al-Radi an aberration and however one might circumscribe the mainstream from the margins, the point of my work is to push for a wider interpretive canvas while examining labors of exegesis that do not take sectarian identity as their point of departure. In pushing for such an approach, I have turned the camera of attention to the internal logics and questions, as well as the intellectual and socio-political terrain, that inspired al-Radi's thought, rather than imposing on his work preconceived notions of the terms, stakes, and points of emphasis that *must* occupy a Shi'i exegete. Ultimately, my attempt to move beyond sectarian framings is animated by the broader project of expanding our understanding of Muslim normativity in a manner that takes seriously the significance of seemingly nonreligious discursive spaces, such as language and literary hermeneutics, in the fashioning of religious imaginaries and arguments. This book seeks to view scholars like al-Radi as vigorous participants in a wide range of the Muslim humanities, rather than as monological agents subdued and subsumed by narrow sectarian concerns. Let me elaborate.

The Conceptual Terrain and Arguments

A figure like al-Radi and his writings alert us to how poets, litterateurs, and a thriving court culture in tenth century Baghdad intersected with heated debates on theology and language. I introduced al-Radi's *Haqa'iq* earlier as primarily concerned with ambiguity in the Qur'an, in which he presents "language" as the hermeneutical key to Qur'an exegesis, especially the Qur'an's ambiguous verses. Which language, though? The tenth century marked a formative moment in the consolidation of several Islamic intellectual disciplines, including language. Muslim scholars were actively debating language's very fundamentals, by taking up questions such as where language originates, what language constitutes, and how language is to be authorized. The theological stakes of these questions raged high; after all, at the center of these debates was the issue of which canon of linguistic rules ought to govern the hermeneutic for reading the Qur'an. Conceived this way, we realize that a work like al-Radi's

Haqa'iq was no ordinary exegesis of the Qur'an. By focusing its discussion on the Qur'an's ambiguous moments in particular, al-Radi's exegesis was, in effect, a treatise on hermeneutics and its protocols. After all, Qur'anic ambiguities represented the most concentrated and decisive interpretive moments; the text literally bore itself open, not just inviting but insisting that the reader make an interpretive claim upon it. In the *Haqa'iq*, al-Radi makes just such a claim, asserting that language is the ultimate arbiter of Qur'anic meaning. Built into al-Radi's claim for language as the hermeneutical key to the Qur'an are his arguments for what language constitutes, where it originates, and who has exclusive authority over it.

Al-Radi's effort to resolve Qur'anic ambiguity through language, which occurs in close conversation with scholars and poets of his period, reveals a set of riveting discussions conceived, imagined, and debated in an episteme where language, poetry, ontology, and theology were all intimately bound. The place and effect of poetry to debates on language meant that writings on the subject were visually rich and throbbing with life. Inhabited by animate and inanimate actors, set in vivid desertscapes, these discussions were rife with emotion. It is worth pausing over the immense distance between the flaccid images that the task of "debating linguistic rules" might conjure up for us today and the intellectual vibrancy connected to this project in early Islamic texts like the *Haqa'iq*. This can partly be explained by our own disconnect from associating the principles of language with a living, breathing universe. Yet, the centrality of poetry to Arabic language for al-Radi and scholars of his period meant that it was through embodied examples of life, articulated in vivid poetic verse, that "linguistic rules" were argued and presented. In this discursive mode, for example, lightning and winds wept to convey yearning, and vast empty lands harkened to the fragility of life.[24] Indeed, it is this aesthetic dimension of the debates on language and their relationship to Qur'anic meaning that the study of a work authored by al-Radi—a tenth-century poet, exegete, political aspirant, and theologian par excellence—critically offers.

Al-Radi's literary investment in and celebration of Qur'anic ambiguity was intimately tied to what Lara Harb has convincingly described as an epistemic turn to "wonder" at this time, permeating a host of disciplines, poetry foremost among them.[25] Wonder, as religion scholar Mary-Jane Rubenstein pithily puts it, "opens an originary rift in thought, an unsuturable gash that both constitutes and deconstitutes thinking as such."[26] And, just so, Qur'anic ambiguity offers a hermeneutical opening, as well as a closure. It is the managing of this dynamic, the Qur'an's simultaneous opening and closing of exegetical labor, that occupies al-Radi in the *Haqa'iq*. In it, he presents his hermeneutical manifesto, both celebrating the possibilities enabled by ambiguity and detailing the task of closing in on its proper meaning. It must be stressed that these two seemingly opposed operations were not at odds in al-Radi's hermeneutical imaginary. Even as al-Radi embraced the notion of a linguistic canon to which all correct linguistic form must refer, this did not carry over into a demand for the singularity of meaning. Put differently, al-Radi's purpose was not simply to rein ambiguity in, at least not to the point of "tranquilizing" it.[27] Rather, he sought to document the *plenitude* of meaning, while also seeking to *circumscribe* it.[28] This may appear to the modern reader as an exercise dogged by contradiction but, to scholars like al-Radi, such a dynamic was perfectly rational and, indeed, characteristic of many arenas and disciplines of the time, even as it manifested in myriad ways.[29] Moreover, for al-Radi, ambiguity carried immense rhetorical and epistemological value in its ability to evoke wonder and to generate, or rather demand, intellectual labor and exertion on the part of the reader.[30]

Conceptually, my reading of this commentary is guided by questions of the following sort: What understanding of language informed al-Radi's hermeneutical moves? How was the question of language connected to the way he understood the interaction of divine discourse and his own temporal authority as an exegete? And what sources of normative authority informed and undergirded his exegetical arguments and explanations? By pursuing this cluster of questions, I aim to sketch a vivid picture of the interaction of language and revelation in al-Radi's Qur'an commentary. Over the course of this book, I will show that al-Radi's invocation of varied grammatical rules and his construction of literary arguments were embedded in a particular epistemological and theological conception of the normative relationship between language and revelation.

My selection of al-Radi's Qur'an commentary for this book is inspired by the larger methodological goal of rethinking Shi'i identity and the predictable way it is often assumed to operate at different historical conjunctures. What is needed is a critical appraisal of our present understanding of religious identity and its operations in the formative period of Islam. I argue against an approach that imagines Shi'ism to have followed a singular trajectory of "development," as if it were an object of zoological evolution that follows a linear or predictable teleology. Of course, by this I do not intend to suggest that the actors we study be dehistoricized altogether. Instead, I propose to

examine how different historical conditions make possible varied arguments
and claims about Shi'i identity. I argue that a productive framing through
which these differences might be conceptualized is through approaching
identity as an ongoing moral argument, invested with particular meanings
and ideological projects at particular historical conjunctures, such as Buyid
Baghdad. Through a close reading of al-Radi's Qur'an commentary, I explore
possible alternatives to frameworks that valorize sectarian and theological
identity as the primary determinant of hermeneutical desires and sensibilities. Instead, I will aim to show that a reexamination of al-Radi's work can
provide fresh insights into the trans-sectarian intellectual confluences that
populated the discursive and institutional terrain of Muslim intellectual history during this particular era.

Qur'an Exegesis and the Problem of Sectarian Identity: Some Further Notes

By approaching al-Radi not simply as a Shi'i scholar but rather as a member
of a particular cultural dialectic and episteme that prevailed at his time, this
book seeks to intervene in current scholarship on early Muslim historiography by making the case for a reevaluation of what is termed "Shi'i identity."
I argue that al-Radi's Qur'an commentary presents a profitable site through
which to trace the multiple processes that enable the construction of contingent religious identities.

The fact that al-Radi's Shi'i identity did not neatly translate into a definable Qur'anic hermeneutic amplifies the conceptual problems attached to
the very category of a "Shi'i hermeneutic," a category that stands authorized
through the unsound assumption that sectarian identity and hermeneutical
imagination readily correspond in a predictable and seamless fashion. It is
precisely this assumption that I challenge and question by describing the multivalent interpretive traditions that informed al-Radi's Qur'an hermeneutic.

In sum, in this book, I seek to question the tendency in the field of Qur'anic
Studies to mobilize terms like "Imami exegesis" in a functionalist fashion as
always signifying a particular notion of Shi'i identity—one that is assumed
to operate in an unchanging discursive and institutional framework. While it
is acknowledged that the main interpretive strategies adopted by the Imami
school evolved over time under changing sociopolitical conditions,[31] I argue
that the assertion that Shi'i authors shared a set of common characteristics that

were subject to the vicissitudes of time is itself problematic. This is because the grouping of Shi'i authors into a single category presupposes a "functional" relationship between a particular school of thought and the interpretive approach that an exegete of that school adopts. Invariably, such a functionalist approach generates a palpably static notion of religious identity.[32] As an alternative to this model that generates a closed system of attribution of the signifier to the signified, in this case, the attribution of Shi'i identity to a Shi'i hermeneutic, and where the signs are assumed to be preceded by a truth or meaning already constituted by and within the notion of "identity," I do not attribute to al-Radi's writings any stable notions of a characteristically Shi'i work. I ask what hermeneutical and epistemological concerns informed the kinds of questions al-Radi raised in his commentary and the kinds of answers he advanced to those questions. In this way, I refer to al-Radi's text not merely to represent his hermeneutical positions but as a site through which to understand the discursive terrain that enabled him to adopt his chosen views and to defend them through distinct forms of reasoning.

Book Organization

The chapters in this book are thematically organized. In Chapter 1, "Competing Memories of al-Radi," I sketch a biographical portrait of al-Radi by presenting an overview of the varied ways al-Radi has been remembered and represented in different types of literature, from biographical dictionaries and literary anthologies to Shi'i genealogical works. I then introduce key components and structural features of al-Radi's Qur'an commentary, the *Haqa'iq*, to give the reader ample sense of the length, style, and organization of the textual field that occupies much of this book.

Next, in Chapter 2, "Buyid Baghdad and al-Radi's Hermeneutical Identity," in preparation for a closer examination of al-Radi's thought in subsequent chapters, I consider the intellectual and political conditions in which al-Radi's career as a scholar unfolded. Writing during a period of immense intellectual fermentation and political flux (during the Buyid dynasty), al-Radi's Qur'an commentary is the discursive product of the vivacious intellectual milieu and literary culture of tenth- and eleventh-century Baghdad. This chapter discusses the intellectual, cultural, and political conditions in which al-Radi composed the *Haqa'iq* and provides the contextual backdrop for what I identify as al-Radi's hermeneutical identity. What were the pressing scholarly debates that consumed major scholars of this era that also informed and shaped al-Radi's exegesis? How were these discussions and debates connected to the imperial setup of the Buyid dynasty? And what are the major historical and political factors and conditions that enabled a heightened spirit of inquiry and intellectual exchange during this moment? These are among the questions I take up in this chapter, with the specific purpose of addressing for the reader the following question: Why, in this setting, did the authoritative claims put forward by the custodians of language, lineage, and poetry, like al-Radi, carry the weight they did?

In my examination of the contextual component of this book, I am mindful of another common problem in the study of Shi'i Qur'an commentaries—that of periodization. As several scholars have pointed out, the assumption that Islamic political history is the primary framework for understanding the socio-historical development of Islamic thought is no longer tenable.[33] Moreover, periodization schemes often lend themselves to narratives of "golden age" and "decline," which do little more than reinforce outdated Orientalist perspectives on the teleological direction of dominant drivers of Muslim history.[34]

According to periodization schemes in the work of recent scholars that outline the development of Twelver Shi'i exegesis, al-Radi's scholarly career coincides with the time when the Shi'i Buyid dynasty was in power, or what Todd Lawson terms a period characterized by a "hermeneutics of compromise."[35] Although the distinct phases of Twelver Shi'i exegesis and the dominant principles that characterize each period may be one way of evaluating the literature, it narrows the scope of comparison to one where the work of a Twelver Shi'i scholar is integral only to the extent that it is part of a history that is imagined to be shared by works that come under the rubric of "Twelver Shi'i exegesis."

In the present study, I defer to the view that not only religious "identity" but "contexts," too, must be interpreted as verbal artifacts, much like the ideas and "texts" they produce. Accordingly, I shift attention from situating the *Haqa'iq* simply as a work authored by a "Shi'i exegete writing during the Buyid period." Instead, I propose to expand the very task of contextualizing the historical actor and text by approaching both as contributing to and constitutive of a larger intellectual and institutional milieu. In so doing, I seek to move away from reductionist understandings of al-Radi's "Shi'i religious identity," as well as from generalized characterizations of "the Buyid dynastic period." Instead, I explore al-Radi's engagement with the multiple intellectual discourses that are inflected in his writings. I bring into focus the way in which al-Radi's hermeneutical choices reflect a distinct understanding of the discourse of which he was a part, and of the specific manner in which he conceived and defined the very problems he sought to overcome.

In Chapter 3, "Ambiguity, Hermeneutics, and Power," I offer a conceptual history of the term "*mutashabih*," focusing specifically on the relevance of this category to various disciplinary traditions in Islamic thought, including philology, theology, and law. I then turn to al-Radi's theorization of this term, bringing attention to the significance of his perspective as a figure situated at the crossroads of Baghdad's poetic, legal, theological, and exegetical traditions. At the heart of al-Radi's exposition, I argue, is his view of ambiguity in the Qur'an as a gateway to experiencing the wonders of language. This, I note, marks a shift from a more defensive approach to ambiguity, as seen in the writings of his predecessors and contemporaries. Al-Radi's *Haqa'iq*, I show, evidences the aesthetic, rhetorical, and epistemological potential of ambiguity while also circumscribing its reach through the critical legal principle of clarity. This process, of moving from the decentering of language, or a hermeneutical opening in the sacred text, to its subsequent closure, is what defines al-Radi's discussion throughout. In this chapter, I carefully illustrate two critical moments in the *Haqa'iq* where al-Radi rehearses the details of his hermeneutical operation. Presented under the rubric of the *mutashabih-muhkam* dynamic, or an unraveling of ambiguity through the clear (verses) in the Qur'an, al-Radi views his hermeneutic as a methodologically rigorous affair. The near-science-like precision with which he demonstrates the literary unfolding of ambiguity is made all the more secure through his articulation of the authoritative lexicon (*asl al-lugha*), or the literary canon, that authorizes each and every one of his claims. With an eye to unpacking the specific arguments by which this seemingly unshakeable canon came to be and by which it was held up as the sovereign source for language, this chapter also dissects its constituent elements. Throughout, I argue that it is through al-Radi's invocation of the lexicon as a normative body on which he could rest his linguistic arguments that he also contributed to its canonization.

Approaching al-Radi as a participant to some of the major intellectual debates of this period and not simply as a peripheral actor whose sectarian identity necessarily places him outside these conversations is one of the central goals of Chapter 4, "The Politics of Language." I begin the chapter with one such debate, on the language-versus-logic question, where scholars argued over the superiority of language versus logic as the fundamental source of knowledge. I argue that the contours and stakes of this exchange provide a crucial window to understanding the intersection of theological, epistemological, philosophical, and ontological concerns of the time, and the way these played out in response to questions pertaining to language. Further, the broader intellectual conversations that surrounded al-Radi's work provide important indications of the kinds of politics that a literary approach to the Qur'an, as we find in the *Haqa'iq*, was invested in. Next, through three illustrative chapters from the *Haqa'iq*, I offer a slow and careful reading of al-Radi's arguments to capture and convey the ambit of ambiguities he wrestles with and the myriad means by which he does so. In addition, I explore what al-Radi's discussion in these examples might tell us about his language philosophy,[36] his stance on interpretive authority, and his overarching hermeneutic. By "language philosophy" I mean al-Radi's position on questions and topics such as the origin and acquisition of language and its relationship to cosmology and ontology. The chapter concludes by reiterating, from a different vantage point, how his hermeneutic exhibits the interplay of scientific exactitude and rhetorical performance.

In Chapter 5, "The Theology of Language," I continue my exploration of the centrality of language to the religious and social landscape of early Islam by shifting my focus to some key debates on the intersection of language and theology that occupied major scholars in this era. For instance, I investigate how early Muslim writings on language navigated the "origin of language" question. Concomitantly, I reflect on ways in which the thriving intellectual tradition of theology shaped dominant understandings of human life and how they, in turn, informed early Muslim theories of language. I also explore how scholars imagined the relationship between language and the empirical realities it sought to represent. In other words, I address the critical question of what, in their view, was the relationship between language and ontology? In the latter half of the chapter, I connect these debates to some specific examples from al-Radi's Qur'an commentary to show and argue that his commentarial labor was both constitutive of and constituted by these broader conversations on the interaction of language and theology in Islam.

Chapter 6, "Is the *Haqa'iq* a Mu'tazili Tafsir?" continues with the theme of sketching a broad picture of the intimacy of language and theology in early Muslim thought but with a much more specific focus: a comparative analysis between the exegetical temperaments and choices of al-Radi and his famous Mu'tazili teacher Qadi 'Abd al-Jabbar (d. 1025). By juxtaposing their exegetical labors, I argue against a commonplace tendency to view the work of Shi'i

Qur'an commentators, especially from this period, as products of Mu'tazili "influence." How might we rethink intellectual relationships such as that of al-Radi's with 'Abd al-Jabbar in ways more nuanced and less predetermined than what the narrative frame of Mu'tazili influence over Shi'ism allows for? This is the central question that guides this chapter, occupied with further close readings of al-Radi's Qur'an exegesis, but this time in intimate conversation with the thought and exegesis of Qadi 'Abd al-Jabbar. Collectively, these chapters seek to reorient our understanding of the Twelver Shi'i Qur'anic exegetical tradition by rethinking the often taken-for-granted assumptions about the correspondence between sectarian identity and hermeneutics. As such, *Beyond Sectarianism* aspires to connect and integrate the literary exegesis of a scholar like al-Radi with broader questions, categories, and intellectual fields critical to the Muslim and indeed Western humanities. I begin by offering a detailed and hopefully enjoyable account of the life and multiple memories of the protagonist of this book: al-Sharif al-Radi.

CHAPTER 1

Competing Memories of al-Radi

Al-Radi: A Poet-Exegete in Times of Change

A thirteenth-century biographer by the name 'Ali ibn al-Yusuf al-Qifti (d. 1248) reports the following exchange that transpired between al-Radi and his teacher Abu Sa'id al-Sirafi (d. 932), a prominent Sunni philologist of the time:

> A young al-Radi not more than ten years of age was sitting in a study circle with his teacher of grammar, al-Sirafi. As is common in such lessons on Arabic grammar, al-Sirafi asked, "if I say *ra'aytu* 'Amr [I saw 'Amr], what is the sign of *nasab* [accusative case] on 'Amr?" Al-Radi replied "*bugd* [hatred of] 'Ali." All those present were amazed at al-Radi's perspicacity.[1]

Al-Radi's clever response is a play on the word *nasab*, which carries the technical meaning of "the accusative form of a noun" but also conveys a general meaning of "having enmity." In addition, al-Radi plays on the name "'Amr," which is a generic character mobilized in the pedagogical context of illustrating or discussing points of Arabic grammar, yet historically a figure by that name is remembered by Shi'i supporters of 'Ali ibn Abi Talib (d. 661) as a bitter rival of his. Specifically, the reference to 'Amr is most likely to 'Amr ibn 'Abd Wadd (d. 627), a formidable warrior of the Quraysh tribe. 'Ali was the only one willing to accept the challenge to fight him in the Battle of the Trench (*Khandaq*). This encounter, in which 'Amr ibn 'Abd Wadd was defeated and killed by a single strike of 'Ali's sword, is memorialized in Shi'i history and literature, most significantly through 'Ali's own account of it.[2] Another intended reference of the term 'Amr could be 'Amr ibn al-'As (d. 664), a governor of Egypt who allied with Mu'awiya against 'Ali. In a particularly memorable confrontation between them at the Battle of Siffin, when things turned in favor of 'Ali, it is said that 'Amr ibn al-'As came up with the ruse of placing Qur'anic leaves on lances, signaling the desire for an arbitrated settlement of the dispute.[3] The eventual arbitration between 'Ali and Mu'awiya was met with much displeasure among some of 'Ali's followers, who left his camp and came to be known as "those who departed (al-khawarij)," one of whom eventually took 'Ali's life in 661. This arbitration thus, proved historically decisive and divisive for the Muslim community.

This brief exchange, frequently cited in several biographical sources, concisely conveys a few key characteristics about al-Radi that came to be remembered in the biographical tradition surrounding him. First, from the outset, this narrative emphasizes al-Radi's linguistic acumen and wit as he playfully challenges the foremost grammatical authority of the time. It also brings into focus his firm allegiance to the Imami Shi'i struggle against unjust rule, a struggle that began with what the Shi'i school regards as the usurpation of power from 'Ali ibn Abi Talib immediately after the death of the Prophet Muhammad in 632. Finally, this exchange captures al-Radi's bravado and eloquence in the authoritative presence of his esteemed teacher. In addition to these details derived from the exchange itself, the transmitter of the report can also be read to serve a critical authenticating function. It is narrated by no less than Ibn Jinni (d. 1002), another towering figure in the discipline of Arabic language, who also happened to be al-Radi's teacher and also a Sunni. Thus, this report plays a critical role in inscribing al-Radi's authority into the intellectual genealogy of leading Arabic grammarians of the time.

Some important insights about the intellectual and social milieu in Baghdad under the Buyids can also be glimpsed from this narrative. Reference to al-Radi's connections to two leading Sunni teachers, al-Sirafi and Ibn Jinni, along with the mention of his affiliation to the Imami Shi'i reflects a literary culture marked by considerable intellectual fluidity and crossover.[4] Religious scholars, litterateurs, and rulers alike participated to create a rich and lively space for scholarly exchange. Similarly, circles of students assembled in mosques, courts, and the shops of book-dealers—transcending differences of faith, school, and sect—to engage in theological, literary, and juridical discussion. Al-Radi benefited from and actively participated in this environment and his sectarian identity did not hinder his movement in Baghdad's multivalent intellectual circles. From a young age, he enjoyed the tutelage of the finest teachers that Baghdad had to offer and distinguished himself in their eyes as a quick learner with a sharp wit. It is important to note that al-Radi's

identification as an "'Alid," the label used at the time to identify Shi'a descend-
ing from the line of the first Shi'i Imam, 'Ali ibn Abi Talib, did not "other" him
in a way that bounded him off from other intellectuals of his time. Al-Radi
received his training with an eclectic group of scholars. In addition to the two
Sunni grammarians already mentioned, Ibn Jinni (who is reported to have per-
suaded al-Radi to establish himself as a poet)[5] and al-Sirafi, al-Radi's teachers
included the Sabian[6] poet and litterateur, Abu Ishaq Ibrahim ibn Hilal al-Sabi
(d. 994), the Sunni Mu'tazili, 'Abd al-Jabbar, the Shi'i theologian, Muhammad ibn Muhammad al-Mufid, known as al-Shaykh al-Mufid (d. 1022), and
the Maliki jurist, Ibrahim ibn Ahmad al-Tabari (d. 1002), to name a few. Al-
Radi's range of writings in scholarly arenas apart from Qur'an exegesis, such
as poetry and history, also reflect the multifaceted range and character of his
scholarship and of the cultural milieu prevalent in Baghdad during that time.[7]

However, not all of al-Radi's writings reflect a humanist spirit free from
exclusivist sectarian sympathies. Whereas on some occasions the cross-cultural
interactions of the time rendered al-Radi's sectarian leanings peripheral to his
scholarly persona, at other moments his affiliation with the Shi'i school was
central to his intellectual life. For example, in addition to works on literary
exegesis, poetry, and history, al-Radi compiled the sermons and speeches
of the first Shi'i Imam, 'Ali ibn Abi Talib (the Prophet's cousin and son-in-
law, d. 661), in a volume titled *Nahj al-Balagha* (*Way of Eloquence*). The *Nahj
al-Balagha* has ensured for al-Radi a permanent place in Shi'i intellectual traditions; the collected sayings of 'Ali ibn Abi Talib are often considered second only to the Qur'an in the rhetorical perfection, guidance, and knowledge
they are understood to contain.[8] This text includes speeches by the first Shi'i
Imam in which he criticizes the first three Sunni caliphs for usurping his
rightful position as the Prophet's successor. But again, even with a text like
Nahj al-Balagha, al-Radi's normative investment in its compilation cannot
be reduced to sectarian motivations alone. Rather, his interest in compiling
the sayings of 'Ali in what became a central text for the Shi'i position on the
illegitimacy of the first three Sunni caliphs was equally tied to the tremendous literary excellence of this text and the way it resonated with the injus-
tices he saw himself to have suffered, in addition to being an effort to exalt
the claims of the Shi'i community against the Sunnis.[9] What is clear is that
the message of the sermons contained in this text put forward strong opposition to existing Sunni authorities. But al-Radi's prominent role in compiling this text did not hinder him from attaining important political positions
either. Thus, his contrasting roles as writer, leader, and scholar illustrate

the variegated and complicated nature of his attachment to the Shiʻi tradition. These competing possibilities point to the complex social fabric of this period, in which the structure, place, and function of religious identity did not conform to the modern anxiety to locate religious identity in a singular and clearly defined domain.

A few other details about al-Radi and his personal and intellectual genealogy occur frequently in the biographical sources. Several references are made to the nobility of his family, especially to the prestige and status of his father, Abu Ahmad al-Musawi (d. 1010), who was well-respected by the Buyid leadership and by the general populace. His wide-ranging popularity can be gauged from the fact that the honorific title "al-Tahir" (the pure) was bestowed on him by the Buyid princes, while the notoriously scornful poet accused of heresy, Abu al ʻAla al-Maʻarri (d. 1058) dedicated an elaborate elegy to him in his poetic collection, *The Spark of the Flint* (*al-Siqt min al-Zand*).[10] Scholars have noted that the important role of al-Radi's father Abu Ahmad in the political bureaucracy of the Abbasid empire reflected the growing influence in the region of the ʻAlid *ashraf* (literally, those of elite lineage and social status, in this case the name given to the collective descendants of al-Hasan (d. 670) and al-Husayn ibn ʻAli ibn Abi Talib (d. 680)). In 965, Abu Ahmad was appointed to three distinguished positions: chief judge over the court of appeal (*Diwan al-Mazalim*),[11] director of the Hajj pilgrimage, and *naqib* (chief) of the ʻAlids (Prophet Muhammad's descendants) in Baghdad.[12] The duties of the *naqib* comprised of "genealogical, material, and moral matters," including "to keep a register of nobility, enter births and deaths in it and to examine the validity of ʻAlid genealogies. He also had to restrain them from excesses. He had other special duties including certain juridical powers."[13] As chief of the ʻAlid community, Abu Ahmad was a crucial mediator between the Buyids, the ʻAbbasid caliphs, and the larger populace. He was often dispatched to settle disputes between the Buyids and neighboring dynasties like the Hamdanids in Syria, and also played an integral role in establishing peace among Sunnis and the Shiʻites after violent struggles in Baghdad. Abu Ahmad's appointment as chief or *naqib* of the ʻAlid *ashraf* class marked the family's century-long ascent in Baghdad.[14] Moreover, his appointment as the director of the pilgrimage for Iraq was significant because that position was usually held by someone from the extended ʻAbbasid family.[15]

These prestigious posts remained in the family between al-Radi and his brother, al-Murtada. Al-Radi was first entrusted as aide to his father in these responsibilities at the young age of twenty-four, in the year 990, when his father was unwell. In 1006, the Buyid prince Baha al-Dawla (r. 989–1012) appointed al-Radi to these positions, independent of his father. And, a few years after his father's death, al-Radi's area of responsibility was expanded to all the lands of the 'Abbasid empire.[16] Significantly, in his study of the *niqaba* office, Qasim Samarra'i notes that the earliest evidence describing the rituals and ceremonies surrounding the appointment of someone to the position of *naqib* comes from al-Radi's *Diwan*. These date from the year 990, when the caliph al-Ta'i' (r. 974–991) first adorned al-Radi with this position at the caliph's court (*dar al-khilafa*).[17]

The catalyst for what would become al-Radi's successful poetic career occurred in the year 980, when his father was captured and imprisoned by the Buyid ruler 'Adud al-Dawla (r. 949–983) and deprived of his properties. Sources suggest that the reason for his imprisonment was ostensibly that of divulging state secrets, but the more probable reason was his mounting prestige, which, according to some, even exceeded that of the caliph.[18] This event proved to be an important milestone in al-Radi's career as a vocal and critical poet. It marked his entry onto the political scene through a powerful literary voice, which he used to plead the case of his father. He criticized the Buyid ruler 'Adud al-Dawla in a style at once bold and eloquent, a style that would come to characterize his poetic verses, as well. Abu Ahmad was released in the year 986 by Sharaf al-Dawla (r. 983–989), 'Adud al-Dawla's son, who succeeded him. At this time, al-Radi used the power of his verses to express his gratitude to the new prince and his vizier Sabur ibn Ardeshir (d. 1025). Over time, al-Radi cultivated close relations with the ruling political elite, including the 'Abbasid caliph al-Ta'i', to whom he dedicated many poems of praise. Baha al-Dawla was the main figure with whom al-Radi had close relations and for whom he wrote a glowing elegy. In return, Baha al-Dawla crowned al-Radi with numerous honorific titles, including the one by which he is remembered until today, al-Radi ("the well-pleasing.")

Like other poets of the day, al-Radi, too, first made his name in scholarly circles through the writing of praise poems dedicated to the Buyid sultans, their viziers, and the 'Abbasid caliph of the period. Since these ruling figures were also the main patrons and hosts for the literary arts, al-Radi's skills put him on friendly terms with the leading political players of Buyid Baghdad. But al-Radi did not only use the power of his poetry and the recognition it enjoyed to shower lavish praise on the leaders. At times, he also condemned the unjust use of political power and expressed his distrust of hypocritical sovereign rulers. When, for example, the 'Abbasid caliph al-Ta'i, with whom he enjoyed good relations, was deposed by the Buyid ruler Baha al-Dawla, al-Radi happened to be present in the court. Although al-Radi himself managed to escape, he captured the humiliating incident that he witnessed in his poetry:

> How wonderful that I should retain my life after
> > it has been attacked by disasters virgin and matron
> And that I should have escaped the day of the palace when others
> > succumbed
> I however, retained some discretion which saved me
> I darted thence swooping like a shooting-star
> Just as the doors of destruction were closing on me
> After the master of the realm had been smiling upon me,
> > each of us affable to the other, I
> Found myself pitying him whom I had envied
> Truly honor and disgrace are near neighbors
> Never shall I be deceived by a sovereign again
> Fools are those who enter sovereign's doors[19]

Al-Radi's resentment and suspicion of political power was also directed at the exaggerated titles that rulers adorned themselves with, and he mocked their self-aggrandizing ways in his verses. However, despite these critiques of the powerful, at other moments, al-Radi was hardly shy at making his own claims to power. Not only did he not object to the flowery honorifics he himself was given by the same rulers, in his poetry, he explicitly aired his desire for acquiring the seat of the caliphate. In one set of particularly controversial lines, he expressed his aspirations for acquiring the seat of the caliphate.[20] Al-Radi felt that his noble 'Alid lineage and esteemed scholarly status entitled him to a position much more expansive than what he enjoyed. No doubt, these political ambitions made al-Radi a detestable presence in the eyes of those figures whose positions he sought and threatened. On several occasions, al-Radi was removed from the political positions he held in retaliation for his critical words (those positions were returned to him by the next generation of rulers). In sum, al-Radi's varied encounters with the courts and his periodic stints of political power as leader of the 'Alid community ultimately left him with more than a hint of discontent. Paradoxically, the force of al-Radi's verses both acquired for him a privileged place amid the personalities he chose to praise and also earned for him periods of political isolation, enforced by those he targeted with his critique.

Noteworthy is that, although the Buyid period is often described as a time of tolerance with regard to the freedom and access granted to Shi'i religious scholars, the narratives and reports presented above suggest that under some Buyid rulers and 'Abbasid caliphs, the 'Alids faced significant challenges, and the political positions granted to them were conditional to their support of the political establishment. Also important to note from the above discussion are what appear to be competing memories of al-Radi's "'Alid identity." What I mean by this is that he does not consistently express his authenticity through symbols of particularistic belonging to the 'Alid cause. Rather than interpret this as al-Radi's decision to "abandon" Shi'i resistance to authority, as some earlier scholars have done,[21] I argue that it is more productive to explore the possibility of a conceptual vocabulary that does not limit the operations of identity, particularly that of a minority group, to mere vacillation between assimilation and resistance. In Chapter 2, I return to this point and examine alternate readings of the relationship between the ruling elites of Baghdad and Twelver Shi'i scholars like al-Radi.

Al-Radi's associations with the courts and leaders suggest that he did not actively challenge the 'Abbasid caliph or the Buyid sovereigns on the basis of political legitimacy. At the same time, we have multiple moments in the *Diwan* where he openly challenged the authority of the 'Abbasid caliphs and presented them as bearers of illegitimate political rule.

What are we to make of the seeming hypocrisy or contradiction in al-Radi's pronouncement of invective poetry against the caliphs, while simultaneously being the occupant of prominent positions granted by the very political establishment that he critiqued? A treatise composed by al-Radi's brother, al-Murtada, titled *The Legality of Working for the Government (Mas'ala fi al-'Amal Ma'a al-Sultan)*, is helpful in this regard.[22] It dealt explicitly with the question of the legality of working with and for the ruling government. In the absence of the Imam, al-Murtada argued, the legitimacy of the office of anyone "ordering what is proper and prohibiting what is reprehensible (*amr bi al-ma'ruf wa nahi 'an al-munkar*)," was derived from the theological position of that person acting on behalf of the Imam, regardless of on whoever's behalf he may nominally be holding his political office. That is, the holder of office is not in fact serving the ruler (who is not an Imam), even if he might appear to be doing so. Rather, he serves the Imam. With regard to his view on holding office at the behest of an unjust ruler (as opposed to a ruler who, though not the Imam, was not unjust either), al-Murtada argued that if someone knows or considers it likely that he will be able to "order what is proper and forbid what is reprehensible," then taking on the responsibility of political office is obligatory (provided it does not result in the shedding of blood or cause significant harm to others).[23] In short, as long as there was some moral benefit and good to be derived from holding a political position, then doing so was not only permissible but in some instances even obligatory.

This trope resonated with a broader Shi'i critique of the Muslim political set up after the death of the Prophet. According to this view, political power had been usurped from the rightful leaders—the members of the Prophet's family. As such, al-Radi framed his objections to the political setup of his time as part of a broader pattern of 'Alid resistance. In some instances, this was achieved by allying himself with the Fatimid caliphs in Egypt on the basis of their shared 'Alid lineage:

I am clothed in humiliation in my enemies' abodes,
While in Egypt rules an 'Alid caliph,
Whose father is my father, whose master is my master,
While [in Baghdad] one distant [in kinship] oppresses me.
My blood is joined to his by the two lords of the people,
Muhammad and 'Ali.[24]

The Sunni historian Abu al-Faraj Ibn al-Jawzi (d. 1200) reports that these provocative words of al-Radi's led to a confrontation between the 'Abbasid caliph al-Qadir (r. 991–1031) and al-Radi's father, Abu Ahmad (who was made to account for al-Radi's impetuosity). Abu Ahmad reassured the caliph that his family's loyalties had always been with them, at which point al-Qadir challenged him to put this affirmation in writing and dispatch it to the Fatimid leader. When Abu Ahmad instructed al-Radi to retract his words and send such a letter to the Fatimids, al-Radi refused, and this led to some discord between al-Radi and his father.[25] Ihsan 'Abbas, in his 1959 Arabic biography of al-Radi simply titled *Al-Sharif al-Radi*, notes that while the sources do not provide much detail, we know that, after this episode, al-Qadir removed al-Radi from his position of *naqib* and al-Radi's father and brother from their posts, as well.[26] It is evident that the caliph, al-Qadir, felt threatened by any show of support for the Fatimids, since it is reported that, in 1011, he assembled a group of scholars and notables and commanded them to declare in a written document that the Fatimid caliph, al-Hakim bi

Amr Allah (r. 996–1021) and his predecessors lacked genuine 'Alid ancestry. Apparently, and likely through coercion, al-Radi also signed this document, along with his teacher, al-Shaykh al-Mufid, and his brother, al-Murtada.[27]

The context of al-Radi's invective poetry against the 'Abbasid caliph can be better understood by considering one of his main functions as the chief or *naqib* of the 'Alids: publicly confirming true 'Alid descent and denouncing false claims through issuing a decree (*mahdar*).[28] As Shainool Jiwa has argued, al-Radi and his brother, al-Murtada, were not only talented poets boasting sacred lineage who were lamenting the twisted fate of their place in the government and leadership of the Muslim community. More than that, it was their job as *naqibs* to make known when a claim to authority derived from that sacred lineage was false. This is the context in which one should place al-Radi's repudiation of the 'Abbasid caliph in his poetry, even as he was selective in his denouncements.

The tragic sensibility at the heart of al-Radi's critique of the political conditions of his time—a point I will return to in Chapter 2—can also be traced, if much less explicitly, in the *Haqa'iq*. While he makes no mention of his caliphal ambitions in the *Haqa'iq*, he does refer to the hostile conditions under which he composed the work. Analogizing his process of writing to a deer desperately grabbing gulps of water while its predator hunts it down, al-Radi presents his position in Buyid intellectual and imperial circles as one that is under constant threat. While justifying the repetition of a theological point in the second chapter of the *Haqa'iq*, he writes:

> Mentioning it again is not redundant because there is a great distance between the beginning of this book and its end. Hence, repetition is helpful and not burdensome to the argument. This is particularly so since much time has passed since I was able to write due to hindrances I had to confront and things that kept me away from it; things like a change in my circumstances and my subjection to severe difficulties. As a result, my task was cut short and I was only able to work in flashes and at opportune moments, like the animal who takes a quick drink from fear of its predator and surroundings.[29]

In addition to the visceral sense of impending political threat that al-Radi's discourse here echoes, one also feels a palpable sense of estrangement in his writings. Estrangement, that is, from both an internal and external other. I have noted, above (and will discuss in more detail in Chapter 2), his discontentment and lack of affinity with the 'Abbasid caliphs, on account of their less than "pure" lineage. But we also see al-Radi estranged from his own community: namely, his father and brother, who did not support him in his critique of the 'Abbasid caliph, al-Qadir. Finally, we also see him lamenting the distance he felt from the 'Alid community, whom he served and oversaw in his role as *naqib*. In his poetry, he points to the ways in which the *niqaba* was hard on him, contrary to the honor and prestige it carries in the eyes of the outsider.[30] In one instance, al-Radi described it as an iron collar round his neck that put him in disfavor among his own people. Another anecdote captures the burden and heavy responsibility of the role: a woman complained to al-Radi of her husband's conduct. When al-Radi meted out justice, as per the law, she was upset with his harshness. In response, al-Radi exclaims that he is not some teacher at a Qur'an school disciplining children at whim, but he's rather acting according to the rules of the Shari'a![31] Aside from the remarkably familiar, comical portrait we get here of the rough and tough ways of Qur'an teachers, what is striking in these lines is al-Radi's depiction of himself: a lone warrior fighting the good fight against injustice in all the places it rears its head, be they in the mundane domestic sphere of 'Alid households or the politically charged imperial courts of the Buyid elite. Most crucially, he presents himself as deeply cynical of the glittery allure of power and, despite his young age, well-aware of its fragile and fickle ways. He writes at another moment in his poetry:

If it [*niqaba*] is bestowed/awarded, I want not of it,
We are cheapened by its value and high price
Generosity in it is not generosity,
Our stinginess in it is not stinginess
He who pursues it is nothing but deceived,
He who is fortunate is he who is free of it.[32]

Al-Radi as a Sayyid Poet-Scholar

Above, I presented a brief sketch of al-Radi's aristocratic background and poetic personality in the political context of tenth century Baghdad. I turn now to the way in which al-Radi has been remembered in the Muslim tradition. Relying on biographical dictionaries, literary anthologies, and historical works, I show that al-Radi has been memorialized first as an outstanding

Arab poet, comparable to the most renowned and esteemed poets in early Muslim history. In addition, he is venerated as a *sayyid*, or descendant of the family of the Prophet, and the significance of this sacred lineage has shaped many of his biographical accounts. Finally, turning to al-Radi's scholarly output, I present his portfolio of writings, and point out how his expertise in language and literary topics permeated all his works, which covered a variety of disciplines.

In the majority of sources that paint a portrait of al-Radi's biography, his reputation as a poet surpasses all his other achievements. One of the earliest (extant) testaments of his poetic abilities is cited in the work of al-Tha'labi's (d. 1035) literary anthology, in which he states that it would not be far from the truth to call al-Radi the best poet from among the Quraysh.[33] The same recognition is accorded to al-Radi's poetic fame by the respected historian and author of the famous book *The History of Baghdad* (*Tarikh Baghdad*), al-Khatib al-Baghdadi (d. 1071).[34] The positive review by al-Baghdadi gains additional significance when compared with his scathing critique of al-Radi's primary teacher in Imami theology, al-Shaykh al-Mufid:

> He wrote many books in their [*Rafida's*] errors and in defence of their beliefs and tenets, as well as polemics against the early generations, the Companions and the Followers, and against the generality of jurists who use *ijtihad*. He was one of the imams of error. A large number of people were ruined by him before God gave the Muslims respite from him.[35]

It is important to note that, unlike al-Mufid, al-Radi was not profiled pejoratively as an Imami Shi'i (or as a *Rafidi*, the derogative label used by their opponents at the time). Instead, in the writings of al-Khatib al-Baghdadi, al-Tha'alabi, and several other Sunni authors, al-Radi's poetic persona overshadowed his sectarian affiliation.[36] The wide circulation of al-Radi's poetic collection, *Diwan al-Radi*, can also be observed from Carl Brockelmann's *Geschichte der Arabischen Litteratur*, which catalogs all existing manuscripts of Arabic literary works. Brockelmann lists numerous copies of al-Radi's *Diwan* as compared to his other writings, thus affirming the popularity and widespread distribution of this work.[37]

In addition to the emphatic statements affirming al-Radi's poetic genius in the majority of his biographical accounts, al-Radi's name is also tied to the purity of the family of the Prophet through genealogical connections. As the title in his name "al-Sharif" (noble) indicates, his parents were direct descendants of the Prophet Muhammad. His father's side of the family traced its lineage to the seventh Shi'i Imam, Musa al-Kazim (d. 799), and his mother's side to the fourth Shi'i Imam, Zayn al-'Abidin (d. 712), thus earning al-Radi the weighty honorific of "*Dhu al-Hasabayn*" (possessor of the two nobilities). Al-Radi's noble lineage is most authoritatively and visually depicted in the biographical sources through a powerful dream narrative. The anecdote appears in recent Shi'i studies on al-Radi and his works,[38] although its earliest mention occurs in a thirteenth-century Sunni source, the Shafi'i Mu'tazili Ibn al-Hadid's (d. 1258) commentary on al-Radi's text, *Nahj al Balagha*.[39] The narrative goes as follows:

> Renowned Shi'i theologian al-Shaykh al-Mufid has a dream in which the Prophet's daughter Fatima comes to him with her two young sons, Hasan and Husayn [the second and third Shi'i Imams, respectively], and asks him to accept them as his students. The following [waking] day, al-Mufid is at the mosque delivering a sermon and the mother of al-Radi, Fatima,[40] enters holding by the hand her two young sons, al-Radi and al-Murtada. She approaches al-Mufid and requests him to take trusteeship of the education of her two sons. On realizing the powerful meaning of this moment, and how it is a realization of his dream from the previous night, al-Mufid is overcome with emotion and moved to tears.

The power of dreams such as this one relies on an understanding of the oneiric imagination not as the realm of individual fantasy and fiction but as an intermediary realm between the spiritual and the material, the divine and the human, the dreamer and multiple others. In Islamicate dream culture, albeit with certain qualifications, dreams function as authentic conduits of communication from the invisible world.[41] In addition, as anthropologist Amira Mittermeier has convincingly argued, dream-stories insert the dreamer into a wider network of relationships and meanings, offer guidance, and place the dreamer in relation to the divine.[42] By calling into question conventional parameters of the "real," they invite a more radical rethinking of community and subjectivity.

Al-Mufid's dream can more explicitly be situated in a tradition of dream narratives specifically concerned with the *sayyids/sharifs*, or the descendants of the Prophet. Kazuo Morimoto has shown that dreams involving the *sayyids* are often of great consequence.[43] To see why this is so, it will be useful to consider the main elements associated with dream-narratives of this kind. Morimoto argues that the dreams invariably feature charismatic figures from the Prophet's family who transform the course of events in a given present despite the long period of time separating them from that present.[44] The significance of the dream and its truthfulness is reinforced by the appearance of members of the Prophet's family. Not only do they vouch for the content of the dream, their presence also differentiates it from satanic dreams. This is so because according to the Shi'i tradition, a dream in which a member of the Prophet's family appears could not have been inspired by Satan. It is worth noting that this has led dream stories to carry authoritative weight comparable to that of *hadith* (written sayings of the Prophet and the Imams).[45] Another important characteristic of dreams concerning the *sayyids* is that, in such dreams, they are not represented as impartial demonstrators of universal norms but as affectionate forebears personally invested in the fate of their family members. Thus, *sayyids/sharifs* in these stories can count on the care and protection of the Prophet's family members with whom they share the most intimate of bonds, a blood relationship.[46] Seen this way, the emotive and, indeed, genetic power of kinship erases the apparent temporal distance separating the family of the Prophet and later *sayyids*. Most often, the proper action that is presented to the dreamer in the stories is that of supporting the livelihood of *sayyid/sharifs*, especially the poor among them.[47] In sum, it is the idea of the existence of a trans-temporal supernatural circuit between *sayyids/sharifs* and their holy and affectionate forebears in all later times that underpins these edifying dream stories.[48]

In al-Mufid's dream, the apparition of the two Shi'i Imams and the daughter of the Prophet all act as authoritative messengers communicating with al-Mufid and instructing him to take al-Radi and al-Murtada into his intellectual tutelage. Additionally, the theme of transmitting knowledge in al-Mufid's dream also evokes the Shi'i conception of the Imams as having access to concealed knowledge.[49] The imagery in the dream, thus, also endows al-Radi's intellectual apprenticeship under al-Mufid and his overall scholarly status with sacred significance. In sum, by visually inscribing al-Radi and his brother in this unbroken chain of knowledge, al-Radi and his family are placed in a sacred connection with the spiritual authority of the Imams. This narrative, presented alongside mentions of al-Radi's noble *sayyid* lineage, effectively posits an inextricable link between his lineal and epistemological purity. In addition, this prophetic dream plays an important role in authorizing the contributions of al-Radi and his brother al-Murtada to Shi'i religious thought.

Al-Radi's noble lineage and scholarly achievements are further supplemented by anecdotes that extol his morally upright character. These narratives not only figure in studies that seek to inscribe al-Radi's authority in the Shi'i tradition. On the contrary, stories of al-Radi's moral integrity are commonly featured across the wide range of biographical literature in which he is represented. In these narratives, al-Radi is projected as an exemplary figure who withstood the temptations of material and political gain under Buyid rule. In his own writing, al-Radi attests to this moral challenge. He explains how he set himself apart from the debauchery that characterized courtly life and describes his own assemblies as "limited and unstained by evil."[50] The biographical accounts convey al-Radi's austerity and moral high ground through the succinct but weighty attestation that he did not accept a single thing from anyone. This assertion is often supported with some or all of the same set of anecdotes; the selected number varies depending on the amount of space the author has opted to give to each individual entry in his work.

Once, on the occasion of a birth in al-Radi's house, the Buyid vizier Fakhr al-Mulk sent him one thousand dinars. Al-Radi refused to accept it. The vizier sent it again as a gift for the nurses. Al-Radi refused it on the grounds that in the family of the Prophet to which he belonged, none but the women of the family were employed on such an occasion. The vizier sent it a third time, requesting the poet to distribute it among the students who attended his academy.[51]

On another occasion, al-Radi was reading the Qur'an with his teacher, the Maliki jurist Ibrahim ibn Ahmad al-Tabari. The teacher asked al-Radi, "Where do you stay?" Al-Radi replied, "In my father's house in *Bab al-Muhawwal.*" Al-Tabari, as a compliment, stated, "Someone like you should not be in his father's house," and then presented al-Radi with a house in Karkh. Al-Radi refused the gift, insisting that he did not accept anything from anyone but his father. To this, al-Tabari argued, "My right over you is greater because I made you memorize the Book of God." Only then did al-Radi accept the house.[52]

Lending further weight to al-Radi's abstinent ways is another narrative that praises him for his immense generosity. Al-Radi is noted as one among a few leading figures of this period to have set up an independent center of learning (*Dar al-ʿIlm*).[53]

> He provided for all the needs of his students, including the oil for their lamps. In a telling anecdote, it is said that one day a student needed oil for his lamp but the caretaker of the *Dar al-ʿIlm* was absent. On learning about this incident, al-Radi had keys made for all the students, so that they could access all the material themselves.[54]

These narratives portray al-Radi as a scholar who was deeply invested in the attainment, production, and transmission of knowledge.

Considering the young age at which al-Radi died (just over forty), his biographers time and again marvel at the number of responsibilities he shouldered for the community, Shiʿi and beyond, during his short life, while managing to produce the variety, number, and quality of works that he did. To remind us, in 990, when al-Radi was only twenty years old, he was appointed as aide to his father in three key positions: *naqib al-ashraf* (chief of the Prophet Muhammad's descendants in Baghdad), director of the annual hajj pilgrimage to Mecca, and chief judge over the petition-and-appeal court.

Between these prestigious government appointments and his scholarly endeavors, al-Radi also devoted himself to mentoring a number of renowned students whom he taught at the house of knowledge (*Dar al-ʿIlm*) that he himself established and financed. I will mention and describe some of these students momentarily. The *Dar al-ʿIlm* housed an impressive library and accommodation for students. Most biographers mention the lengths to which al-Radi went to ensure that his students were taken care of materially so that they could focus entirely on their studies. Perhaps what made al-Radi all the more passionate in his commitment to the students' educational cause was the difficult childhood he had himself experienced, during which his father was imprisoned and his mother was left alone to provide for and educate her two sons.

Several notable scholars of law, poetry, and other Islamic disciplines benefited from al-Radi's mentorship and care during his short life. Some among the many names of al-Radi's students that biographers mention include the famous poet Mihyar al-Daylami (d. 1036–37), a Zoroastrian who converted to Islam and studied poetry under al-Radi's guidance; al-Qadi ibn Qudama (d. 1108), a Shiʿi jurist and scholar of moral etiquette, poetry, hadith, and other Islamic disciplines; al-Mufid al-Nisaburi (d. 1066), an influential Imami scholar who traveled extensively and learned from various teachers during his travels, including the Sharif brothers and al-Shaykh al-Mufid; Abu Bakr al-Nisaburi (d. 1087), a well-known jurist and scholar of hadith and the grandfather of Abu al-Futuh al-Razi (author of the famous Persian Imami Qur'an exegesis *Rawd al-Janan*, d. 1157). Some sources mention that Shaykh al-Tusi (d. 1066) was also al-Radi's student but al-Tusi's time in Baghdad likely occurred after al-Radi passed away (in 1015).[55]

Al-Radi's Scholarly Oeuvre

In terms of al-Radi's own scholarly output, in addition to the *Haqa'iq* (again, composed in 1011), which is best described as a literary analysis of the Qur'an, al-Radi also dedicated two other treatises on the literary trope of metaphor: one on the Qur'an, *Economy of Eloquence in the Metaphors of the Qur'an* (*Talkhis al-Bayan fi Majazat al-Qur'an*), completed in 1010,[56] and the second on Prophetic hadith, *Prophetic Metaphors* (*Majazat al-Nabawiyya*), completed between 1010 and 1015 (al-Radi indicates that it was completed after his studies on Qur'anic subjects).[57]

Al-Radi also turned his attention to the enterprise of biographies. For instance, in his father's honor—his father being a man he held in great esteem and to whom he was also intellectually indebted—al-Radi authored a biography called *Sirat al-Tahir* (*Biography of al-Tahir*).[58] Next, al-Radi focused on a short biographical survey of the twelve Imams, with mention of which I began this book, *Khasa'is al-A'imma: Khasa'is Amir al-mu'minin* (*The Specialties of the Imams: The Specialties of the Commander of the Faithful*, completed 994). Al-Radi began this work with the intention of covering the qualities of all twelve Imams but could only complete the section on the first Imam, 'Ali ibn Abi Talib. In the *Khasa'is*, al-Radi presented an account of 'Ali ibn Abi Talib that fluctuated between descriptive retelling of key moments in the latter's life, especially his eventual martyrdom, discussion of 'Ali's views on legal and ethical problems, normative pronouncements on the obligation of befriending 'Ali (*ijab al-wala'*), and analysis of 'Ali's contributions to Arabic rhetoric, idioms, and to the art of delivering sermons. In comparison, his teacher al-Shaykh al-Mufid's text on the twelve Imams, *al-Irshad* (*The Guidance*), is generally more comprehensive than al-Radi's, since it includes discussion of all twelve Imams. Moreover, its chapter on 'Ali ibn Abi Talib is also considerably more detailed. In addition to the aspects of 'Ali's life covered by

al-Radi, al-Shaykh al-Mufid also engages ʿAliʾs role and importance at different stages of the Prophetʾs career, ʿAliʾs miracles, and even his encounters with
Jinns. The one distinctive aspect of al-Radiʾs *Khasaʾis*, perhaps, and one that
connects nicely with his Qurʾan exegesis that is the subject of this book, is its
explicit focus on the traditions of Arabic poetry attached to ʿAli and on the
significance of ʿAliʾs discourse to the Arabic language and rhetoric.

It was while compiling this section on ʿAli for the *Khasaʾis* that al-Radi
came across the speeches and sermons of ʿAli ibn Abi Talib, to which he then
turned his full attention and compiled the famous *Nahj al-Balagha*. Completed
in 1010, this was a monumental contribution of "232 orations, 78 epistles, and
429 sayings attributed to ʿAli b. Abi Talib, selected by al-Radi for their eloquence."[59] Scholar of Arabic literature Tahera Qutbuddin, who is completing
a critical study and translation of the *Nahj al-Balagha* states that the work
has enjoyed enormous currency through the ages, generating hundreds of
commentaries by medieval and modern Shiʿi and Sunni scholars."[60] And, as
Suzanne Stetkevych poignantly explains, the title *Nahj al-Balagha*, translated
as *Way of Eloquence* or simply *Rhetoric*, means "showing the way to salvation
by means of eloquence" and its intent is to establish the words of ʿAli ibn Abi
Talib as the proof of the precedence of ʿAli and Ahl al-Bayt on the basis of the
rhetorical force of its moral message rather than military-political might."[61] I
will return to Stetkevychʾs important insight shortly.

Al-Radi also left an indelible mark on Arabic literature with his two volumes of poetry, entitled *Diwan al-Radi*. The collection is comprised of 391
odes and covers his poetical compositions from the time he was a young pre-
teen until a couple of years before his death. The majority of compositions
fall under the themes of panegyric, self-praise, elegy, and love-poetry. The
themes of the injustice of Husaynʾs martyrdom and the usurpation of power
from the ʿAlid family also appear frequently in his poetry.[62] The eleventh-
century scholar al-Thaʿlabi emphasized al-Radiʾs mastery over the craft of
composing elegies.[63] Contemporary scholars of Arabic poetry have argued
that the works of al-Mutanabbi (d. 965), al-Buhturi (d. 897), and Abu Tammam (d. 845) were critical in shaping what would become al-Radiʾs distinct
poetic style.[64] An ingredient of his poetic corpus especially critical for the
purposes of this study relates to al-Radiʾs renown for using complicated
metaphors drawn from the traditional poetic heritage, which further attests
his investment in and command over the Arabic language.[65]

The insights and arguments of Suzanne Stetkevych in her two articles
focusing on al-Radiʾs poetry resonate in particularly important ways with the

arguments of this book.[66] On the question of poetic influences and markers of individual style in al-Radi's poetry, Stetkevych argues that "the influence of al-Mutanabbi's grand heroics is perceptible in al-Radi's madih and fakhr, as are the ease and fluidity of his style," but where al-Radi's poetry stands out is in his lyric-elegiac prelude to the *qasida*, the *nasib*, which was not necessarily al-Mutanabbi's strong suit. For the *nasib*, she traces the influence on al-Radi's poetry to the Umayyad period's genre of 'Udhri ghazal, defined by the theme of the erotic suffering of unrequited love, and to the lyrical development of this theme in the hands of the 'Abbasid master-poets (namely al-Buhturi and Abu Firas al-Hamdani, d. 968) in the opening *nasib* section of the full *qasida* as well as in ghazal. Stetkevych also emphasizes two varieties of al-Radi's compositions as the most striking and moving examples of his lyrical power. First, "his poems for 'Ashura', in which the Shi'i rituals of mourning the martyrdom of al-Husayn at Karbala' serve as a framework to explore the poetics of loss and 'Alid dispossession at both personal and political levels." And, second, "his lyrics on the Iraqi pilgrimage route, called al-Hijaziyyat, in which the traditional nasib and ghazal place-names are replaced by those of the Iraqi pilgrimage route, so that the nostalgic yearning for the beloved and the places associated with her and her tribe now take on an evocative metaphorical dimension." Particularly germane to this book is Stetkevych's argument that it is possible to trace an overarching theme, that of a sense of loss and dispossession, in al-Radi's poetry, which is connected in significant ways to his compilatory work of the *Nahj al-Balagha*. As she puts it:

> I would like to propose that the combined delicacy and ardor of al-Radi's lyrical gift, whether the introductory *nasib* sections of his full *qasidahs* or his free-standing lyrical *Hijaziyyat*, reflect not merely al-Radi's profound mastery of '*ilm al-balaghah*, a field that encompassed and analyzed all the most revered sources of the Arab language—Qur'an, *Hadith*, and poetry, but are intimately connected with the sense of loss, dispossession, and bereavement inherent in his 'Alid heritage, and inherent, too, in the rhetoric of dispossession expressed in many of the *khutbahs* he has chosen to include in *Nahj al-balaghah*.[67]

It is important to ask how al-Radi's writings on the Qur'an tie up (if at all) with this theme of loss, so palpable in al-Radi's poetry and selections in the *Nahj al-Balagha*. Stetkevych's insights on the *Nahj al-Balagha* are critically helpful for making this connection. She writes:

Just as the formulation of *i'jaz al-Qur'an* established the Qur'an's unmatchable rhetorical power and beauty as evidentiary proof of its veracity (i.e., divine origin) and of the Prophet Muhammad's divine mission, it is the rhetorical power and beauty (which are the same thing) of *Nahj al-balaghah* that ultimately confer authenticity and establish the veracity of the 'Alid claim to Islamic moral and/or political legitimacy and dominion.[68]

Stetkevych captures here the immense social currency and power of language in the epistemic milieu of tenth-century Baghdad, where the demonstration of linguistic mastery was effectively a claim to power. In the *Haqa'iq*, al-Radi carefully unraveled each ambiguity in the Qur'an and in doing so indexed the special access he had to the beauty, power, and inner secrets and subtleties of the Arabic language. In effect, the linguistic and rhetorical power on display in the *Haqa'iq* reaffirmed his claim to 'Alid authority and was valorized by the view that linguistic mastery was tied to genealogical descent.

This important theme of the intimacy between language and lineage is discernable throughout al-Radi's intellectual oeuvre, and will feature prominently in the analysis I conduct in this book. Taken together, al-Radi's varied works point to his deep investment in and commitment to demonstrating the linguistic mastery of the Qur'an, the Prophet, the Imams, and himself. As I will argue throughout the book, this theme is very much a reflection of his understanding of language as the master discipline that sets the terms for making sense of all things and through which all forms of authority (religious and temporal) could be claimed and established.

Some of al-Radi's other works, mostly non-extant, include three works on the poetry of leading poets of his time, Ibn al-Hajjaj (d. 1001), al-Sabi, and Abu Tammam. The titles of these works are as follows: *The Best Poems of Ibn al-Hajjaj* (*al-Jayyid min shi'r Ibn al-Hajjaj*),[69] *Selections from Abu Ishaq al-Sabi's Poetry* (*Mukhtar Shi'ir Abi Ishaq al-Sabi*), and *Additions to the [collected] Poetry of Abu Tammam* (*al-Ziyadat fi Shi'ir Abi Tammam*).[70] Another important genre through which al-Radi displayed his literary skills was that of ornate Arabic prose, exemplified in literary exchanges. Al-Radi's correspondences were collected in a text titled *Letters of al-Radi* (*Rasa'il al-Sharif al-Radi*). Although this book is not extant, his letters to al-Sabi have been put together as a text titled *Rasa'il al-Sabi wa al-Sharif al-Radi* (*Letters [between] al-Sabi and al-Radi*).[71] Finally, on the topic of Arabic language, specifically, al-Radi authored a text called *Annotation on Abu 'Ali al-Farisi's 'Elucidation'* (*Ta'liq 'ala Idah Abu 'Ali al-Farisi*),[72] a commentary on this renowned grammarian's book, *The Elucidation* (*al-Idah*).

Al-Radi also sought to document features of his own historical period, through a history of the judges of Baghdad, *Reports on the Judges of Baghdad* (*Akhbar Qudat Baghdad*). Finally, he also penned a juridical work that has not survived, titled *Annotation on the Jurists' Disagreements* (*Ta'liq Khilaf al-Fuqaha'*),[73] which one can surmise from the text's title dealt with pertinent legal topics and debates of his day; this text may well have represented an annotation on al-Tabari's well-known *The Jurists' Disagreements* (*Ikhtilaf al-Fuqaha'*).[74]

The Textual Field: al-Radi's Qur'an Commentary (the *Haqa'iq*)

Al-Radi's predilection for literary composition and analysis is evident from his scholarly oeuvre described in what just preceded. In the *Haqa'iq*, al-Radi combines his aptitude as a litterateur with his training in a host of religious subjects and other ancillary disciplines. Thus, the coalescence of al-Radi's multiple intellectual genealogies is most vividly observed in this exegetical work. The *Haqa'iq* also most thoroughly captures al-Radi's Qur'an hermeneutic, in which he employs the classical method of organizing his discussion under distinct queries or questions (*masa'il*), to give the text a clear and lucid organization. As Walid Saleh has argued in his critical contribution to the study of the classical *tafsir* tradition, the act of organizing Qur'anic material by means of the *mas'ala* or question/point of investigation heading signaled the entry of scholastic mentality into the discipline of exegesis.[75] Moreover, Tariq Jaffer has shown how the tool of *mas'ala* allowed the leading eleventh-century scholar Fakhr al-Din al-Razi (d. 1209), to record, organize, and classify vast amounts of knowledge. Similarly, in al-Radi's exegesis, the dialectical tool of dividing and organizing material into different problems or *masa'il* allows al-Radi to prioritize specific questions pertaining to a specific verse, without letting those questions be overshadowed by other exegetical material that would naturally make its way into a traditional commentary.

In contrast to a typical verse-by-verse commentary, which was the custom for exegetes of this period, al-Radi selects for analysis only those verses that result in "ambiguities" (*mutashabihat*). Yet, his Qur'an exegesis straddles multiple genres. On the one hand, it is not a traditional verse-by-verse Qur'an commentary, in that it focuses solely on the ambiguous verses. Certainly, works that conduct a selective commentary on specific verses are still categorized as exegesis in the traditional sense, Sufi exegeses being a case in point. Structurally and thematically, though, al-Radi's *Haqa'iq* is different in a few ways. First, its chapters are divided by the Qur'anic verses being discussed moving in an ascending order (chapter one deals with verse 3:7, chapter two deals with verse 3:8, chapter three deals with verse 3:18, and so on). Second, the chapters themselves are dedicated to answering a broader question that a particular verse raises. Al-Radi's answer to those questions fits partially into a scheme termed the question-and-answer (*masa'il wa ajwiba*) style common to theological argumentation during this period, and partially with the Qur'an commentary or *tafsir* genre. The question-and-answer format is premised on the disputational style of "if they were to say . . . then I would say."[76] The beginning of each chapter in al-Radi's commentary follows this scheme of staging and then engaging the question of a hypothetical interlocutor. However, the *Haqa'iq* fits with traditional *tafsir* schemes in its comprehensive presentation of scholarly opinions on the verse in question before presenting (if at all) al-Radi's own interpretation. Clearly, the two genres were related and a work like the *Haqa'iq* nicely illustrates the interconnection between varied disciplines and genres. So, to answer an anticipated question, is this even a Qur'an exegesis or is it just a literary text peppered with conundrums derived from the Qur'an? I would argue that yes, the *Haqa'iq* is best categorized as a work of *tafsir* or Qur'an exegesis because, despite some of its distinctive organizational features, its underlying objective was ultimately the explication and resolution of the ambiguities populating the Qur'an and, by so doing, privileging a canonical notion of the Arabic language as the key to addressing Qur'anic ambiguities.

The single surviving volume of al-Radi's exegesis includes his commentary on the entire third sura (chapter) of the Qur'an, titled "Household of 'Imran" (*Al 'Imran*). It also includes a small portion of his commentary on the first few verses of the fourth Qur'anic sura, titled "The Women" (*al-Nisa'*).[77] The title of the third Qur'anic chapter, "Household of 'Imran," refers to the narratives this chapter contains on Moses, Aaron, Zachariah, Mary, and Jesus.[78]

The entire third sura consists of two hundred verses, of which al-Radi identifies and explains thirty-one. These verses are selected by al-Radi on the basis of the ambiguities they raise. From the fourth sura, only the first forty-eight verses fit in this surviving volume and, of those, al-Radi narrows down a total of six verses as ambiguous. In sum, the fifth volume of al-Radi's commentary is framed by thirty-seven questions (masa'il) that correspond to thirty-seven ambiguous verses. Al-Radi devotes approximately ten to twelve pages of discussion to each question. The number and selection of verses that al-Radi categorized as "ambiguous" is important, since even though many exegetes shared the exegetical principle of structuring their commentaries according to the clear/ambiguous verses, they differed on the question of which verses would count as ambiguous. In other words, the "ambiguous" verse in contrast to the "clear" verse may have been a common exegetical principle, but the nature of "Qur'anic ambiguity" and the different forms that it could take varied considerably. The reason for these variances, as I will argue, is that authors were informed by multiple intellectual factors and conditions, not limited to their sectarian and theological affiliations.

My study of the thirty-seven questions raised through the ambiguous verses in the Haqa'iq will enable us to discern how al-Radi understood the category of Qur'anic ambiguity and to appreciate the multiple types of ambiguity that, for him, come under this grouping. In my analysis of this work, I identify four primary forms of ambiguity that frame al-Radi's discussion of the mutashabih or ambiguous verses. In Figure 1 below, I map the thirty-seven issues (masa'il) under these four themes. Although the classifications adopted in this figure are not conclusively impervious or mutually exclusive, the purpose of this chart is to provide the reader a bird's-eye view of the different kinds of topics covered in the Haqa'iq, as well as the weight that al-Radi gives to each one. Since al-Radi himself does not divide the masa'il according to the themes that I have enumerated, the reader should keep in mind that this thematic division reflects the conceptual scheme that I see as governing al-Radi's broader discussion. The breakdown in this figure has also guided my selection of specific discussion topics (masa'il) in the rest of this book. Given the impossible task of addressing all the topics contained in al-Radi's exegesis, I have chosen those themes that occurred most frequently in his exegetical discourse.

My four-fold division of al-Radi's approach to ambiguity in the Qur'an is based on the nature of the query that is built into the majority of the questions (masa'il) posed at the start of each chapter, which take various forms. Some directly challenge the Qur'an's coherence, like "Why does the Qur'an state the obvious?" Others express concern with verses that insinuate a prophetology that is theologically problematic (for al-Radi), such as "How can the Qur'an say that prophets exhibit doubt?" Still others remain occupied with preserving the linguistic perfection of the Qur'an and ask, "How can

Figure 1. Types of Ambiguity in the *Haqa'iq al-Ta'wil fi Mutashabih al-Tanzil*

Theological	Grammatical
Q. 3.8 - God as cause of human deviation? (*Haqa'iq* 3.2)	Q. 3.7 - Use of singular noun "mother" (*umm*) to describe plural noun "verses" (*ayat*) (*Haqa'iq 3.1*)
Q. 3.14 - God as beautifier of desires? (*Haqa'iq* 3.4)	Q. 3.45 - Jesus as the word of God, mismatched gender of pronoun (*Haqa'iq* 3.10)
Q. 3.26 - God gives power to the unjust? (*Haqa'iq* 3.6)	Q. 3.61 - *Mubahala* verse; how can the Prophet invite himself? (*Haqa'iq* 3.12)
Q. 3.40 - Zachariah's doubt on having a son (*Haqa'iq* 3.9)	Q. 3.91 - Superfluous letter '*waw*' (*Haqa'iq* 3.18)
Q. 3.60 - Prophetic doubt (*Haqa'iq* 3.11)	Q. 3.110 - Repetition of God's name (in discussion section) (*Haqa'iq* 3.23)
Q. 3.83 - Forced submission? (*Haqa'iq* 3.16)	Q. 4.22 - First clause in present tense, second in past tense (*Haqa'iq* 4.2)
Q. 3.90 - Repentance of the unbelievers not accepted? (*Haqa'iq* 3.17)	
Q. 3.102 - Obeying God as He ought to be obeyed (*Haqa'iq* 3.21)	
Q. 3.109 - All actions must return to God—were they ever detached? (*Haqa'iq* 3.22)	
Q. 3.128 - No actions are from you (*Haqa'iq* 3.25)	
Q. 3.154 - What has been written down will happen (*Haqa'iq* 3.29)	
Q. 3.178 - Respite for unbelievers so they increase in sin (*Haqa'iq* 3.31)	
Q. 4.48 - Forgiveness for sins, except sin of associating others with God (*Haqa'iq* 4.6)	
Total 13	**6**

Logical	Ethical/Social
Q. 3.13 - God reduced the number of believers in the eyes of the polytheists (*Haqa'iq* 3.3)	**Q. 3.26 - God gives power to the unjust? (*Haqa'iq* 3.26)**
Q. 3.18 - God testifies on Himself? (*Haqa'iq* 3.5)	Q. 3.28 - Taking unbelievers as allies? (*Haqa'iq* 3.7)
Q. 3.36 - The man is not like the woman (*Haqa'iq* 3.8)	Q. 3.64 - People of the Book taking other gods? (*Haqa'iq* 3.13)
Q. 3.81 - Prophets must recognize earlier prophets? (*Haqa'iq* 3.15)	Q. 3.75 - Unreliable cheaters from the People of the Book (*Haqa'iq* 3.14)

Logical	Ethical/Social
Q. 3.96 - Mecca as the first house? (*Haqa'iq* 3.19)	**Q. 3.90 - Repentance of unbelievers not accepted? (*Haqa'iq* 3.17)**
Q. 3.97 - Equating unbelievers with believers unable to perform Hajj (*Haqa'iq* 3.20)	Q. 3.110 - "Best *umma*" as reference to past community? (*Haqa'iq* 3.23)
Q. 3.111 - It won't hurt you except it will pain (*Haqa'iq* 3.24)	Q. 3.145 - Equivalence between those who seek reward in this life and the Hereafter? (*Haqa'iq* 3.28)
Q. 3.133 - Breadth of paradise equal to heaven and earth (*Haqa'iq* 3.26)	Q. 4.43 - Forbidding intoxication while in prayer (but permitting it when not in prayer?) (*Haqa'iq* 4.4)
Q. 3:143 - Vision of death? (*Haqa'iq* 3.27)	
Q. 3.175 - Satan fears his allies? (*Haqa'iq* 3.30)	
Q. 4.3 - Link between "doing justice to orphans" and "marrying women?" (*Haqa'iq* 4.1)	
Q. 4.42 - The disobeying wish the earth is leveled with them (*Haqa'iq* 4.3)	
Q. 4.47 - God's promise of disfigured unbelievers not coming true (*Haqa'iq* 4.5)	
Total 13	8

*Two numbering schemes are used in this figure. The first refers to the sura and verse numbers in the Qur'an. For example, "Q. 3.8" refers to verse 8 in Sura 3.

The second scheme reflects the sura and question (*mas'ala*) in the *Haqa'iq*. For example, *Haqa'iq* 3.2 refers to question number two in his discussion of Sura 3.

**Bold and highlighted verses cover more than one theme and therefore appear more than once in this figure.

a feminine pronoun be used to refer to a masculine noun?" This question-and-answer structure was characteristic of the "writerly culture"[79] of tenth-century Baghdad, during which time books continued to function as written records of personal lessons and where the form and structure of a hypothetical exchange in person was preserved.

Having sketched critical lineaments of al-Radi's biographical cum scholarly persona and literary output, in the next chapter, I turn to a discussion of the sociopolitical context in which he operated—that of Buyid Baghdad.

CHAPTER 2

Buyid Baghdad and al-Radi's Hermeneutical Identity

There are two main purposes that inform this chapter and that also, in turn, inform its structure and sequence. The first is presenting an overview of the sociopolitical context during the Buyid period. And the second is outlining the conceptual approach that I plan on employing as part of my examination of al-Radi's Qur'an commentary over the course of this book. With regard to the first purpose, that of contextualizing al-Radi's thought and discourse on the Qur'an, I try to offer and work with a notion of "context" that does not presume neat or conclusive correspondence between extant political policies and trends of religious thought. Specifically, I alert the reader to the problematic conclusions this framework has generated with respect to the history of Twelver Shi'i thought under the reign of the Buyid dynasty.

As for the second purpose and part of this chapter, connected to the conceptual position I take throughout this book, I will argue for approaching al-Radi's exegetical work as a moral argument that is situated in a particular question-and-answer space. I show that this framing shifts our attention to his understanding of the problem or question to which he saw his commentary as a response. The historiographic depth that this approach affords is that it opens avenues for viewing al-Radi's Qur'an commentary as informed by and responding to the wider intellectual currents and conversations that encircled his career as a poet and exegete. What were the sorts and sources of dissatisfaction that he found in the intellectual and political world he inhabited, and in what ways did he imagine and frame his Qur'an exegesis as a response and resolution to those dissatisfactions? This question, central to how al-Radi wielded his religious authority as a scholar and writer, is also central to my engagement with his exegetical project. Such a question-and-answer-based approach also allows me to interrogate the interaction of different aspects and modalities of his thought that might otherwise be foreclosed through a predominantly sectarian reading of his work.

Most notably, I have in mind the pivotal importance of his role as a renowned poet of his time for the sort of hermeneutical scheme he advances. The critical link between his poetic persona and the interpretive moves he makes in his Qur'an commentary, I will show, is his view of language. This is because he regarded language as the hermeneutical key for interpreting the Qur'an and, in this distinct historical juncture under the Buyids, poets had emerged as the authoritative custodians of language. Thus, I suggest that al-Radi's role and experience as a well-known and well-regarded poet in Baghdad's literary circles profoundly informed his hermeneutical identity as a Qur'an exegete, at many times outweighing his theological and sectarian leanings and sympathies.

In fact, in al-Radi's epistemological vision, the very task of responding to and resolving conundrums posed by Qur'anic ambiguities was inextricably bound to the larger question of mastery and expertise over the Arabic language. To him, the Qur'an was first and foremost an *Arabic* text that ought to be understood through the mastery of a critical linguistic canon. Moreover, and this again is among my central arguments in this book, in al-Radi's thought, the work of Qur'anic exegesis was both informed by and contributed to the formation of the Arabic linguistic canon. The resolution of the Qur'an's ambiguous verses and the canonization of the Arabic language were synchronous imperatives. Capturing this mutually reinforcing relationship between language and hermeneutics is among the major purposes of this book. And, to successfully execute this task, it is important that one resists adopting as one's analytical point of departure the assumption of seamless correspondence between hermeneutics and sectarian identity. Al-Radi's Shi'i identity did not neatly translate into a definable Qur'anic hermeneutic nor into a definitive conception of language. This is how the central argument of this book, having to do with establishing the intimacy of language and hermeneutics in exegetical projects like al-Radi's, and the central conceptual intervention of this book, to do with questioning and showing the limits of sectarian-driven readings of Qur'an commentary traditions marked as Twelver Shi'i, connect together. Ultimately, what I aim to amplify over the course of this book are some of the glaring conceptual problems attached to the very category of a "Shi'i hermeneutic," a category that stands authorized through the unsound assumption that sectarian identity and hermeneutical imagination readily

correspond in a predictable and seamless fashion. By describing the multivalent interpretive traditions that informed al-Radi's Qur'an hermeneutic, it is
precisely this assumption that I challenge and question.

But, in preparation for a closer examination of al-Radi's thought, it is
imperative to first consider the intellectual and political conditions in which
al-Radi's career as a scholar unfolded. It is to this task that I now turn.

Grand Narrative of the Buyid "Golden Age"

In the field of Islamic studies, the tenth century, in particular, has attracted a
great deal of scholarly attention. It has been described as an age of intellectual
"renaissance," a blueprint for a distinctly Islamic "humanism," and a century
that saw an unprecedented efflorescence of cosmopolitanism in Islam.[1] The
decentralized rule of the Buyids, which paved the way for multiple networks
of patronage under different dynasties, played a critical role in this culture of
intellectual dynamism, and Twelver Shi'i scholars were among the major ben-
eficiaries of this climate of scholarly exchange and fertility.[2] Scholars of this
period, like Claude Cahen, have argued that the background of the Buyid rulers as Persian Daylamite Zaydi Shi'is, and their later adherence to the Twelver
sect of Imami Shi'ism, led them to favor prominent Shi'i personalities.[3] Specifically, this meant including them in their smaller circles of advisers, prop-
ping them up as appointed leaders of highly coveted posts, such as chief judge
of the courts of appeal (*mazalim* courts) and director of the Hajj pilgrimage.
Buyid Shi'ism is said to have translated into a general climate of tolerance,
such that previously privatized and persecuted Shi'i beliefs and practices were
provided a safe space for public articulation. In other words, the Buyids are
given credit for offering Imami Shi'i intellectuals a taste of freedom not previously available, thus marking the Shi'i "coming out," so to say, from their
previous state of *taqiyya* (dissimulation). For example, Meir Bar-Asher, the
author of what is, to date, the only comprehensive study of Twelver Shi'i exegesis (until the tenth century), describes this development as follows:

> A dramatic change in the fortunes of Imami Shi'ism occurred soon
> after the Major Occultation with the rise to power of the Buwayhid
> dynasty in Baghdad, the heart of the 'Abbasid state. . . . Whatever their
> relationship to Imami Shi'ism, it seems beyond doubt that during their

rule (334/945-447/1055), Imami Shiʿism thrived. In fact, the reign of this dynasty marks a golden era for Imami Shiʿism, which had earlier experienced continual persecutions. The legitimization accorded to Imami Shiʿism under the Buwayhids brought about an important cultural shift, characterized by extensive literary activity and far-reaching innovations in Imami doctrine. In studying early Imami literature a distinction must therefore be drawn between works composed prior to the rise of the Buwayhids (or up to the Major Occultation) and those written during their period.[4]

More recently, in Western scholarship, aspects of this grand narrative of Shiʿi emancipation under the Buyids from the previous clutches of Sunni persecution have been successfully challenged. In the extant historiography, the flourishing of intellectual activity during the Buyid period in the varied realms of Muslim social, political, and intellectual life is still generally agreed upon. It is also acknowledged that there was an increase in the participation of scholars from multiple schools of thought in the realm of public debate. However, the use of romanticizing and triumphalist categories to describe the Buyid period such as "renaissance," "age of humanism," or "golden age" are no longer held viable. Such categories and the analytical frameworks they generate are problematic because they serve to evaluate Muslim historical currents and actors through the narrow terms and filter of a distinctly Euro-American lens. Moreover, and equally importantly, tying scholarly cross-sectarian intellectual activity and productivity under the Buyids to modern ideals of pluralism represents an anachronistic and thus misleading gesture.[5]

An important work that offers an effective correction to this problem is Arabic scholar Samuel England's *Medieval Empires and the Culture of Competition*.[6] In his comparative study of Muslim and Christian medieval empires, including that of the Buyids, England calls for the decentering of religious and ethnic identity (and the stubbornly modern notions of the self it entails) as the critical lens through which to approach this period. The privileging of identity in Mediterranean studies, he insists, has produced an academic emphasis on pluralist multiculturalism or an innate othering as the dominant historiographic terms of evaluating the medieval past. Although these positions stand at opposite ends of the spectrum, they share a common heritage: post-Orientalist Western historiography dating from the latter half of the twentieth century. England's work shifts away from identity as an ethnic or religious question as the central pivot around which to frame his questions and analysis and, instead, focuses on competition and its operation in the vastly separate Islamic and Christian empires of the medieval period. The central argument of his book that also offers a useful contextual backdrop to my analysis is this: it is not the striving for tolerance and pluralism, both thoroughly modern desires, that fueled the thriving culture of intellectual discourse and debate at imperial medieval courts such as that of the Buyids. Rather, the "culture of competition," as England calls it, was integral to the maintenance of imperial political sovereignty. In fact, a vibrant court featuring literary contests served as a critical means for maintaining some semblance of political stability, *particularly* during a moment otherwise marked by political vulnerability.[7] Put differently, the social capital acquired through the patronage of a culture of intellectual competition served to stave off the threat of looming competitors to political power. These insights are crucial for grasping the background picture of the intellectual and political climate in which al-Radi's *Haqa'iq* was composed, a work in which language and poetry function as the most authoritative arbiters of Qur'anic meaning.

Another Western scholarly text that has shown, in particularly instructive ways, the conceptual poverty of positing a neat correspondence between contemporaneous political policies and religious thought and identity during the Buyid period is Kambiz GhaneaBassiri's unpublished (as a monograph) but extremely important 2003 dissertation, *A Window on Islam in Buyid Society*. In this work, GhaneaBassiri presented a trenchant critique of Euro-American research on the development of Muslim religious thought under the Buyid dynasty. He argued that most of the Western scholarship on the Buyid period produced during the latter half of the twentieth century perpetuates the unsound view that the religious thought and disagreements of Muslim scholars during this period is reducible to or can be readily mapped onto the ongoing dynamics of imperial politics, namely the decentralization of power under the Buyids and its impact on the institution of the caliphate. He points out that in doing so these studies "exemplify a prevailing trend in Islamic studies that is based on the assumption that religion and politics are one and the same in Islam."[8] Questioning the salience of this approach, which views Islamic political history as an all-encompassing framework for understanding the sociohistorical development of Muslim religious thought and discourse, GhaneaBassiri argues for a reevaluation.[9] This reevaluation, he argues, ought to be achieved by "examining the way in which Muslims of varying schools of thought, who lived within a similar historical context,

sought to practice their personal understanding of humanity's ideal relationship with both God and the world."[10]

What, though, does the application of GhaneaBassiri's call for a reevaluation look like in practice? A recent study, focusing on the question of what
it meant to be Sabian in tenth-century Baghdad, provides us an excellent
such example. Alexandre Roberts's article on Abu Ishaq Ibrahim b. Hilal al-
Sabi (d. 994)—a close friend and mentor of al-Radi's—proposes to explore
how one Sabian scholar who moved among the intellectual elite of tenth-
century Baghdad operated in his social role as an intimate associate of Muslim scholars like al-Radi and others while adhering to a "pagan" cult with
few adherents.[11] Moving away from an effort to uncover the "true" motives of
his protagonist, al-Sabi, Roberts instead documents interreligious scholarly
exchanges in which al-Sabi maintained his distinction as a Sabian even as
he simultaneously cultivated cultural assimilation with the religious "other."
So, for instance, while at times we find al-Sabi adeptly employing Muslim
tropes in his expressions of piety, at yet other moments we see him playing
along with the image of Sabians as having exclusive access to the science
of astrology. Let me share a fascinating anecdote that captures the delicate
dance through which al-Sabi negotiated his religious identity in a Muslim
imperial setting.

> One day al-Sabi was present at [Abu Muhammad al-Hasan] al-
> Muhallabi's [d. 963, vizier to the Buyid Amir Mu'izz al-Dawla, d. 967]
> table, but then declined to eat, on account of some fava beans which
> were on [the table], since they are forbidden to Sabians, along with
> fish, pork, camel-meat, dove-hens, and locusts. Al-Muhallabi said to
> him, "Don't be tedious, eat these fava beans with us." But [Ibrahim]
> replied, "O vizier, I do not wish to disobey God in anything I eat,"
> which pleased [the vizier].[12]

As Roberts notes, the vizier's initial displeasure with al-Sabi's refusal to eat
quickly turns into approval when he hears the explanation behind the latter's dietary choices: avoiding disobedience toward God. In other words, by
taking the rules of his own religion seriously, al-Sabi gains the respect of his
most powerful companion, the Muslim vizier, whose wish al-Sabi had been
compelled to deny. Another telling example of interreligious friendship is
found in the eulogy al-Radi, a sayyid Muslim, penned for al-Sabi, a *dhimmi*
[non-Muslim under Muslim political rule] Sabian,[13] after the latter's death:

By virtue we were bound together, since
   no bond was my nobility or birth.
Though you were not my family or my tribe,
   you hold my love the tightest of them all,
and though your origins were not so high,
   great auspices replaced strong ancestors.[14]

These words from al-Radi were not the expression of some open-ended or universalist pluralism, but rather the manifestation of a form of everyday friendship and intimacy that exceeded the theological limits of interreligious difference. Al-Sabi's example helps reiterate the point that access to elite intellectual circles in the court were not determined solely by one's affiliation to a particular sect or religion. As Samuel England has shown while studying Buyid imperial courts and the ethos of competition that sustained them, what mattered most when it came to the ability to rise to the top as a courtier was one's intellectual ability to outdo others. At any rate, the point I want to emphasize through this discussion is twofold. First, religious thought, discourse, and debate, while obviously informed by the political conditions and policies of a moment, cannot be reduced to them. And second, in the specific case of the Buyid period, while recognizing the noticeable efflorescence of intellectual exchange and competition across scholarly, sectarian, and even religious boundaries, it is important to view this phenomenon through a nuanced perspective on power and politics that does not resort to anachronistic explanations of tolerance or medieval cosmopolitan humanism. I now turn more specifically to some necessary contextual comments on Shi'i scholarly traditions during the Buyid period.

Twelver Shi'i Scholars During the Buyid Period

The reign of the Buyid dynasty marked a transitional period between the cohesive political structure of the 'Abbasid dynasty that came before and the mostly independent Islamic states that arose afterward, in the eleventh century. Historians describe this period as one marred by immense political fragmentation; several independent dynasties scattered a landscape that had previously been united under the 'Abbasids. The Buyids (Shi'i) occupied the southern and western parts of Iran and all of Iraq; the Samanids and, later, the Ghaznavids (both Sunni) neighbored them in the east; the Hamdanids

(Shiʿi) had their stronghold in Aleppo and Mosul; while Egypt and Syria had come under the rule of the Fatimids (Ismaʿili-Shiʿi).

The Buyid conquest over the ʿAbbasids represents a dramatic and decisive moment in Islam's political and religious history. This is so because, as adherents of the Twelver Shiʿi school, the Buyids could have put an end to the institution of the caliphate, altogether. The fundamental objection and criticism of the Shiʿi school, from the time of its earliest form, was that the caliphs were illegitimate rulers who had usurped power from the rightful successors of the Prophet—that is, the Imams. In other words, the only acceptable sources of authority for the Shiʿi community were the divinely designated Imams. Upon seizing power, the Buyids made no attempt to revise the situation by deposing the caliph. In fact, not only did they not put an end to the caliphate, they emerged as the first Shiʿi dynasty to create a principality that was, on the one hand, independent of the caliphate, but, on the other hand, parallel to it.

When the Buyids came into office, they significantly curtailed the caliph's power and mobilized the religious authority invested in that position to assemble their own legitimacy as the new political rulers. By claiming honorifics such as *"shahanshah"* (king of kings), the Buyids also revived the Persianate tradition of kingship (sultanate). The symbolic transfer of sovereignty, from caliph to king, was also facilitated by practices such as the caliph's bestowing of honorific titles on the Buyid rulers (titles often selected by the ruler himself). But underlying such political maneuvers and strategies was a fundamental ambiguity: the Shiʿi doctrinal position that only the Imams possessed the sovereign authority for political leadership. So how did the Buyids uphold the institutions of the caliphate and sultanate without subverting Shiʿi dogma on the Imams' encompassing authority? The answer to this question lies in the subtle yet significant shifts within Shiʿi intellectual traditions during this hinge moment in Muslim history. The Buyids ascended to power in the years just after the twelfth and final Imam's occultation, in 941. This crisis compelled Twelver Shiʿi scholars to revisit and rethink their established positions on acceptable forms of political authority. Previously, they had categorically rejected any form of illegitimate, meaning non-Imami, rule. But, under the unusual and unprecedented circumstances of the tenth century, whereby the Imam was no longer among them, the Shiʿi community did not protest the Buyid configuration of sultanate-caliphate-occult imamate. Since the Imams were no longer around, their doctrinal status and prestige were not diminished by the political rule of non-Imams.

In addition to doctrinal innovation, the Buyid era also witnessed important shifts in the intellectual and political milieu in which Shiʻi scholars
operated. Under the Buyids, Twelver Shiʻi scholars benefited from a general
climate of intellectual exchange and were organized into an autonomous
body, so as to counterbalance the ʻAbbasids. Formerly, the ʻAlid family unit
was integrated into and dominated by the ʻAbbasids.[15] But, under the Buyids,
although they were never permitted entry to the high ranks of sultan, caliph,
or vizier, Twelver Shiʻi scholars nonetheless took part in the literary assemblies and scholarly circles that flourished at that time.[16]

The intellectual vitality of Twelver Shiʻi scholars during this period, as seen
in their numerous public positions and scholarly contributions, has led some
contemporary historians to conclude that the tolerant attitude of the Buyids played a formative role in what has been called "the critical turn" in Shiʻi
thought: namely, the increasingly public role of Shiʻi scholars and a concomitant rationalization of Shiʻi doctrines.[17] According to this narrative, a tradition
that was previously hidden in the shadows of dissimulation assumed visibility during the Buyid reign. And, as a result, so the narrative goes, the exaggerated and hyperbolic features of the Shiʻi tradition, such as the association
of supernatural qualities with the figure of the Imam, made way for a more
"rationalized" and sober expression of Shiʻism. Such a reading of Shiʻi history
is conceptually wanting for a few reasons. The fundamental shortcoming of
the view that Shiʻism transformed from a dissimulated to a public and, cor-
respondingly, an "irrational" to a "rational" tradition during the Buyid era is
the assumption that Shiʻism represents a linear category, the passage of which
from one state to another is readily available for disciplinary canonization.
According to this view, a fixed and unchanging category called the "Shiʻi position" simply shed off its dissimulated past as it saw the light of publicity under
the Buyids. Moreover, as Shiʻism became more public, it also became more
"rational"; the opening up of Shiʻi scholars and scholarly traditions to other
currents of Muslim intellectual thought (read: Sunni thought) enabled Shiʻism
to become more moderate, public, and rational. In other words, having been
exposed to normative patterns of "orthodoxy," Shiʻism assumed a more orthodox form. What is lost from such a teleological approach toward religious
identity is the a priori canonization of what counts as "rational" or "orthodox"
prior to the intellectual arguments and discourses through which the boundaries of such categories are articulated, presented, and contested.

Implicit in this reasoning is the argument that Shiʻi membership in a
more cosmopolitan *and* more Sunni milieu led them to cast off the more
"radical" or "heterodox" elements of their doctrinal apparatus. In other

words, increased social interaction, exchange, and exposure led Shiʿi scholars to *concede* or *conform* to the majoritarian view. For instance, the recent entry on the Buyids in the *Encyclopedia of Islam* illustrates this trend quite well:

> At no time did the Buwayhids plan the persecution of the Sunnis by the Shiʿis—both sects were represented in their army; rather they intended to set up a sort of ʿAbbasid-Shiʿi condominium, which freed the Shiʿis from the obligation of a certain *taqiyya* and provided them, as well as the Sunnis, with an official organization.... Without the smallest doubt, Twelver Shiʿism owes to the Buwayhid regime not only this organisation, but even a part of its doctrinal structure.[18]

It is evident that the author is referring to the appointment of elite Shiʿi figures like al-Radi's family to prestigious administrative posts as evidence of the new conditions in which the Shiʿis actively participated in the governance of their own community, as well as that of the Muslim community at large. But it would be hasty to associate the nominal Shiʿi prominence in the public sphere with a desire on the part of the Buyids to be more tolerant toward the minority Shiʿi community.

As I outlined in the introduction, in this book, my approach to understanding religious identity begins by arguing against a view that ascribes a predetermined essence to "Shiʿism," and against a framework that fails to account for the ways in which the very structure of religious identity gets constituted under shifting intellectual and institutional conditions. Instead, I turn attention to particular historical conjunctures of authoritative debates, discord, and disagreement in which Shiʿism as an "embodied argument" is made possible and centrally visible. The post-occultation Buyid period is one such conjuncture that brings into view different configurations of a Shiʿi identity and enables certain versions to be inscribed and persist. Thus, rather than remain focused on a singular, pre-constituted Shiʿi identity and the change it underwent at the hands of external causes—in this case, the freedom granted by Buyid rulers—the reframing I am proposing demands that we turn our attention to the very *conditions* that enabled certain components of Shiʿi identity to come into central view.

Accordingly, I argue against the view that it was Buyid tolerance that led the official Shiʿi position to take the turn that it did toward a position that came to increasingly resemble the majority Sunni school. What such a narrative does not account for are the shifting alliances and strategic moves characterizing the political landscape of Buyid Baghdad. As noted earlier, the Buyid decision to organize and prop up the Twelver Shiʿi community, independent from the 'Abbasids, was a pragmatic political strategy that earned the rulers greater legitimacy, on the basis of which they further distinguished themselves from the 'Abbasid caliph. Crucial to note here is that, since the Buyids adhered to the Twelver School, it was precisely the Twelver Shi'i scholarly elite who represented their most formidable competitors. This can be witnessed in the cautious reserve with which they decided on which Twelver Shi'i scholars were to be given which administrative and official posts, and for what duration. Al-Radi's political career constitutes a series of cycles where he was granted certain leadership positions and then removed from them. Al-Radi's father, as well, Abu Ahmad, was famously employed by different Buyid rulers to serve as an intermediary on their behalf and conduct dialogue with their most threatening adversaries in the surrounding regions. But, after Abu Ahmad achieved success at his assigned task and became popular as a result, another Buyid leader imprisoned him for seven years—he saw Abu Ahmad's sudden rise in popularity as an imminent political threat. Thus, it is critical to note that Buyid attitudes toward Twelver Shi'i scholars were far from uniform or predictable, making it very difficult to posit a linear or predictable relationship between the political orientation of the Buyids and fluctuations in Shi'i thought during this era.

Another problem with reading Shi'i scholarly productivity during this period as a product of Buyid tolerance is that this view does not take into account the significant shift in historical circumstances that occurred around the same time. As mentioned earlier, the Buyid rise to power occurred just a few years after the occultation of the twelfth Imam. Thus, it remains to be asked to what extent the increase in Shi'i scholarly participation can be tied to the fact that the Shi'i community was no longer bound by the doctrinal covenant that prevented them from serving any ruler other than the Imam. These markedly altered conditions, in the absence of the Imams, complemented by a new political leadership whose rulers adhered to Shi'i principles even as they paid subservience to the Sunni 'Abbasid caliph, may very well have enabled a new willingness on the part of the Shi'i community to be associated with the establishment.

Political Fragmentation and Narratives of Sunni/Shi'i Strife

Above, I have demonstrated the conceptual limitations of broaching Twelver Shi'i thought in the tenth century as the product of Buyid tolerance, and pointed out that this view results from the problematic assumption that religious currents in Islam neatly correspond with extant political conditions. I want to turn now to another prevailing assumption in existing narratives of Buyid history, according to which, sectarian difference is uncritically posited as the primary cause for division and discord between Sunnis and Shiʻites during this period.

The fragmentation of political authority was an important development during the Buyid era.[19] The Buyid Empire comprised of three separate principalities ruled by different members of the same family. From a political standpoint, this meant that measures undertaken by the different leaders were executed with consideration to the particular interest of individual principalities rather than that of a collective Muslim empire. Fragmented political objectives, in turn, led to significant internal strife within the three principalities, which manifested in the form of fierce rivalries between competing claimants to political authority. Historians have typically depicted this division as a sectarian battle between the majority Sunni and minority Shiʻi schools. The fact that this historical interlude was dominated by the reign of Shiʻi dynasties has also led scholars to label the period as "the Shiʻi century."[20]

Yet this label blurs the vast difference between the political ambitions and modalities of governance adopted by the various Shiʻi empires. If anything, to refer to the period as some kind of Shiʻi "golden age" is to employ the language of the Seljuqs in the thirteenth century, who cast themselves as the revivers of an "orthodox" Sunni Islam, destined to free Muslim society from the stronghold of the heterodox Shiʻi sect. Recently, scholars such as Richard Bulliet and Omid Safi have brought to our attention the way in which depictions of this historical period as a momentous showdown between Sunni and Shiʻi forces represent uncritical recapitulations of the traditional Sunni narrative.[21] Their reevaluation of the source material suggests that much more than a sectarian battle between the Sunni and Shiʻi sects, it was a dramatic and caustic intra-Sunni contestation between the Shafiʻi and Hanafi legal schools that dominated the political landscape of this era.

Intellectual and Cultural Life Under the Buyids

From a cultural perspective, the political fragmentation under the Buyids catalyzed an unprecedented boon. The establishment of regional principalities resulted in the expansion of impressive courts and cultural centers that were on par with the flourishing city of Baghdad. One medium through which each of the courts competed for power was patronage of the arts. Thus, if a talented person in one region faced hardships under a particular regime, it was possible to seek high positions in the court of a different ruler. Developments in the cultural and intellectual infrastructure of the empire also energized the scholarly life of the Muslim community. For instance, important schools were established, such as the Dar al-'ilm (House of Learning) founded by the vizier Sabur ibn Ardeshir (d. 1025), hospitals were set up in Baghdad and Shiraz, and impressive libraries were built in Shiraz, Rayy, and Isfahan by successive generations of Buyid leaders. Although the first generation of Buyid leaders had inadequate knowledge of Arabic, they equipped themselves with the most illustrious Arabic scholars of their day. Moreover, the courts frequently hosted the finest Arabic poets. Persian poets, too, were welcomed. For example, the preeminent Persian poet Abu al-Qasim Ferdowsi (d. 1020) was invited to the court of the Buyid ruler Baha al-Dawla. Other notable scholars who benefited from this practice of patronage and from the culture of scholarly exchange cultivated during the Buyids included the philosopher/historian Miskawayh (d. 1030) and the celebrated philosopher Ibn Sina (Avicenna) (d. 1037), to name just two. Treasuries of Arabic literature, such as Abu al-Faraj al-Isfahani's (d. 967) Book of Songs and Ibn al-Nadim's (d. 995) Kitab al-Fihrist, were also compiled during this time. Scholars of different stripes were invited to come and publicly debate at the courts for the pleasure and learning of the vizier, who served as their host. Moreover, distinguished scholars were well-received by the Buyid rulers and by their viziers, especially those scholars whose expertise could be put to practical use, such as geographers, astrologers, physicians, and mathematicians.[22]

Professionalization of the Poetic Enterprise

All of these developments were part of a broader reconfiguration of patronage relations that took place under the Buyids between scholars and the political elite. As social historian Roy Mottahedeh has aptly argued, in his landmark study of the Buyid period, both individual ties as well as ties based on genealogy or occupation contributed to the cultivation of loyalties between political patrons and their scholarly benefactors, including poets, in tenth and eleventh-century Baghdad.[23] Accordingly, the value of an individual in Baghdad's intellectual circles was increasingly tied to a person's ability to demonstrate the knowledge he possessed. In other words, relationships of proximity to powerful patrons were acquired through one's worth or capacity and inherited through one's lineage. This shift enabled a much wider group of scholars to vie for power and prominence in the imperial court and beyond, which, in turn, produced a climate of fierce competition among the scholarly elite.

Similar insights can be gleaned from Erez Namaan's recent publication, *Literature and the Islamic Court*. Namaan fixes his attention on the distinct space of courts[24] and examines the impact of court patrons in shaping literary output during the Buyid period. Arguing along similar lines as Mottahedeh, Namaan holds that ties of kinship and social affiliation that had previously enjoyed a certain degree of legitimacy were fundamentally reconfigured during this moment. More specifically, unlike the past, when inherited relationships were central to one's place and status in imperial circles, in the newly configured lines of patronage, particularly between patron and poet, the focus of attention turned to the significance of acquired relationships. Poetry thus emerged as the prime "commodity" and the court as a key "market" for such modes of exchange between poets and political patrons.[25] The concomitant economy of poetry sustained not only the patron-poet relationship. Moreover, poetry emerged as a key instrument for the performance of the politico-theological authority of key members of the imperial court, as well. For instance, it is often through poetry duels that the vizier expressed his gratitude to God for the divine blessings bestowed on him and the courtier, in turn, modeled his gratitude for the worldly benefits accorded to him by the vizier.[26]

An important discursive ingredient in this mix was that of praise poetry, through which poets employed innovative techniques for glorifying the caliphs, sultans, and their viziers, and thus signaled their poetic expertise to their royal patrons. With the establishment of a wider patronage system, and increased contact with diverse peoples inhabiting the fringes of the empire, the intellectual climate was imbued with a new vitality, which consequently enabled a professionalization of poetry that had not previously existed. In this environment, poetry came to function as a social and political commodity, attracting a host of claimants motivated by the desire to attain power and place in the courts.[27] What is crucial to note in this development—where poetry became a professional enterprise—is the way the professionalization of poetry threatened the intimate connection between noble lineage, purity of language, and the mastery of Arabic poetry, which formed the foundation of the older poetic tradition. I will return to this critical point in a moment.

The economy of poetry generated by these developments was not always viewed with celebration by poets themselves, both prominent and lesser

known. Take, for instance, the case of Abd al-Wahhab al-Maliki (d. 1031), a
struggling poet who, like many others, came to Baghdad in search of an intellectual community and recognition for his talents. Instead, he registered his
despondency with the state of affairs he found in the city by composing the
following verses about his experience:

> Baghdad is a delightful residence for those who have money,
> But for the poor it is an abode of misery and suffering.
> I walked all day through its streets bewildered and desolate;
> I was treated with neglect like a Qur'an in the house of an atheist.[28]

Similar notes of resentment are recorded even in writings of much more
famous poets, such as the redoubtable Abu Hayyan al-Tawhidi (d. 1023) and
al-Ma'arri (d. 1058), both of whom lamented their destitute poverty and the
tragic reception they received in the bustling cultural center of the Buyid
empire. The sad fate of these struggling scholars is symptomatic of a broader
trend sweeping the literary culture of Baghdad during the tenth and eleventh
centuries: the increasing professionalization of the poetic enterprise.[29]

A Conceptual Interjection

So far, in this chapter I have sought to argue that approaching al-Radi's hermeneutical identity through a narrative that positions him as a Twelver Shi'i
scholar who was given a voice under the Buyids, so that a hitherto hidden
Shi'i position was made public, is fraught with conceptual and historiograph-
ical problems. I have shown that this approach assumes a rigid notion of religious identity and views Islamic political history as the singular explanatory
factor for understanding the development of religious thought. By moving
away from such a reading of Shi'i religious identity and from reductionist
conclusions about Islamic political history, I have made a case to explore
al-Radi's engagement with the multiple intellectual discourses and currents
inflected in his writings. In so doing, my objective is not to historicize al-
Radi *better*, but to reorient and expand our understanding of the very task of
contextualizing a historical text by viewing it as part of a larger intellectual
field inhabited by a variety of discursive conditions. Put differently, I refrain
from attempting to identify and precisely locate the historical "context" of

al-Radi's Qur'an commentary and instead subscribe to the view that "contexts" must be interpreted as verbal artifacts, much like the ideas and "texts" they produce.

My conceptual approach is indebted to the work of the anthropologist David Scott, and especially his reading of the historian cum theorist Reinhart Koselleck. Scott invoked a conceptual relation between what Koselleck called the "space of experience" and the "horizon of expectation" to discuss how concrete histories are always produced within the medium of particular experiences and expectations.[30] For Koselleck, "space of experience" refers to the "present-past," that part of the past that has been preserved and remembered in the present. On the other hand, "horizon of expectation" signifies "the future made present," meaning the expectations, desires, and anxieties that are projected to an imagined future. For Scott, crucial to Koselleck's theory is the idea that moral arguments are constructed by positing a particular temporal relationship between the past that is to be preserved or overcome and the future that is to be attained. A moral argument, in other words, not only provides an "answer" to a problem. More importantly, as I explained earlier, the persuasiveness and moral force of an argument depends on how it describes the "problem" or the "question" that is to be resolved and answered. The idea of a "question-and-answer" space in which moral arguments are embedded proves fruitful in analyzing and describing the religious thought of a scholar like al-Radi. As a moral argument, his Qur'an commentary was situated in a particular problem-space that he navigated. Al-Radi's hermeneutical choices served as a response to his understanding and framing of the problems and the dissatisfactions he sought to address and overcome. Rather than reading al-Radi's hermeneutics as neatly correlated to or reducible to his historical context, I instead focus on the question-and-answer space that animated his hermeneutical enterprise. In this context, I have highlighted that the professionalization of poetry, and its disentanglement of language and lineage, represents an important source of dissatisfaction that al-Radi strived to redress through his poetry and his Qur'an commentary. I next turn to a more detailed elaboration of this point by more closely considering how he understood and described the problem or the question to which he saw his Qur'an commentary as a response. The crucial significance of the intimacy of language and lineage and, in al-Radi's view, the threat posed to this relationship during his life will again be central to my analysis.

Discontentment and Caliphal Ambitions

Al-Radi's ties to a noble sayyid lineage from both of his parents granted him an important place in Baghdad's intellectual aristocracy. At times, al-Radi used his poetry to lament the fate of the poetic enterprise. In doing so, he argued for the critical relationship between the purity of an individual's lineage and the purity of his/her language. He was openly critical of the increasing professionalization of the poetic enterprise and the many claimants it produced. These views are nicely captured in the following verses penned by al-Radi:

> Buy stature with what you want, but real stature is not for sale,
> With some gold if you like, or with long nights of discourse,
> Lacking in intelligence is the deceived, who tries to purchase stature
>   with wealth,
> For the price of high station, wealth is a despicable thing[31]

As a vocal critic of the effects of the democratization of knowledge and increasing social mobility made possible under the various political dynasties scattered across the Muslim lands, al-Radi argued for a fixed literary and linguistic canon and for the exclusive authority of elite scholars to interpret that canon. In so doing, al-Radi asserted his privileged place in society by arguing for the inextricable link between specialist knowledge of language, social capital, and the capacity of making claims to political power.

Although al-Radi was opposed to the social mobility granted to poets who didn't uphold the strictures of a pure Arabic language during his time, it is critical to note that he himself benefited from and actively participated in tenth-century Baghdad's distinctly polysemous literary culture. In this regard, Suzanne Stetkevych's article, titled "Al-Sharif al-Radi and the Poetics of 'Alid Legitimacy: Elegy for al-Husayn ibn 'Ali on 'Ashura', 391 A.H.," represents a particularly helpful study that identifies al-Radi's poetic writings as expressions of his discontentment with his fate in Baghdad's political landscape. In her convincing analysis of al-Radi's fifty-eight line *qasida* about the martyrdom of the third Shi'i Imam al-Husayn b. 'Ali, Stetkevych argues that this poem goes beyond the strictures of an "elegy," which is how it has commonly been described and classified. Instead, she contends that it is a polythematic poem and in it al-Radi has "masterfully manipulated classical Arabic *qasidah* conventions, including form, genre, imagery and diction, to promote a politico-religious claim for 'Alid legitimacy—his own imminent

Imamate—and to create, at the same time, a meticulously crafted and per-during work of the poetic art."[32]

The crux of Stetkevych's argument is that, in this poem, the distinction between the elegizer and elegized collapses. This is because she interprets al-Radi's lament on the usurpation of the caliphate from al-Husayn by the Umayyads as a reflection of al-Radi's own ambitions and frustrations under 'Abbasid caliphal rule. Thus, this poem nicely illustrates al-Radi's aspirations of becoming the leader of the larger Muslim community. In addition to this specific poem, Stetkevych notes that the "poetics of loss" evident in al-Radi's poetry, where an intense sentiment of dispossession produces an extraordinary lyric-elegiac strain, is also strikingly expressed in the sermons of 'Ali in the *Nahj al-Balagha*, which al-Radi himself compiled. Stetkevych's reading of al-Radi's *Diwan*, together with the *Nahj al-Balagha*, leads her to argue that the principle of selection al-Radi used in his compilation was not the historical textual authenticity of the sermons but their performative rhetorical power.[33] To explain, Stetkevych turns to the key argument that echoes through her numerous studies of this period: this was a time of "the extreme valorization of rhetoric," when rhetorical power *was* a key ingredient in assembling, maintaining, and defending imperial power.[34]

Stetkevych also offers other examples from al-Radi's *Diwan* (collection of poems) to illustrate al-Radi's shifting loyalties in the hope of receiving recognition and a position to which he felt his talent and 'Alid lineage entitled him. For example, she cites the verses where he is unequivocally critical of the 'Abbasids and proclaims the superiority of his lineage over theirs:

Return the inheritance of Muhammad, return it!
For neither the staff nor the [Prophet's] mantle are yours!
Does blood like Fatimah's flow in your veins,
Or do you have a grandfather like Muhammad?[35]

Also, in the final lines of another *qasida*, which al-Radi had dedicated to the 'Abbasid caliph al-Qadir (d. 1031 CE), he boldly declares:

When men compete in glory there is no difference between us
At all: each of us is of the noblest origins—

Except for the Caliphate: I am deprived of it
While you are crowned![36]

In these verses al-Radi invokes his spiritual genealogy through the Imams to connect himself to the Prophet. This argument provides a helpful glimpse into how 'Alid lineage continued to command critical clout in the claim to legitimate rule in tenth-century Baghdad. As noted earlier, this period in early Islamic history is characterized by the political shakeup wrought by the Persianate Buyid dynasty from the time they took power in 945, stripped the 'Abbasid caliphs from any real political control, and introduced the sultanate as a way of invoking the political authority of Persian kingship.[37] Since the Buyids had assumed the role of the political sovereign while making no decisive claims about religious authority, it opened up the space for a discursive battle over religious legitimacy between the 'Abbasids and 'Alids without posing any direct threat to the Buyid sultanate.

The air of aristocracy that al-Radi exudes in his poetry is legitimized by the purity of his lineage. But unlike other theologically grounded writings by 'Alid scholars on the legitimacy of 'Alid rule, such as that of his brother al-Murtada, al-Radi's argument for his own candidacy for political rule does not concern itself with theological explanations. Another curious detail about al-Radi's claim to the caliphate is that, according to the biographers, it was al-Radi's friend al-Sabi[38] (the Sabian) who convinced him to pursue these political aspirations. Al-Radi's relationship to al-Sabi resembles that of a protégé to an older mentor, particularly since al-Sabi was a famous litterateur employed by the Buyid courts and had remained a close companion of al-Radi's father.[39] An extant work titled *Rasa'il al-Sabi wa al-Sharif al-Radi* showcases a literary exchange between al-Radi and al-Sabi in highly ornate Arabic poetry and prose. In these writings, it is evident that, despite their difference in age and religious orientation, al-Radi and al-Sabi shared a talent and passion for the Arabic letters. Al-Sabi's poetic exchange with al-Radi for which he is credited (or blamed) for planting the seed of political ambition in al-Radi reads as follows:

O Abu Hasan! In the matter of men I have intuitive knowledge
    ['ilm al-firasa],
It fails me not in speaking the truth,
It has informed me that you are a man of nobility who will rise to the
    highest rank,
So I gave you full honor before it was due, praying "may God
    prolong the life of Sayyid!"
Not revealing yet a phrase which I kept secret, until I see myself free
    to spell it out.[40]

These words, coming from a figure like al-Sabi, carried immense divinatory value. After all, the science of prophesizing was seen as a specialty of the Sabian community. As mentioned earlier, al-Sabi is said to have actively cultivated and put his astrological prowess on display as a way to acquire social capital. For instance, as part of his self-branding as an astrologer, he was fond of describing his contemporaries through an astrological idiom in his poetry and also often extended gifts that corresponded to the same theme.[41]

A contemporary biographer of al-Radi, 'Abd al-Ghani Hasan, reports that al-Sabi denied uttering these words after their dissemination, since he feared punitive repercussions by the caliph.[42] If true, then this further complicates reading the Buyid period as one where scholars of all schools of thought were granted "freedom," since what was permissible for al-Radi to utter as an 'Alid was considered dangerous for his Sabian friend.

Irrespective of the credibility of this account, it is worth noting that the narrative it forms successfully isolates al-Radi's individual claim for the caliphate from the more sustained and systematic body of literature that came to represent the Shi'i canon. According to this literature,[43] arguments for 'Alid legitimacy begin with 'Ali ibn Abi Talib and end with the twelfth Shi'i Imam. Consequently, there was no place in canonical Shi'ism for a figure like al-Radi, writing some fifty years after the occultation of the twelfth Imam, to seek the position of what was rightfully considered the jurisdiction of the Imam in occultation. Al-Radi's claim to the caliphate, as well as his refusal to deride the first three caliphs, has led some early biographers and contemporary scholars to identify him as a Zaydi.[44] One factor that might lend support to this thesis is that Sunni sources do not malign al-Radi in the way that they malign his brother, al-Murtada. Yet, these same Sunni sources say nothing of his doctrinal affiliations, either. Another factor may be the positive Zaydi reception of al-Radi's compilation of 'Ali's speeches and sermons in the *Nahj al-Balagha*, a point that is not unconnected to the politically activist tone of those speeches and sayings and the favourable reception they would receive in Zaydi circles.

Critical here, given the absence of any explicit evidence of al-Radi's Zaydi leanings, is whether there is enough material to support such a view and the question of by what criteria such a claim could be supported to begin with. To put it simply, short of having an explicit statement from al-Radi announcing his Zaydi affiliation, is it possible to know if he was or was not Zaydi? As recent scholar Hanadi Za'al Mas'ud al-Hindawi has shown, if we go by what we know about al-Radi in his writings, we would have to conclude that he both supported *and* rejected important tenets of the Zaydis, in that he asserted the need for political revolution while also arguing that it should come from the "right" lineage.[45]

Also relevant for this discussion is al-Sharif al-Murtada's treatise outlining the permissibility of working in the government in the absence of the Imams—be the rulers just or unjust. As discussed in Chapter 1, al-Radi, his brother al-Murtada, and their father Abu Ahmad held influential positions in the Buyid political establishment. It is valuable to consider that the reasoning and justification that al-Murtada provides to argue for the legitimacy of working for the ruler (who is not the Imam) can theoretically be extended to claim the position of the ruler, as well. So, even as al-Murtada did not stake the claim for the caliphate as al-Radi did, his treatise does offer juridical justification for that claim. Scholars who attribute to al-Radi a Zaydi affiliation do so in order to make sense of the perceived dissonance between his claim to the caliphate and official Imami doctrine that reserves such a role for the Imam. But al-Murtada—whose own position as an Imami was never questioned—through his treatise, sheds some doubt on the extent to which that claim conflicted with what was deemed permissible according to Imami logics of the time. Thus, rather than pronounce al-Radi a closet Zaydi, I would argue that his writings suggest that he was an Imami who toed a line that came close to the Zaydi position. He articulated this position in order to align himself with the view of the twelfth Imam as Mahdi, to return and establish justice (as he mentions in one of his odes in the *Diwan*)[46] while making a provisional exception for someone like himself to take up that fight in the twelfth Imam's absence.

Outright contestations for power between 'Alid and 'Abbasid leaders, as well as the intellectual exchange between al-Radi and al-Sabi, offer critical snapshots of the political and intellectual culture that thrived under the Buyids in Baghdad in the late tenth and early eleventh century. As I have already discussed, historians have described this period as a time of political fragmentation, since it was the first time that a non-Arab dynasty had taken control of the majority of Muslim lands. But this political fragmentation produced conditions for tremendous intellectual fermentation that transcended boundaries of religious, ethnic, and linguistic difference, which also had the effect of dislodging the Arab-centrism that had characterized earlier discourses on political authority.

In al-Radi's writings it is possible to discern a critical response to this changing political climate. Not only did he express discontent with the

'Abbasids' claim to spiritual rule over the 'Alids, he also mourned the impact of the diminishing influence of Arabic letters in scholarly circles. In particular, he made explicit his lament of the infiltration of an uncultured class in an otherwise pure and noble tradition of classical Arabic poetry. Disgruntled by the increasing influence of scholars unfamiliar with the nuances of the Arabic language preserved in the rich oral tradition of poetry, al-Radi produced writings that can be interpreted as a plea for the return of political and religious power to the 'Alids—a people pure in both lineage and language.

In trying to explore the questions that al-Radi's Qur'an commentary may have been a response to, or the specific question-and-answer space it was a part of, I have noted al-Radi's overall discontent with the marginalization of lineal and linguistic purity. I pointed to his lament against the conditions of his time, where political power lay with a family that was not of a pure and sacred lineage like his own. Additionally, he expressed his opposition to the social mobility granted to poets who didn't uphold the strictures of a pure Arabic language. Part of al-Radi's resistance to Buyid decentralization of power was his affiliation to the literary circle of poets and the authority they wielded as custodians of the Arabic language, particularly in terms of the threat they faced in light of competing disciplines of knowledge in tenth-century Baghdad. Clearly, then, the intellectual and political context in which al-Radi wrote was more complicated and nuanced than what a sectarian reading of this moment, conducted through a binary prism of an a priori Sunni/Shi'i division, would suggest.

It is important to consider that, although the Buyids were strong supporters of Arabic literature, they themselves were of Persian descent and their early generations of leaders in fact communicated with the help of translators between Arabic and Persian.[47] Thus, these changed circumstances played a critical role in how poets like al-Radi imagined their own role as the new custodians of Arabic language, which was regarded as the key for interpreting the Qur'an.

Conclusion

In this chapter, I began by describing the transformed sociopolitical and cultural conditions under the Buyids. I highlighted the way in which political fragmentation had the corollary effect of creating multiple patronage networks, which led to intensified cultural and intellectual productivity during this period in history. I also demonstrated the conceptual limitations of drawing neat correlations between the central visibility of al-Radi's thought in the Buyid public sphere and general characterizations of the Buyid rulers as enablers of free intellectual discourse and debate. I noted that the problem with such a narrative is that it assumes an unchanging entity called "Shi'ism," which, subject to external conditions, can be readily concealed and revealed. Instead, I argued for an altogether different approach to thinking about the operations of religious identity, as an embodied argument that responds to the specific historical conditions in which it is constituted. I proposed that the task of identifying al-Radi's hermeneutical identity must situate his work in the multiple intellectual discourses in which he participated and identify the concerns and questions that animated these traditions.

Accordingly, I suggested that al-Radi's position as a poet is the most instructive vantage point from which to understand the hermeneutical choices he made. With this proposal, my goal is not to simply assume that his interest in a literary approach to the Qur'an is a reflection of his literary profession. Rather, it is to argue that the role of the poets in tenth-century Baghdad under the Buyids reflects an emergent group of voices who sought to preserve the purity of the Arabic language. Al-Radi, in particular, tied his own authority as an exegete to the "purity" of his lineage, which traced back to the Prophet. To reiterate: this is not to say that al-Radi's position as a Shi'i scholar played no part in his hermeneutical choices. However, what I have sought to argue is that al-Radi's Shi'i identity cannot be abstracted from the multiple intellectual traditions that thrived and came into view in tenth-century Buyid Baghdad. His hermeneutical identity did not neatly correspond to his sectarian identity as a Shi'i scholar, nor was his sectarian identity the overarching driver of his hermeneutics. In the next chapter, I continue to develop this underlying argument through a close reading of al-Radi's Qur'an commentary, to explore ways in which he imagined the interaction of language, revelation, and interpretive authority. I show how al-Radi's literary approach to the Qur'an, which seeks to interrogate and resolve Qur'anic ambiguity, is tied to a theology of language that locates interpretive power in the hands of the exegete. The fact that al-Radi's hermeneutic made no attempt to reconcile the absence of the Imams and his own authority as an interpreter of the Qur'an indicates that he did not view this situation as contradictory.

CHAPTER 3

Ambiguity, Hermeneutics, and Power

Historicizing al-Radi's Interpretive Method:
Ambiguity and its Operations

The opening pages of al-Radi's *Haqa'iq* are no longer extant. What might we have found in those introductory pages?[1] It is possible that al-Radi's introductory words would be dedicated to explaining why he chose to compose a work that identifies, compiles, and resolves the ambiguous verses of the Qur'an. It is very likely that, as part of that discussion, he would also have announced his own superlative qualifications for composing such a work, which, as he states throughout the book, requires nothing short of a mastery over the Arabic language. To be sure, he would waste no opportunity to perform this mastery, and express all of the above in the finest lyrical prose!

In addition to being deprived of the sheer literary value of the *Haqa'iq's* starting act, the loss of his introduction has also meant that current scholars do not have in their possession al-Radi's clearest exposition of his "interpretive method." Consequently, even the fundamental task of determining how al-Radi understood the term "ambiguity"—the central concept in the *Haqa'iq*—demands some excavation, as well as extrapolation. This chapter seeks to perform this crucial task through two forms of analysis. First, I examine the broader intellectual networks of al-Radi's time and earlier that cultivated the epistemological terrain that informed the varied meanings and valences of the category of ambiguity circulating in al-Radi's midst. And second, toward the end of the chapter, by turning to some particularly illustrative fragments from the *Haqa'iq*, I try to piece together and describe al-Radi's own conception of "ambiguity" in the Qur'an. A key motif of this chapter is to demonstrate the intimate connections between Muslim scholarly conceptualizations of ambiguity during this period and the emergence of a literary canon of the Arabic language, a canon of which al-Radi and his Qur'an commentary were major benefactors and to which they amply contributed as well. This chapter thus continues the work of the previous chapter to historicize al-Radi's exegesis but through a more intensive focus on reconstructing his understanding of what is arguably the single most important concept governing his hermeneutic: that of ambiguity, which is also the central feature of the Qur'an's ambiguous verses (*mutashabihat*). The analysis conducted in this chapter therefore serves as the conceptual platform undergirding the more detailed readings of the *Haqa'iq* conducted in the subsequent chapter. And, by situating al-Radi's conceptions of ambiguity in the larger intellectual networks and currents of which he was a participant, cutting across varied disciplinary formations and sectarian identities, this chapter further advances the underlying thrust of this book to argue for nonsectarian readings of the commentarial tradition. Throughout this chapter, keeping in view the ease of reading, I use the English word ambiguity and the Arabic term for the genre of the Qur'an's ambiguous verses, the *mutashabih* (pl. *mutashabihat*) interchangeably.

My main argument in this chapter is that the *Haqa'iq* should be read as a detailed illustration of the semiotic process that the literary quality of ambiguity entailed and demanded. Accordingly, I place the *Haqa'iq* as a critical contribution to the field of *bayan*, a genre dedicated to highlighting the communicative abilities of various forms of speech.[2] Framing my reading of the *Haqa'iq* as part of this wider conversation, I show that al-Radi's discussion on ambiguity reflects and highlights the epistemological cross-pollination between the exegetical, philological, theological, and legal traditions in late tenth- and early eleventh-century Baghdad.

Today, the term "*mutashabih*" is typically translated into English as "ambiguous" (as I also have) and its sister term, "*majaz*," is translated as "figurative" or "trope."[3] At the time that al-Radi was writing, categories like "*mutashabih*" and "*majaz*" were not employed in a uniform way, primarily because the stabilizing and systematizing effects of published works on literary criticism were yet to come. Considering the number of meanings in circulation for the term *mutashabih*, I begin this chapter with a discussion of what al-Radi intended by this term and how his usage of it compared with that of other scholars. I direct this recuperative task of identifying key categories and interpretive devices in al-Radi's *Haqa'iq* toward two main goals. The first is for the heuristic purpose that it serves; a solid grasp over al-Radi's governing interpretive principle is critical to understanding the conceptual architecture that undergirds the commentary that fills the later extant pages of the *Haqa'iq*. The second is that isolating al-Radi's deployment of a key literary category like ambiguity offers an important snapshot for tracing the conceptual history of this term. I should note that, unlike 'Abd al-Qahir al-Jurjani (d. 1078) and other later theorists of language, al-Radi did not fashion the *Haqa'iq* as a work of Arabic literary criticism. Yet, as I hope to show, al-Radi's work on the *mutashabih* and its sister category *majaz*, conducted in the authoritative literary register of *tafsir*, represents a critical moment in the interpretive trajectory of these terms. Specifically, what al-Radi's writing ultimately offers is not just a particular conceptualization of ambiguity, but rather a particular theory of language that places ambiguity at its center.

The Power of Ambiguity

The title of al-Radi's Qur'an commentary, *Haqa'iq al-Ta'wil fi Mutashabih al-Tanzil*, nicely captures the dual goals behind his composition of this work. On the one hand, it makes a claim about the value of the method he employs and the interpretations that result from it: *Hermeneutical Realities [for Uncovering] the Ambiguities of Revelation*, as if to say "this is the correct hermeneutic that will guide you through the Qur'an's ambiguities."[4] On the other hand, the same title can be read as a reflection of al-Radi's important claim about the critical epistemological role of ambiguity in the Qur'an: *The Truths of Interpretation [Are in] the Ambiguities of Revelation*!

In the *Haqa'iq*, al-Radi's discussion of what ambiguity *is* and by extension how one ought to define the Qur'an's ambiguous verses was tied to the vexing question about the role and place of ambiguity in a text like the Qur'an. How did the presence of ambiguity in the Qur'an sit together with its inimitability? Critically, for al-Radi, ambiguity served as the primary linguistic tool through which the Qur'an generated and communicated awe-inspiring meanings. Far from viewing ambiguity as something to be "endured" or "overcome" through the rationalizing efforts of exegetes, al-Radi made a case for the benefit of the strenuous intellectual labor that ambiguities demand from their readers and for the epistemological gains that come from such an exercise. Ambiguities demand extensive efforts from readers because they require that one move from a state of unknowing, where meaning remains open, unsettled, or misunderstood, to that of knowing, marked by an ambiguity's settlement and correct understanding. Or, in al-Radi's words, it entails the movement from a *mutashabih*, or ambiguous verse, to its corresponding and clarifying *muh-kam*, or clear verse. Al-Radi saw the steps for this semiotic movement between ambiguity and clarity as built into any given ambiguous phrase or word. There-fore, theoretically speaking, meaning was available to any discerning reader. However, not every ordinary reader was capable of parsing it out. Thus, while al-Radi *did* regard the answers to Qur'anic ambiguities as inherently available in language, he argued that access to this knowledge was *only* possible under the guidance of a learned teacher like himself. The ordinary individual might read an ambiguous verse in the Qur'an and see no ambiguity in it, for example. Without explicitly saying so, al-Radi cautions the unknowing reader, urging him or her to tread carefully; what appears to be a clear verse may in fact be not only profoundly complex, but also the key to accessing the Qur'an's deepest secrets. Matters of language were no child's play; they required proper guid-ance and supervision. In the *Haqa'iq*, the work of unraveling the ambiguous verses entailed an unsettling of the familiar. To this end, an element of decen-tering was involved; the preliminary reading, at first taken for granted, now assumed the power to dismantle meaning, even to astonish. Al-Radi argued that the additional intellectual labor required to tease out an ambiguous verse actually contributed to the epistemological rewards rendered by that verse. And, in tenth-century Baghdad, in the intellectual and imperial spaces that al-Radi frequented, the immense power invested in a literary feature like ambi-guity bore implications far exceeding its rhetorical value. Let me explain.

The vibrant display and performance of poetry in the competitive context and setting of the imperial courts tied together rhetorical might with sover-eign might. Crucial and especially important to my analysis is Stetkevych's argument that, in this context, it was not far-fetched for a claimant of abso-lute rhetorical ability to also make a claim to absolute political power.[5] In other words, the capacity to master language signaled the capacity to control the affairs of society.

For al-Radi, thus, the opportunity that a commentary on the Qur'an's ambiguities afforded to display linguistic mastery, and to evoke wonder and humility, made it a particularly conducive site for making a claim not only to linguistic but also to political authority. Given the reach of al-Radi's political aspirations (detailed in Chapter 1), the political power that linguis-tic authority wielded partially explains why al-Radi would choose to com-pose this specific work.

It is most fruitful to view the *Haqa'iq*, a work on Qur'anic ambigu-ity, as part of a broader literary oeuvre through which al-Radi performed, displayed, and affirmed his linguistic prowess as a way to authorize his claim to the caliphate. As part of this endeavor, the *Haqa'iq*—a step-by-step guide on the operation of the *mutashabihat* or the Qur'an's ambiguous verses—was no small feat. To claim mastery over the linguistic mysteries of the Qur'an carried enormous intellectual and sociopolitical weight, at this historical juncture. As for al-Radi's other writings, in his poetic compendium (*Diwan*), he spoke uninhibitedly and critically about the 'Abbasid leadership and was categorical about his ambitions for caliphal office. In his compilation of 'Ali ibn Abi Talib's sermons (*Nahj al-Balagha*), he found the ideal exemplar for a demonstration of the mutually reinforcing effects of linguistic and political power. What all three of these otherwise distinct genres had in common, thus, was not only the claim over and display of rhetorical excellence. More than that, it was through the display of rhetorical excellence that an author laid claim to political excellence and power.

Ambiguity and Wonder

What may have given a work like the *Haqa'iq* further traction in this climate where literary might opened avenues for political power was its focus not on any feature of the Qur'an's linguistic excellence, but on ambiguity specifically. As Lara Harb has convincingly argued, this moment marked a critical shift with regard to how eloquent speech was measured and evaluated. Namely, a poet's ability to evoke "wonder" (as opposed to "truthfulness") emerged as the new criteria for eloquence. Harb argues that "wonder was the aesthetic on which classical Arabic criticism was anchored, at least after the fourth/tenth century"[6] Literary critics of this period argued that a poet's ability to produce wonder in the reader/listener through literary devices such as metaphor was what distinguished them from others as true masters of their craft. This literary context, in which the argument for experiencing poetry through wonder held immense significance lent further weight to al-Radi's hermeneutic, the centerpiece of which was ambiguity and the promise of its resolution.

The interlocking of ambiguity, wonder, and power was not only central to al-Radi's authority as an exegete. Moreover, throughout the *Haqa'iq*, we find al-Radi acutely alert to and invested in the evocation of affective responses like awe and wonder (*i'jab*) as part of his exegetical program. Why? Because, for al-Radi, moments of ambiguity in the Qur'an posed not simply a theological dilemma whereby the divine text emerged as a source of confusion through the resolution of which the exegete restored and preserved its fault-lessness. In addition to this theological and hermeneutical mandate, which was certainly important, the Qur'an's ambiguous verses also extended an invitation to such affective states as awe and wonder. As I will show in this chapter, through my reading of specific passages in the *Haqa'iq*, al-Radi saw the aesthetic quality of ambiguities and the salience of their wonder-inducing features as pivotal to accessing the Qur'an's most profound teachings. In his view, the aesthetic value and potential in language was inextricably tied to its epistemic value and potential. Al-Radi regarded ambiguous verses, by means of the affect they produced on being discerned, as repositories of the most subtle features of language, communicating the Qur'an's deepest truths.

Before turning in more detail to al-Radi's argument for ambiguity as an epistemological category, let me pause and reiterate the larger stakes of situ-ating and reading al-Radi as part of a broader context of multiple intellectual conversations in his midst, including but certainly not limited to literary crit-icism. Contemporary biases that ascribe and circumscribe the substance of Shi'i scholarly writings, including Qur'an commentary, to theological apolo-gia have obscured the substance and value of al-Radi's work by reducing it to a work engaged in sectarian polemics. I question the preemptive ascription of al-Radi's attention to literary devices like *mutashabih* and *majaz*, both of which point to a different register of meaning, as reflections of a "charac-teristically Shi'i" inclination towards *batini* (hidden) meanings in the text.[7] Instead, I attend closely to the arguments that inspire and sustain al-Radi's use of literary categories and show that his hermeneutical project, even as it ultimately did make a case for 'Alid authority, did so using the tools and argu-ments that held critical normative and aesthetic purchase at the time. This contrasts with an approach that continues to prevail in Islamic studies, where Shi'i scholars, regardless of when and where they lived and wrote, are seen as drawing on fixed templates like "*batini* meaning" or "hidden meaning" to make consistent arguments about Imami authority. Casting the Shi'i exeget-ical tradition into predictable templates of reactionary theological projects undercuts this tradition of its intellectual vitality by foreclosing a number of alternate analytical questions and possibilities. It also reinforces a majoritar-ian view of how a minority discursive tradition ought to operate. Instead, in this chapter and throughout this book, I show that al-Radi's distinct herme-neutical posturing alerts us to a wide array of intellectual disciplines from which he drew his positions and to which he actively contributed. My objec-tive here—as it is throughout this book—is to probe the questions that may have led al-Radi to privilege one argument over another and to understand the critical purchase of these arguments at the specific historical juncture during which he lived and wrote.

It is worth reiterating that to call for a non-sectarian reading of al-Radi is not to argue that we purge al-Radi's writings of their political motivations. Quite to the contrary, I will affirm and show how the *Haqa'iq* can be read as a politically charged manifesto through which al-Radi sought to announce his own supreme candidacy for the office of the caliphate. There is no reason to deny the political stakes and purpose of his exegetical work. Even so, however, the crucial point to note is this: it is perfectly possible for a Shi'i scholar, as did al-Radi, to make political claims and launch political projects while occupying one of the most important leadership positions in the 'Alid community and yet, *at the same time*, not rely on a predetermined (Shi'i) pattern of argument. Al-Radi might come across as idiosyncratic and an aberration in this regard not because he necessarily was so, but because of the contemporary normalization of a dominant understanding of Sunni and Shi'i identities and politics whereby the latter are often assumed as invariably driven by the normative pressure of theological defense and apologia. The task of rendering al-Radi's example intelligible, therefore, is intimately connected to the broader purpose of rethinking and rescuing from the hold of majoritarian biases the terms and operations of religious identities in settings like tenth-century Baghdad. Before I get to some specific examples from al-Radi's commentary to elaborate this argument, though, some necessary preparatory comments historicizing the very concept of ambiguity in the Qur'an are in order.

A Brief Conceptual History of the *Mutashabihat*

Although the *mutashabihat* are now commonly understood as "ambiguous" verses of the Qur'an, in contrast to the *muhkam or* "clear" verses, this was not always the case.[8] Ibn 'Abbas (d. 688), for example, the Prophet's cousin and commonly known as the "father of exegesis"[9] to whom many exegetical dicta are attributed, had understood the *mutashabih* as a reference to that which one believes but does not act upon, such as oaths and abrogated verses.[10] Meanwhile, other scholars distinguished the *muhkam* and *mutashabih* verses on the basis of their content; the *muhkam* were thought to concern definitive issues of law, punishments, or proofs of the Prophet's message, and the *mutashabih* with "the rest" of the verses.[11] Or, the *mutashabih* were associated with the isolated letters that precede some chapters of the Qur'an[12] and repeated stories about past peoples and prophets.[13]

It was only by the turn of the ninth century, when the Qur'an came to be regarded as a closed, unchanging text, that the *mutashabih* began to carry the meaning of rhetorical ambiguity. Let me explain this point in more detail. As we can well imagine, ascribing ambiguity to the Qur'an had major theological consequences. It suggested that *lack of clarity* could be a defining feature of the text. To characterize the Qur'an—God's guidance to humanity—as unclear was to raise a host of questions about the nature of God's justice. Most prominently, how could a just God hold humanity accountable for its actions if the very source for distinguishing right from wrong is confusing? Clearly, Qur'anic ambiguity could have grave consequences for how divine justice and divine guidance would be conceived. But, once the Qur'an acquired the status of a fixed, closed entity, the threat of ascribing ambiguity to it was also curtailed. How? What were previously considered alternate *readings* of a text that was not-yet-closed now came to be understood as varied *explanations* of a bounded book. And what were previously regarded as linguistically stable but inaccurate verses due to changes that occurred through their transmission now came to be seen as linguistic transgressions in an otherwise stable text. The uncertainty of the text, in other words, was displaced. Sources of uncertainty were previously understood to be the result of errors in recitation and transmission. Now, those same sources of uncertainty became characteristic *features* of the text and opened the way for hermeneutical inquiry and explanation.

A cautionary note: this shift, from viewing the Qur'an as an unstable open text to one that was closed and fixed, should not be confused as a shift from the oral to the written. After all, variance in the readings of the Qur'an were not (yet) done away with in favor of a single authoritative reading. They continued to hold an important place, but their role had changed. Rather than operate as viable fragments of an open text, the variant readings became a hermeneutical tool for the exegete to draw upon in interpreting an otherwise stable Qur'an. It was this altered attitude toward the Qur'anic text as an unchanging entity that also set the stage for a particular meaning to be associated with verse 3:7's mention of ambiguity.[14] In line with this new conception of ambiguity as the uncertainty of hermeneutical inquiry rather than textual discrepancy, the reference to ambiguity in verse 3:7 also came to be understood as a reference to the text's *rhetorical* ambiguities. One of the earliest indications of this shift is found in the work of the Baghdadi

Mu'tazili theologian, Abu Ja'far al-Iskafi (d. 854).[15] Al-Iskafi defined the *muh-kam* as verses with only one possible apparent meaning and the *mutashabih* as admitting more than one meaning. After al-Iskafi, other influential think-ers who affirmed this association between *mutashabih* and textual ambiguity included the prominent theologian Abu al-Hasan al-Ash'ari (d. 935) and the legal theorist Abu al-Hasan al-Karkhi (d. 952). Henceforth, verse 3:7 came to be regarded as an affirmation of rhetorical ambiguity in the Qur'an.[16]

The *Mutashabihat* and Other Lexicographical and Grammatical Writings

Al-Iskafi is best remembered for making the critical link between verse 3:7's reference to *mutashabih* and ambiguities in the Qur'an. However, well before al-Iskafi, scholars had already been scrutinizing the Qur'an's ambiguities from a philological standpoint, as part of a genre that concentrated on the "difficul-ties in the Qur'an" (*mushkil al-Qur'an*). As I noted above, prior to the ninth century, textual difficulties were seen as discrepancies that scholars sought to "correct" by offering alternative linguistic readings.[17] By the turn of the ninth century, though, the Qur'anic text had come to be regarded as an unchang-ing given and scholars were wary of making claims against its accuracy. The theological stakes and consequences of such a claim had also elevated sub-stantially. To impute to the Qur'an discrepancies no longer merely signaled the need to gather more accurate information about the Qur'anic text; it now signified committing the much graver act of threatening divine sovereignty. In this setting, discrepancies had to be explained and justified, rather than "corrected." The grammarian and exegete Abu Zakariyya al-Farra' (d. 822), for example, stated that he did not wish to differ from the Book, and that he preferred to justify a grammatical irregularity rather than accept a proposed correction.[18] Crucial here is that, with the works of al-Farra' and several oth-ers like him, a significant body of literature was generated that was dedicated to *explaining* the problematic passages in the Qur'an.[19] The *mushkil al-Qur'an* genre evolved more into an exercise of textual interpretation than that of tex-tual correction. The chief architects of this emerging genre at the turn of the ninth century were al-Farra', Abu 'Ubayda (d. 825), and Abu 'Ubayd al-Qasim ibn Sallam (d. 837).[20] Of central concern for these scholars was the effort to provide more sophisticated explanations of semantic puzzles in the Qur'an by turning to a more nuanced analysis of the Arabic language. Abu 'Ubayd and, later, the famous scholar Ibn Qutayba (d. 889) also extended this effort to the hadith literature by composing separate works dealing with linguistic difficulties in the collected sayings of the Prophet.[21] An explicit link between the *mutashabihat* and the *mushkilat* was established by Ibn Qutayba and Ibn Manzur (d. 1311) in their texts, *Ta'wil Mushkil al-Qur'an* and *Lisan al-'Arab*, respectively, where they described the *mutashabihat* as synonymous with *mushkilat* (difficult passages), which are subject to myriad interpretations.[22]

In addition to specific works on the *mushkil al-Qur'an* (difficulties in the Qur'an), another genre of literature relevant to Qur'anic ambiguity included the compilation of lists enumerating the variety of linguistic phenomena to be taken into account while interpreting the Qur'an. One such early list is attributed to Ibn 'Abbas and includes the *muhkam/mutashabih* verses. The most important of such lists is again ascribed to Muqatil and includes an enumeration of thirty-two phenomena of Qur'anic speech.[23] Other congruent genres of writing that dealt with ambiguities included *wujuh* works, which represented an acknowledgement of the problem of homonymous or polysemous verbal forms, such as the treatise authored by Muqatil ibn Sulayman (d. 767). In this work, Muqatil listed words that occur in the Qur'an with more than one meaning, defined each meaning, and then cited passages in the Qur'an where the listed words appear with each of the identified meanings.[24] I will return to the important connection between al-Radi's *Haqa'iq* and the tradition of composing *wujuh* works, shortly. What I wish to note here is the way in which these and other writings marked the emergence of the ancillary disciplines of lexicography and grammar,[25] and also included the sustained effort to explain Qur'anic language through an Arabic lexicography based on Arabic poetry.[26] Concurrently, by the beginning of the tenth century, the Arabic grammatical tradition constituted two major types of writing: a descriptive account of the Arabic language and an explanatory account invested in the explanation of why the Arabic language was what it was.[27] So, with the works of grammarians like Sibawayhi (d. 796) in the late eighth century and al-Mubarrad (d. 898) in the late ninth century, who sought to account theoretically for the grammatical peculiarities of the Qur'an rather than correct those peculiarities, as had their predecessors, Arabic grammar as a formal discipline received a major impetus.[28] Consequently, the works of scholars like al-Zajjaji (d. 948) and Ibn Jinni (d. 1002) pushed the inquiry and consolidation of grammar as a full-fledged discipline even further, as they sought to *explain* the principles or secrets that underlay the rules of the Arabic language, moving beyond description to issues of methodology and epistemology.[29] These linguistic developments formed the critical backdrop for the fashioning of al-Radi's hermeneutical vocabulary populated with homonymy, poetry, and textual ambiguities.

Al-Radi and the Philological Tradition

In the preceding discussion, I sought to present a general picture of the intellectual activities in the fields of language that dominated the scene in tenth-century Baghdad. Beyond this shared literary milieu, there are significant overlaps that I want to discuss between al-Radi's work on the ambiguous verses and specific treatises and genres related to the category of the *mutashabih*. Of the many linguistic arguments al-Radi employed to explain the ambiguities he identified, some of the most common included ellipsis (*nuqsan*), pleonasm (*ziyada*), reversal of normal grammatical or logical order, indirect reference, lack of grammatical agreement, and metaphor (*isti'ara*). To this extent, a striking similarity exists between al-Radi's work on the ambiguities in the Qur'an and Abu 'Ubayda's (d. 824) *Majaz al-Qur'an*, written two centuries earlier.[30] John Wansbrough, in his survey of Qur'anic exegesis, described this work by Abu 'Ubayda as the earliest exegetical work that entailed a sustained analysis of grammar and syntax (as opposed to lexical explanations or variant readings). In this work, Abu 'Ubayda enumerates thirty-nine subcategories of *majaz*, explaining that certain ways of "transgressing"[31] the boundaries of normal expression are legitimate, and proceeds to translate these transgressions into equivalent normalized expressions.[32] In his terminology, *majaz* has no counterpart *haqiqa*, and it belongs to a more generic category, which can be termed "explanatory writing."[33] Thus, Abu 'Ubayda's rendering of *majaz* as "linguistic transgression" comes close to al-Radi's rendering of *mutashabih* in the *Haqa'iq*. And, like Abu 'Ubayda, al-Radi sought to disambiguate ambiguous Qur'anic expressions by locating equivalent examples in what he regarded as the authoritative linguistic canon. Abu 'Ubayda and al-Radi also shared the exegetical strategy of taking recourse for grammatical explanations in the poetic canon.[34] However, an important difference between the two works lies in the specific terminology employed by the authors. Abu 'Ubayda, writing almost two centuries earlier, used *majaz* as the collective category to refer to a wide range of linguistic transgressions,[35] whereas al-Radi placed linguistic transgressions (in the Qur'an) under the broader Qur'anic category of *mutashabih*, since by al-Radi's time the term *majaz* had acquired the more technical meaning of "figurative usage." The convergences and divergences between al-Radi and Abu 'Ubayda's works are instructive, as they show the ways in which the category of *majaz* represented an important component in the intellectual genealogy of the concept of *mutashabih*.

Reading Ambiguity as "Trope/Metaphor": *Mutashabih, Majaz,* and *Isti'ara*

In the previous section, I showed the genealogical links between al-Radi's use of the term *mutashabih* and Abu 'Ubayda's earlier use of the term *majaz*, whereby both scholars intended the broader meaning of a linguistic transgression from normative expression. But what about the relationship between *mutashabih* and *majaz* in al-Radi's own works? Were the two terms interchangeable for al-Radi? If not, then what was it that distinguished one from the other? To answer these questions and further unpack al-Radi's conception of *mutashabih*, or Qur'anic ambiguity, I turn to the way in which he imagined the similarities, differences, and the overall relationship of *mutashabih* (ambiguity) to *majaz* (linguistic transgression).

The most immediately striking thing to note in al-Radi's treatment of *majaz* and *mutashabih* is that he dedicated separate treatises to these two literary themes and did not examine them in the same work. The *Haqa'iq* text is exclusively concerned with the *mutashabih* verses of the Qur'an. Al-Radi also authored two works on *majaz*: the first was dedicated to the metaphors (*majazat*) in the Qur'an, *Economy of Eloquence in the Metaphors of the Qur'an* (*Talkhis al-Bayan fi Majazat al-Qur'an*); the second was dedicated to the *majazat* in the prophetic Hadith, *Prophetic Metaphors* (*Majazat al-Nabawiyya*).[36] In both works, he employs the term *majaz* in its more restricted sense of metaphor.[37]

Recently, scholars have traced the practice of interpreting *majaz* in its narrow meaning of "metaphor" as compared to its general meaning of "linguistic transgression" (as was the case in Abu 'Ubayda's work) to the Mu'tazili tradition.[38] What was it that led Mu'tazili scholars to focus their use of the term *majaz* to a special type of linguistic transgression—that is, figurative language, especially metaphor?[39] *Majaz* offered a solution to theological dilemmas in the Qur'an that concerned Mu'tazili scholars like 'Abd al-Jabbar, including verses that described God in anthropomorphic terms and verses that undermined the principles of divine justice and its corollary themes, such as the agency of human beings and the sovereignty of God. By the end of the ninth century, scholars (theologians in particular) had instituted a clear binary opposition between literal (*haqiqa*) and figurative (*majaz*) usage, around which they developed theoretical discourse.[40] The Basran Mu'tazili masters Abu 'Ali al-Jubba'i (d. 915) and Abu Hashim (d. 933), for example, disputed whether a word can have both literal and figurative meanings at the same time.

In extant scholarship, the exegetical practice of dedicating separate studies to the *mutashabih* verses of the Qur'an is regarded to have emerged from the tradition of figurative readings of anthropomorphic verses by Mu'tazili scholars. This interpretive method, therefore, posited an important relationship between these two literary themes, whereby *mutashabih* described the ambiguous quality of the verse and *majaz* was the literary tool through which to resolve its ambiguity. 'Abd al-Jabbar, for example, argued that *ta'wil* (interpretation) is the operation through which we can unveil the hidden aspects of the *mutashabih*, by returning them to the *muhkam*, and that *majaz* is the main tool for this operation of *ta'wil*. By connecting *majaz* and *mutashabih* with the operation of *ta'wil*, 'Abd al-Jabbar thus posited that lexical reasoning (*istidlal lughawi*) went hand-in-hand with intellectual reasoning (*istidlal 'aqli*).[41] Moreover, he affirmed the central place of *majaz* within the broader category of *mutashabih*.

The use of *majaz* in the meaning of metaphor was not universally shared by all scholars; it was the distinct practice of Mu'tazili scholars. Other scholars of the time argued for a differentiation between *majaz* and *isti'ara*, such that *isti'ara* referred to analogy-based metaphor, and *majaz* encompassed a wide range of idiomatic expressions.[42] Such variation in the conception and application of *majaz* was possible since the systematization of Arabic literary theory as a formal and fully theorized discipline had not yet gained prominence. An example of such an expansive view of literary themes is reflected in the work of Abu Hilal al-'Askari, who simply listed the various opinions on *majaz* without contesting them. Al-Radi, like some of his Mu'tazili contemporaries, employed the term *majaz* interchangeably with *isti'ara*. But al-Radi departed from his Mu'tazili contemporaries in important ways, as well, most notably by choosing to keep the discussion of *majaz* verses separate from that of what, to him, counted as the ambiguous or *mutashabih* verses. For the reader's benefit, presented below is a figure that depicts clearly and in detail al-Radi's classification of the verses in the third Qur'anic chapter, Sura Al 'Imran, according to their metaphors and ambiguities.

Figure 2. Al–Radi's identification of *mutashabihat* in the *Haqa'iq* compared with his identification of *majazat* in the *Talkhis al–Bayan fi Majazat al-Qur'an*

*Shaded areas indicate convergences between the two texts.
† The notation "*Haqa'iq* 3.1" points to the first *mas'ala* (issue) in Sura 3.

Ambiguities (in the *Haqa'iq*)

Q. 3:7 – Use of feminine plural "they" (*hunna*) for feminine singular "mother" (*umm*) (*Haqa'iq* 3.1†)

Q. 3:8 – Can God be the cause of human of deviation? (*Haqa'iq* 3.2)

Q. 3:13 – Did God reduce the number of Muslims in the eyes of polytheists? (*Haqa'iq* 3.3)

Q. 3:14 – Is God the beautifier of desire? (*Haqa'iq* 3.4)

Q. 3:18 – Does God testify on himself? (*Haqa'iq* 3.5)

Q. 3:26 – Does God give power to the unjust? (*Haqa'iq* 3.6)

Q. 3:28 – Taking unbelievers as allies (*Haqa'iq* 3.7)

Q. 3:36 – Redundant statement: the man is not like the woman (*Haqa'iq* 3.8)

Q. 3:40 – Did Zachariah doubt God's word that he would have a son? (*Haqa'iq* 3.9)

Q. 3:45 – Jesus as the word of God, mismatched gender of pronoun (*Haqa'iq* 3.10)

Q. 3:60 – Prophetic doubt (*Haqa'iq* 3.11)

Q. 3:61 – *Mubahala* verse; How can the Prophet invite himself? (*Haqa'iq* 3.12)

Q. 3:64 – People of the Book taking other gods? (*Haqa'iq* 3.13)

Q. 3:75 – Unreliable cheaters from the People of the Book (*Haqa'iq* 3.14)

Q. 3:81 – Must prophets recognize earlier prophets? (*Haqa'iq* 3.15)

Q. 3:83 – Is there forced submission? (*Haqa'iq* 3.16)

Q. 3:90 – Is the repentance of unbelievers not accepted? (*Haqa'iq* 3.17)

Q. 3:91 – Are there superfluous elements in the Qur'an? Superfluous letter 'waw' (*Haqa'iq* 3.18)

Q. 3:96 – Mecca described as the first house? (*Haqa'iq* 3.19)

Q. 3:97 – Are unbelievers equal to believers unable to perform Hajj? (*Haqa'iq* 3.20)

Q. 3:102 – Obeying God as He ought to be obeyed (*Haqa'iq* 3.21)

Q. 3:109 – All actions must return to God— but were they ever detached from God? (*Haqa'iq* 3.22)

Q. 3:110 – Repetition of God's name (in discussion [*fasl*] section) (*Haqa'iq*, 3.23)

Q. 3:110 – Is "best *umma*" a reference to a past community? (*Haqa'iq* 3.23)

Q. 3:111 – It won't hurt you except it will pain (*Haqa'iq* 3.24)

Q. 3:128 – No actions are from you (*Haqa'iq* 3.25)

Q. 3:133 – Breadth of paradise equal to heaven & earth (*Haqa'iq* 3.26)

Q. 3:143 – Vision of death? (*Haqa'iq* 3.27)

Q. 3:145 – Equivalence of reward seekers of this life and the Hereafter (*Haqa'iq* 3.28)

Q. 3:154 – What has been written down will happen (*Haqa'iq* 3.29)

Q. 3:175 – Satan fears his allies? (*Haqa'iq* 3.30)

Q. 3:178 – Respite for unbelievers so they increase in sin (*Haqa'iq* 3.31)

Metaphors (in the *Talkhis*)

Q. 3:7 – "*Umm*" (mother) of the Book is metaphor for the main part (*asl*) of the Book.

Q. 3:7 – *Rasikhun* is a metaphor for the firm in knowledge.

Q. 3:12 – *al-Mihad* (bed) is metaphor for what you prepare.

Q. 3:22 – *al-Habt* (disease that rots the insides) is a metaphor for wasted deeds.

Q. 3:27 – *al-Ilaj* is a metaphor for the entering of day into the night and night into the day.

Q. 3:27 – "The dead" are a metaphor for the unbelievers and "the living" are a metaphor for the believers; bringing to life refers to a rejuvenated religiosity.

Q. 3:39 – Jesus as Word of God is a metaphor for Jesus as bearer of good news

Q. 3:54 – "Plotting of God" is a metaphor for God's bringing down punishment.

Q. 3:72 – "*Wajh al-Nahar*" is a metaphor for first part of the day.

Q. 3:73 – God is expansive/wide is metaphor for God's expansive giving, or for the wide routes through which to gain knowledge of him, or for the width of his dominion.

Q. 3: 77 – "They will not see God" is a metaphor, and its *haqiqa* (true meaning) is that God will not have mercy on them.

Q. 3:103 – *Habl Allah* (God's rope) is a metaphor for God's commands.

Q. 3:103 – "On the brink of a fiery abyss" is a metaphor for person on the brink of death due to bad deeds since here too his fall is from the slipping of the foot.

Q. 3:109 – To God return all things—"return" here is a metaphor for the transfer of ownership of all things to God.

Q. 3:112 – "*Duribat*" is a metaphor for a tent that surrounds and spreads over its people.

Q. 3:118 – "Do not take for your intimates outsiders to Devotion"; the term "*bitana*" (lining of cloth, "thing put beneath" on a camel) is a metaphor for intimate friend.

Q. 3:127 – "*Li-yaqta'a tarafan*" (to cut the sides) is used metaphorically for reducing their number by cutting a number of them and weakening them.

Q. 3:143 – Vision of death is metaphor for vision of its signs.

Q. 3:144: "Turn back on your heels" is a metaphor for reverting to doubt in the Prophet's message.

Q. 3:156 – "*Darabu fi al-ard*" is a metaphor for journeying to far–off places; the similarity is between the wanderer of the earth and the swimmer in the sea, since he slaps with his hands and legs (*atrafihi*) to combat the depth of the sea.

Q. 3:163 – "They are degrees/levels"; "*darajat*" is a metaphor for possessors of levels.

Q. 3:185 – "*Mata' al-ghurur*" illusory pleasure is a metaphor for the pleasure of this world as a fleeting shadow and fading dye.

Q. 3:185 – "Taste death" is used metaphorically to refer to human proximity to death.

Q. 3:186 – "*'Azm al-umur*" (determination of actions) is used metaphorically for strength of actions.

Q. 3:187 – "*Nabadhahu wara'a zuhurihim*" (tossed it behind their backs) is a metaphor for their neglecting from remembering it and busying themselves from understanding it.

Q. 3:188 – *Bi-mafazatin min-al-adhab*" is metaphor for place that is far from punishment; "*mafaza*" is a remote desert.

Q. 3:196 – "*Taqallub fi al-bilad*"; *taqallub* here is used metaphorically for journeying and for movement from one condition to another.

As Figure 2 illustrates, al-Radi's separate treatment of the literary themes of *mutashabih* and *majaz* is evident from the fact that the verses he identified as *majaz* in the *Talkhis* text were not the same verses that he identified as *mutashabih* in the text of the *Haqa'iq*. In addition, even if there existed occasional overlap between the verses discussed in the two books, the element of ambiguity that al-Radi identified in a given verse discussed in the *Haqa'iq* was different from its metaphorical quality engaged in the *Talkhis*. In his introduction to the *Talkhis*, al-Radi highlighted two main goals he sought to accomplish through this work: first, to gather all instances of *majaz* in the Qur'an in one place, so as to show how it bolsters and improves the intended meaning of a given instance of divine speech; and second, to present a paradigmatic template of the literary features of *majaz* that might serve as a beneficial point of reference for orators, poets, and any other interested parties. At this juncture, al-Radi gestures to his other work, the *Haqa'iq*, and how it, too, belongs to the same category (*jins*). In other words, and this is critical, he sees the *Haqa'iq* as fulfilling the same goals as the *Talkhis*, even though, as I have just highlighted, the content and accent of these works were noticeably different. I would argue that by "belonging to the same category" al-Radi did not mean that they are both works about *majaz*. Rather, he seems to have drawn a conceptual analogy between *majaz* and *mutashabih* as literary devices through which the meaning and affect of Qur'anic discourse is enhanced.[43]

To better and further elaborate al-Radi's conception of the interaction (or lack thereof) between *majaz* and *mutashabih*, let me turn more specifically to his treatment of verse 3:7, which, to remind the reader, states: "It is He who revealed to you the scripture, part of which is definite [*muhkam*] verses; these [*hunna*] are the mother of the book. Other [verses] are ambiguous [*mutashabih*]." In the *Haqa'iq*, al-Radi identified the ambiguity in this verse as a lack of agreement in the female plural pronoun "*hunna*" used to describe the singular female noun, "mother of the Book." By contrast, in the *Talkhis*, he identified the *majaz* with the term "mother," which he argued represents a metaphor for "foundation" or "root" (of the Book). Examples such as this suggest that the two texts advanced markedly distinct hermeneutical projects and operations. However, there are some exceptions. There were some verses where metaphorical usage was what made a verse ambiguous. One example is the verse that says, "You were longing for death before you met it; now you have seen it, while you were seeing" (Qur'an, 3:143). Al-Radi explains the ambiguity in this verse through the metonymical use of the term "death," for "the causes of death," and, in an unusual case of overlap, he cites the same explanation in the *Talkhis*, where death is used in its metaphorical meaning for causes of death.

The exact relationship between al-Radi's two works, *Talkhis* and *Haqa'iq*, can thus be summed up as follows. Based on al-Radi's organization of the material and the distinct selection of Qur'anic verses discussed in each text, it seems that al-Radi regarded *majazat* and *mutashabihat* as two separate literary categories, whereby *majazat* represented a sub-category of the *mutashabihat*. Most likely, he chose to devote a separate treatise to the *majazat* since they were numerous and shared a common literary function. In any case, the point I want to impress here is that al-Radi's separate treatment of these two categories clearly suggests that he was acutely attuned to the varied yet overlapping hermeneutical registers connected to the tropes of *majaz* and *mutashabih*.

Polysemy and Ambiguity

Another genre of works closely related to al-Radi's *Haqa'iq* were those addressing polysemy in the Qur'an (henceforth *wujuh* works), as well as treatises
on antonyms (*addad*), synonyms (*mutaradifat*), and etymology (*ishtiqaq*) in
language. *Wujuh* works essentially accounted for the philological category of
mushtarak (homonymous polysemous words),[44] also described by the phrase
"what agrees in form and differs in meaning" (*ma ittafaqa lafzuhu wa ikhtalafa ma'nahu*). This phrase encompassed multiple phenomena:

(a) homonymy (when two different words with two different mean-
    ings have the same spelling);
(b) polysemy (when the same word carries more than one meaning);
    and
(c) antonymy (when the same word carries two opposite meanings).

As with the category of ambiguity in the Qur'an, the assertion of
mushtarak terms as constituent elements of the Arabic language came with
theological consequences. Namely, the presence of such features in the Arabic language could be understood to mean that an intrinsic feature of the
Arabic language (and by extension that of the Qur'an) was a lack of clarity.
Thus, some scholars strongly opposed the idea that language could contain
multiple words for a single meaning or a single word with several meanings,
due to the threat this might pose to its intelligibility and, by extension, to the
justness of the Creator of a language that was not intelligible.[45]
    Some of the ways that scholars who did accept the presence of these liter-
ary features in the Arabic language worked around the problem (of insinuat-
ing that the Qur'an was unclear) were the following: by limiting the number of
possible meanings any single word could carry; by consolidating the sources
by which those meanings could be determined; and by outlining with great
specificity the steps that each literary operation entailed. This same impulse
of circumscribing ambiguity was what gave rise, for example, to the genre
of enumerating word lists with accompanying meanings: *wujuh* works. Two
important *wujuh* works that acknowledged polysemous verbal forms include
the treatise authored by Muqatil ibn Sulayman (d. 767), *Meanings [of Words]
and the Analogous Passages [in Which They Occur]* (*al-Wujuh/al-Ashbah wa
al-Naza'ir*),[46] and, more than a century later, that of al-Mubarrad (d. 898),[47]
titled *Words That Agree in Their Utterance but Differ in Their Meaning in the*

Glorious Qur'an (Ma ittafaqa lafzuhu wa ikhtalafa ma'nahu min al-Qur'an al-Majid).[48]

In a succinct and insightful study, Andrew Rippin examined al-Mubarrad's treatise alongside that of Muqatil and identified the common assumptions underlying the work of both of these scholars,[49] which, as I show here, also apply to al-Radi's Haqa'iq. Like al-Mubarrad and Muqatil, al-Radi acknowledged the multiple instantiations of "mushtarak" words, and he relied on this feature to explain and resolve the ambiguity associated with select verses. In theory, al-Mubarrad, Muqatil, and al-Radi shared the premise that the Qur'an is not indecipherable but is, rather, directly intelligible by humans, once the code of language is figured out. Yet, "it was recognized that it did contain some degree of uncertainty on a semantic level—vagueness, indefiniteness, ambiguity—and that it used a wide range of rhetorical devices."[50] Muqatil listed words that occur in the Qur'an with more than one meaning, defined each meaning, and cited passages where the word occurred with each meaning. For example, the book commences with the seventeen different wujuh (aspects/senses) of the term huda (often translated simply as guidance). After mentioning each wajh (singular for wujuh), he supplies the relevant Qur'anic verses where that meaning is in effect. No further commentary accompanies these lists. As Rippin (following John Wansbrough and other scholars) has noted, divisions of the sense of words (wujuh) in Muqatil's text correspond more to their context of usage than what we might understand as different root senses or meanings.[51] So, for example, the term kufr (covering up/denial) is said to carry four different senses in the Qur'an: al-kufr bi tawhid (denial of the oneness of God), kufr al-hujja (denial of God's proof), kufr al-ni'ma (denial of God's blessings), and al-bara'a (exemption from).[52]

Al-Mubarrad's work, written a century after Muqatil's, classifies words and meanings in their various possibilities: synonyms, homonyms, and single words with opposite meanings (addad), and includes poetry and prophetic hadith as evidence for determining their specific meanings. The text then proceeds to examine various instances of polysemy in the Qur'an. The examples from the Qur'an are not limited to individual words but extend to certain larger utterances and their rhetorical features. Also, as Rippin points out, al-Mubarrad also "treats expressions in which the meaning does not seem to be the same as what is intended as a consequence of the use of standard Arab idioms, not an issue of polysemy at all but of language usage creating textual ambiguity."[53] Such treatises served the dual purpose of allowing authors to assert their authority as legitimate interpreters of the

Qur'an by first identifying and then resolving the uncertainties that they deemed it to contain.

Al-Radi's *Haqa'iq*, composed a good century after al-Mubarrad's work, is of course organizationally quite different, in that it is a commentary on those verses al-Radi identifies as ambiguous, and ambiguity for al-Radi encompasses much more than instances of polysemy. Moreover, the work is structured into chapters divided on the basis of the larger question that each ambiguous verse raises, be it grammatical, theological, ethical, or logical. In other words, in terms of its structure, the *Haqa'iq* most resembles works of the *masa'il*, or the question-and-answer genre. Yet, al-Radi's method for deriving explanations for these ambiguities is very similar to that of al-Mubarrad, to whom al-Radi appreciatively refers on numerous occasions. In its treatment of grammar, its citation of poetry and speech of Arabs, and its invocation of shifts in meaning in particular usages, al-Mubarrad's work is an important predecessor to the discussion we find in al-Radi's *Haqa'iq*. One key difference is that, unlike al-Mubarrad, al-Radi does not refer to Prophetic hadith as an authoritative source for language.

As for the category of antonyms (*addad*), this was another critical concept of language that permeated al-Radi's linguistic maneuvers. Early treatises on this linguistic phenomena include the work of Basran philologist Abu Hatim al-Sijistani (d. 869),[54] Abu al-'Abbas Ahmad ibn Yahya al-Tha'lab (d. 904)'s *Kitab al-Fasih*, and several others who are mentioned as linguistic authorities in Ibn al-Anbari's *Kitab al-Addad*.[55] Al-Radi, too, freely invokes this phenomenon as an explanation for ambiguity in the Qur'anic verses, as we will see in the subsequent chapters of this book.

My objective in juxtaposing the *Haqa'iq* with these related works is to situate as well as historicize al-Radi as an important interlocutor and contributor to the Arabic philological tradition in early Islam. In addition to his invocation of many features like polysemy and antonymy as explanations for Qur'anic ambiguities, there is another connecting thread between the *Haqa'iq* and these rhetorical writings. Specifically, for some scholars during this formative period for the theorization of Arabic language, the very existence of literary features like ambiguity, polysemy, homonymy, and antonymy carried the risk of undermining the coherence of the Arabic language (and, in turn, that of the Qur'an). In his defense of the existence of antonyms, for example, Ibn al-Anbari argued that their existence is not a reflection of the deficiency of the Arabic language. Rather, when read in their respective contexts, the meaning of these words becomes quite clear. This explanation is similar to what we also find in al-Mubarrad's discussion of polysemy, where he states that whenever multiple meanings are possible, there must also be present an indication (*dalil*) of the intended meaning.[56] As we will see, al-Radi argues along similar lines in his discussion of ambiguous verses claiming that they are clear when read alongside the right *muhkam* verse. We will see over the course of the discussion that follows that the exegetical prerequisite of a built-in indication or *dalil* for every instance of ambiguity takes on an extremely significant role in the developing hermeneutical apparatus of scholars like al-Radi.

The fact that a defense of the Qur'an's coherence was one of the goals and motivating conditions for the composition of several works like those discussed above has had, I would argue, a rather stultifying effect on secondary scholarship on these writings. The tendency has been to stop at describing theologically motivated writings as apologetic. Rippin, for example, in seeking to answer why scholars like al-Mubarrad and Muqatil would create inventories of words as they did, argues that this method suggested an effective containment and circumscription of the problem of ambiguity. Thus, Rippin understood the purpose of Muslim scholarly writings on homonymy (like those of al-Mubarrad and Muqatil) to be primarily apologetic, or part of an effort to defend the Qur'an from any allegations of imperfection. In an effort to situate al-Mubarrad's work, Rippin refers to the following view of Gregor Schwarb on the task of Muslim exegesis:

> The standard procedure for identifying and controlling the indeterminacy of meaning in general and the meaning of God's speech in particular was to systematize and classify the whole range of linguistic and epistemological difficulties that are prone to impair its understanding, and to attribute to each of these difficulties a set of interpretive rules so as to regulate the process of meaning construction and bring about clarity (*bayan*) by way of disambiguation, specification, qualification, and so forth.[57]

While I agree with the general insights regarding the theological motifs undergirding these writings on homonymy, I find the descriptor "apologetic" of little analytical value. If anything, it forecloses further avenues of inquiry. Certainly, as I have shown here, al-Radi's *Haqa'iq* arose in a context similar to that of his predecessors al-Mubarrad and Muqatil. Yet I argue that to read the *Haqa'iq* simply as a work of apologia and to go no further would miss the weight of al-Radi's intervention—namely, the effort to privilege ambiguity as a fundamental way of knowing, the subject to which I now turn.

The *Muhkam/Mutashabih* Dynamic as Interpretive Device

While it is possible to read al-Radi as an exegete, in the *Haqa'iq*, or as a poet, in the *Diwan*, or as a judge, in his role as *qadi* of the 'Alid community, in reality, he embodied all of these disciplines at once. Yet, for him, the stakes to permit ambiguity as a feature of language when writing as a poet were very different from when as a judge he was tasked with legislating lives on the basis of a divine text. It is this issue to which I now turn: How did a figure like al-Radi— straddling the markedly different positions that he did—account for ambiguity in the Qur'an? How did he proclaim the beauty of the hermeneutical openings that Qur'anic ambiguity makes available while also demarcating the limits of such ambiguity so as to avert the possibility of hermeneutical chaos?

By the turn of the ninth century, in Muslim intellectual traditions, divine speech or revelation was approached not only as a form of guidance but also as the fundamental source of law;[58] discourses on language and revelation went hand-in-hand with emerging theories on law and jurisprudence.[59] The first chapter of works on legal theory, for example, was dedicated to hermeneutics. In general, the overlap between legal and grammatical traditions was extremely important, and many treatises attest to this relationship.[60] Al-Radi's approach to these three important concepts—namely, language, law, and revelation—is thus critical for grasping his understanding of the hermeneutical trope of ambiguity that was central to his exegesis. For al-Radi, the ambiguous or *mutashabih* verses in the Qur'an were not limited to metaphorical or figurative expressions; they encompassed several other types of linguistic transgressions. Even as ambiguity was transgressive by nature, an important theological principle oversaw and sought to circumscribe its departure from normative speech. This was the theological principle of "clarity" (*bayan*). This concept was most comprehensively formulated by al-Radi's Mu'tazili teacher, Qadi 'Abd al-Jabbar. The theological system articulated by 'Abd al-Jabbar centered on the principle of God's justice. Accordingly, within this justice-centered system, the pairing of revelation with law led 'Abd al-Jabbar to assign to revelation the necessary property of absolute clarity.[61] In other words, 'Abd al-Jabbar argued that if God's revelation is to be understood as God's law, and God is just, then revelation must have been expressed in an absolutely clear language.

The "principle of clarity" thus came to define the very nature of revelatory language for ʿAbd al-Jabbar and his followers. But if from a theological perspective the Qurʾan was understood as absolutely clear, then how was this clarity achieved in language? In other words, how was one to understand and measure "clarity?" For ʿAbd al-Jabbar, the principle of clarity was mainly expressed as a denial of deferred clarification (taʾkhir al-bayan). In other words, whenever God uses a word non-literally or transgressively in his revelation, he must provide rational or revealed evidence of what it means, and this evidence must accompany the transgressively used expression; it cannot be revealed at some later time.[62] Therefore, although ʿAbd al-Jabbar recognized the category of transgressive usage, which, on the one hand, suggests the opening up of a space for ambiguity and reinterpretation, he also insisted that the clarifying text must be revealed at the same time as the transgressive one. In this way, his theory of transgressive usage remained under the firm control of his principle of clarity.[63] Of crucial importance here are the ramifications of ʿAbd al-Jabbar's emphasis on the principle of clarity on his understanding of the operations of literary devices such as metaphor and ambiguity. Most critically, in order for ʿAbd al-Jabbar to assign absolute clarity to language and also maintain that language is composed of literary features like ambiguity and metaphor, he had to firmly establish and regulate the operations of these literary devices.

We see strong echoes of ʿAbd al-Jabbar's argument on language and the limits of ambiguity in al-Radi's writings. For al-Radi, not only did the literary motifs of ambiguity and metaphor represent rhetorically powerful devices, similar to ʿAbd al-Jabbar's view, the extent to which these devices could be allowed to defer meaning was also determined and limited by the overarching principle of clarity. Al-Radi's literary arguments on the import of the Qurʾan's ambiguous verses were both bolstered and limited by what he upheld as a fixed linguistic canon. Moreover, for al-Radi, the principle of clarity demanded that all literary operations (metaphors and beyond) were part of the samʿ, or the received transmission of language, meaning that literary hermeneutical devices were lexicalized and could not be freely formed by analogy.[64] The "principle of clarity" thus determined al-Radi's overarching view of language, including its ambiguities, as fixed in a literary canon. In al-Radi's view, following ʿAbd al-Jabbar, the principle of clarity was also primarily expressed as a denial of deferred clarification (taʾkhir al-bayan), such that the evidence of a linguistic transgression had to be present in the specific expression in question. For al-Radi, therefore, the evidence of linguistic transgression in the

Qur'an was located in the clear verses (*muhkamat*), thus making the *muhkam-mutashabih* dynamic central to his interpretive process.

This principle of returning the *mutashabih* to the *muhkam*, the ambiguous to the clear, that we find centrally featured in al-Radi was not without precedent. For instance, the highly influential and much referenced Muslim historian and exegete Muhammad ibn Jarir al-Tabari (d. 923) cited Muhammad Ibn al-Zubayr (d. 728–38) as saying:

> The *muhkamat* are verses that can only be interpreted in one way, while the *mutashabihat* are verses that allow for various interpretations. . . . Then they refer the interpretation of the [*aya*] *mutashabiha* to what they know of the interpretation of the [*aya*] *muhkama* that admit only one interpretation. The book is thereby harmonized by what they say, one part confirming another. By means of it, the proof [*hujja*] is established, victory appears, falsehood departs and infidelity is refuted.[65]

The Literary Canon

At this juncture it is instructive to clarify the kinds of sources that constituted for al-Radi "the literary canon" on the basis of which he constructed and supported his exegetical arguments. Ultimately, scholarly exchanges between grammarians—who were actively in conversation with the sources, tools, and methods of the legal tradition—provided the intellectual scaffolding for al-Radi's conceptualization of a linguistic canon. Al-Radi's interpretive method in the *Haqa'iq*, therefore, further reinforces the inextricable links between law and language as fields of thought and practice at this historical juncture.

The primary scheme by which Arab grammarians of the time established the canonical rules that governed the Arabic language were: *ijma'* (consensus), *sama'* (attested materials), and *qiyas* (analogy).[66] Each of these were similarly upheld by al-Radi as the major discursive sources and knowledge traditions for constituting a literary canon and onto which he would graft his literary hermeneutic of Qur'an exegesis. Let me explain what each of these categories referred to.

Ijma', in the context of grammatical writings, referred to the explicit agreement of Basran and Kufan grammarians.[67] Functioning as the established authority on questions of language, *ijma'* can be seen as a force of continuity expressed through a voice of authority.[68] But *ijma'* could also refer to the implicit agreement of the grammarians, which might simply mean the absence of any *disagreement*. In this second meaning, *ijma'* or consensus was of course not as normatively weighty as the former. In the *Haqa'iq*, time and again, we see al-Radi turn to *ijma'* or the authority derived from a consensus among grammarians as a way to undermine competing interpretive claims.

Sama', or the corpus of collected data (attested materials), included transmitted texts and elicited data.[69] Transmitted texts consisted mainly of authorized readings of the Qur'an, a historically delimited field of poetry, and a small portion of generally accepted prose materials. Elicited material was data elicited from Bedouin speakers and collected by the grammarians. In culling this material, the grammarians were constantly engaged in evaluating and selecting which poets/poetic writings and which speakers, for example, could be regarded as normative.[70] In al-Radi's *Haqa'iq*, we find that he was comfortable drawing on the Qur'an's variant readings as an authoritative source, a position similar to that of his teacher, Ibn Jinni, and to that of the Kufan school of grammar.[71] Poetry, a crucial transmitted text for grammarians, was an indispensable reference for al-Radi, as well. It is important to note the shifting function of ancient Arabic poetry as it went from a foundational source of all knowledge to a repository for knowledge of the Arabic language during this time. This transformation reflected the attempt by scholars to reconcile Qur'anic verses in which Prophet Muhammad was clearly distinguished from the "poets." In his study of Arabic poetics in early Islam, Vicente Cantarino pointed out that by establishing Arabic poetry as a grammatical and linguistic canon, scholars who responded to the Qur'anic denunciation of poetry strove hard to assert poetry's "falsity" as compared to the Qur'an's "veracity." The intention here was to separate the two forms of writing by such dramatic strokes so as to have the effect of protecting the poetic tradition from being completely superseded by the Qur'an. As long as the two were never held to be similar or comparable by the critical measure of "truth," the poetic tradition could be kept alive and appreciated as a source of grammatical reference.[72] What is crucial to note here is that the preservation of Arabic poetry as a literary tradition hinged precisely on its status as an authoritative repository of Arabic grammar and rhetoric. Moreover, that status also enabled Arabic poetry to function as proof text to illustrate unusual applications of the language.

Not all poetry was regarded as a suitable reservoir of data for linguistic analysis and description, however. Rather, poetry had to undergo a process of selection, in which the principle of eloquence (*fasaha*) applied as a criterion of relevance. What eloquence meant in practical terms was fluid. For some, it was defined by the period in which the poetry in question was produced. For others, thematic and stylistic excellence were its true markers.[73] The array of poets that al-Radi cited, from Dhu al-Rumma (d. 735) to Kuthayyir (d. 723) and others, is an important indicator of where he stood on this critical issue on the limits of eloquence in the poetic tradition. Finally, with regard to elicited data, practically speaking, this represented information initially acquired by grammarians from Bedouin informants through in-person meetings in the marketplace or visits to the desert for the purpose of data collection.[74] Although, by Ibn Jinni's time (d. 1002), this mode of data collection had become obsolete, given that he reportedly declared it almost impossible to find a speaker whose ordinary linguistic behavior could validly be characterized by eloquence or *fasaha*.[75]

Irrespective of the "authenticity" of elicited data,[76] its prestigious place in the canon secured a link between the notion of pure speech to desert life. This link, not dissimilar to the claim that pure speech derives from pure lineage, would develop into a familiar trope for poets and scholars alike. Al-Radi himself relied on this trope in varied ways throughout the *Haqa'iq*. For example, aside from directly quoting Bedouin speech, it can be noted that a number of the poetic verses that al-Radi cited drew on the visual imagery of Bedouin life. For the most part, the *authors* of these verses remained unnamed. But more consequential and crucial than the identity of these poets was the authorizing work performed by their poems, by laying on display subtle visual cues from Bedouin life.

It is in the third and final source of authority for grammarians, that of *qiyas* (analogy), that we find the most pronounced imprint of the juridical hermeneutical model. In the work of Ibn Jinni and others, the very idea of grammar as a whole was understood as analogy, and that was what justified the use of this tool in grammar. How can "grammar" as a whole be understood as "analogy?" Let me briefly explain. If language is imagined as a system that utilizes finite means to generate an infinite number of utterances, then analogy is the tool through which the finite rules can be used to generate these infinite applications. Similarly, *qiyas* was foundational to jurisprudence: the application (through analogy) of fixed, authoritative legal cases to an infinite number of situations.

And how exactly did *qiyas* work in the linguistic context? The key concept through which to trace the process of analogy is "*ta'lil*," or linguistic reasoning, the individual components of which are as follows: (1) the base (*asl*), (2) the subsidiary (*far'*), (3) the rule (*hukm*), and (4) the rationale (*'illa*). The base or *asl* was an attested entity that conformed to regular patterns of language.[77] The rule or *hukm* was a linguistic property or feature shared by the *asl* and the subsidiary or *far'* by virtue of a common rationale or *'illa*. The rationale, the most important component of analogical analysis or reasoning, was the rational basis that justified the ascription to the subsidiary of the rule that was originally applicable to the base or *asl*.[78] Analogical reasoning or *qiyas* as a hermeneutical tool was at the very heart of al-Radi's interpretive framework. The specific examples from the *Haqa'iq* that I will next analyze illustrate the centrality of *qiyas* to the *muhkam-mutashabih* hermeneutic that al-Radi outlined and implemented in his work.

In al-Radi's own words, the fundamental principle that authorized and governed his tightly sealed interpretive method was the inextricable relationship between the *muhkam* and the *mutashabih*, whereby the Qur'an's ambiguous verses (the *mutashabihat*) were to be understood by establishing their link to verses whose meaning was clear and apparent (the *muhkamat*). Al-Radi, of course, was by no means alone in adopting such an approach to interpreting the *mutashabih* verses; he had the company of several other exegetes on this score.[79] However, where he differed from many was on the details of how this principle was to be applied. To explicate the contours of this difference, I want to turn to an important exegetical example in the *Haqa'iq* whereby al-Radi walked the reader through his application of the fundamental hermeneutical principle of *muhkam/mutashabih* in the context of verse 3:7 while explaining the steps through which the *muhkam* illuminates the meaning of the *mutashabih*.

Illustrations from the *Haqa'iq*

By the time of the *Haqa'iq*'s composition in the tenth century, verse 3:7 had assumed a critical function in the Muslim exegetical tradition. Its specific references to revelation, interpretation, and authority created an important conceptual space through which exegetes could convey their hermeneutical (and sectarian) positions. But, for al-Radi, this verse does not serve as an opportune moment or space for making explicit any normative "Shi'i" position on the Imams' exclusive claim to interpretive authority. Quite to the contrary, even while he adhered to a reading of verse 3:7 that accords interpretive authority not only to God but also to "those rooted in knowledge," he argues that "those rooted in knowledge" refers to the *'ulama'*, or scholars, without any mention of Imami authority. In other words, for al-Radi, the ambiguity in verse 3:7 was not to be found on the issue of interpretive authority, the most commonly understood issue at stake in this avidly contested verse. In fact, it was only in the "discussion" (*fasl*) section of this chapter that he even felt the need to bring up interpretive authority. So, unlike the Qur'an commentaries of many of al-Radi's predecessors, his discussion of this verse did not center on the obscure language with which the Book is described as a composite of clear and ambiguous verses.[80] For al-Radi, then, where was the ambiguity in verse 3:7 to be located? It was located in the domain of Arabic grammar.

Specifically, as I had briefly mentioned earlier, while tackling verse 3:7, al-Radi focused his exegetical energies on the following linguistic conundrum: How was it that the plural feminine pronoun (*hunna*) was used to refer to the single feminine noun, "mother of the Book" (*umm al-kitab*)? To repeat for the reader's benefit the relevant part of the verse: "It is He who revealed to you the scripture, part of which is definite verses; these [*hunna*] are the mother of the book [*umm al-kitab*]." The apparent lack of grammatical agreement in this sentence, whereby a plural pronoun referred to a singular object, represented al-Radi's main concern. In responding to this dilemma, though, while seeking to resolve the specific puzzle at hand, al-Radi also offered some important insights on his broader understanding of the relationship between the *muhkam* and the *mutashabih*, the elucidation of which, in turn, is my central concern. I quote al-Radi at some length due to the passage's importance:

The pronoun [*hunna*] refers to the entirety of the verses [in the Qur'an], and the joining of some of them to others in their revelation is what the "mother of the Book" [*umm al-kitab*] refers to. Each verse in the Book does not count as the *umm* [mother/foundation] on its own. Describing the singular with the plural is permissible when they are deeply connected to each other and when their meanings are conjoined. Because if God had said, "they are the mothers of the Book," the listener would have [mistakenly] assumed that every single verse is the mother [*umm*] for the entire Book. This is not the [intended] meaning [of this verse]. Rather, the meaning is what I have said about the essence of the verses in their entirety being the "mother of the Book," not just some [of the verses]. The meaning of their essence as the mother of the Book is that from which one learns what is intended by the Book with respect to the clarification of the markers of religion [*min bayan ma'alim al-din*]. So, the expression "mother of the Book" does not refer back to each and every [*muhkam*] verse, but rather to all the [*muhkam*] verses in their totality. Therefore, *umm* here takes the meaning of "the foundation" [*al-asl*] to which [meaning] returns and rests on. *Muhkam* is the foundation for the *mutashabih*; it is illuminated by it [*yuqaddihu bihi*] such that it makes clear what is hidden in it [*maknunahu*] and extracts what is buried in it. And this is why a mother of a human is called *umm* because she is the root [*asl*] from which a human is born and then grows.[81]

There are a few points worth highlighting from this quote. First, notice how al-Radi insists that the foundational character of the *muhkam* verses is a feature that describes the verses as a collective whole and not as individual constituents.[82] Critical to this assertion is al-Radi's refusal to accept any difference between the verses on the basis of their epistemological value. Al-Radi was adamant in insisting that there was no hierarchy separating different verses of the Qur'an on the basis of their epistemological value. This position aligns well with al-Radi's broader effort to preserve the "principle of clarity" and its application to all parts of the Qur'an. It also captures the place of ambiguity in al-Radi's view of Qur'anic language: as an integral component of divine speech that complicates language and elevates its rhetorical value, and not as a source of confusion that can threaten its absolute clarity. Al-Radi clearly articulated this all-important principle of clarity of the Qur'an in several sections of the *Haqa'iq*. He also frequently argued that the purposefulness of each part of the Qur'an contrasts with the work of poets. The poet, for al-Radi, freely employs the device of superfluity in order to bring balance to his verses. But in the revelatory text, no word or letter is without meaning.[83]

The second important point highlighted in the passage from al-Radi cited above is his explicit reference to the principle of referring the ambiguous verses back to the clear verses to determine their meaning. Indeed, for al-Radi, it is precisely the relationship between the *muhkam* and the *mutashabih* that held the key to resolving the ambiguities inhabiting the *mutashabih* verses. This represented a foundational principle and approach to the question of ambiguity in the Qur'an. For al-Radi, the fundamental feature of the *muhkam* is that it makes visible the inner contents of the *mutashabih*. The imagery associated with the term *muhkam*, as that which brings forth or gives birth to the inner contents contained in the *mutashabih*, works well to establish the governing principle of al-Radi's hermeneutic: the answer to every *mutashabih* verse lies in its *muhkam* equivalent. And a small detail is significant here. Al-Radi describes the *muhkam* as "making clear what is hidden in it [*maknunahu*]." The term *maknun* carries the meaning of that which is contained inside, as opposed to something hidden. Often, it is used to describe the child in the mother's womb. So, the meaning of the *mutashabih* is conceived of as something that is already present, though in need of being pushed forward. What is required from the exegete, then, is not the capacity to resolve an error or confusion, but rather the skill of an individual who is able to kindle this subtle meaning by placing it alongside the appropriate *muhkam* verse. What we see here, then, is al-Radi adeptly using the Qur'anic description of the *muhkamat* as *umm al-kitab* as a means for outlining his overarching hermeneutic.

A sectarian reading of al-Radi's discussion might push a reader to the hasty conclusion that al-Radi's language is grounded in an esoteric Imami logic of concealed knowledge crying out for uncovering by the authoritative Imams. But we must remind ourselves that, ultimately, al-Radi makes no explicit reference to Imami authority in the *Haqa'iq*, nor to the moral or spiritual practices of charismatic teachers as crucial mediators of meaning. Instead, fragments of al-Radi's language imaginary, such as his description of language as "a repository of secrets," is better found in the writings of other (Sunni) grammarians. Kees Versteegh, in describing Zajjaji's *Book of Explanation of the Secrets/ Causes of Grammar* (*Kitab Idah li Asrar/'Ilal al-Nahw*) notes such a title was in keeping with "a fundamental notion in Arabic linguistic studies: behind the linguistic rules there is a hidden truth, reflecting God's hand in the creation of language. It is the task of the grammarian to reveal these secrets, be it in the domain of phonology as in Ibn Jinni's *Sirr al-sina'a*, or in the domain of rhetoric as in [Ibn Sinan] al-Khafaji's (d. 466/1073) *Sirr al-fasaha*."[84]

Let me turn to another clarifying example from the *Haqa'iq* that shows the inextricable link between the *mutashabih* to the *muhkam* in al-Radi's thought: his discussion of verse 3:178, which forms problem (*mas'ala*) thirty-one of the *Haqa'iq*. The verse reads as follows:

The disbelievers should not think that it is better for them that We give them more time: We give them more time [so that] they become more sinful [*innama numli lahum li-yazdadu ithman*]—a shameful torment awaits them.[85]

The dilemma posed by al-Radi's hypothetical interlocutor is that, according to an apparent reading of this verse, the term "so that" (*li*) leads to the absurd conclusion that God actually desires disbelief from the disbelievers. The term "so that" (*li*) seems to posit here a causal correlation between God's granting respite to the disbelievers and them increasing in sin. How could that be true?

Al-Radi responded to his interlocutor's puzzlement by reiterating the centerpiece of his hermeneutic: the *muhkam/mutashabih* rule. He then explains how the rule applies to this particular verse. I translate and quote a sizable fragment of his discussion below, as it is quite illustrative of his larger hermeneutical assumptions and operation:

> In the beginning of this book, while discussing the principles of *muhkam* and *mutashabih*, I presented a rule [*qa'ida*], which must serve as the foundation [*al-bina'*] and underlying point of reference [for problems of interpretation]. This rule is that the *mutashabih* verses must revert [*wajaba raddaha*] back to the *muhkam* verses. The verse, which is the subject of [this] discussion, is *mutashabih*; its root [*asluha*], according to which it must be interpreted, is the *muhkam* verse with which we responded to the questioner. The verse [51:56] states: "I created jinn and mankind so that they worship me."[86] Clearly, this verse counts as a *muhkam* verse, which is compatible with rational proof, since the letter *lam* in "*li ya'buduni*" [so that they worship me] occurs in a way that reflects its intended meaning [the worship of jinn and mankind]. The earlier verse [3:178] is counted as *mutashabih*, which opposes rational proof because the *lam* in the phrase "so that they increase in sin" occurs in a way that does not reflect its intended meaning [the increase in sin]. Therefore, we argued that its interpretation should be carried out in a way that is compatible with rational proofs and principles of justice. This is the foundational principle of religion [*asl min usul al-din*] that must be applied and relied upon.[87]

Let me briefly analyze the passage. What we see here is that, for al-Radi, the first step and order of business while interpreting such ambiguous verses was to refer them back to the clear verses. The purpose of such a referral was to find instances of *muhkam* verses in which the ambiguous parts of the ambiguous verses, such as the construction "so that" in verse 3:178, were not employed with any ambiguity. In his view, for a verse to count as *muhkam* or apparent, its structural soundness must be coupled with the balanced and rational logic of its message. These qualities invest *muhkam* verses with the power of referential authority, in the sense that an exegete can refer to them as model statements that fulfill the criteria that are necessary for their apparent sense to count as the intended meaning. So, for instance, as a first step in his attempt to clarify and remove the ambiguity raised by verse 3:178 regarding the apparently illogical use of the construction "so that," al-Radi mobilized another *muhkam* verse in which this construction was operative along similar modalities. To execute this task, he turned to verse 51:56, which reads as follows: "I created jinn and mankind so that [*li*] they worship me."

According to al-Radi, this verse clearly counts as a *muhkam* verse that was compatible with rational proof since "the letter lam in '*li ya'buduni* [so that they worship me]' occurs in a way that [unambiguously] reflects its intended meaning [the worship of jinn and mankind]." So how was this verse connected to verse 3:178, the ambiguous verse in question? By representing a parallel model of a *muhkam* verse that shared the ambiguous construction of 3:178, the term "so that," without being crippled with any ambiguity.

Once the *muhkam* was used to identify the *mutashabih*, al-Radi was then in a position to argue for an alternate grammatical reading of the ambiguous word or sentence in question. For example, in this particular case, he turned to non-Qur'anic sources to argue that even though *lam*, in the language of the Arabs, can carry the meaning of "in order to," it can also carry the meaning of "recompense." For this task, al-Radi drew on his background as a renowned poet of his time, by highlighting another meaning of the preposition *li* from the poetic lexicon. He proposed his readers observe the following poem that also seemed to articulate contradictory uses of the preposition *li*.

We gather our wealth so that [*li*] it can be passed on as inheritance
We build our houses so that [*li*] they decay with time
For [*li*] imminent death does every wet nurse raise [the child]
For [*li*] ultimate destruction do humans build civilizations anew

Al-Radi showed that the causal meaning of *li* in these verses is not rationally sound, since human beings raise children for life and not for death. Similarly, they build houses to last, not to decay, and they collect wealth to benefit from it for themselves, not to transfer it to someone else. But, when this is the ultimate fate of these actions, then it is more eloquent for the poet to use *li* in the way that he does, al-Radi contended. So, in light of the use of *li* in this poem, when one turns to the verse that says. "We give them respite *li* they become more sinful," it becomes obvious that the relationship between the provision of respite and the condition of becoming sinful is not causal but is rather resultative, or the outcome of the respite of life.[88]

According to al-Radi's *muhkam-mutashabih* hermeneutic, then, the Qur'anic text was approached as a single literary unit, such that a *muhkam* verse from one part could be brought forward to make sense of a *mutashabih* verse in an entirely different section. Moreover, this relationship between one part of the Qur'an to another was not bound to any chronological (temporal order of revelation) or sequential (order of placement in the text) pattern. A *mutashabih* verse from an early chapter could be unveiled by means of a *muhkam* verse that came after it.

There are two critical points that we can draw from the above example. First, it shows how a *mutashabih* verse is identified as such when it is read in conjunction with its *muhkam*. Second, it illustrates how the linguistic transgression in the *mutashabih* is identified and the ambiguity is thus resolved, when it is read in conjunction with a poetic source. Al-Radi's interpretive act thus comprised of two tasks: (1) referring to a *muhkam* from within the Qur'anic text and (2) referring to a model of linguistic transgression from within the linguistic canon (which includes but is not limited to the Qur'anic text). This is how, for al-Radi, the operation of hermeneutically wrestling with the Qur'an's ambiguities both drew from and contributed to an emerging canon of the Arabic language.

Conclusion

In this chapter, I have shown that al-Radi's interpretive method represented a confluence of multiple intellectual currents and positions, mediated by the intellectual and social milieu of Buyid Baghdad. Through an interrogation of the term *mutashabih* in al-Radi's Qur'an commentary, I have demonstrated the interconnections between his work and the philological tradition of interpreting grammatical difficulties in a text.

At this juncture, it is important to point out that philological approaches to interpreting the Qur'an were not restricted to an exclusively Sunni tradition of exegesis that al-Radi had to have "borrowed" from or "conceded" to. To frame it this way would be to fall prey to an exclusively sectarian reading of al-Radi's work, as well as that of his contemporaries. In addition, such a framing reinforces a majoritarian reading of Muslim intellectual history. It should be noted, for example, that the Shi'i Imams were respected for their knowledge of Arabic grammar and for their application of this knowledge in Qur'anic exegesis.[89] Therefore, it would be inaccurate to conclude that al-Radi's thought was subsumed by an orthodox Sunni approach or that his recourse to linguistic authority (as opposed to Imami) somehow validates an attitude of compromise.

Having said that, it is also evident that al-Radi was not drawing connections to early Imami precedents of attributing grammatical explanations for Qur'anic ambiguities. In fact, it is evident throughout the *Haqa'iq* that al-Radi did not consider it necessary to rest his hermeneutical decisions on the authority of what is now regarded as an exclusively Imami tradition of interpretation. But, on the other hand, to treat this citational absence as evidence of his defection to an orthodox Sunni view uncritically accepts that religious identity in tenth-century Baghdad entailed an interaction of self-conscious "majority" and "minority" groups. This strictly majority/minority driven framework assumes that the structure of identity is inherently dichotomous, such that any diversions from a minority position must entail an act of being subsumed by the dominant majority.[90]

I challenge this assimilative narrative of identity formation. Instead, I argue that the way in which al-Radi on the one hand affirms Imami authority and on the other hand appears to undermine it suggests that for him there was no contradiction in doing so. I interpret al-Radi's ambivalent attitude as a reflection of his intellectual climate, in which sectarian identities did not operate according to a modern logic of accountability. While al-Radi was no doubt a Shi'i, his identity as a scholar was not bound to any predetermined or a priori assumptions on what being a Shi'i scholar entailed.

What these discourses on language do clearly exemplify is the fundamental concern of early Muslim scholars to establish the relationship between language and revelation on theological grounds. The theological demands on the text meant that al-Radi's challenge was to explain what *work* ambiguity performed, since, as a rhetorical feature adopted in the revelatory text, it had to be purposeful. At the same time, al-Radi's discourse of ambiguity was mediated by the fundamental theological principle of clarity, according to which it was impossible for the Qur'an to remain inaccessible. Thus, the literary devices of metaphor and ambiguity in al-Radi's interpretive framework were regulated by an overarching linguistic canon, which limited the possibilities of meaning to an identifiable reference. Al-Radi's transgressive use of language thus was at once circumscribed and informed by the imperative of linguistic canonization. These two contrasting yet interlocking features of his hermeneutic reflected his embeddedness in a scholarly milieu that was captivated by the dynamic of wonder, dominated by a culture of ambiguity, and governed by a hermeneutic of concealing and revealing, each authorized in none other than the Qur'an and its ancillary disciplines.

CHAPTER 4

The Politics of Language

During the decades prior to the composition of the *Haqa'iq*, a range of sche-
matic studies on Arabic grammatical theory appeared, and these works were
broadly of two different types: descriptive accounts of the Arabic language
and explanatory accounts that informed readers why the language is the way
that it is.[1] Moreover, grammarians sought to argue for the coherence and correspondence of grammar and its laws with a wider cosmological, material,
and, indeed, political universe.[2] In philosophical writings, the ontological
nature of human beings (the rational soul) came to be conceived as intimately
connected to the cosmological structure of the universe (most significantly as
articulated by the late ninth-/early tenth-century doyen of philosophy, Abu
Nasr al-Farabi [d. 950]).[3] Similarly, scholars of language argued for the inextricable relationship between the structure of Arabic and the ontological and
social realities to which it corresponds. During this period, for instance, the
underlying purpose of language—its form and content—came to be imbued
with a clear epistemological value.[4]

　While the *Haqa'iq* is not structured as a formal treatise presenting the
underlying rationale for grammatical rules, al-Radi draws extensively from
foundational works on the topic. In the frequent explanations al-Radi provides for why a particular grammatical formulation is the way that it is, he
does not build his case on the basis of arguments of practical necessity, such
as "ease of pronunciation," etc. Rather, much like his contemporaries in the
grammatical tradition, al-Radi sought to tie the laws of grammar to laws of
nature and to show that the secrets of language corresponded to the subtle
secrets of social realities. All the while, he conceives of language as a thoroughly logical system, the underlying logic and laws of which a scholar of his
erudition and pious lineage can successfully deduce. We will see this line of
thought and reasoning on ample display in the examples that follow.

Al-Radi's hermeneutical choices were deeply rooted in the debates on language that dominated the intellectual landscape of Islam in tenth-century Baghdad. At the heart of these debates was the question of the authority of language over logic as a source of knowledge. One such famous debate took place in 932 between the prominent Muslim philologist of that time, Abu Sa'id al-Sirafi (d. 979), and leading Christian philosopher Matta ibn Yunus (d. 940), who was also the teacher of al-Farabi. The alluring high stakes of this duel are evident, propelled by the seemingly bifurcated choice between philosophy and language. Which is the superior discipline for accessing truth? But it is critical to clarify here, as scholars already have,[5] that it would be misplaced to approach this debate in binary terms, as one that pitted Arabic language against the Greek sciences or logic against language. In fact, the goal of al-Sirafi (the grammarian) was not to question the validity and importance of logic (or that of reason) as a critical epistemological tool. Rather, he sought to challenge the very premise that logic can be separated from language and hailed as a universal tool capable of being applied to any cultural and linguistic context. Al-Sirafi's main contention was that logic is, in fact, inseparable from language. This is so because, in his view, the language in which a thought is articulated shapes that thought. Thus, contrary to Matta's assertion, logic cannot be universal. And to argue for the universality of logic is to ascribe to Greek logic the exceptional status of transcending language. According to al-Sirafi, then, logic does not stand outside or above language; rather, it is part of language. He argues that it is the grammar and syntax of language that makes thought logical. To reiterate: by upholding the role of grammar and language as primary, al-Sirafi did not question the inherent value of logic or reason per se. Rather, he argued that they, too, were mediated by language. Thus, as Muhsin Mahdi insightfully states in his study of this iconic debate, Matta, in his facing of al-Sirafi, "is confronted by a dialectical theologian versed in popular Platonism rather than a grammarian who despises logic or the Greeks or reason as such."[6]

Scholar of Arabic Shukri Abed has argued that al-Sirafi's view, that logic is derived from a particular natural language—that, in fact, there is no logic except the logic of a given language—is similar to what in modern linguistics is called *linguistic relativity* or, alternatively, the "Sapir-Whorf hypothesis" (since it is closely associated with twentieth-century linguists Benjamin Whorf and Edward Sapir). Whorf, for example, believed that "a change in language can transform our appreciation of the Cosmos."[7] Language, according to Whorf, influences the very way people perceive the world. Similarly, al-Sirafi argued that logic, in its broadest sense, cannot be separated from the language in which it is expressed. The opposing view, Abed continues, held by al-Farabi and his fellow logicians, comes very close to the modern notion of *linguistic universals*, brought into current vogue by Noam Chomsky. In an almost Kantian vein, for example, al-Farabi posits that all human beings have fixed categories of the mind that determine their perception of the world, regardless of the language they speak.[8]

In addition to challenging the universalist claims of philosophers like Matta, another important critique that al-Sirafi presented against the philosophers centered on the issue of accessibility. He argued that Greek logic was inscrutable, bogged down by its technical jargon, and deliberately rendered unyieldingly complicated by its proponents. They did so, he continued with disdain, only to confound the public and draw from them a hefty fee for their teaching. Underlying this criticism was the theological argument that truth, as presented through the world and by religion, must be accessible. This principle of prioritizing the clarity and accessibility of knowledge, as I will show in this chapter, was also critical to al-Radi's exegetical thought and outlook. An ambiguity that did not seem to ruffle al-Radi or al-Sirafi was that this promise of access was nonetheless limited to an exclusive scholarly elite whom they regarded as the ultimate custodians of language. This apparent tension also serves as a useful reminder that al-Radi's push for the accessibility of knowledge cannot be characterized as a championing of unbridled populism. The broader matrix of religious authority that undergirded his view of language and knowledge was indelibly rooted in an elitist vision. For al-Radi, his authority to interpret the Qur'an's ambiguous verses derived from an index of expertise that combined his mastery of Arabic language and poetry with his pedigree boasting a noble Sayyid lineage. Thus, in al-Radi's social imaginary, language and lineage were mutually entwined.

The intellectual context described in what has preceded serves as an important backdrop to al-Radi's theory of ambiguity and the mobilization of language as his principle hermeneutical device. Leading Aristotelian philosophers like Matta ibn Yunus and his student al-Farabi played a pivotal part in connecting logic with the domain of poetic speech, primarily through the poetic syllogism.[9] Their thought made deep imprints on al-Radi's efforts to define the semiotic process that ambiguity entails, and to conceive of it as a markedly logical operation involving linking the *mutashabih* to its *muhkam*, on the basis of a common cause or *'illa*. In addition, al-Radi's hermeneutic worked to strengthen the relevance of grammar as a source of authority by attaching it to a fixed body of sources, which simultaneously contributed to its canonization.[10] His position of valorizing the authority of language as the foundational source of knowledge closely aligned with the arguments of his teacher, al-Sirafi. All of this is not to say that al-Radi's position as a "Shi'i" scholar played no part in his hermeneutical choices. The point is, however, that al-Radi's Shi'i identity cannot be abstracted from the multiple knowledge traditions and debates that thrived and came into view in the contested intellectual landscape of tenth-century Buyid Baghdad.

To reiterate, it is critical to view the *Haqa'iq* in the context of the ongoing intellectual debates of which it was a part and to ensure that we approach the writings of a Shi'i scholar like al-Radi as more than a neat reflection of his sectarian identity. Examining al-Radi's role as a participant in the intellectual conversations of his time not only does justice to his thought but also expands our analysis of critical exchanges beyond their representation by exclusively Sunni authors. Too often, in Western Islamic studies, the perspective of scholars marked as Shi'i are siloed away or deemed "beyond the scope of the present study." This persisting attitude, ostensibly a humble acknowledgement of the limits of one's expertise, does much to reinforce the untenable view that "they" (Shi'a) inhabited an altogether alternate universe, one that must take another lifetime to study! And so, along with the contributions of the works themselves, the intellectual formations made possible through these writings and their wider relevance to Muslim intellectual thought are rendered illegible. As a case in point, even remarkable and otherwise sophisticated work like Thomas Bauer's *A Culture of Ambiguity* does not escape this modern sectarian bias, despite being poised to confront and challenge the persistent reliance on Eurocentric frameworks of analysis and categories in the study of medieval Islam. Bauer states:

> The diversity of Islam—even in the realm of the Mamluks, which also had Shiite subjects—cannot and will not be taken into consideration here. It may suffice to point out that the cultural ambiguity studied here, which will focus on the "orthodox" Islam of Sunni scholars, would be many times multiplied if all the ways of life and ways of thinking of all people in the premodern Islamic world were taken into account. . . . *Finally, Shiite Islam remains almost entirely outside the scope of this book.*[11]

Bauer's formidable study challenges conventional histories of Islam by presenting case after case (exclusively from Sunni works) to accomplish his goal of studying Islam on its own terms, unburdened by the baggage of Eurocentric categories and categorizations. The crux of Bauer's contribution lies in his perceptive argument about the fundamental value and "tolerance of ambiguity" in the culture of premodern Islam, marked by the embrace of competing (but consistent) interpretations, the porousness of normative boundaries, and the celebration of complexity.[12] But by excluding altogether Shi'i perspectives and contributions to the development of this culture of ambiguity in premodern Islam, Bauer misses an important opportunity to use his analysis for the purpose of complicating sectarian identities and binaries in this context. In other words, how would considering the contribution of Shi'i actors to what Bauer calls Islam's culture of ambiguity disrupt dominant understandings of the relationship between sectarian identity and texture and orientation of religious thought?

This question is especially critical with regards to the reason/revelation debate that forms an important theme of this chapter. It is critical to interrogate the discursive mechanisms through which multiple participants from varied sectarian orientations assembled their respective arguments in a nuanced fashion that does not magnify sectarian identity as a decisively explanatory variable. My aspiration through the question-and-answer space I highlight in this chapter and throughout this book is to shift away from a paradigm that is attentive to sectarian identity only when it is made evident through discord and difference. The current paradigm in Euro-American studies on Shi'ism, for example, has been to focus on individuals, doctrines, and historical moments that seem to mark the splitting off of the Shi'i community from the larger Sunni majority. As a paradigmatic example of this trend, one can point to the many articles by Etan Kohlberg,[13] whose studies Robert Gleave (in his overview of current research on Shi'ism) describes as "of such importance that they take on almost canonical status in the study of the history of early Imamism."[14] Another illustrative example of this phenomenon is found in a recent anthology, titled *Shi'ism*, put together by Paul Luft and Colin Turner.[15] Divided into four volumes, the subject headings of this anthology read as follows: 1. Origin and Evolution; 2. Theology and Philosophy; 3. Law, Rite and Ritual; and 4. Shi'ism, State, and Politics. The articles included under this generic and neatly compartmentalized heading include surveys of Shi'i views on the Qur'an, *jihad*, the doctrine of dissimulation (*taqiyya*), the Mahdi and messianism, Muharram rituals, revolutionary ideology, and "heterodox" splinter groups, etc. As one ploughs through this work, it becomes increasingly apparent to the reader that the very selection of material and topics considered relevant by the editors for an anthology on Shiʻism are informed by a conceptual orientation toward Shiʻism as a reified identity and "heterodox other" that can be neatly separated from an "orthodox" Sunni Islam.

Moving away from this approach of examining Shiʻism solely through the looming shadow of its Sunni "other" enables the opening of a window into a spectrum of ideas, discourses, personalities and events that were equally significant in the formation of religious identities in early Islam. Critical to this shift is the recognition that religious identities and affiliations such as that of Shiʻi and Sunni do not represent unchanging and predictable entities, such that a firm grasp of their "origin" or "splitting off" from their supposed "others" suffices for an understanding of how they operate. It is thus with the premise that religious identities cannot be isolated from the larger sociopolitical and intellectual networks of which they are an integral part that I examine and present al-Radiʼs literary Qurʼan exegesis in what follows.

In this chapter, I will explore the politics of al-Radiʼs literary approach to interpreting the Qurʼan as a way to begin the process of situating debates such as the reason/revelation debate in their wider discursive contexts. In adopting a literary approach, al-Radiʼs work privileges language as the primary hermeneutical key to determining the meaning of the Qurʼan. But how does he conceive of "language"? And how might we understand the contours of his language philosophy, including its temporal and/or transcendental nature, its relationship to time and alterity, and its function on the path of acquiring knowledge? And how do his views on these questions intersect with the intellectual currents of other disciplines of his time? These are the questions I will address in this chapter through a close reading of select sections from the Haqaʼiq.

I will discuss illustrative examples of ambiguous Qurʼanic verses that constitute three separate chapters in the Haqaʼiq. The rationale for selecting al-Radiʼs discussion of these verses over others is twofold. First, of the many "types" of ambiguity that al-Radi invokes (see Figure 1 in Chapter 1), these verses reflect three of the most common types of ambiguities found in the Haqaʼiq: grammatical, logical, and ethical/moral. Second, al-Radiʼs discussion of these ambiguous verses is particularly illustrative of his overarching language philosophy.

My study of al-Radiʼs discussion on individual Qurʼanic verses will include different levels of analysis. At the most elementary level, I will provide the specific interpretive problem that the verse in question posed. Second, I will summarize the views of other exegetes, as enumerated by al-Radi, as a way to provide a general overview of the issue at stake for exegetes of the period. Third, I will outline al-Radi's argument on the existing debate and identify the key hermeneutical tendencies and principles that characterize his particular combination of interpretive rules and invocations of authority. This should help provide readers a vivid picture of how al-Radi imagined the task of interpretation and the degree of control over meaning he allocated to other authors, texts, and interpreters. Fourth, and most importantly, I will reconstruct his assumptions about language, epistemology, divine speech, human agency, divine sovereignty, and the role of exegetes in the absence of the Imams. In order to frame my subsequent illustration of the operations of al-Radi's hermeneutic, let me begin by returning to verse 3:7, the iconic and much-contested point of entry for any exegete of the Qur'an interested and invested in its ambiguous verses.

Interpretive Authority and Hermeneutics

Earlier, I examined al-Radi's discussion of verse 3:7 in relation to the grammatical conundrum it raised, the seeming lack of correspondence in the pronoun used to describe *umm al-kitab*. In the "discussion section" (*fasl*) of the same chapter in the *Haqa'iq*, al-Radi turns his attention to the contentious question of the addressee of the phrase "those firm in knowledge" (*al-rasikhun fi al-'ilm*), and the equally contentious question of its placement in the verse. Al-Radi, for his part, places this section under the separate heading of *fasl* and, in doing so, indicates to the reader that he does not consider this clause as ambiguous at all. Rather, we assume that it is included here due to the critical stakes involved in its interpretation. What were those stakes? The long-standing scholarly debate surrounding the phrase "those firm in knowledge" has been critical to conversations on interpretive authority more broadly and is consequently a familiar Qur'anic reference in primary and secondary sources. Briefly stated, commentators committed to upholding the authority of Imams, Sufi saints, or religious scholars, argue that the conjunction "and" (*waw*) joins the first part of the sentence to the second, which results in granting these groups the authority to interpret the *mutashabihat*. Others, who sought to limit interpretive authority to none other than God, argued that the mention of "those firm in knowledge" was the beginning of a new clause, unconnected from the previous. Al-Radi argued for the former. However, in a departure from previous Shi'i commentaries, he identified the firm in knowledge not with the Imams but with the scholarly religious class (the 'ulama').

Al-Radi begins by painting an instructive typology of the groups that differ on the meaning of this verse. There are, for him, two extreme positions and the middle view. The first group he describes are those who limit interpretive authority to God alone.

> They exclude the 'ulama' from knowing the truth of the ta'wil and knowing the state of its inner meanings, of excavating its obscurities, and extracting its secrets. In doing this, they undermine them [the 'ulama'] of their deserving stature [rutba], which they are worthy of fulfilling and worthy of the knowledge of its honor. God is the one who has granted them access to the right way [nahj al-sabil] and given them the light of proof [diya' al-dalil] by which to unravel [yaftatihun] the opaque [mubham] and shed light on the dark, all of which is possible through God's gift upon them and God's hoisting for them the lighthouse of proofs [manar al-adilla]. And so, their knowledge is supported by God's knowledge, praise be to Him, and there is no meaning in taking away from them this station and preventing them from reaching their highest stature.[16]

Particularly striking here is the fact that al-Radi's laudatory acclaim of the stature of the al-rasikhun or "those firm in knowledge" and of the divine favor that is the cause of their exclusive knowledge is made in reference not to the Imams but to the 'ulama', among whom al-Radi most likely counted himself.[17] Moreover, from a literary standpoint, while rehashing the opponent's view of circumscribing the authority of those privileged by virtue of their knowledge, al-Radi cleverly steers the conversation into an argument for the extensive *reach* of their authority!

The second group, al-Radi explains, read the verse as: "no one knows its ta'wil except God and the firm in knowledge." Thus, the exception (of knowing the ta'wil) is extended to God and the 'ulama'. This group grants the 'ulama' excellence of knowledge in the ta'wil of the Qur'an and knowledge of what is in it and what is external to it, in the styles of its arguments and methodologies. This view is espoused by Ibn 'Abbas and Mujahid ibn Jabr al-Makki (d. 722) and al-Rabi' (d. 756). This group occupies the other extreme

for al-Radi, whereby the 'ulama' are granted unconditional authority to interpret the Qur'an's ambiguous verses.

Finally, al-Radi refers to a third group of scholars, whom he names the
"truthful ones" (muhaqqiqun) from among the scholars; these are the uphold-
ers of the middle position (manzila wusta), or the third way (tariqa muthla).
He explains:

Neither do they exclude the 'ulama' from knowing any of the ta'wil,
nor do they give them the stature of knowing it in its entirety. Rather,
they say that from the ta'wil there are some things that the 'ulama'
know, and there are some things only God knows. That which only
God knows includes the specifics of minor sins, the time of the Hour
[Judgment Day], that which lies between us and the last Hour in
terms of time and the measuring of recompense for our actions, and
things similar to this.[18]

Hasan al-Basri and Abu 'Ali al-Jubba'i were some of the scholars identified with this position. Al-Radi argues that their reading of 3:7 is informed by
their understanding of the term ta'wil. The meaning of ta'wil, for them, was
"recompense for one's actions." Thus, what they sought to circumscribe as
exclusively divine knowledge were the specifics of reward and punishment.

Turning to another view, al-Radi explained that none but God knows
the ta'wil in detail or the specifics of the mutashabihat because many of the
mutashabihat carry multiple meanings (wujuh).[19] Al-Radi, in effect, tethered
the Qur'anic usage of the term ta'wil in this verse with the linguistic operation of unraveling the ambiguities by sifting through the multiple facets of
its meaning.[20] This is in contrast to the earlier view he cited, where ta'wil was
limited to the disclosure of details of reward/punishment. Instead, he argues
that the work of the interpreters or practitioners of ta'wil (muta'awwilun) was
to mention all the wujuh or facets of meanings. This they did, he argues, even
though it remains unclear which of these meanings God intended, since only
God knows what is truly intended by Qur'anic discourse. He continues:

[The next clause of the verse], where the rasikhun say "we believe in
it, all of it is from our Lord," is proof of their submission to that which
they don't know from the ta'wil of the mutashabih, which God alone
knows. This includes the time of the Last Hour, the specifics of the
minor and grave sins and similar [such] things. What is clear is that in

the *ta'wil* of the *mutashabih* is some of what they don't know even as they know much from it.[21]

Thus, for al-Radi, the proclamation of the *al-rasikhun* in verse 3:7 underscores what he described as the "middle position," specifically that there were some matters on which the *'ulama'* were authorized to speak (the *wujuh*), and others on which they acknowledged the limits of their own knowledge.[22]

The relationship that al-Radi draws here (through the unnamed views he cites) between the *mutashabih* and *wujuh* is essential to understanding his overarching hermeneutic. It is to an elaboration of this relationship that he next turns in his discussion. Al-Radi cites Qadi 'Abd al-Jabbar's presentation of two equally plausible grammatical renderings of verse 3:7 (both of which carry the same meaning, where the *al-rasikhun* share in the knowledge of the *ta'wil*).[23] In the first reading, the grammatical function of the clause "they say 'we believe in it'" is that of a predicate to the exceptional term *illa* (except).[24] In the second reading, the grammatical function is that of describing the state of the subject (the firm in knowledge).[25] We can capture 'Abd al-Jabbar's explanation as follows:

Reading 1:

None know its *ta'wil* except [*illa*] God and the firm in knowledge [predicate 1 of *illa*], they say, "We believe in it; all of it is from our Lord" [predicate 2 of *illa*].

Reading 2:

None know its *ta'wil* except God and the firm in knowledge; [while they are in a state of knowing its *ta'wil*] they say, "We believe in it; all of it is from our Lord."

These are two possible readings of this verse. After establishing that there are two plausible readings or *wujuh*, 'Abd al-Jabbar argues that since they are both grammatically acceptable, we must assess them on the basis of their meaning. If it is possible to establish with proof the soundness of one of the meanings, then that meaning applies. If it is possible for both meanings to be applicable, then they both will apply, as long as they are not contradictory.

In a critical move, al-Radi next turns to a proof text for the view that 'Abd al-Jabbar has just stated. For this, he turns to al-Jubba'i. Al-Jubba'i says: "If it is possible to carry two different readings, both are feasible."[26] The proof for this is verse 18:86, in which God says: "Until, when he reached the place of the sun's setting, he found it setting in a pool of hot water [*fi 'aynin hami'atin*], and there he found a people."[27] Al-Radi continues:

> In this verse, two meanings can apply as adjectives for the word "*'ayn*" [water]. The term describing the water can either be read as *hami'atun* [water with bad smell], or as *hamiyatun* [very hot]. Both meanings can apply [since they are not contradictory]. All speech can carry two meanings [*haqiqatayn*] and since, in this case, there is no indication which of the two is the intended meaning, both must apply. If it were the case that either of the meanings did not apply, then God would necessarily indicate with a proof [*dalala*] as to which one is intended. If this weren't the case, then the speech would be of no purpose.[28]

From this discussion, we learn that, according to al-Radi, all speech can have multiple meanings (*wujuh*), including the speech of God. Either all the meanings are intended or one meaning is intended in a way that it cancels out all other meanings. If this is the case, and one meaning is intended over others, then there must be what can be termed an indication (from the speaker) that refers the reader to a model or precedent in which that intended meaning is in effect. Most critically, this indication that authoritatively determines the proper meaning can be located *elsewhere*. That is, the model or precedent can be located in the same body of speech (other parts of the Qur'an), or in authoritative, eloquent speech, in general (the verses of renowned ancient and contemporary Arab poets or everyday speech of the Bedouins). The difference between these different registers of knowledge is collapsed in an interpretive gesture whereby all of them can present themselves as the indication or proof for the Qur'anic register. The common idiom of this shared normative reservoir of language effectively dissolves any semblance of hierarchical difference between the linguistic authority (even if not theological) of these otherwise rather varied genres of discourse.[29] In this section, I described al-Radi's stance on the question of interpretive authority (in a context defined by the absence of the Imams) and detailed his overarching hermeneutic for interpreting the Qur'an's ambiguous verses. Let me now turn to specific examples from the *Haqa'iq* to show how he operationalized this hermeneutic.

The First Ambiguity, Verse 3:143:
Rhetorical and Ethical Conundrums

I begin with al-Radi's discussion of verse 3:143,[30] described by him as ambiguous on account of the logical, rhetorical, and ethical conundrums it raises.
It reads:

> You were longing for death before you met it; now you have seen it
> [ra'aytumuhu], while you were seeing [tanzurun].

The historical occasion recorded by commentators for the context of this
verse is the famous Battle of Badr that took place in the year 624 between the
Prophet's newly formed Muslim community and the Meccan Arabs, which
concluded with the followers of Muhammad successfully defeating the Mec-
cans. This historical context, however, is not the focus of al-Radi's discussion.
For him, this verse can be broken down into three ambiguous components
that require clarification. The first question that is raised is a logical-rational
one: How is it possible for anyone to "see" death? This poses the problem of
plausibility. The second question concerns the linguistic features of the verse,
and how the phrase "now you have seen it, while you were seeing," seems
redundant. Although two different verbs for "seeing" are used in the Arabic
text (ra'-a and na-za-ra), the questioner argues that mention of just one of
these terms would suffice. So, the second question that emerges from this
verse is how can any part of the Qur'an be without purpose? This would raise
doubt about the Qur'an's rhetorical coherence. Finally, the third issue that
arises from this verse is ethical, since the clause "you were longing for death"
refers to a group among the believers who were seeking their own martyrdom and, in doing so, they were seeking their own death at the hands of
the unbelievers. This results in the moral dilemma of the believers effectively
wishing for a grave sin. The presence of these three pertinent questions—
namely, the plausibility of a Qur'anic statement, the rhetorical value of a
Qur'anic statement, and the moral implication of a Qur'anic statement—lead
al-Radi to designate this verse as part of the category of "ambiguous" verses.
To respond to these questions, al-Radi referred to the tripartite literary canon
he regarded as the authoritative source for the Arabic language: the Qur'an,
the poetic tradition, and the everyday speech of Arabs.

In response to the first question concerning the plausibility of seeing
death, al-Radi shows that the term "death" in this verse is used metonymically

to mean the causes of death. He explains that the trope of correspondence between death and its causes permits the substitution of one with the other. So, what the verse really intends to say is that the believers saw the signs of death, such as a lance or stone, and not death itself. For al-Radi, this metonomyical use of the term death is authorized by a phrase from everyday speech: "I saw death with my own eyes!" (*qad ra'aytu al-mawt 'iyanan*),[31] which implies that the speaker is expressing how she or he was under extreme duress, hence the intended meaning is "I faced the causes of death, like intense agony and severe hardship." Al-Radi also refers to the lines of two poets.

Dreamers walk under their flag
While death awaits under the flag of the family of Muhallim

The second poem is a reference to the verse by the Umayyad poet Kuthayyir ibn 'Abd al-Rahman, more commonly known as Kuthayyir 'Azzah:

If you see the fate of death as evident,
Do not be a direct target for it, abandon its path[32]

For evidence from the Qur'an, al-Radi refers to verse 37:105 about Abraham's sacrifice of Isma'il, in which God refers to Abraham's dream of the sacrifice as credible (*musaddaq*), even though, historically, the sacrifice was never completed: "'You have fulfilled the dream.' This is how We reward those who do good."[33] Al-Radi points out that because Abraham exhibited all the signs of the sacrifice, such as laying Isma'il down, taking the knife, and binding Isma'il's legs, the grammatical rule at play in this verse is the same, which is the substitution of the *cause* of sacrifice with its *effect*.

To respond to the second question, on the redundancy of the terms *ru'ya* and *nazar*, where both seem to convey the same meaning of "seeing," al-Radi draws on an interpretive strategy that represented a signature approach for him: that of identifying a key term that extends lexical and, subsequently, hermeneutical flexibility. The term from which he gains this mileage here is that of *nazar*. He argues that the term *nazar* can have multiple meanings, one of which is to contemplate, look at, or "direct the eye to that which you wish to see."[34] He points out that what is critical in the act of *nazar* is the individual's *desire* to see. The poem that al-Radi selects to justify this distinction is from the early Islamic poet Dhu al-Rumma, and it visually captures this meaning of "desire to see" that he is trying to explain. The verse reads:

Oh Mayya, will I be compensated for my bitter tears,
and my breaths that travel to you like zephyrs?
And when will I be honored by the side that you are on,
in the meantime, I am the seeker of vision [*nazir*]

Al-Radi explains that the last line, where the poet self identifies as a *nazir* (seer), must communicate the meaning not of a seer but that of the seeker of vision. This is so because no lover who succeeds in gaining a glimpse of his beloved seeks compensation for it. Only the one who suffers from the *desire* for such a glimpse, the *nazir*, can claim a reward for his suffering. Applying these arguments of al-Radi's back onto the verse in question, it would read: "You were longing for death before you met it; now you have seen [the signs of] it [*ra'aytumuhu*], while you were [in the state of] seeking it [*tanzurun*]."

The third conundrum with respect to verse 3:143 is ethical. In the verse, the believers are described as seeking death in battle, which is essentially another way of saying that they are seeking to be killed at the hands of unbelievers. Now, we know that unbelievers killing believers amounts to a grave sin. So, does this mean that believers seeking martyrdom in battle are, by extension, desiring that a grave sin be committed? Al-Radi does not think so. And, again, his argument hinges on language. He argues that an individual's desire for death cannot be equated with his desire to be killed because the doer of the two actions is not the same. Death goes back to no one other than God, whereas the act of killing is a human act. This fundamental difference of human versus divine authorship of an action prevents us from making an analogy between the desire to die at the hands of God and to be killed at the hands of the unbelievers.

Through al-Radi's brief discussion of this verse, we note the different types of scenarios that can render a verse ambiguous for him. We also see that the sources that al-Radi used to defend his position, namely, Qur'anic verses, Arabic speech, and early Islamic poetry, transcend sectarian, theological, and disciplinary lines precisely by relying on the overarching rules of *language*. The critical point to keep in mind here is that at the heart of al-Radi's exegetical discourse was the question of the authority of language over logic as a source of knowledge. During his time, scholars were pushed to clearly articulate the role of language in mediating the relationship between revelation and history. It was within this context that al-Radi wrote his commentary on the Qur'an's ambiguous language and used literary arguments drawn from early Islamic poetry and the oral tradition to explain these ambiguities. And it was within this context, when the significance of a poetic lexicon came to represent the authoritative source for a canonical Arabic language, that al-Radi made the self-confident assertion that his text was the hermeneutical key for interpreting the Qur'an. Thus, al-Radi's hermeneutic worked to strengthen the relevance of grammar as a source of authority by attaching it to a fixed body of literature, which simultaneously contributed to its canonization.

The Second Ambiguity, Verse 3:61 (*Aya Mubahala*): A Threat to Qur'anic Eloquence?

The second ambiguity, to which I now turn, is tied to the question of the Qur'an's grammatical and linguistic eloquence. In chapter twelve of the *Haqa'iq*,[35] al-Radi discusses verse 3:61, commonly referred to as the *mubahala* (mutual invocation of a curse) verse.[36] I have chosen this particular verse as an example not only because it nicely elucidates major aspects of al-Radi's interpretive maneuvers and my analysis of those maneuvers, but also because this is the one verse discussed in his Qur'an commentary that is potentially most amenable and susceptible to a sectarian reading. So, I want to demonstrate why, even in this case, where a sectarian reading seems imminently plausible, such a reading would yet be problematic and would conceal more than it would reveal. Turning to the verse itself, it reads as follows:

> If anyone disputes this with you [Prophet Muhammad] now that you have been given this knowledge, say, "Come, let us gather our sons and your sons, our women and your women, ourselves [*anfusana*] and yourselves, and let us pray earnestly and invoke God's rejection on those of us who are lying."[37]

Historically, the verse refers to an incident that took place in the year 632, where the Prophet participated in what may be called an "embodied argument," in its very literal sense. Two parties, namely the Prophet and the Christians of Najran had disagreed over the nature of Jesus Christ (whether he is human or God). As a way of "resolving" their disagreement, they agreed on participating in the tradition of "the mutual invocation of a curse," meaning they would meet at an agreed upon place and then whoever was wrong would be cursed to destruction through God's wrath. In this scenario, the destruction of the body through the affliction of God's curse signified belonging to the lying party, while being left unblemished demonstrated allegiance to the truthful. Moreover, in a theatrical event of this kind, the companions who accompanied the leader of each party functioned as the guarantors of that leader's claim regarding the issue under dispute. Significantly, the Prophet took with him his daughter Fatima, his cousin and son-in-law 'Ali ibn Abi Talib, and their sons Hasan and Husayn. Together, they waited for the rival Christian delegation to arrive. But the delegation never showed up. Their failure to take on the challenge was interpreted by exegetes and historians as a victory for the message of the Prophet. Now, this verse and the incident it narrates has captured the attention of several scholars in Muslim intellectual thought. It has also represented a recurring motif in Muslim visual culture in the premodern and modern periods.[38]

The Reception of the *Mubahala* Verse Between Western and Traditional Scholarship

Before turning to al-Radi's discussion of this verse, it is important to first examine some of the recent literature surrounding this unusual incident. There are two main topics through which the *mubahala* verse has been treated in recent scholarship. First, the *mubahala* event has piqued the interest of several scholars for the way in which it vividly illustrates the themes of "divine designation" and "substitute-sacrifice."[39] The view of the *mubahala* as a *shared* mission between the Prophet as leader and his family as the guarantors of his mission gave rise to the concept of a *substitution* between the two groups. Scholar of mysticism Herbert Mason, in his biography of the mystic Husayn ibn Mansur al-Hallaj (d. 922), points to the significance of the theme of "substitution" in the *mubahala* event:

> They [the 'Alids] were his [Muhammad's] private heirs according to the unwritten Arab law, but also, and especially, that they were established publicly as his juridical "substitutes," acting in this capacity vis-a-vis his clients as his debts of blood. This substitution dates, as the whole of Shi'ism affirms and the Qur'an and historical data agree, from a public test of an ordeal, the *mubahala* of 21 Hijja 10/March 22, 632. On this particular day, in Medina, Muhammad had challenged the Christian Banu 'Abd al-Madan emissaries of the Balharith of Najran to a "judgment of God" (seized with fear, the Christians declined it the

next day, signing a *musalaha*, "capitulation," the first between Christianity and Islam). For this "judgment of God," Muhammad had placed as hostages of his sincerity (about the negation of the Incarnation) and of his faith (in his own mission), "his own people," the "five whom he covered with his mantle" (*ashab al-kisaʾ*): his two grandsons, Hasan and Husayn, his daughter Fatima, his son-in-law ʿAli, [and himself]. Henceforward this solemn judiciary substitution was to transfer to each of them the expectation of justice and the devoted service that the true friends of Muhammad had pledged to him; and it also transferred equally all vendetta, all of the hatred that the Umayyads, of the Quraysh, nurtured against the founder of Islam for their pagan dead killed in cold blood after Badr (in AD 624).[40]

This theme of substitution and specifically substitute-sacrifice also emerges as a trope in Sufi discourses. For example, Louis Massignon, whose biographical reconstruction of al-Hallaj has dominated how he is now remembered, notes a provocative exchange between al-Hallaj and the vizier who condemned him:

Al-Hallaj: I will die attached to the Cross!
Vizier: Do you think you are taking up the *mubahala* of the
    Christians of Najran?

Through this conversation, Massignon gestures toward the Christ-like character of al-Hallaj and how, through his martyrdom, he became a substitute (*badal*) for the Christians of Najran who had not dared to confront the trial themselves.[41]

An emphasis and interest in the way in which this verse highlights the substitution or interchangeability between ʿAli and Muhammad can also be found in Shiʿi works aimed at outlining the virtues and qualities of ʿAli (*manaqib* literature). In his *Kitab al-Irshad*, for example, al-Shaykh al-Mufid presents a fascinating account of the incident in which the Najrani Christians make peace with the Prophet and sign a peace agreement that al-Mufid cites. Most relevant for our discussion here is the end of al-Mufid's account, where he states, "Through this incident, God, the Exalted, gave judgement in the verse of the contest of prayer on behalf of the Commander of the Faithful, peace be on him, that he was of the same (station) as the Apostle of God, thus revealing the great extent of his outstanding merit and his equality with the Prophet."[42] Going further, the famous Shiʿi theologian, historian, astrologer, and bibliophile, Ibn Tawus

(d. 1266), in his *Iqbal al A'mal*, states, "God makes evident through this verse that 'Ali ibn Abi Talib is the *nafs* of the Prophet and that he is equal in his essence and attributes, and his meaning [*murad*] is also 'Ali's meaning. Even as they differ in form [*sura*], their meaning is one in terms of all their qualities."[43]

The second approach most frequently found for studying the *mubahala* verse is in the domain of traditional Shi'i scholarship, where authors seek to support the argument that 'Ali is the rightful successor to the Prophet and the household of the Prophet are the authoritative interpreters of the tradition.[44] According to this view, the family members who accompanied the Prophet acted as guarantors of his claim and they, too, were infused with authority and conferred with a "divine right" like that of the Prophet. The *mubahala* is thus celebrated as a public demonstration of this investiture of authority. What is interesting is how this investiture is understood as visually communicated, such that the Prophet's companions offer their bodies as sites for the public confirmation of his claim. In doing this, their own right to share in the authority of the Prophet is assured. The *mubahala* event has been remembered in the Shi'i tradition alongside two other pivotal moments. The first of these is the *Hadith al-Kisa'* (report of the cloak), which narrates how the Prophet gathered the same five family members under his cloak, immediately after which the Qur'anic verse 33:33 is said to have been revealed: "God wishes to keep uncleanness away from you, people of the [Prophet's] House, and to purify you thoroughly."[45] The *Hadith Kisa'* is accordingly invoked as proof of the purity and infallibility of the family of the Prophet. The second crucial incident to which the *mubahala* is connected is the occasion known as *Ghadir Khumm* (Pool of Khumm), which is the location where the Prophet publicly proclaimed 'Ali as *mawla* (master) of the Muslim community. By interpreting *mawla* as "successor," Shi'i scholars have argued that this incident is evidence of 'Ali's succession to the Prophet. Together, these three events, namely, the *mubahala*, *Hadith Kisa'*, and *Ghadir Khumm*, form a powerful cluster of publicly witnessed events where members of the family of the Prophet were not only distinguished by the Prophet but physically made to *share* in his mission.

The Prophet's Life as an Illustration of Arabic Grammar

Now let me turn to al-Radi's interpretation of this verse. To be absolutely clear, he would not have disagreed with the import of seemingly sectarian readings of this verse invested in the Shi'i doctrine of establishing 'Ali as the

Prophet's successor and his family as the most worthy inheritors of his legacy. But, as I hope to show, limiting his exegetical program to sectarian investments and affirmations precludes the possibility of approaching commentarial texts through less predictable and more productive analytical horizons. Let me explain. Al-Radi's interpretation of this verse does not hinge on an effort to demonstrate the status of the Prophet's family as divinely appointed. While he certainly alludes to this point, as we will soon see, it is not central to his interpretive scheme. Rather, in his commentary, al-Radi was most interested in examining the seeming incoherence of the grammatical structure of the sentence that made up this Qur'anic verse.

The underlying linguistic puzzle that al-Radi sought to resolve was this: How, asks al-Radi's self-staged interlocutor, can God's injunction (Say!/*qul!*) direct the Prophet to state, "let us invite our sons and your sons, our women and your women, ourselves [*anfusana*] and yourselves?" The ambiguity here concerns the last part of the sentence, having to do with inviting "ourselves": How can anyone invite one's own self when this possibility was not grammatically available according to the conventions of the Arabic language? Who exactly was this term ourselves referring to here? In order to tackle this puzzle, al-Radi first went through a process of elimination. He gives his readers a visual depiction of all the people present, including details of their physical arrangement in relation to the Prophet. Standing before the Prophet (*bayna yadayhi*) was the commander of the faithful, 'Ali, behind the Prophet was Fatima, to his right was Hasan, and to his left was Husayn. Al-Radi then proceeds to decipher the Prophetic invitation of the term "ourselves" through a careful process of elimination. "Our sons" refers to (*masrufan ila*) Hasan and Husayn, "our women" refers to Fatima, which leaves the term "ourselves" and its reference to either 'Ali or the Prophet. So, the only possibility left was that the Prophet's self here metaphorically represented the self of 'Ali, since there was no one else present in the congregation to whom this could apply and it was grammatically impossible for the Prophet to have invited himself. The linguistic rule underlying this impossibility is that an individual cannot invite, command, or forbid him or herself.[46]

But a question that emerges here is this: How could the term "ourselves" not refer to one's own self but rather serve as a metaphor for someone else? In addressing this question and in providing a sustained defense of the linguistic prohibition against the use of the term "ourselves" in this verse with reference to the Prophet, al-Radi turned to three bodies of sources: other moments in the Qur'an, Arabic poetry from pre-Islamic and the early Islamic eras, and the oral speech traditions of the Arabs, the three sources that in his view constituted the preexisting literary canon. Quite remarkable, in this discussion, is what was perhaps the most fascinating and illustrative example of a form of evidence that al-Radi mobilized in this context, having to do with a narrative from the Prophet's own life. Specifically, he refers to a narration by al-Waqidi (d. 823) in his book on the battles and expeditions of the Prophet (*maghazi*). When the Prophet left Badr in 624, with him were the prisoners from the hypocrites, including Suhayl ibn 'Amr, who was tied to the camel of the Prophet. However, when the Muslim army returned to their hometown of Medina, Suhayl ibn 'Amr somehow managed to unshackle himself and fled. At this point, the Prophet said to his companions that whoever finds Suhayl ibn 'Amr should kill him. As it turns out, the Prophet himself found Suhayl hiding under the cover of a tree branch, and he brought him back (instead of killing him). Now, one might be tempted to read this moment from the Prophet's life as an example of his kindness or generosity for having spared the life of a fugitive prisoner of war. But, for al-Radi, this episode only confirmed that the Prophet's experiences and life can be read as a manual for grammatical rulings. Al-Radi argued that the Prophet did not kill Suhayl ibn 'Amr, the prisoner of war who had escaped, because the Prophet himself had ordered that 'Amr be killed if found; that order thus did not apply to his own self, much like he was grammatically prohibited from inviting his own self to the Mubahala curse contest against the Najrani Christians. Thus, quite remarkably, al-Radi extracted a historical moment from the Prophet's life to the performative illustration of a linguistic rule! In al-Radi's social imaginary, then, the grammar of the Prophet's body and experience and the grammar of the Arabic language were inextricably tied, the latter at once regulating and elucidating the former. Indeed, if taken to its conclusion, al-Radi's hermeneutics had, in effect, rendered the Prophet's life subservient to the rules and protocols of the Arabic language. Of course, al-Radi's emphasis on the linguistic and grammatical harmony of the Prophet's life does not preclude the possibility that it carried other ethical-moral meanings. Yet the purpose of the *Haqa'iq* was to creatively forge a correspondence between the revelatory sources (Qur'an and Prophetic *hadith*) and a preexisting literary canon, and this is what al-Radi successfully achieved.

To further bolster his position on the grammatical incoherence of an invitation in which the speaker invites him/herself, al-Radi cited a tradition that records a conversation between the 'Abbasid caliph 'Abdullah al-Ma'mun (d. 833), Qasim ibn Sahl al-Nushjani (death date unknown), and the eighth

Shi'i Imam, 'Ali al-Rida (d. 818). The scene is set in Marv. Al-Ma'mun asks al-Nushjani: "Which of the stories praising the companions [*fada'il*] is the best?" Al-Nushjani replies, "The Mubahala verse, since in this verse God fuses the self of the Prophet with the self of 'Ali". Al-Ma'mun, who is apparently familiar with varying interpretations of this verse, quizzes al-Nushjani on what his response would be if an opponent were to argue that people understand *al-anfus* to mean the Prophet himself. Al-Nushjani is stumped by this query. Al-Ma'mun then turns to 'Ali al-Rida for his opinion. Al-Rida explains that "The Prophet extended the invitation, and the one who invites cannot include himself in the invitation; he can only invite others. Thus, the Prophet invited the sons and women, but it was not correct for him to invite himself." Al-Rida continued, saying that "the only plausible reference for his invitation to selves is 'Ali ibn Abi Talib, since there was no one else present to whom this invitation could refer. If it were not this way, then the verse would not make sense." At this moment al-Nushjani intervened, with the gleeful proclamation "Now this has become clear to me!" Al-Ma'mun paused and expressed his satisfaction for al-Rida: "O Abu al-Hasan, when the target is hit, no questions are left unanswered!"[47] In this narrative, Imam al-Rida's explanation establishes the unity of the self of 'Ali and the self of the Prophet through a logical process of elimination that is premised on the same grammatical rule that was outlined by al-Radi.

It might be tempting to read al-Radi's invocation of 'Ali al-Rida's astute response to al-Ma'mun as a characteristically Shi'i hermeneutical move. Certainly, by channeling the authority of a prominent Imam, al-Radi could be said to draw on a reservoir of religious authority imbued with Shi'i imaginaries of charisma. However, this move also serves as a useful example to further underscore my underlying argument that reducing al-Radi's interpretive strategies to a sectarian template obscures more than it reveals. A couple of observations will be useful in seeing how this is the case. First, this was a rare instance in al-Radi's Qur'an commentary in which he explicitly referred to the report of an Imam to advance his argument. But, even then, the focus of al-Radi's mobilization of al-Rida centered on establishing an argument that was decidedly of a linguistic nature. It is telling that al-Radi's reference to an Imam occurs precisely during a moment where the latter was advancing a linguistic argument, thus fitting nicely with the larger literary hermeneutic that undergirded al-Radi's exegetical project. Again, the point here is not to measure how well al-Radi's discussion aligns with or departs from a fixed template of Shi'i hermeneutics. Nor is it to claim that a Shi'i hermeneutic is mutually exclusive to a literary one. Rather, the point is to broaden one's analysis of a scholar's exegetical labor in a manner that does not reduce that labor to predictable patterns of sectarian readings.

Sources of a Literary Hermeneutic

As I stated earlier, al-Radi saw three major discursive sources and knowledge traditions as constituting a literary canon: the speech of Arabs, Qur'anic verses, and the Arabic poetic tradition. It was by drawing on these literary sources that al-Radi sought to argue that justifications for substituting one individual "self" for another were intimacy (*qaraba*) and a shared religiosity (*al-ijtima' fi 'aqd al-diyana*). This argument clearly carried significant weight, since it implicitly made the case for 'Ali's substitution for the Prophet in the *mubahala* verse on the basis of a shared religiosity. For other examples of this rule, al-Radi first turns to the Arabic usage of the term *nafs* in the meaning of an intimate friend, and how a close relative can be called the "self" of the person with whom she or he shares that relation. From the Qur'an, he referred to verse 49:11: "... And do not defame yourselves [*anfusakum*], or insult one another with nicknames."[48] Al-Radi explains that the verse intends to state that believing Muslims should not slander their believing brothers. Critically, al-Radi argues that their brotherhood in religiosity (*al-ukhuwwa bi al-diyana*) becomes the basis for their brotherhood in intimacy (*al-ukhuwwa fi al-qaraba*).

Al-Radi also brings in a verse by pre-Islamic poet Dhu al-'Asba' Hurthan al-'Adwani:[49] "as if on the Day of Qurra ... we were killing ourselves [*iyyana*]." Al-Radi explains that the poet intended a substitution between the selves (*nufus*) of a person's kin with his own self (*nafs*), on the basis of their marital connections (*shawabik al-'isam*), paternal relations (literally "relations of the flesh" [*nawa'it al-luham*]), and maternal relations (literally "relations of the womb" [*atit al-raham*]).

Finally, al-Radi refers to the Qur'anic verse 24:61, which states: "When you enter any house, greet yourselves [*anfusakum*] with a greeting of blessing and goodness as enjoined by God."[50] Al-Radi employs this use of *anfusakum* to explain that the intended meaning is "for some of you to greet others, since it is not possible for a person to greet him or herself. The use of the term yourselves, then, is fitting, since the selves of all believers coalesce into a single self, due to the bond of a shared religiosity and the common language of the Shariʿa [*nufus al-muʾminin tajri majra al-nafs al-wahida li al-ijtimaʿ fi ʿaqd al-diyana wa al-khitab bi al-lisan al-shariʿa*]. So, when one of them greets his brother, it is as if he has greeted himself, because of the removal of difference and the mixing of their selves."[51]

Legal Implications of the *Mubahala*

Another notable component of the *Haqaʾiq* text that the *mubahala* chapter illustrates is that, while the text is structured in a straightforward question-and-answer format, an equally rich discussion is woven in through al-Radi's numerous "digressions," which take him onto varied paths well outside the strictures of the questions his interlocutor poses. In this chapter, al-Radi turns to two corollary questions that arise from the *mubahala* verse that hold special importance in the Shiʿi context. The first issue concerns the status of the Prophet's *daughter's* sons, given that the Prophet had no son. Al-Radi uses the *mubahala* verse to argue in favor of extending the term "sons" to include the "sons of daughters" and, in doing so, stakes a claim for the children of Fatima as legitimate references for the posterity of the Prophet. Although al-Radi does not mention the relevance of this issue in his commentary, it can be inferred that it had immediate relevance in justifying the legal stipulation of a stipend being paid to the children of the Hashimites.[52] In his discussion, al-Radi also acknowledges the view of Sunni scholars on this point. He presents the opinion of Hasan ibn Ziyad al-Luʾluʾyi, an important pupil and transmitter of the works of Abu Hanifa (d. 767), the eponymous founder of the Hanafi school of law. Ibn Ziyad agreed that the sons of a person's daughters, as well as the sons of a person's sons, were implied when a will spoke of inheritance to the "sons" of an individual. Al-Radi simply mentions (without overtly rejecting any of these claims) that his teacher, Abu Bakr Muhammad ibn Musa al-Khwarazmi (d. 993),[53] told him that this view of Ibn Ziyad differs from that of Muhammad ibn al-Hasan,[54] who held that it only referred to the sons of a person's son. It is not fully clear what al-Radi intended for his readers to gain from such casual references to scholarly opinions, where his objective was neither to offer a comprehensive summary of views nor to present his own argument. However, what is striking is al-Radi's examination of sources that transcend differences between sects, in an effort to interrogate the issue of the posterity of the Prophet, an extremely sensitive and delicate issue for Shiʿi theologians and jurists.

Another corollary question raised through the *mubahala* verse was that of how Hasan and Husayn, as minors, could participate in an affair that involved mutual imprecation, "since children were not deserving of a curse even if they were the children of the hypocrites, because they could not commit sins that would make them deserve such a thing." Even the editor of the primary printed edition of the *Haqa'iq*, Muhammad Rida Kashif al-Ghita, a contemporary scholar from Iraq, seems to have been taken aback by al-Radi's approach to positing and resolving these corollary questions.[55] In a footnote, he expresses his admiration for al-Radi's neutrality when addressing these issues. He explains that, generally, Imami exegetes use two arguments to answer the question of Hasan and Husayn's young age. First, they posit that maturity was not a condition of the *mubahala*. Second, they assert that participation in the *mubahala* has to do with the perfection of the intellect and discernment, regardless of age. The age of Hasan and Husayn at that time, seven and five, did not prevent them from attaining the perfection of intellect. Al-Ghita further informs the reader that Imami scholars complete their responses by adding that it is possible that God also made Hasan and Husayn extraordinary by elevating their intellect and distinguished them with this quality that others don't possess to make clear the proof of their status. Thus, he argues that it is remarkable that the author of this text (al-Radi) managed to maintain impartiality to any group, sect, or creed in his interpretation. As al-Ghita put it: "Indeed it is rare to find an exegete of the Qur'an who passes over this noble verse without being bold about his creed and digressing to his inner belief."[56] These opinions on the part of the editor are telling. The "age question" was a pressing issue in the context of Shi'i theology. It is echoed in the context of the eligibility of the twelfth Imam as the leader of the Imami Shi'i community, since he was of an extremely young age at the time of his father's death and his subsequent succession.[57] Al-Ghita seems well aware of the theological implications of this verse and appreciative of al-Radi's ability to defend the challenges posed by opponents without falling back on apologetic arguments. Instead, al-Radi's interaction with a variety of teachers and scholars from multiple schools of thought is celebrated as evidence of a nonpartisan defense of a crucial theological question.

Returning to al-Radi, the only "response" he offers to the interlocutor's question on the age of Hasan and Husayn is in the form of citing the opinion of his Mu'tazili teacher, 'Abd al-Jabbar. 'Abd al-Jabbar had argued "the rule of Divine punishments by elimination for falsifying the prophets was a universal rule that included children, even if recompense was in the form of a trial, not a penalty. This could occur through the infliction of diseases, illnesses, bone injuries, and types of death." Al-Radi makes no additional comments to this proclamation and, instead, presents an opposing view, where the last sentence of the same Qur'anic verse, 3:61, is put forward as evidence that children cannot be cursed: "Let us invoke God's rejection on those of us who are lying." The hypothetical opponent uses transitive logic to make his point: "Since the verse indicates that God's curse is for those who falsify, and those who falsify are those who tell lies about God and the Prophet, and children cannot be attributed with these qualities, it is clear that children cannot be deserving of a curse."[58]

Al-Radi does not respond to this objection, perhaps because he is satisfied with 'Abd al-Jabbar's response cited earlier. He moves on to his final point, which is also connected to the last clause of the Qur'anic verse 3:61: "Let us invoke God's rejection on those of us who are lying." He explains that the verse is saying the following: "We ask and you all ask God (may He be glorified) in our prayer and your prayer, to necessitate the curse on the liar among us and among you all."[59] By rephrasing the verse this way, al-Radi emphasizes how the statement is in the form of a supplication to God, and argues that no one is entitled to give God's curse to another person except God, who is the Creator of His curse. Thus, only God can curse the deserving party and attach a curse to the person who quite literally asks for it. With this logic, he concludes that it is permissible for the meaning to be, "Let us invoke the *name* of God on the liars," since it is God who conducts the necessary action upon them of retribution, torment, banishment, and exile.

The discussion above shows that, in al-Radi's work, logical, doctrinal, and theological ambiguities are resolved by reference to an authoritative Arabic language, the operations of which al-Radi regarded as fixed. Thus, I have tried to push for a reading of al-Radi's hermeneutic that takes seriously its literary emphasis, rather than approaching al-Radi exclusively as a Shi'i exegete.

Here one may raise a doubt that I should like to address. One could argue that, despite al-Radi's focus on the question of language, he nonetheless directs his linguistic energies to the service of his sectarian desires. For instance, one might argue that, in al-Radi's linguistic framing of the puzzle surrounding the referents of ourselves (*anfusana*) in verse 3:61, the theological and mystical implications of his interpretation were yet of a decisively Shi'i leaning. Such a line of argument might point to the possibility that, for all the literary hermeneutics of al-Radi and his mobilization of language, ultimately the eventual upshot of his hermeneutics remains in service of his sectarian Shi'i desire to establish 'Ali's intimacy with Muhammad and to privilege the status of the Prophet's family. It could be further argued that not only the outcome but also the method of al-Radi's exegesis, invested in excavating the hidden meaning of a text, as exemplified by his claim that the term "ourselves" represents a metaphor for 'Ali, only underscores his commitment to a Shi'i sectarian narrative. While not without merit, these observations make for rather simple and easily digestible understandings of exegetical projects in early Islam. Such an analytical lens tethered to sectarian readings prohibits a more nuanced understanding of the wider intellectual currents, conversations, and contestations that inform and inflect labors of exegesis like al-Radi's Qur'an commentary.

The critical question that arises here is this: must we preemptively ascribe al-Radi's attention to literary devices like *mutashabih* (ambiguity) and *majaz* (linguistic transgression), which point to a different register of meaning, as reflections of a "characteristically Shi'i" inclination toward *batini* (hidden) meanings in the text? I think not. There are several important questions and avenues of inquiry that such a decidedly sectarian approach would foreclose. To begin with, al-Radi's hermeneutical posturing alerts us to the multiple intellectual conversations from which he drew his positions. Further, rather than simply situating his arguments within any given sect, discipline, or school, it is important to understand the critical purchase of his arguments at the specific historical juncture during which he was writing.

So, to return to the example of the *mubahala* verse, it is useful to observe that al-Radi justifies his reading of this verse, whereby the souls of 'Ali and Muhammad are fused, not by referring to any doctrinal explanations of the Imamate, but rather by drawing on the oral linguistic tradition of the Arabs. This again reinforces my central argument: al-Radi's hermeneutical temperament did not neatly embrace sectarian binaries and boundaries. I should clarify here that my argument should not be taken as a replication of Joel Kraemer's celebration of tenth-century Buyid Baghdad as the site of the "renaissance of Islam," marked by the efflorescence of "individualism," "cosmopolitanism," and "secularism"—one where these features and conditions of a society are seen to be in an oppositional relationship to "religion," by which is implied Islamic law.[60]

I do not wish to pursue the anachronistic objective of positing al-Radi as a premodern example of a scholar who fulfilled the modern liberal secular ideal of overcoming religious and sectarian difference. Such a projection would be at once anachronistic and conceptually unsound. The lack of focus in al-Radi's exegesis on hot-button issues one might today associate with a sectarian Shi'i leaning does not equate on his part to a negation of his sectarian identity. Certainly al-Radi identified as a Shi'i Qur'an exegete, even as his exegesis complicates the idea of a predictable and fixed template of what a Shi'i Qur'an exegesis looks like. Al-Radi's self-imagination as a Shi'i exegete and his affirmation of his Shi'i identity manifested in ways that were particular to his individual temperament and to the sorts of scholarly conversations and commitments in which he saw himself as contributing. Thus, to the exact contrary of Kraemer, rather than projecting modern sensibilities and desires onto premodern actors, my project is inspired by the inverse task of provincializing modern sectarian expectations by showcasing the complexities and nuances marking the thought of a premodern Muslim scholar. So, in contrast to Kraemer, who imposes Europe on Baghdad, I am more interested in having Baghdad speak back to Europe.

The Third Ambiguity, Verse 3:8:
Challenging Qur'anic Coherence

Al-Radi's discussion in the above two examples dealt with varying types of ambiguities: the grammatical conundrum posed by the Prophetic command that included himself in the *mubahala* verse, and the rhetorical and ethical dilemmas presented by the Qur'anic verse where believers expressed their desire to "see" death. The concerns and issues that interested al-Radi as an exegete in these examples were wide-ranging. But I have argued that al-Radi's hermeneutical energies remained focused on establishing how a mastery of language can illuminate meaning and how language in its authoritative sense for him meant a canon composed of Qur'anic verses, oral speech of the Arabs, and poetic verses. To be more accurate, he did not see the logic and beauty of language as separable from other disciplines and domains of life like theology and politics. Quite to the contrary, language was an overarching source of knowledge set in a relationship of intimate correspondence with other fields and ways of knowing.

The next example from the *Haqa'iq* I take up illustrates this point. It also highlights another sort of ambiguity found in the *Haqa'iq*, concerned with questions of theology. More specifically, the example I will soon discuss relates to a deeply contentious issue that attracted ample and often heated responses from tenth-century Muslim theological circles concerning the fundamental question about human agency: Are humans possessors of free will, capable of choosing their own future, or are they actors in a world prewritten by a divine sovereign? To make matters more complex, supporters of each position found equally weighty proofs in the Qur'an that, in their view, endorsed their respective positions. Unsurprisingly, the positionality of scholars on this burning question often proved decisive in determining their intellectual, political, and religious affiliations. For example, the view that human beings are capable of choosing their own actions and, in turn, responsible and accountable for those actions was one of the principle teachings of the Mu'tazili school of thought. Further raising the stakes of the free will/predestination debate was that it was entangled with other basic questions, such as "Who is the cause of human deviation?" and "What is the source (and purpose) of evil in the world?"

Chapter two in the *Haqa'iq*, which is al-Radi's commentary on verse 3:8, is perhaps his clearest and most explicit exposition on these hot-button issues.[61] Significantly, al-Radi tackles these theologically charged questions precisely through a language-centered hermeneutic based on his theory of the critical interplay between the ambiguous and the clear that I have tried to elaborate throughout this chapter. Turning to the verse, it reads as follows:

Our Lord, cause not [*la tuzigh*] our hearts to deviate after You have guided us. Grant us Your mercy: You are the Ever Giving.[62]

The ambiguity enveloping this verse is captured in al-Radi's chapter through a hypothetical interlocutor who raises the following objection: "If God is not the one who *causes* the straying of the hearts, then this verse has no meaning, since that is what the supplicant in this verse asks God not to do! And if, as is stated in this verse, God *does* cause them to go astray *prior* to their own deviation and seduction, then this is in line with the position of your opponents!"[63] In sum, the interlocutor poses to al-Radi a catch twenty-two, or so it seems.

At first, the allegation is indeed indicting. The structure of the sentence threatens the viability of a position that upholds human agency. And in addition to questioning this central tenet of Mu'tazili theology (the moral responsibility and free will of all human beings), the questioner also shows that to argue otherwise would be to strip the Qur'anic verse of any epistemological value or purpose. To declare any part of the Qur'an as redundant or without meaning would undercut its ability to serve as a guide for humankind, ultimately rendering God as unjust for holding human beings accountable without providing necessary, purposeful guidance. And to cast doubt on the doctrine of God's justice was to threaten the very foundation of Mu'tazili thought which rested on the necessity of a just God. How an exegete interpreted this verse, in short, held immense theological significance.

Al-Radi's response—its structure, tone, and tenor—reflects his keen awareness of the gravity of the allegation and of what was at stake. He began by purposefully alerting his readers to the importance of the topic at large: the *cause* of human deviation. This he did by reminding them how frequently the discussion about *al-zaygh* (deviating) and *al-izagha* (to cause to deviate), and *al-idlal* (to cause to stray) and *al-dalala* (straying), have appeared in his commentary (even though the reader is at this point only on the third chapter of a total of a hundred and fourteen chapters).

Mapping Scholarly Opinions

After this brief digression, al-Radi turns to the task of a step-by-step dismissal of the opponent's allegation. But first, he presents a bird's-eye view of the debate by enumerating the spectrum of already existing arguments on this verse. I present a selection of these scholarly opinions below, as they alert us to two critical details: first, how al-Radi's decision to leave out the names of the actual individuals or groups who held these views abstracts them just enough to bring into focus the individuality of his own argument, which immediately follows; and second, how al-Radi saw his arguments to be embedded in and contributing to an ongoing conversation, even as he sought to establish the superiority of his own position within that conversation. To remind us, these are different readings of the clause, "Cause not our hearts to stray after you have guided us."

(1) [Unnamed]: This is like saying, "Oh God, continue your divine favors [*altaf*] on us and keep us in the protection of your guidance so that our hearts don't waver." Although in the phrasing of this request the supplicators refer to themselves as waverers, the attribution is coincidental. It is not because wavering is inevitable for them or a part of their being. It is similar to the expression *adlaltu fulanan* [literally, "I made the person a deviator"], when you find someone to be straying, or *abkhaltuhu* [literally, "I made him stingy"], when you find a person to be stingy.[64]

(2) [Unnamed]: It is like saying, "Don't test us with a difficult thing." The idea is that they are tested after God has guided them, at which point they may be led astray, so they ask not to be tested.[65]

(3) Some say it is to ask God not to turn their hearts away from reward, or to ask that God increase them in guidance and divine favor. Both these supplications refer back to the same meaning because an increase in guidance and divine favor is [equivalent to] reward. The evidence for this is the verse [47:17]: "But those who are guided, He increases them in guidance and grants them their reverence."[66] What this means is that they ask God to bestow His favor on them through successive ideas and strong exhortations in the matter of faith, such that they maintain their faith throughout their lives—that they don't abandon their faith and commit disbelief and become deserving of God causing their hearts to stray from reward, which would be their recompense. They can't ask God not to recompense them [la yuʿaqqibahum] if they are believers, except with this meaning. As for reward, which God bestows upon people's hearts, it is that which God mentioned as an expansion of the chest and the inscription of faith in the heart. The opposite of this is recompense, which is what the disbelievers' hearts undergo, a tightening, narrowing, rusting and covering up of the heart. This is the view of Abu ʿAli [al-Jubbaʾi]. . . .[67]

(6) Some [unnamed] say, "As for guidance, we know it is of different types, but in all its variations it entails reward [thawab]." We know that God doesn't [make man] deviate from faith [iman], so the issue must entail His turning [humans] away [izagha] from reward and its different types, which open the heart and help the soul on its journey. Evidence for this comes from another verse [64:11]: "Whoever has faith in God, He guides his heart [wa man yuʾmin bil-lahi yahdi qalbahu]." The phrase "He guides his heart [yahdi qalbahu]" can refer to two things: either "He guides his heart to faith [iman]," which is impossible because that would mean that the actions of responsible agents are not connected to faith, when [in fact these actions] serve a purpose, just like moral responsibility serves a purpose, and faith is what comes after. It is necessary—and there is a consensus of the community on this—that God guides a person's heart based on his/her actions, which God made him/her responsible for. Thus, the phrase

"He guides his heart [*yahdi qalbahu*]" must refer to the strengthening of the heart in its faith.[68]

(7) Some say it means not to change the form of a person into something bad because, according to the authoritative lexicon [*fi asl al-lugha*], "*al-zaygh*" means to incline toward and to transform a thing into a worse form. What is meant by this is the seeking of forgiveness from the deserved recompense that one fears. [Al-Radi intervenes here to offers his two cents on this position:] This is a very forced explanation. I only chose to mention it for its strangeness. Other views are more reliable.[69]

(8) Qadi 'Abd al-Jabbar: Not everything that someone asks of their Lord not to do points to what God has chosen to do. So, the meaning of this supplication could be: do not make trials severe such that their hearts would be led astray after [receiving] guidance. Or it could mean not keep them away from or deprived of guidance and divine favor.[70]

Ambiguity as a Key to Theological Resolution

After enumerating the variety of different opinions on this question, al-Radi turns to his own view. Al-Radi does not simply present his view as more persuasive than the opinions of others. Much more than that, he made it a point to offer a resolution to the theological problem at hand by returning to the fundamental principle that undergirded his larger framework of engaging the Qur'an's ambiguous verses: that is, in conjunction with their clear or *muhkam* counterparts. Thus, the opportunity of intervening in a matter of theological significance emerged for al-Radi as also an opportunity to further authorize and consolidate his hermeneutical method and posture. Moreover, such an approach, interlocking theology and hermeneutics, also enabled al-Radi to create an air of scientific rigor around his method, presenting the process of interpreting ambiguity as anything but arbitrary.

Next, al-Radi addressed the pivotal question of what it is that makes this particular verse ambiguous. Of course, the act of determining which verse was ambiguous and why was in itself an interpretive act. Al-Radi's first rationale for why verse 3:8 ought to be considered ambiguous was that, in its apparent meaning, it makes the untenable assertion that God leads human beings astray from faith (*iman*). Al-Radi confidently rehearses the many proofs that render this statement false. The first of these is based on a universally accepted assumption about the nature of God: since leading humans astray would be an ugly or reprehensible act, it cannot be attributed to God, since God transcends such a noisome quality. The second proof relies on the view of God as just toward human beings. "Since God has commanded *human* beings to have faith, has inclined us toward it, and has forbidden us from unbelief [*kufr*] and cautioned against it, therefore it is not possible for God to lead us away from that which he has commanded or to establish for us that which he has forbidden." Al-Radi safely presumes that his readers would agree on both these counts: that God transcends the ugly and that God is just. These, for al-Radi and his readers, are truths that require no justification.[71]

And so, with incontrovertible evidence in hand, al-Radi concludes that the verse cannot be taken in its apparent sense and is therefore from among the ambiguous verses or the *mutashabihat*. He reiterates here, as a reminder for his readers, that the primary features of an ambiguous verse are (a) that you cannot draw its meaning from its apparent sense, and (b) that it must be returned to what has come from clear verses like it. Notable here is his use of the term *awwala*, "to return," which shares the same verbal root as the term *ta'wil*. This term was not exclusively used to describe the process of interpreting the ambiguous verses. Rather, it came to refer to a deeper register of understanding—the Qur'an's esoteric or inner meaning—and, in this sense, it could apply to any and all verses. The *ta'wil* of a verse also came to be differentiated from its *tafsir*, or exoteric and apparent meaning. And this difference between *ta'wil* and *tafsir* was most commonly employed in Qur'an commentaries that sought to move beyond linguistic, historical, and legal explanations toward providing more inward-oriented, mystical insights on the verses' meanings. This process, too, was often described as one that sought to return the verse to the underlying core of its message.[72]

For al-Radi, though, the journey of returning the ambiguous verse to the clear verses that resemble it took a different direction. For al-Radi, this process entailed moving horizontally across the Qur'anic lexicon to locate the appropriate *muhkam*, or clear verse. And the link that tied a *mutashabih* to its *muhkam*, as we will soon see, was ultimately a linguistic one. Thus, the process of "returning" the ambiguous to the clear, even as it is understood by al-Radi as a returning of the verse to the core of its message, stands in some contrast to what later came to be associated with the term *ta'wil*, which went beyond language and beyond historical context. That was closer to an excavation beyond external truths to reveal their inner realities. This is not to say that al-Radi doesn't employ the language of "inner meanings" to describe his interpretations. He does occasionally draw from what is retrospectively seen as the stock register of Sufi terminology, such as unveiling (*kashf*) and the inner (*batin*). But, for al-Radi, the inner meaning consistently corresponds to an inner truth about the operations of language. The *asl* or foundation of language was for al-Radi something that required unveiling, and what was revealed were ultimately the inner truths about language itself.[73] Of course, this begs the question of how, if at all, for al-Radi, the inner realities of language corresponded to or were related to inner truths and realities of the material world, including nature, law, ritual, and the human being more broadly. I will argue (in Chapter 5, in a section titled "Language and Reality") that, for al-Radi, the two were intimately tied. Hence, to argue for the inner linguistic meaning was not unconnected from making larger claims about ontological reality. But I return for now to verse 3:8.

The *muhkam* verse that al-Radi argued as the key to unlocking verse 3:8 reads as follows: "And when they deviated, God caused their hearts to deviate [*fa lamma zaghu azagha Allahu qulubahum*]" (61:5). There are two things that al-Radi needed to establish here in order for his argument to cohere: first, that this verse is indeed clear and not itself ambiguous, and second, that there existed a connecting link by which it can function as the *muhkam* referent for verse 3:8. The critical difference between 61:5 and 3:8, which for al-Radi is what makes one come under the category of *muhkam* and the other under *mutashabih*, is that 61:5 first mentions the deviation of the people and only after that follows the clause "God caused them to deviate." This allows al-Radi to argue two things: first, that the people brought God's action upon themselves, and second, that the thing from which *they* deviate and the thing from which *God* causes them to deviate are two distinct things. In his own words:

> The first is ugly [*qabih*] and sinful, whereas the second is good [*hasan*] and a recompense [*jaza*]. If the two were the same, the statement would not have any benefit. The implied meaning would be: when they deviate from guidance, we make them deviate from guidance.

Thus, with the principle of the Qur'an not being a redundant text set into motion, finding an alternate reading becomes necessary. With this hermeneutical opening, al-Radi is able to justify the view that, while their deviation is from belief, God's causing them to deviate is from the path to paradise and from reward. Moreover, he reiterates that the category and quality of actions are not equivalent, even as they may appear to be so. Whereas God's action belongs to the category of recompense, the action of the people is that of sin. One is good, the other ugly.[74]

Al-Radi then further clarifies his criteria for differentiating the ambiguous from the clear, the *mutashabih* from the *muhkam*. What if someone were to say, al-Radi preemptively asks, that this verse is also from among the *mutashabih* because it is not understood by its apparent meaning but rather by its inner meaning (*batin*), which needs unveiling (*al-kashf*)?[75] Al-Radi responds to this possible doubt by arguing that this is not a *mutashabih* verse because the presence of the first clause "when they deviate" allows us to read the next clause "God deviates their hearts" in its apparent sense. This is so because it is clear that the second mention of deviation refers to a different type of deviation. In other words, to sum up, this verse does not fulfill the established criteria of a *mutashabih* verse.

Here al-Radi raises another fascinating possible objection to the *muhkam* verse that he has referred 3:8 back to:

> If they object to our bringing this verse [61:5] . . . on the basis that this verse occurs at the end of the Qur'an, whereas the verse in question [3:8] is at its beginning, what makes their conjoining permissible is that their discursive content [*kalam*] is shared, and the arguments for both are similar. I will mention that aspect of the *ta'wil* [interpretation] that is specific to the verse to show the benefit of [approaching the verses] together. And I will present the foundations of the argument, God willing![76]

In the statement quoted above, al-Radi asserted that a verse from any part of the Qur'an can be brought forward to clarify a *mutashabih* verse. In his view, a *muhkam* verse was not one that did not merit any further discussion. Rather, its defining quality was that it could be read in its apparent sense. This becomes clear when al-Radi next turns to a lengthy linguistic analysis of the *muhkam* verse itself, in which he pinpoints the specific grammatical operation at play in the sentence that comprises the verse. To do this, he refers to the concept of linguistic extension (*ittisa'*).[77] He explains that this is where "an action is attached to a doer when its occurrence is subsequent to his command, even though what occurs is contrary to his command." According to this rule, it is the sequence of events—a command followed by an action—that authorizes the grammatical link between them. This is so, even when the command compels actions that are contrary to the action performed subsequent to it.[78] Al-Radi further elaborated this subtle point by turning to another Qur'anic example, verses 23:109–110):

> Among My servants there were those who said, "Lord, we believe. Forgive us and have mercy on us: You are the most Merciful of all!" But you kept on laughing at them: so intent were you on laughing at them that they made you forget My warning.[79]

The point to be distilled from this verse for al-Radi was this: grammatically, it is permissible to describe the pious group of God's servants as the cause for making the second group forget God's remembrance. This is so because the second group was so preoccupied in deriding the pious servants of God that in the process they became forgetful of God. Here too, grammatically, the pious ones become the agents of an impious action that they themselves never wished for and nor willfully performed. Al-Radi argues that the operation of linguistic extension or *ittisa'* goes even further. Taking it back to the original verse under discussion on God as the cause of deviation, al-Radi explains that, through linguistic extension, the cause of deviation comes to be called the deviator even though there is no invitation for him to deviate from. In support of this point, al-Radi turns to the Qur'an, verses 14:35-36:

> Remember when Abraham said, 'Lord, make this town safe! Preserve me and my offspring from idolatry, Lord, the [idols] have led many people astray! Anyone who follows me is with me, but as for anyone who disobeys me—You are surely forgiving and merciful.[80]

The key point here is that inanimate objects incapable of any movement, be it obedience or invitation to sin, are associated in this verse with misguiding the people of Abraham. Al-Radi next turns to an example from the everyday speech of the Arabs, another major component of the linguistic canon. His example came from everyday discourse about a passionate lover:

> When a man is passionate about a woman and his love for her is great and he is afraid of losing her due to this passional love, he says to

her: "You made me sleepless, Layla, and you made my heart sick, and made unstable the purity of my life." Meanwhile, it is possible that she knows nothing of what she did, and is not aware of his fear of losing her or of his sleeplessness. But because he believed her to be the cause of these states, even though she did neither, it is permissible to associate her with these actions.[81]

Al-Radi next refers to what appears to have been a common reading of the term *zaygh* or deviation as *'udul* or turning away from a thing, and contributes to this view by providing scriptural and poetic proof (by Labid ibn Rabi'a [d. 661 CE]) for the interchangeability of the two terms. The term *za'igh* (the one who deviates), al-Radi explains, is the *'adil* (the one who turns away) from a thing. God is the *'adil* for the *kuffar* (one who keeps the *kuffar* away from) his spirit, mercy, reward, and paradise, due to them having turned away from his obedience and command. This allows al-Radi to emphasize a critical point: that God is the deviator or *muzigh* for their hearts. Not for their intellect or actions, but for their hearts. He states:

It is better to specify the hearts because of the way the sentence is structured. Had God said: "When they [the hearts] deviated from the truth, we strayed them further from the truth," or "When they doubted religion [*al-din*], we increased their doubt in it," then the critic may have a case to make and something to pierce. But, since the sentence does not specify what they have turned away from, we have to return to the proof that gives the verse meaning and [consider what] would be applicable for God to turn them away from; we searched and found that *reason necessitates* that the one who turns away from the path of worshiping Him turns away from the path to His reward.[82]

Al-Radi's underlying position, thus, was that God's action of deviating from reward is of a totally different category from that of the people who deviate from obedience to God. And, in his view, this verse invites this reading by leaving unspecified the thing from which either group deviates. But al-Radi did not stop here. He sought to seal his argument by referring to a scriptural proof, from Sura Isra' verse 17:72: "those who were blind in this life will be blind in the Hereafter, and even further off the path."[83] The point of comparison is this: in this verse, as well, there is reference to two instances of the state of blindness. And what al-Radi stresses is that the thing from which people are blinded in this world and the next cannot be the same. He argues that in the Hereafter there is no blindness from faith or *iman* and nor is there any behavior of unbelief (*kufr*) or misguidance (*al-dalala*). This is so because in that realm all will have attained knowledge of God. He affirms that on this point there is no objection or difference. Al-Radi then continues: as for the reference to blindness in this world, it is a reference to them being ignorant of the truth. To this God informs them that He will make them blind in their sight of paradise, the places of bounty and happiness, in the meaning of turning them away from these. Al-Radi concluded by tying these verses together: God described their deviating and then being cut off from divine rewards (*thawab*) as blindness and, similarly, he described the turning away of humans from obedience and then their being turned away from the path of rewards and paradise as deviation.

The juxtaposition of these two verses allows al-Radi to hone in on the crucial point that the deviation (*zaygh*) of the deviants (*za'ighin*) is of their doing, and God's causing them to deviate or turn away (*azagha*) is God's doing. In addition, their deviation represents deviation from faith and God causes them to turn away from divine rewards or *thawab*. Critically, al-Radi turns to yet another linguistic argument for this point. Had deviation (*al-zaygh*) and causing to deviate (*al-izagha*) been the same, then God would not have used different verbs. Finally, al-Radi turns to the end of the verse, which states "God does not guide the sinful community [*al-qawm al-fasiqin*]." This, for him, further solidifies the point that it is the people who first become sinful (*fasiq*), after which God does not lead them to his rewards.

This example began with a hypothetical opponent challenging al-Radi on the threat verse 3:8 posed to the coherence of a central theological tenet: belief in a just God who grants creation with free will to choose right over wrong. Al-Radi's response was comprehensive and multivalent, as we have seen, marshaling grammatical evidence from the Qur'an and poetry, as well as logical evidence based on what, for him, was the exercise of reason. For al-Radi, these discursive resources were not at odds with each other. He did not clarify whether he found grammatical evidence as weightier and more authoritative than reason or not. But what his discussion does make clear is that, for him, the logic of language functioned as the empirical confirmation of logical truths.

Conclusion

Scholar of Arabic linguistics Michael Carter has argued that "linguistic ability" in Baghdad's intellectual milieu in the tenth century had become synonymous with social power and had given rise to a scholarly elite that aggressively defended a full-fledged grammatical orthodoxy.[84] Under these conditions, the knowledge of grammar became a handy tool with which to discredit one's opponents, without engaging their ideas. Thus, Carter suggests that critiques of poor linguistic ability were often convenient tactics by which to sidestep and eliminate an opponent's ideas. In this context, it should be noted that al-Radi's *Haqa'iq* also conforms to such a "disputational style," and it is in the sections where al-Radi seeks to defend a grammatical point that he adopts a distinctly belligerent tone. Carter's observations suggest that a work like al-Radi's could hold immense social purchase in this context. Al-Radi's well-supported and firmly delivered rebuttals of his opponents on linguistic grounds represented a powerful tool for enhancing his political station and for politically damaging his opponents. But yet the search for "underlying" or "real" motives is best resisted. Such a pursuit can have the effect of stripping the discourse of a thinker like al-Radi of any intellectual value and that of viewing it as yielding no critical force other than that of the instrumentalist mobilization of polemical banter for political gains. Furthermore, the quest for "underlying motivations" of early Muslim arguments over language can also function as another framing through which identity politics are privileged as the primary governing principle and template for approaching these texts.

As I have stated above, Carter's insights are crucial for capturing the wider social implications of literary battles in the intellectual context of tenth-century Baghdad. Yet, in my discussion of the *Haqa'iq*, I have moved away from a singular line of reasoning that seeks to draw a direct line between al-Radi's presumed sectarian or political motives and his exegetical discussion. While not dismissing the power that individual motives may impress upon any author, I have argued that, too often, what these motives might be—particularly when we are dealing with Shi'i scholars—is taken as an a priori fact. Furthermore, I argue that it is crucial to consider the constitutive and productively conditioning features of these exchanges by shifting our attention from the ideological motivations of the actors to the conditions of possibility or what can be termed as the discursive terrain that makes these debates thinkable and possible in the first place. Accordingly, the *Haqa'iq* can be understood as "a piece of living action or an ideological maneuver that takes up a position and puts forward a move in a particular historical-discursive context of argument."[85] With this shift in focus, it is possible to explore how al-Radi's theories on reading the ambiguous verses, according to the linguistic interpretations that he proposes, carried significant discursive and social power.

The case studies of Qur'anic ambiguity discussed in this chapter provide important insights into al-Radi's religious imaginary and into larger questions of language and revelation in early Islam. I have shown that, while engaging the Qur'an's ambiguous verses, al-Radi's hermeneutical energies were primarily focused on how literary devices can illuminate meaning. Moreover, I have also shown that al-Radi's linguistic imaginary is characterized by a marked tension between its definite structure that allow certain rules of grammar to be identified, recognized, and verified, and by its subtle mysteries, access to which is limited to an exclusive few. This accorded well with the scholarly ethos of Baghdad, where the display of linguistic excellence represented a central mechanism of showcasing one's religious and, indeed, political authority.

The commanding voice of al-Radi in the *Haqa'iq*, which points to riddle after riddle in the Qur'anic text, only to masterfully "resolve" them, one by one, points to his view that the language of the Qur'an had to be accessible through the rules of language, established by human convention. And it is language that shaped the parameters of the extent and sorts of liberties one could take while exercising one's exegetical will. By deriving the meaning of Qur'anic ambiguities from a fixed literary canon, al-Radi argued for an unshakeable linguistic ontology. In this way, although al-Radi's literary approach to the Qur'an argued for a linguistically "transgressive" interpretation of certain verses, the clearly defined linguistic sources for his interpretation achieved a rhetorical lockdown on the text's hermeneutical possibilities. Lest this give the impression that al-Radi's exegetical operation was devoid of any aesthetic value, let me clarify that, even as al-Radi's sought to argue for fixed linguistic truths, he was equally invested in the exercise of evoking wonder and delight in his reader. Masterfully guiding the reader into the labyrinthine world of language, he sought to make visible its subtle inner workings and the secrets it harbors about human beings and the worlds they inhabit. An apparent feature of al-Radi's exegetical accounts is the eloquence

and style with which he delivers his arguments. Lyrical Arabic prose peppered with internal rhyme and rhythm scaffolds and bolsters his exegetical
and literary claims.[86] There is no conflict between al-Radi's literary poetic
self, who on the one hand celebrates ambiguity for the wonders it illuminates, and his exegetical self, who explains it with categorical conviction. In
other words, it is through his effort to document and explain ambiguity that
al-Radi puts on display its aesthetic and wonder-producing qualities.

CHAPTER 5

The Theology of Language

Introduction

In preceding chapters, I have established the salience of language in the late tenth-/early eleventh-century milieu from an intellectual and cultural standpoint, as well as the critical social power that its mastery wielded in the courts in particular. To remind us: in addition to serving as a critical social and cultural marker of power, the theorization and analysis of language was also a high-stakes discipline, due to its inseparability from other disciplines, like law and theology, all of which together were foundational to the conceptualization and enactment of social, political, and cultural norms. In this chapter, I continue my exploration of the centrality of language to the religious and social landscape of early Islam by shifting my focus to some key debates on the intersection of language and theology that occupied major scholars in this era. In the latter half of the chapter, I then connect these debates to some specific examples from al-Radi's Qur'an commentary to show and argue that his commentarial labor was both constitutive of and constituted by these broader debates on the interaction of language and theology in Islam.

Among the most critical and contentious issues that hovers over the encounter of language and theology, in the Muslim tradition and otherwise, is the debate over "the origin of language." This debate centers on the following question: Does human language represent an arbitrary phenomenon and process or does there exist an underlying rationale that governs the application of a particular word to its referent? Clearly, this question was and remains significant not just to Muslim thinkers or to the Muslim intellectual tradition. Its significance stretches across all religious traditions and time periods, even though the stakes of this debate have varied. More recently, this question and the theories of language it engenders has attracted the attention of a number and range of theorists who have shown its profound significance in shaping twentieth-century Western epistemologies of knowledge. However, the contribution of Muslim thinkers to the debate over the origin of language remains rather scantily addressed in contemporary Euro-American theoretical and philosophical discussions on this issue. This represents an unfortunate omission that is not only significant in terms of signaling a historiographic lacuna; more significantly, it profoundly skews the texture and vectors of grand narratives regarding the global unfolding of the "origin of language" debate. Let me illustrate this point with two prominent and representative examples of recent Western academic engagements with this topic.

In his recent book, *The Fall of Language*, Alexander Stern presents a discursive analysis cum intellectual history of key shifts in Western philosophical views on language, with a focus on the thought of two doyens of post-Enlightenment thought: Ludwig Wittgenstein and Walter Benjamin. Stern's narrative plot pivots on a crucial contrast he proffers between what he terms "enchanted" and "disenchanted" understandings of language. Stern's argument is that a previously enchanted imaginary of language, as held by ancient Greek philosophers, was eventually supplanted by a disenchanted notion of language in the post-Enlightenment period, as best exemplified in the language philosophies of Wittgenstein and Benjamin. In Stern's account, language, not too long ago, was understood as the vestibule that carried the meaning inherent in our spiritually enlivened and enchanted world. Language, in other words, was endowed with spiritual meaning while also representing a repository of the meaning invested in a spiritually enchanted universe. Moreover, and this is a crucial point, the very functionality of language, in its enchanted view, was tied to its capacity to capture the essence of what it referred to and described. Names and essences were intimately entwined. But, according to Stern, this enchanted imaginary of language was radically altered in the wake of the Enlightenment and its intellectual aftermath and made way for a disenchanted view of language that in turn corresponded with a disenchanted universe. Objects of life were no longer thought to hold an essence, as the relationship between language and essence was disentangled. Language henceforth was reduced to a medium of communication rather than an enchanted receptacle of meaning. In Stern's own words:

> A world endowed with spiritual meaning promises a tight connection between things and the names we give them. Plato's Cratylus goes as far as to argue that names are "correct" insofar as they grasp the

essences of the things they name and that we can thus come to knowledge of things through their names. Etymology is, for Cratylus, first philosophy. In modern, disenchanted nature, by contrast, the names we assign the furniture of reality can't hope to have much to do with the things themselves, mute and meaningless as they are on their own.[1]

Stern's grand narrative of this shift from enchanted to disenchanted views of language is mirrored in philosopher Charles Taylor's recent book, *The Language Animal*, though through a different analytical vantage point. If Stern's study focuses on shifts in how language has been imagined in Western philosophical thought, Taylor examines shifts and changes in the significance accorded to the very category of language and its associated philosophical conundrums over time.

Taylor argues that debates on language were not that important to the ancients, while garnering palpable interest in the thought of seventeenth-century early modern thinkers like Thomas Hobbes and John Locke, and eventually assuming the status of "obsessional" interest by the twentieth century when the "origin of language" question came to consume the intellectual energies of almost all major Western theorists and philosophers. As Taylor puts it:

Are linguistic signs arbitrary or motivated? What is it that signs and words have when they have meaning? These are very old questions. Language is an old topic in Western philosophy, but its importance has grown. It is not a major issue among the ancients. It begins to take on greater importance in the seventeenth century with Hobbes and Locke. And then in the twentieth century it becomes close to obsessional. All major philosophers have their theories of language: Heidegger, Wittgenstein, Davidson, Derrida, and all manner of "deconstructionists" have made language central to their philosophical reflection.[2]

While Stern and Taylor argue for critical shifts in Western philosophical attitudes toward the category of language, they both employ a remarkably symmetrical historiographic frame wedged between the ancient and the modern worlds. Their sweeping historical frame begins with Greek philosophy and ends with modern Western thought, sidelining in the process discourses, traditions, languages, and commentaries that occupy the centuries in between. Also critically missing in their narrative is an account of

how scholars from other non-Western intellectual traditions sought to theorize and philosophically wrestle with the nature of the relationship between
language, community, and theology. That is precisely the sort of lacuna this
chapter seeks to address, with a focus on the context of early Islam.

Bringing Muslim intellectual perspectives on the theology of language
into central view also allows us to disrupt the "enchanted premodern" and
"disenchanted modern" binary. Indeed, the dizzying spectrum of positions
on the language question populating Muslim scholarly tradition from the
ninth to the eleventh centuries—which is when this question held particular sway and importance—does not accord with the view that "premodern
scholars" imagined language primarily as imbued with enchanted spiritual
meaning readily contrastable with a disenchanted modern present. As an
example, take the case of al-Radi's brother and contemporary, al-Sharif al-
Murtada. A devout theologian, jurist, poet, and literary scholar, al-Murtada
felt entirely comfortable arguing for the inherently non-unique nature of
Qur'anic speech, let alone general speech, even as he may have belonged to
an episteme saturated with spiritual meaning.[3] This among other examples
highlight the importance of attending to the specific arguments, logics, and
assumptions through which scholars across varied religious traditions and
historical conjunctures articulated their respective theories of language.
Moreover, what this also shows is that non-Euro-American actors like key
Muslim scholars and theologians who expended their intellectual energies
in theorizing language and its beginnings hold the potential of serving as
useful and instructive interlocutors in the humanistic study of the interaction of language, theology, and knowledge. Put differently, they offer us the
opportunity to decolonize the study of religion and language by enlarging
and diversifying our canvas of analysis. This is among the political and theoretical aspirations of this chapter, as it is of this book as a whole.

However, despite the geographic and cross-cultural limitations of their
work, Taylor and Stern nonetheless offer some critical conceptual tools, categories, and problems to clarify language theory broadly, and the stakes and
forms of reasoning that inform Muslim intellectual encounters with language more specifically. For instance, in his discussion, Taylor introduces a
useful distinction between what he calls "enframing" and "constitutive" theories of language. By "enframing," he means a notion of language whereby
language is understood as always enmeshed with and responding to a framework of "a picture of human life, behavior, purposes, or mental functioning"[4]
that precedes language. In other words, language in this scheme is enframed

and enshrined in a discursive repository of meaning, behavior, purpose, and mental functioning that is not language itself. Put yet differently, language is informed and determined by the picture that enframes it, not the other way around. In contrast, according to the "constitutive theory" of language, it is language that makes possible "new purposes, new levels of behavior, new meanings," and is hence "not explicable within a framing picture of human life conceived without language."[5] Put more simply, in this reading, language generates and constitutes meaning rather than being enframed and constituted by an external frame or picture of meaning. There is no language without language; there is no language outside of language. Taylor's larger argument is that this fundamental division between *enframing* and *constitutive* theories of language map onto broader and more profound divisions regarding the interaction of language and human ontology. This is also a key theological concern of Muslim scholars in early Islam. Taylor's concept of a constitutive notion of language mirrors and can be usefully folded with Stern's observation regarding Ludwig Wittgenstein's emphasis on "showing what language does, instead of speculating about what it might mean." Wittgenstein, Stern helpfully and pithily adds, "puts language back into the world."[6] Though belonging to a very different context, that of twentieth-century Western philosophical thought, the categories and associated conceptual questions introduced by Taylor and Stern offer potentially productive keys and avenues for examining the intersections of language, theology, and ontology in early Muslim thought. In turn, examining how Muslim scholars approached these issues provides the opportunity of a dialogical encounter between Western theory and the Muslim humanities.

For instance, drawing from Taylor's insights, one may ask: In early Muslim writings on language, do we find a dominant a priori framework of life that *preceded* theorizations of language, or was language itself understood as generating or constituting new forms and frameworks of life? Concomitantly, how did the thriving intellectual tradition of theology shape dominant understandings of human life, and how did they, in turn, inform early Muslim theories of language? Building on Stern's work: How did early Muslim scholars imagine the relationship between language and the empirical realities it sought to represent? In other words, what, to them, was the relationship between language and ontology? Was language seen as essentialized and in a fixed relation to the world or as an ever-changing entity that makes possible different ways of being in the world? Were Muslim scholars invested in the question of what *work* language *did* in the world, or were they primarily invested in articulating the sources and methods for determining what it *means*? Which aspect was privileged?

In what follows, I briefly address these questions as they are reflected in the writings of key Muslim scholars from the ninth and tenth centuries. My aim is not to present a comprehensive account of the multiple threads of conversations connected to these questions, a task both impossible and outside the scope of this chapter and book. Neither do I aspire to capturing the wide spectrum of positions held by individual scholars nor in detailing the specificities of their arguments. What I hope to do instead is to present illustrative fragments of critical moments and examples that might help sketch an overarching picture of the intellectual milieu that informed al-Radi's discussion on similar topics in the *Haqa'iq* and to which he in turn contributed. My goal, then, is to foreground and provide the intellectual context of al-Radi's thought on the encounter of language and theology in Islam, the binding theme of this chapter. With the context in place, in this chapter's latter segment I proceed to a close reading of selections from the *Haqa'iq* to argue that al-Radi represented an important participant in these conversations. How? In the *Haqa'iq*, he offers (at minimum) an explanation of Qur'anic ambiguities. But he also makes an important argument about what ambiguity *is* to begin with. My exploration of the ways in which al-Radi's theory of ambiguity was tied to theological concerns helps us understand further the intersection of language and theology in Muslim thought at this formative moment in early Islam. But, before I get to al-Radi, let me offer a brief genealogy of early Muslim intellectual expenditure on the question of language. Situating al-Radi in this ongoing tradition of intra-Muslim discourse is also connected to my overall argument in this book: that the stakes and significance of the varied aspects of his Qur'an exegesis are best understood and appreciated when placed in conversation with the wider intellectual currents of his time. And these currents, as I have argued throughout, extend well beyond the confines of Shi'i circles.

Language Imaginaries: Intersection of
Language, Law, and Society

In examining early Muslim theorizations of language, one of the most striking features one finds in abundance is the conceptualization of language as analogous to society. That is, early Muslim grammarians often discussed elements of language as if they personified members of society who behaved and acted according to a set of preestablished norms. Words represented agentive entities, capable of acting on and being affected by others. Moreover, and perhaps more crucially, much like human subjects in a society, language was also subject to moral evaluation and judgment. The conceptualization of language as a morally culpable living system, in other words, drew heavily from discourses on law and ethics.

For example, as Kees Versteegh has explained, the title of prominent grammarian al-Zajjaji's famous work *Linguistic Causes* (*'ilal al-nahw*) reflects an understanding of linguistic units as mirroring the functioning of a society. How? The causes governing linguistic rules and laws are determined by the interrelationship between various language units, metaphorically corresponding with the members and unfolding of a human society. Language has its own laws, and from these laws linguistic units derive certain rights and duties, much like human actors live and exist with others according to particular set of shared laws and norms. In addition, theologically, since language is among God's creations, it cannot exhibit any arbitrariness; for every phenomenon, and for every apparent exception, there must exist a viable explanation.[7] The idea of language as simulating human behavior is nicely captured by scholar of Arabic Michael Carter in his useful study of arguably the most renowned early Muslim grammarian Sibawayh's widely read text *Al-Kitab*: "Behavior is a way of doing things, and *nahw* means exactly that—a way of speaking. Because of this, the act of speaking is judged by the same standards that Arabic uses to judge other acts, as 'good' (*hasan*), 'bad' (*qabih*), 'right' (*mustaqim*) and 'wrong' (*muhal*)." Carter helpfully adds:

Everything I have so far said about the *Kitab* points toward a sustained social metaphor as the basis for its grammatical system. Not only are the criteria the same as those of ethics and law, and not only are the parts of speech personified into "sisters," "mothers," and "daughters," but there are also numerous other personifications which, since some of them have already been pointed out by Weiss, I will content myself with merely listing here. Weiss notes that the *Kitab* uses the terms *'amila fi*, meaning "to have an effect on something," that words are said to have a "power" (*quwwa*), an "effect" (*ta'thir*, but I have not found it in the *Kitab*) and that a word may be "occupied" (*mashgul*) or even "idle" (*farigh*). . . .

We have, as a result, two parallel processes which come under Sibaway-hi's consideration: the behaviour of the speaker as he uses his language, and the internal "behaviour" of the words which make up what he says. Both are extensions of the ethical methods that I have shown to be used by Ibn al-Muqaffaʻ, and we may now make a useful distinction between the transference of ethical ideas to the domain of man's linguistic behaviour, which remains a perceptible social act, and the problem of the behaviour of speech itself, to which ethical methods can only apply as pure metaphor.[8]

Here, Carter advances a useful distinction while analyzing Sibawayh's view of language: the behavior of the speaker, and the internal behavior of the words he or she uses. From a theological standpoint, this distinction between the behavior of words and that of the speaker was significant. This was so because, according to Muʻtazili teachings, the foundation of any theory of language was premised on the assumption of understanding language as primarily the action of the speaker. This shift to the agency of the speaker as the primary producer of language was critical to the cogency of the Muʻtazili view that held the Qurʼan as created (and not eternal). Why? Because if one acknowledged that language is fundamentally an action of the speaker, then God's speech in the Qurʼan rendered that speech God's—that is, the speaker's—creation. Therefore, viewing the Qurʼan as a *product* of God's speech aligned nicely with the doctrine of the Qurʼan as created.[9] For the Muʻtazilis, upholding God's transcendence and separation from what they regarded as a temporally produced text, the Qurʼan, was crucial. And they sought to simultaneously establish this separation while still maintaining the intimacy of the speaker with the text through their argument about the nature of language itself. For them, language was inextricably attached to the speaker. It was specific to the speaker. It did not represent a generalized abstract entity available for any speaker to draw from. Rather, language represented an intimate act or product of the speaker's making. To put it simply, language constituted the "making of speech" by the speaker.

Language and Reality

Another important consideration regarding the interconnections of language and theology in early Muslim thought concerned the relationship between language and reality. This question again related to the overarching *function* of language and its relationship with the world it sought to represent. Is there an intrinsic connection between names and their referents? More specifically, do names and their referents share a common identity? Or are they onto-logically distinct?[10] Theologically, these were high stakes questions. Why? Because they were tied to arguably *the* most burning theological problem: the nature of God. How one understood the encounter of language and reality, names and its referents, carried profound implications for how one under-stood the relationship of God's names and attributes to his essence. Was there a unity of identity between the names of God and his essence? In a nutshell, despite varied views on these questions, an abiding assumption in early Mus-lim thought that informed the way these questions were addressed was that the relationship of God's names to his essence was conceptually analogous to the relationship of language to the empirical realities in the world that it rep-resented. In other words, language, ontology, and theology are inseparably entwined. The primary objective of this chapter is to elaborate this point and argument, and to demonstrate its reflection in and significance to al-Radi's exegetical project.

Qur'an scholar Mustafa Shah, in a series of articles, has explored the convergence of language and theology as seen in the two major schools of Muslim theology: the Ash'arites and the Mu'tazilites. For the Ash'arites, God's names and attributes exist hypostatically within God's essence; there exists a unity of identity between the name and the thing named. In their view, divine names and attributes reflected the ontological reality of divine essence. The names and attributes that described God symmetrically corresponded with God's being.[11] The Mu'tazilites on the other hand, Shah argues, held that initially God had neither name nor attributes: the names and attributes that describe God were created and designated at a later point in time. As a cor-ollary, names and their referents, language and reality, did not form part of a unified identity. Names were attached to their referents through a process of naming (*tasmiya*); they were not intrinsically bound together. That is to say, for the Mu'tazilites, names are what humans use to describe God. The main ambiguity connected with this position, as opponents of the Mu'tazilites often relished in pointing out, was that if language was assumed to represent a human convention, then divine knowledge became subject to the human capacity to name God as knowing/able.[12] In other words, divine sovereignty was rendered subordinate to human language, a theological impossibility.[13]

The influential Mu'tazili thinker 'Abd al-Jabbar's (whom we've already met extensively in this book) discussion on this question of language's relationship with reality is significant as well as instructive. He argued that knowledge is not a given, but rather a quality that one acquires through intellectual effort and exertion. The acquisition of knowledge thus requires work and application on the part of human beings, a process that 'Abd al-Jabbar categorized as *taklif* or the moral obligation on humans to strive for God's knowledge. Tying this *taklif* logic to language, 'Abd al-Jabbar advanced a distinction between the name, the named entity, and purpose (*ism/musamma/qasd wa al-irada*).[14] For 'Abd al-Jabbar, what validates the connection between a name and its referent is the act of *qasd* or divulging the intended purpose of naming. This paradigm automatically rules out the position of *tawqif* or divine creation of language. Because "if God had created language (the *tawqif* position) then he would have to reveal the intention behind the use of language; he would have to reveal knowledge of God before the imposition of religious obligation." 'Abd al-Jabbar, in effect, argued that if humans were acquainted with God's purpose through a divinely created language that they have been taught, then *taklif*, the divine act of imposing moral obligation, would be rendered futile.[15]

Central to 'Abd al-Jabbar's conceptualization of language was the premise that speech can only be performed by a speaker. Thus, the quality of speaking, for him, meant "making speech."[16] For 'Abd al-Jabbar, of primary significance was the role of the speaker's intention and will in determining speech. In his own words:

Speech can only occur as command (*amr*), prohibition (*nahy*), or information (*khabar*) because of the influence which the intention and state of intending have on this speech. This state can only have influence on the acts which the subject that is in this state performs. Therefore, the speaking (and commanding, prohibiting, and informing) subject must be the subject who made speech, and who made it belong to one of the "parts of speech" by the concomitant will.[17]

In effect, the various parts of speech are determined by the will of the speaker.[18] In sum, 'Abd al-Jabbar's answer to the origin of language question hinged on presenting a case and argument for what language itself constitutes. And here, rather than only consider the relationship between names and referents, he introduces a critical additional component: the speaker and his or her intention, without whom speech/language is impossible. Privileging the subjectivity of the speaker as the centerpiece of the possibility of language, therefore, necessitated that language was suffused with intentional-ity. Without intention, there was no language.

Notice that 'Abd al-Jabbar's argument is irreducible to an Aristotelian view of words that signify objects lying out there in the world and is instead closer to resembling Wittgenstein's approach to language "not simply as a thing aligned or misaligned with the world but a part of the complex, inde-terminate ways that humans inhabit the world by forming and reforming their life."[19] Of course, there are important differences between Wittgenstein and 'Abd al-Jabbar. For starters, as Talal Asad explains, "what is important for Wittgenstein is not simply how "meaning" is to be determined but whether and if so how something becomes intelligible—and usable— in given situa-tions."[20] And, "Wittgenstein doesn't simply argue that meaning is necessarily determined by use . . . but that the multiple ways in which language is used— by sender and by receiver—require us to investigate the complex relation-ships of discourse to life through the idea of 'grammar.'"[21]

Putting 'Abd al-Jabbar in conversation with Wittgenstein (via Asad) thus makes visible the insight that the relationship between language the-ory and theology is often complex, unavailable for neat, predictable theori-zations fitting with modern dichotomies of ancient/modern, East/West, and rationalist/traditionalist.

What is Language? The Role of Theology in
Early Muslim Debates about Language

Debates on language in early Islam, as I have shown, were deeply entangled with theological questions. Before developing this point further, it might be useful to begin however by clarifying what it is we are even talking *about* when we use the term "language," often translated as such from the Arabic term *al-lugha*.[22] What are we referring to when we ask, for example, what a scholar like al-Radi's philosophy and theory of language may have repre-sented? And, most crucially, how were the connotations attached to the term *al-lugha* in early Islam during al-Radi's life different from its later connota-tions leading to the present?

Lugha constituted the essence of language and its lexical vocabulary in the sense that it represented an argument about what meanings a series of sounds/vocables carried. Now, a crucial point that must be introduced here is this: *lugha* (linguistic datum) was understood to have been instituted, in that it was regarded as a product of placement or ordering (*wad'*). *Wad'* or the institution of language is a crucial category for my purposes, as it signals and serves as a key link between language and theology, the central theme of this chapter. So, what is *wad'*? Put simply, *wad'* refers to the placement or institution of an articulated sound (*lafz*) to a particular meaning.[23] More technically, it is defined as "the primitive assignation of an articulated sound (*lafz*) to a certain significance (*ma'na*)."[24] Theologically, the crucial and thorny question generated by *wad'* was this: Who was its agent? Ash'ari and Mu'tazili theologians were split over this question. For the Mu'tazilis, *wad'* was a product of human convention, whereas for the pioneers of the Ash'ari school, it represented a divine institution.

But the institution of language, or *wad' al-lugha*, as it was called, did not always represent a settled matter of normative acceptance. Some scholars, like the early Mu'tazili thinker 'Abbad ibn Sulayman (d. approx. 864), disputed the notion that language was instituted (and arbitrary); he instead argued that linguistic sounds or vocables and meaning were interlocked in a motivated relationship of natural affinity. This position effectively challenged the view that language was instituted, such that the correlations between vocables and their meanings were based on a primordial institution or *wad'*, and not on the basis of innate internal affinity between them.

Over time, however, as Bernard Weiss has pointed out, 'Abbad's view lost its purchase among the Muslim intellectual elite and the doctrine of *wad'* assumed the character of a widely held normative proposition. But aside from the shifts and transformations in the intellectual history of this category, *al-lugha* brings into view three central conceptual problems and issues.

First, at stake in the debate over whether language was externally instituted, primordially found, or contextually derived, or what one might call the *wad'*/non-*wad'* debate, was the question of the relationship between sound and meaning. The majority position, or the *wad'*-affirming position that ultimately acquired normative status, was premised on the assumption that there existed no inherent relationship between sound and meaning. Rather, that relationship was instituted or put in place (*wad'*). While there were disagreements about the details and history of this lexical placement and the degree of divine involvement, most agreed that this was the structure within which language was created and existed.[25] The short-lived minority position of 'Abbad held that there was indeed an intrinsic or motivated relation between sound and meaning, and that they were intimately interlocked in a relationship of correspondence. Thus, there was no need to rely on an external cause like a preestablished code to explain why words held the meaning they did; that cause was not connected to any external institution but was rather found internally within the words and meanings themselves. A third and later position, held by Ibn Taymiyya (d. 1328) was to argue that relations between vocables and mental content were borne entirely out of specific contexts and usage by human beings. In other words, for Ibn Taymiyya, a word taken on its own without its context did not signify anything. Building on this, he argued that there was no such thing as metaphorical speech, since it is context that fixes the meaning of speech and, since all speech has its own context, it must therefore all be literal/real. What undergirded these arguments was Ibn Taymiyya's view that the origin of language did not entail a process of lexical placing (*wad*). This is because to adhere to a narrative of lexical placing as the origin of language was to assume that "the real meaning of a word is its original meaning, the meaning that is apparent by itself without any context."[26] This was an untenable assumption for Ibn Taymiyya on the grounds that the meaning of *all* speech was contingent to its context.[27]

This position forms an integral part of Ibn Taymiyya's treatment of the ambiguous verses in the Qur'an. He demands that the meaning, or the resolution to these ambiguities, does not lie in a language that can be separated from or stand outside its speakers and their lived realities. Talal Asad has drawn instructive parallels between this position of Ibn Taymiyya's and the arguments on language put forward in a very different context by Wittgenstein. What draws a figure like Asad to Ibn Taymiyya's non-rationalist position is that Ibn Taymiyya refuses to *concede* meaning to language. The Qur'an's ambiguities do not demand an intellectualized hermeneutical resolution, but rather one premised on the embodied experience of language. In Asad's words: "For 'traditionalists,' the Qur'an is not a text that addresses God's existence as a problem requiring a solution: it is a demand for a practical engagement with an essentially indescribable force, an engagement that includes the complex passion of dread-awe-reverence, by which one's form of life is oriented and deepened."[28] And, "while tradition may involve the making of new meanings, traditionalists do not puzzle over meanings in the Qur'an but try to respond to its demand for a specific form of life as they learn it in the tradition."[29]

For Asad, thus, a figure like Ibn Taymiyya privileges an embodied over a hermeneutical response to the Qur'an and its ambiguities even as the embodied experience inspired by the Qur'an is not bereft of hermeneutical engagement and complexity. But, to extend Asad's analysis, what should we make of scholars like 'Abd al-Jabbar and al-Radi who seemingly fall under the rationalist camp and for whom ambiguity is indeed resolved through language? More specifically, it is rationalized away into a non-ambiguity? One might respond to this question by noting that al-Radi's discussions on Qur'anic ambiguities, especially his mobilization of wonder as a receptacle of thought and imagination, complicates the division of language and embodied life and that of rationalist and non-rationalist hermeneutics. How? For al-Radi, even though ambiguity is resolved through language, this process is intimately bound to the life of language in everyday experience. His mobilization of such discursive fragments as oral speech, performed poetry, and the recited Qur'an work precisely to establish the intimacy of language and embodied life and the underlying connection of language to ontology. This is found most clearly in the multiple instances in which al-Radi argues for a particular reading of a Qur'anic ambiguity based on a grammatical rule that stands authorized through what, to al-Radi, are the operations of ontological reality. As I will show, in one among numerous examples, one may cite verse 3:36 in which, for al-Radi, the reference to a female witness with a male pronoun actually conveys the empirical reality of the aspiration of the weaker sex to attain sameness with the stronger sex.

Returning to the central conceptual problems brought into view by *al-lugha,* even if one agreed on the instituted nature of language, and accepted that language ultimately constituted a predetermined code by which certain sounds came to represent certain meanings, the second question that emerges is this: How and through what process was that code instituted in the first place? Was it a divinely determined act (*tawqif*) or a process channeled by human and social conventions (*istilah*) that were eventually embraced and accepted by its users? One might categorize these questions as reflections of an intra-*wad'* debate.

Third, another question that arose from within the *wad'* camp had to do with the conundrum of how a view of language as preestablished could allow for or explain changes that occurred within language over time? How could a phenomenon that was a product of originary institution undergo change and transformation? This puzzle was eventually answered with the following resolution: although the meanings of vocables changed over time, the original, primordial assignment of vocables to meanings, or *wad'*, remained in place. To borrow from Bernard Weiss, "*Wad'* produced the basic language or code in relationship to which all subsequent semantic development amounted to extension, accretion or modification, and not true invention."[30] In simpler words, changes and transformations in language did not constitute substantive departures from the original institution of language; rather, they represented extensions and modifications that seamlessly connected with the moment of origin.

As a way to round off this preparatory discussion, before I get to moments from al-Radi's exegesis again, let me briefly return to the origin-of-language question with which this chapter began. In an informative article-length study, Bernard Weiss has argued that intra-Muslim theological debates over the origin-of-language question peaked in early Islam during the tenth century, and were engaged with particular purpose by two prominent figures: the Mu'tazili Abu Hashim al-Jubba'i[31] and the eponymous founder of the Ash'ari school of theology, Abu al-Hasan al-Ash'ari (d. 936).[32] On the one hand, Abu Hashim argued that language represented a product of social convention, a position that came to be known as the conventionalist theory or *istilah*.[33] Critical to this position was the view that the choice of names given to objects, or the relationship between language and the object of language was ultimately arbitrary, and the result of contingent conditions. Al-Ash'ari, on the other hand, argued for a systematic and predetermined divine role in the placement and ordering of language, a view that took the name of revelationist theory or *tawqif*. Eventually, by the early eleventh century, over time, this debate seems to have simmered off and lost its earlier bite and purchase. So for instance, Abu Bakr al-Baqillani (d. 1013), al-Radi's contemporary and a leading exegete of Ash'ari leanings, gestured toward a stalemate when he pronounced that no conclusive resolution to this issue existed.

Here, an important qualifier is in order: the position of individual scholars on the question of the origin of language did not always neatly correspond with their theological leanings, much as sectarian identities did not always correspond with exegetical choices, as I have argued throughout this book. Certainly, the conventionalist position/theory commonly associated with the Mu'tazili school was often held by important Mu'tazili thinkers, including al-Radi's teacher 'Abd al-Jabbar. This was primarily so because, in their view, the opposing revelationist theory, by divesting any role for human agency in the institution of language, infringed on the doctrine of free will.[34] However, yet, even among the Mu'tazilites, there were several figures who in fact argued for the revelationist theory while also proffering the createdness of the Qur'an. In so doing, they often cited the Qur'anic verse that refers to God as "teaching Adam all the names," clearly upholding the revelationist view. Notable Mu'tazili figures who accepted the revelationist view included the Persian grammarian Abu 'Ali al-Farisi (d. 987) and also the eminent grammarian cum exegete Mahmud ibn 'Umar al-Zamakhshari (d. 1144). The Mu'tazili shift to the conventionalist view assumed greater prominence in the next generation of scholars such as 'Abd al-Jabbar.[35]

More recently, Mustafa Shah has dedicated a series of articles that investigate the extent to which tenth-century intra-Muslim scholarly debates on language were driven by theological affinities. He pursues this question by examining prominent threads of Muslim intellectual discussions on the origin of language and on specific linguistic features like synonymy, polysemy, etc. After a rather thorough analysis, Shah concludes that the link between philological positioning and theological affiliation was, in fact, quite nominal.

Shah further argues, and this is the critical point I wish to underscore, that the revelationist/conventionalist or *tawqif/istilah* positions did not always represent a binary choice. Take the example of Ibn Jinni. On the one hand, he left traces that suggest his affinity with the position that language was a product of human conventions. For instance, his famous study of morphological change in language (*tasrif*), titled *al-Munsif*, included an important tract on morphological derivation or etymology (*ishtiqaq*), a feature of language that assumes parts of speech to have been derived from other parts of speech, a position clearly more disposed to a view of language as based on human convention.[36] But still, Ibn Jinni avowedly announced himself as an upholder of the *tawqif* position that ascribed to language divine origins.[37] How could an esteemed Mu'tazili scholar like Ibn Jinni simultaneously play a pioneering role in the theoretical study of etymology, while also expressing his attachment to the *tawqif* position? Shah explains this seeming contradiction in Ibn Jinni's stance by pointing out that during the latter's career, the revelationist or *tawqif* position had assumed the mantle of normativity to the extent that Mu'tazili thinkers like Ibn Jinni and al-Farisi did not consider it necessarily contradictory to their theology. More specifically, while writing on questions of philology, they were perfectly capable of bracketing their theological commitments and proclivities and keeping them separate. Theological views and commitments need not have enmeshed with linguistic and philological imaginaries; theology and language could occupy distinct intellectual domains for a particular thinker. But such decoupling was not always the case; in many instances, theological inclinations and philological understandings, especially on the origin-of-language question, did indeed coincide and correspond.

So, for example, early eleventh-century grammarian Abu Hilal al-'Askari's opposition to synonyms (*taraduf*) in language, in his important work *Furuq al-Lughawiyya*, was clearly based on the premise that synonyms defied a single stage of *wadʿ* and, by extension, the wisdom of the institutor of language, or the *wadiʿ al-lugha*, which of course is God. Similarly, prominent scholars like Thaʿlab and Ibn Faris also questioned the occurrence of synonyms in language for similar theologically driven reasons. Therefore, the very concept of synonyms or *taraduf* and attempts to critique it were deeply implicated in the larger theological schema of the divine origin of language. This was just one of many examples that highlighted the intimate entanglement of language and theology.

The broader point I have wished to highlight and impress through what has preceded is this: the view of language as "established by convention" was not considered *contradictory* to that of language as divinely instituted. While different scholars proffered a range of views on this matter that covered a wide spectrum, the sedimented thrust of human conventions often interacted in productive tension with the force of divine power.

Bruce Fudge, in his instructive study of a later Shiʿi scholar and exegete, al-Fadl ibn al-Hasan al-Tabrisi (d. 1154), has shed useful light on this "tension" between what he calls linguistic convention and epistemological essentialism by arguing that partly what made this tension workable was that language as established by convention was viewed as having a linear teleology that went from the Bedouins to pre-Islamic poets to the Qur'an to the language of the Arabs.[38] In other words, while language was understood to be constituted in the world, it was done so only during a particular time and by certain authorities.

A synergetic rather than oppositional understanding of the relationship between conventionalist and revelationist views on language also informed al-Radi's interpretive aesthetic. What was his opinion on the origin of language question? There is no conclusive evidence in the *Haqa'iq* that definitively answers that question. So, explicitly at least, al-Radi's discussions in the *Haqa'iq*, like Ibn Jinni's, kept separate the relationship between grammar and theology. But what is clear, however, is that al-Radi's intellectual genealogy linked him on the one hand to the conventionalist view of language through ʿAbd al-Jabbar *and* to the quasi-revelationist view through Ibn Jinni, both of whom were his teachers and mentors.[39] In the *Haqa'iq*, al-Radi draws liberally from both ʿAbd al-Jabbar and Ibn Jinni's arguments and linguistic positions. For example, his interpretive method relies heavily on Ibn Jinni's concept of linguistic etymology (roots of words and the string of related terms they generate)—a concept well in line with the conventionalist or *istilah* position. At the same time, his constant references to the "hidden secrets" of the Arabic language and his frequent marshalling of what he regarded as the subtleties of Arabic that invoke awe and wonder seem more in line with the revelationist or *tawqif* position. It appears that al-Radi's position on the origin of language may have been similar to that of Ibn Jinni's—that is, a position that combined the admission and attribution of a special, almost sacred status to the Arabic language on the one hand, with an acknowledgement of the etymological social development of that language on the other.

In al-Radi's case, the seeming disparity involved in upholding both positions simultaneously stood resolved to a certain extent by the fervent effort to circumscribe what counts as permissible and prohibited according to an authoritative linguistic canon, as we have seen through numerous examples from the *Haqa'iq* during the course of this book. By extrapolating meanings of Qur'anic ambiguities from a fixed literary canon, al-Radi argued for an unshakeable linguistic ontology. In this way, although al-Radi's approach to the Qur'an argued for a non-literal interpretation of certain verses, and invoked literary concepts like ambiguity, metaphor, metonymy, and synonymy, the clearly defined sources for his readings served to achieve a rhetorical lockdown on the ambit of hermeneutical possibilities available in the text. The ambiguities invested in revelation went together with the canonicity of the discursive field through which those ambiguities were engaged and resolved. Thus, somewhat paradoxically, ambiguity and canonicity were mutually reinforcing.

In the remainder of this chapter, I will present and analyze some more specific examples from the *Haqa'iq* that highlight the interaction of language and theology in al-Radi's thought. To be sure, the *Haqa'iq* is not a didactic treatise on language per se, as were many of the early and medieval Muslim texts discussed in this chapter so far. Yet, even while not explicitly focused on the question of language and its origins, I argue for the importance of approaching and engaging the trope of *mutashabih*, and al-Radi's discussion on ambiguity in the *Haqa'iq* specifically, not just as a tool that organizes and assembles the Qur'an's architecture or simply as an arena of polemical contestation whereby competing doctrinal claims are advanced and contested, such as for instance Ash'ari/Mu'tazili debates on anthropomorphism. Rather, as a close reading of illustrative examples from the *Haqa'iq* will show, the conceptual force of the category of "ambiguity" lies precisely in its inextricability to the very epistemic grounds on which the interpretive possibilities of the Qur'an are staged and encountered. In what follows, I will present some illustrative ways in which this intimate entanglement of ambiguity and epistemology plays out in the medieval exegetical tradition, with a focus on the work of a less studied litterateur and Qur'an exegete, al-Sharif al-Radi.

Guarding the Qur'an from the Stain of Superfluity

In what follows, I examine al-Radi's contribution to the theme of language by engaging his understanding of linguistic "ambiguity" and the work that he envisioned it to perform. Specifically, I will elaborate his conception of the very *purpose* of ambiguity in the Qur'an, beyond the task and mandate of resolving those ambiguities.

How could a revealed text that announces itself as clear and conclusive be riddled with ambiguities? This question, at the heart of the relationship between language and theology, haunts al-Radi's exegesis. Indeed, much of his Qur'an commentary is invested not only in trying to resolve the puzzle of ambiguous verses in the Qur'an; perhaps more importantly, critical to the formative motif of his project is the attempt to explain and justify the very *purpose* of ambiguity in a revealed text that by its nature is supposed to be clear and accessible. Let me turn to an example of a verse examined by al-Radi that further amplifies and clarifies this conundrum and al-Radi's approach to addressing it: Q. 3:91. It reads as follows:

Those who disbelieve and die disbelievers will not be saved *even if* they offer enough gold to fill the entire earth. Agonizing torment is in store for them, and there will be no one to help them. (*Inna alladhina kafaru wa matu wahum kuffarun falan yuqbala min ahadihim mil'ul-ardi dhahaban wa-law iftada bihi ula'ika lahum 'adhabun alimun wa ma lahum min nasirin.*)[40]

Here, al-Radi's interlocutor expresses his puzzlement by the seeming redundancy of the Arabic letter *waw* between the two clauses of this verse, as in "even if [*wa-law*] they offer enough gold to fill the entire earth."[41] Now, Arabic grammar admitted a category known as the "extra or superfluous" letters (*al-huruf al-mazida*), which was a critical tool for poets of Arabic to achieve the rhythmic harmony in the composition of their verses. Many Qur'an commentators had held that such instances in the Qur'an also represent examples of extra or superfluous letters, as they appeared in Arabic poetry. Al-Radi's interlocutor probed him about the usefulness of such a category of "excess language." In his response, al-Radi disagreed with the application of such a category on verses such as the one under question. In so doing, he advanced an important principle of eloquent speech. That principle was this: since the Qur'an constituted a text of purposeful guidance from God, it could not contain any superfluity. So, then, what explained the presence of this seemingly superfluous *waw*? Al-Radi sought to resolve this conundrum by arguing that the presence of the *waw* represented a linguistic trace for that part of a verse's meaning that was left unsaid.[42] So, for instance, in verse 39:73:

> Those who were mindful of their Lord will be led in throngs to the Garden. When they arrive, they will find its gates wide open.[43]
> *Wasiqa alladhina ittaqaw rabbahum ila-l-jannati zumaran hatta idha ja'uha wa futihat abwabuha. . . .*

The *waw* in this verse reaffirmed the occurrence of that which is left implied in the verse. Al-Radi argues that, in this case, the *waw* before the phrase *futihat* (were opened) implies that they entered paradise (*dakhaluha*).[44] As for the original verse under discussion, Q. 3:91, al-Radi argues that the purpose of the *waw* there is to clarify that the *general* attempt to turn to God at the time of one's death as an unbeliever will not be accepted by God. The presence of the *waw*, al-Radi argues, generalizes God's refusal beyond the specific instance of a group offering enough gold to fill the earth as ransom.[45] So, the *waw* is not just a superfluous prosthetic that is not adding to the intended meaning of the verse. Exactly to the contrary, it is the *waw* that lends meaning to what follows it, thus making visible a form of meaning that is otherwise absent from the apparent text of the verse. *Waw* emerges as the carrier as well as the adjudicator of ambiguity in the Qur'an. Put differently, the seeming prosthetic of the *waw* indexes the significance of ambiguity as an epistemic register intimately interwoven into the Qur'an's texture and interpretive fabric.

The above example illustrates al-Radi's attempt to convey the meaningfulness of an ambiguous instance in the Qur'anic text. But he didn't stop there. It was crucial for al-Radi to not only demonstrate the presence of meaning in each element, but to argue that ambiguity as an epistemic register and linguistic device itself carried meaning. In other words, even as al-Radi defended the ambiguities from the charge that they diminished meaning, another question loomed large: if every element of the Qur'an was infused with meaning, then what additional purpose did the property of ambiguity serve? It is to al-Radi's response to this conundrum that I now turn. We will see that critical to addressing this question is to observe that al-Radi's hermeneutical project on the ambiguous verses was not only directed at removing doubt or confusion about their meaning. Much more than that, by positioning ambiguous verses at the heart of his hermeneutical enterprise, he valorized these verses as the primary repositories of the most subtle secrets of the Qur'an, which were only accessible through the equally subtle mysteries of the Arabic language. This is how ambiguity worked as a normative hermeneutical principle in al-Radi's exegetical project and imaginary.

The Interlocking of Language and Ontology

The debate over the value of Qur'anic ambiguity was thriving among al-Radi's contemporaries, and scholars presented a variety of explanations in response to this issue. Some argued that the function of the ambiguous verses was to distinguish the learned from the masses. Others held that the presence of ambiguity in the Qur'an had been generative in enabling the emergence of numerous disciplines dedicated to deciphering meaning. Finally, some maintained that the ambiguous verses were a means through which exegetes could expend intellectual effort as they wrestled with the challenges the verses posed; overcoming these challenges served as opportunities through which they could hone not only their interpretive skills but also their relationship to the text.[46] It was along the lines of this third justification that 'Abd al-Jabbar, who, as we saw previously, was a critical figure in al-Radi's intellectual training, argued that the *mutashabih* verses were part of "acquired knowledge" as opposed to "necessary knowledge." Accordingly, his reasoning for why the *mutashabih* verses are beneficial was closely tied to the logic of the benefit of God's division of knowledge into two types: acquired and necessary. Thus 'Abd al-Jabbar emphasized that the value of ambiguity lay in the intellectual effort required in elucidating it.

Turning to al-Radi, the purpose of Qur'anic ambiguity for him was closely connected to the intimate relationship between language and ontology. Language, he explained, was a reflection of ontological reality, such that subtleties of linguistic expression represented the key through which realities of the world could subsequently be accessed and validated. The idea of such correspondence between language and ontological reality profoundly impacted the way in which early Muslim custodians of language imagined the scope of their authority and the issues that came under their jurisdiction.

Approaching language as a mirror of the social world accorded well with the intellectual ethos in Baghdad and other major centers in the Buyid Empire. For example, the grammarians of Basra, whose school came to dominate the discipline of grammar, posited a direct correlation between the words and structures of Arabic on the one hand, and the realities that they expressed on the other.[47] As a corollary to this theory, it was necessary to account for speech that departed from normative expressions. Grammatical theorizing offered a way to explain the Qur'an's many violations of the mirror character of language, including techniques such as concealment, ellipsis, indirect reference, non-apparent meaning, redundancy, repetition, inversion of word order, and figurative language. The notion of a transgressive language (*majaz*), more specifically, represented therefore a corollary to the grammarian's concept of a natural correlation between language and reality.[48]

A particularly fascinating example of the intimacy of language and ontology in al-Radi's hermeneutics is found in his discussion of verse 3:36, which reads as follows:

But when she gave birth, she said, "My Lord! I have given birth to a girl"—God knew best what she had given birth to: the male is not like the female—"I name her Mary and I commend her and her offspring to Your protection from the rejected Satan."[49]

This verse raises some pressing theological questions. For instance, how, asks the hypothetical interlocutor in al-Radi's commentary, can the verse state "the male is not like the female?" He argues that this seems to have no instructive purpose and only states the obvious. So, the question or ambiguity that emerges from this verse is how any part of the Qur'an can be redundant, since this would raise doubt about the Qur'an's rhetorical value.[50] Al-Radi's discussion is framed as a response to this charge that the revelatory text is redundant. During the course of his explanation, al-Radi drew on his understanding of language and its relationship to the realities it represents. He asserted that the name of a thing (in the language of the Arabs) can represent that which the thing aspires toward and desires to become. To paraphrase, al-Radi posits that language not only reflects fixed essences or substances, it can also convey the process of becoming. For al-Radi, this aspect is one of the subtle mysteries of language, available only to the exclusive few endowed with the ability to traverse its multiple layers of meaning.

With this context in place, al-Radi described the specific kind of male/ female difference emphasized in this verse and explained why that difference might exist. He argued that the statement "the male is not like the female" does not refer to a difference in essential traits, since that would be to state the obvious. Rather, the verse pointed to the varied social conditions that exist for males and females. These include restrictions on women to serve in the Holy Temple, because of "menstruation and childbirth and the need for her to protect her adornments from the people. And because if she were to intermingle with men, they would be seduced by her [iftatanu biha] and her status would attract them [wa istadarru bimakaniha]."[51]

Al-Radi tied this restriction to a broader generalization of women's failure to effectively fulfill social contracts. He argued that women are intellectually weaker and more feeble than men in this regard. Al-Radi connects this supposed inadequacy on the part of women to the legal stipulation that their word is not counted as equal in weight to that of men in the affair of giving testimonies. Most crucially, after establishing this variance between the sexes in the realm of social affairs, al-Radi sought to establish a correspondence between what he viewed as ontological realities and their linguistic equivalents. It is here that we most clearly find the interplay of language and ontology at work in al-Radi's hermeneutic.

Al-Radi noted that Abu al-Hasan al-Akhfash (d. 825–35), who was the student and transmitter of Sibawayh's teachings, stated that Arabs, when referring to women, say "this is a witness [shahidi]" with a masculine construction, even though they mean a woman.[52] Crucial here is al-Radi's assertion that the use of a male label for a female or the employment of the term "witness" in its masculine construction (shahidi) in place of the feminine construction (shahidati), unveils a subtle secret of the Arabic language. The secret is that, through this label, the Arabs seek to complete the deficiency in the woman's meaning by attaching a male descriptor to her. In al-Radi's view, the similarity drawn between "her" and "him" in this verse was akin to how the Arabs named a person who was stung (ladigh) as healthy (salim), and referred to the person who was destroyed (mahlaka) as victorious (mafaza).[53] Qur'an and gender studies scholar Ash Geissinger has pointed out that late medieval Muslim writings were informed by the Galenic notion of viewing free, able-bodied males as the most complete examples of what it means to be human and female bodies as deviations from this norm. Moreover, male and female bodies were thought to differ in degree rather than in kind.[54] Al-Radi's discussion corresponds to this understanding of gender, described by contemporary historians as the "one-sex body" and, most notably, he goes on to show how this reality was also reflected in the Arabic language.

Al-Radi was, of course, no different from his medieval contemporaries in his less-than-egalitarian views on male-female relations. However, the critical point to underscore here is this: al-Radi imagined the rules of language (of the Arabs) as a repository for subtle social realities. Moreover, he regarded the subtle references of language to have been perfected in the revelatory text, which, for him, demonstrated a harmonious relationship between grammatical literality and ontological reality. Each element of language, including conjunctions, prepositions, particles, and other grammatical operations, was imbued with ontologically manifested meaning. Underlying al-Radi's appreciation for these epistemological connections was the idea that language ultimately mirrored both ontological realities (incomplete female aspiring toward the complete male) as well as social realities (legal equivalence of one man with two women).

One could mention in passing that this notion of there being an intimate connection between language and the reality it represents arose in a variety of genres at the time. Al-Hakim al-Tirmidhi (d. 912), in his *al-Furuq wa Man' al-Taraduf*, for example, sought to argue that there are no synonyms in the Arabic language.[55] He did so by enumerating a hundred sixty–plus conceptual pairs that appear to be synonyms but which he argues have subtle differences between them. To elaborate these differences, he turns to the centerpiece of his argument, that individual words correspond to separate experiences or functions of a human being's internal spiritual organs: the carnal soul and the heart. Specifically, most relevant to our discussion on the inextricable relationship between language and ontology is al-Tirmidhi's analysis on differences in language that to him serve as a basis for discussing the human condition and the ills and whisperings of Satan it suffers. In short, al-Tirmidhi's text on lexicography simultaneously functions as a guide to overcoming human weakness and to cultivating a virtuous self. For al-Tirmidhi, language is the key to accessing the subtle realities and conditions of the human being.[56]

A second example that captures the extent to which language and ontology were seen as mutually intertwined is concentrated in the literary term *majaz* (metaphor)[57] and its counterpart *haqiqa* (literal reality). One instance of this coalescence of the linguistic and ontological dimensions of the *haqiqa/*

majaz dyad occurs in the work of al-Nashi' al-Akbar (d. 906), a poet and Mu'tazili theologian who made the claim that certain descriptive terms, such as "living" and "hearing," apply literally to God but only figuratively to humans.[58] Wolfhart Heinrichs has situated this intermingling of language and ontological conditions by al-Nashi' to the Basran cultural milieu, Basra being the headquarters for many prominent mystics.[59] Although Heinrichs, in his remarks about al-Nashi's application of the *haqiqa*/*majaz* relationship, does hint at the pervasive effect of ideas across boundaries set by discipline, school, and sect, he does not pursue this possibility any further. Building on Heinrichs's inkling, my examination of the interaction of *haqiqa* and *majaz* in al-Radi's work is directed at addressing how this approach constituted and was constitutive of a broader cultural and hermeneutical episteme.

Al-Radi's interpretive method also represents a confluence of multiple intellectual currents and positions, mediated by the intellectual and social milieu of Buyid Baghdad. I have demonstrated the interconnections between his work and prevailing discourses that reflected the fundamental concern of early Muslim scholars to establish the relationship between language and revelation on theological grounds. The theological demands on the text meant that al-Radi's challenge was to explain what work ambiguity performed, since, as a rhetorical feature adopted in the revelatory text, it had to be purposeful. At the same time, al-Radi's discourse on ambiguity was mediated by the fundamental theological principle of clarity, according to which it was impossible for the Qur'an to be inaccessible. Thus, the literary device of ambiguity in al-Radi's interpretive framework was regulated by an overarching linguistic canon, which limited the possibilities of meaning to an identifiable reference. Crucial to such a hermeneutical operation was the philosophical premise that language represented a mirror for reality—that language and ontology were inexorably bound. Let me conclude this analysis and argument with a final and rather dramatic example.

Language, Ontology, and Theology

A fascinating issue that al-Radi took up in the *Haqa'iq* that encapsulates the intersection of language, theology, and ontology in particularly vivid ways hovered around the following question: What kinds of speech are possible in the afterworld when the body has severed the soul? Specifically, how does the transformed ontological state of the inhabitants of hell affect the kinds of speech they are capable of uttering? The most striking feature of al-Radi's discussion was his assumption that, even in the afterworld, the laws of language remained operative and intact. Despite the death of the body, the intimacy of language and being, or language and ontology, was not disentangled.

Obviously, the question of the status of language in the afterworld was connected with the ontological status of human beings after death, a topic of considerable interest and concern for theologians and philosophers alike. In what form are human beings resurrected? Where is their identity located? How do their identities carry over after death and resurrection? Owing to these conundrums, eschatologically oriented passages in the Qur'an, in which a variety of scenes from the afterworld were depicted, thus emerged as important sites of contestation. Some passages portrayed various limbs and parts of an individual's body as key witnesses that would testify against them. Other Qur'anic passages captured the intensity and immensity of punishment in the afterworld, in the form of dramatic proclamations of regret aired by those confronting recompense for their actions in this world. In both these types of passages, the status of the physical body in the afterworld featured prominently, as did the role of speech.

One such instance in the Qur'an, which was also engaged by al-Radi in the *Haqa'iq* as a site of ambiguity, is verse 4:42. It reads as follows:

> On that day, those who disbelieved and disobeyed the Prophet will wish that the earth could swallow them up: they will not be able to hide anything from God.[60]

The key clause in the above verse is God's statement that the deniers of truth or the unbelievers (*kafirun*) will not conceal anything from God on that day. This poses an issue of Qur'anic coherence. Specifically, al-Radi's hypothetical interlocutor asks: How God could state in this verse that the unbelievers will not hide things from God when in other verses we are informed that they did in fact hide some things. For example, in verse 6:24 they exclaim: "By God, our Lord, we were not idolators," to which God replied, "See how they lie to themselves." How, then, are we to reconcile these seemingly opposed descriptions?[61]

The main problem or ambiguity reflected here is that the Qur'an appears to be contradicting itself. Concomitantly, al-Radi's goal in his discussion is to preserve the Qur'an's consistency as an eternal guide for all humankind. In signature fashion, he begins by laying out a selection of prominent and varied readings or interpretations (*wujuh*) of the verse. These interpretations alternate between a focus on the verse in question, 4:42, and the verse that seemingly contradicts it, 6:24, which was also cited by the interlocutor. For instance, according to one interpretation presented by al-Radi, the statement "they shall not conceal from God anything that has happened" (*wa-la yaktumun allaha haditha*) in 4:42 does not mean that these unbelievers in question were announcing their as yet concealed views and beliefs of their own volition or choice. To the contrary, it is God who reveals their secrets on that day and unveils their hidden matters. Al-Radi further elaborated his argument through some illustrative analogies from varied discursive domains. This statement, al-Radi reasoned, is similar to when a person says to his companion, "Hide from me what you want; by God you can't hide from me your thoughts." Or when the poet says, "Your eyes report to me what your heart conceals; you cannot cover up hatred and glares from the corner of your eyes." "Don't you see," Al-Radi continued, in his rehearsal of this argument, that the statement "your eyes report to me" indicates that such a person does not want or choose to reveal what is hidden in his heart through his eyes? But the emotion of hatred, when it appears in the corner of one's eyes, speaks with one glance as if the heart were speaking. Similarly, in this Qur'anic verse, al-Radi completed his thought—the unbelievers, much like eyes filled with hate that speak even without wanting or choosing to speak, are not able to hide things in the afterworld; their secrets are manifested and revealed by God.[62]

The next view presented by al-Radi was that of Hasan al-Basri. Al-Basri's discussion illustrated the entwinement of language and ontology in particularly fascinating ways. He argued, as narrated and tacitly endorsed by al-Radi, that the varied stages and sequences of punishment or reward in the afterworld were symmetrically aligned with corresponding articulations of sound and language. In other words, the eschatological apparatus of the afterworld was founded on language. And it is this intimacy between language and eschatology that held the key to solving the puzzle surrounding the seeming contradiction between the speech of the inhabitants of hell in verses 4:42 and 6:24. So, for instance, al-Basri explained, the moments described in these two verses corresponded with two different states and stations of the afterworld, each marked by distinct sonic qualities. For example, he elaborated, there is the place in hell marked by an astonishing absence of sound. It houses a bell that makes no sound; you hear nothing but a soft sound generated by the movement of feet. Then there is the place where one can speak and also lie. This is where the unbelievers say "we didn't commit any evil" and God replies to them, "Indeed God is all knowing of what you did." Or, when they say "By God, our Lord, we were not idolators" (6:23), God replies, "Behold how they lie against themselves, but that which they used to fabricate has forsaken them" (6:24).[63] Then there is the station where they become aware of their mistakes in the world and ask that they be returned to the world: "Would that we were sent back! Then we would not deny the signs of our Lord, but we would be among the believers!"[64] (6:27). Then there is the last station, where their mouths are finally sealed and their skins and limbs give witness of their deeds. To this dreadful scene, al-Basri adds his commentary: "God protect us from this place of shame."[65]

Striking in the eschatological portrait sketched by al-Basri is the critical role of sound in expressing the hierarchy as well as the embodied experience of punishment in the afterworld. The state and condition of the inhabitants of hell are reflected precisely by the kinds of speech they are capable of uttering. At one extreme is the station dominated by the absence of sound altogether. Then next comes a station in which the unbelievers act as hypocrites, indicated by their ability and inclination to construct false statements and lies. And, below them, al-Basri describes a group of unbelievers gripped by the pangs of remorse and regret, whose sorry state is expressed through the wish-statements (*tamanna*) or "if-only" statements they utter. And then, the most severe station, the pinnacle of punishment, if you will, involves a site where it is not *sound* that is absent but *speech*. Stripped of the ability to defend themselves through speech, it is the limbs and skins of the unbelievers that emerge as their final arbiters and witnesses. The crucial point to underscore is this: in al-Basri's scheme, the theological question of eschatological consequences in the afterworld was intimately interwoven with linguistic qualities and articulations that materially manifested those consequences. And, again, it is this synchronicity between language and theology that unraveled the puzzling ambiguities populating the Qur'an.

A similar yet different articulation of the intimacy of language and theology that al-Radi also discussed concerned the views of one of his teachers, Ibn Jinni. More specifically, al-Radi presented Ibn Jinni's reading of Qur'anic verse 43:77: "*wa nadu ya maliku li-yaqdi 'alayna rabbuka qala innakum makithun*" (They will cry, 'Malik, if only your Lord would finish us off,' but he will answer, 'No! You are here to stay.')[66] According to Ibn Jinni's reading, in this verse, the word *malik* is cut off, and simply read as *mal*, so the verse would read as "*wa nadu ya malu li-yaqdi 'alayna rabbuka*."[67] Ibn Jinni explained his interpretation as a case of what is called *tarkhim* or the "lightening/softening" of speech. But why would the speech of hell's inhabitants be muffled? Because, Ibn Jinni elaborated, they find themselves in a condition of deep anguish from the punishment they are enduring. Hence, they are incapable of properly enunciating their words. Ibn Jinni's explanation and reading caused a fair bit of consternation and controversy among his scholarly peers. In fact, in a remarkable moment, al-Radi admitted that, when he learned about Ibn Jinni's interpretation, he was doubtful about its applicability, as it seemed to go against the import of the verse that clearly included the verb "they called" or *nadu*, which does not imply a muffled sound. How could Ibn Jinni claim that the speakers' anguish dimmed their voice when, in the same instance, they were crying out loud (to Malik)? Al-Radi informed the reader that, when he brought this conundrum to Ibn Jinni, the latter, unfazed, confidently replied: "Where's the problem? Don't you know that for the occupants of hell, their punishment continues even as neither their bodies remain nor their selves? When this happens their skin is restored and their bodily strength returns, but only so they may experience suffering with embodied intensity. As God has said in his book: "Every time their skins have been burned away, We shall replace them with new ones so that they may continue to feel the pain" [4:56].[68] What exactly is the objector objecting to when [it is clear that] their [the inhabitants of hell] inability to complete the word [Malik] corresponded to the moment when they lost their bodily strength and their crying/calling out loud occurred previously during the moment that their strength had returned to them and their skins had been replaced."[69] Thus, for Ibn Jinni, there was no contradiction or cause of puzzlement in the coexistence of muffled speech and loud cries in the same instance; these bodily reactions corresponded to two distinct moments of the same verse.

Rather than endorsing or siding with Ibn Jinni's position, Al-Radi instead concluded this discussion in active ambivalence by noting without championing one over the other competing view on this matter. But what is striking in these discussions, to conclude this section, is the remarkable syncopation between language and theology that marks the thought of al-Radi, Ibn Jinni, and al-Hasan al-Basri. For the latter two, expressions and articulations of language mapped onto different states and stations in the afterworld. While al-Basri connected the soundscape of the afterworld with its eschatological hierarchy, Ibn Jinni read the language of the Qur'an with an eye on the physical experience of punishment suffered by the inhabitants of hell. Crucially, for them as for al-Radi, the mutual boundedness of language and ontology was not limited to the temporal world; it extended even to the afterworld.

This was just one of the many instances and examples outlined in this chapter that highlights the intimacy of language and theology in early Muslim intellectual thought.

The Width of Heavens

Chapter twenty-six of al-Radi's commentary focuses on verse 3:133; it centers on a rather unusual problem. Unlike previous verses, which read as familiar cases of theological and linguistic dissonances, here the questioner takes issue with a strange visual that the Qur'anic verse conjures about the mathematical dimensions of paradise. The verse reads: "Hurry towards your Lord's forgiveness and a Garden, as wide as the heavens and earth prepared for the righteous."[70] Why would paradise be described by its width (and not its length?), asks the questioner? What is the meaning of such a phrase?[71]

Like all the *mutashabih* verses, this one, too, has many possible *wujuh* or meanings. What makes this discussion a particularly useful place to observe al-Radi's hermeneutical apparatus is the way it illustrates the marrying of theology and literature in his thought. His position makes for a fascinating dialogue between poetic and theological reasoning. Let me elaborate.

First, al-Radi enumerates the views of other scholars, and I mention some of them here to show how he builds on them to climax with his own position.

The first group (Ibn 'Abbas and Hasan al-Basri, his two oft-quoted sources), resolve the issue by identifying a syntactical solution. The meaning of this verse, they argue, is that the width of paradise is "like" the width of the seven heavens and the seven earths, if they were all to be joined and flattened. Of course, the actual verse does not contain the particle "like/similar to" (*kaf*), but they justify this reading by referencing verse 57:21, which does include *kaf* (similar to), to state "the width of paradise is *similar to* the width of the heavens and earth." They argued that verse 57:21 is the root (*asl*) of the verse at hand, in that it explains why in verse 3:133, the particle *kaf* has been dropped, even as its meaning is implied. They further bolstered this position by citing other Qur'anic verses in which the particle *kaf* was dropped but the meaning still applied. So, we see that this first approach resolves the ambiguity by transforming the phrase "the width of which is [like] the heavens and the earth," into a similitude.

A second group of exegetes concerns itself with the lexical meaning of the term *al-'ard* or width itself. By identifying the meaning most suitable in this verse to be "vastness," they proceed to provide other instances from the speech of the Arabs and from Arabic poetry where al-'ard was invoked with that meaning. This included the Prophet's saying "You all went in it [the battle of Uhud] 'aridatan," meaning "the earth had the ability to contain all of you." They also reference poetic verses such as "the hand of Hajjaj can't reach me the way a fast camel reaches its victim because the earth is wide." Verse 3:133, they thus argued, was similarly using the term al-'ard in its meaning of vastness (and not width).[72]

Another view posits that this is a figure of speech, through which the speaker is able to exaggerate and emphasize the immensity of what is being described. This is to say that it is by *not* mentioning the length of paradise that God alerts us that the length is even greater than its width. It is as if to say, "If this is its width, imagine what its length would be!" Similar to this is verse 55:54, "reclining upon couches lined with brocade,"[73] in which God specifies the elevated status of the outer by pointing to the elevated status of the inner (lining of a garment), as if to say "If this is the description of the lining, imagine what the garment is like!" To sum up, for this group, the peculiarity of the Qur'anic expression that singles out width to describe greatness of size (over length) is resolved by interpreting it as an instance of purposeful rhetorical flourish.[74]

In the three interpretive stances just described, we find what one might call a syntactical solution, a lexical solution, and a rhetorical solution, respectively. The next position is different, in that while presenting an explanation for the Qur'anic phrase of heaven's width, another group of (unnamed) scholars also express a slight critique of the word choice in the phrase "the width of which is that of the heavens and the earth." Al-Radi takes immediate objection to this. Some, he explains, associate verse 3:133 with verse 41:51: "Whenever We are gracious to man, he goes away haughtily, but, as soon as evil touches him, he turns to prolonged prayer! [fa dhu du'a 'arid]"[75] They argue that, had the verse used the term "long" (tawil) instead of "broad" ('arid), it would have been clearer, since it is possible to describe something that has no width or breadth (like prayers) by its length. For example, you say "long story" (hadith tawil) or "extended speech" (kalam tawil) or "prolonged issue" (amr tawil), whereas you only really use the term 'arid when you want to suggest both length and width. Al-Radi, displaying resolute determination to refute any attempt to question the perfect eloquence of every part of the Qur'an, argues that "the term 'arid is actually more appropriate than the term tawil in describing prayers because it carries the meaning of vastness. The term tawil, on the other hand, only points to length." How does he justify this? Instead of turning to his usual literary sources, he approaches the term "length" as a technical mathematical term. Accordingly, by referencing competing theories of the line (and what these imply about the relationship between length and breadth) al-Radi supports his argument for what *tawil* means. The critical point here, for him, is that length (*tawil*) *only* points to length, irrespective of whether you adhere to the school that argues that, in a line, the length is separate from breadth, or whether you adhere to the school that prohibits the occurrence of length without breadth, where the line is as per its breadth. In sum, mentioning width implies a mention of length, whereas had the verse only said length, this meaning of length would not have been communicated.

After presenting these varied explanations, al-Radi shares a different question that was asked in relation to this verse. The question, he tells us, was posed by Hercules, leader of Rome, to the Prophet: "We heard that you invite to a paradise, the width of which is like the heavens and the earth. [If this is so] then where is hell?"[76] The problem being expressed here is that, if the heavens and the earth (in their width) cover all space, this leaves no room for hell. The Prophet replied: "Glory be to God! When the day comes, where is the night?" Al-Radi triumphantly asserts that this fitting reply dealt a blow to the question and its questioner because He who has the power to make the day go as He pleases has the power to make hell as He pleases.

Al-Radi then cites another report in which the polytheists pose a similar query to the Prophet about the location of paradise, if its width was equivalent to the heavens and the earth. Al-Radi explains that in response God revealed verse 36:81 to cut right through the antagonists' question. In this verse it is asked who will give life to the bones when they die, and God replies: "Is He who created the heavens and earth not able to create the likes of these people? Of course He is!"[77] Al-Radi explains that, through the verse, God conveys the point that his "giving life to the dead and returning of mortal remains is not more wondrous than the extraction of fire from green trees, and in this way He combines the burnt with the green and blessed be God, the Lord of the Worlds." Once again, al-Radi celebrates this reply to the polytheists, arguing that "God can create paradise above the heavens and hell under the earth or He can increase the width of the heavens and earth and place paradise or hell there, and the vastness of paradise could be the dimensions of the vastness of the heavens and the earth before He adds to them." Ultimately, al-Radi's point in citing these verses and reports is to argue for the continuity and infinitude of God's power. He further clarifies:

This is the meaning of the Prophet's analogy [*tashbih*] of the heavens and hell with the day and night. The day is an expression for the time when the sun is visible without any obstruction and the veil is removed from it and night is an expression for the times when the sun is invisible and its light is eclipsed; and it is known when the sun rotates, day happens and becomes night in the end; so, there is no interruption in God's power and it is the same with heaven [*janna*] and hell [*nar*; literally, fire].[78]

Here, notice how a question about the physical arrangement of the different elements that make up the material world is resolved for al-Radi—through poetic means. The prophet's striking of a similitude between objects of time and space is a powerful and more-than-sufficient answer for al-Radi to an otherwise rather concrete, empirically grounded question. Through language, the prophet's similitude challenges a finite, temporal conception of time and space (day/night, this life/hereafter). Most intriguingly, al-Radi's explanation of the Prophet's analogy suggests that time occupies a visible space in the eye/mind of the human being. Two visuals of time (day/night) are staged in the phenomenal world, making it appear that they are part of a linear sequence, one proceeding after the other. But the truth, as we understand from al-Radi's explanation, is that in reality there is no such distinction between night and day and that they both always exist. The same, he seems to suggest, is the case for heaven and hell. What makes this line of argument particularly illumining is that it presents the question (Where is the space for hell?) as one that makes sense only if we imagine time and space from within the parameters of a finite, limited, human understanding. But none of these limits apply to God's power.

Conclusion

The question of the origin of language, as well as that of how one ought to understand and resolve ambiguous verses, operated at the nexus of language and theology. However, I sought to show in this chapter that the relationship between language and theology was not always predictable or predetermined, much as that between sectarian identity and Qur'an exegesis is often not, as this book has argued throughout. Affiliation to particular theological schools was not always a definite guide to one's language philosophy, even if some correspondence between the two was commonly found. Ultimately, what this chapter has tried to show and argue is that in early Islam (and perhaps even later), the problem of the Qur'an's ambiguous verses was not only deeply theological. Moreover, at stake in it was precisely the question of how one imagined and approached the relationship and entanglement of language and theology. Beyond sectarian identity, theology and theological dispositions represented another critical discursive site intimately connected to the conundrum of identifying and resolving ambiguity in the Qur'an.

What one made of ambiguity in divine speech depended on how one conceived the encounter of language or speech and representations of divine authority or theology. This enticingly simple proposition contains many layers of theological, linguistic, and hermeneutical complexities, which I have labored to demonstrate. In this chapter, I examined in some detail specific moments and case studies from al-Radi's exegesis, while sketching a broad picture of the intimacy of language and theology in early Muslim thought. In the next chapter, I continue this theme but with a much more specific focus: a comparative analysis between the exegetical temperaments and choices of al-Radi and his famous Mu'tazili teacher, Qadi 'Abd al-Jabbar. By juxtaposing their exegetical labors, I will argue against a commonplace tendency to view the work of Shi'i Qur'an commentators, especially from this period, as products of Mu'tazili "influence." How might we rethink intellectual relationships such as that of al-Radi's with 'Abd al-Jabbar in ways more nuanced and less predetermined than what the narrative frame of Mu'tazili influence over Shi'ism allows for? This is the central question that animates the following chapter, occupied with further close readings of al-Radi's Qur'an exegesis, but this time in close conversation with the thought and exegesis of Qadi 'Abd al-Jabbar.

CHAPTER 6

Is the *Haqa'iq* a Mu'tazili-Shi'i *Tafsir*?

In a famous polemical treatise aimed at discounting the beliefs of the Imami Shi'i school, fourteenth-century Hanbali scholar Taqi al-Din Ahmad Ibn Taymiyya wrote:

> As for their [Rafidi] reference to reasoning [*nazar*] and rationality [*'aqliyyat*], the later generation of Rafidis relied on [*i'tamadu 'alayh*] the works of the Mu'tazila [for it] and agreed with them on the issues of [God's] Attributes and [human] capacity. In general, the Mu'tazila are more intelligent and truthful. . . .[1]

> It is known that the Mu'tazilites are at the root of this thesis [of God's justice and human freedom] and that the shaykhs of the Rafidites such as al-Mufid, al-Musawi, al-Karajaki and others merely took it [*akhadhu dhalika*] from the Mu'tazila. For the rest, none of this is found in the discussions of the early Shi'is.[2]

The underlying logic in Ibn Taymiyya's assertions can be summarized as follows: because the principles of reason and speculation in the work of later Shi'i scholars were borrowed from the Mu'tazilis, this confirms the inherent inadequacy of the *original* Shi'i belief framework.

Ibn Taymiyya was not the first to level such a charge against the later generation of Twelver Shi'i scholars. Even prior to him, Imami Shi'i scholars were often pejoratively labeled as "takers" of what were deemed as originally Mu'tazili ideas. Writing in the tenth century, for example, the leading Imami scholar of this period, al-Shaykh al-Mufid (al-Radi's teacher), defended himself from a similar accusation of unoriginality. He urged that Mu'tazili teachings were *not* the inspiration for the rational basis of Imami theology. Rather, al-Mufid insisted, it was the sayings of the Shi'i Imams (*hadith*) that endorsed and legitimized the importance of rational inquiry.[3] At stake in Ibn Taymiyya's charge of taking/borrowing and al-Shaykh al-Mufid's defense of ownership was the authority of the Twelver Shi'i Imams and the coherence of Imami theology as a whole. This was so because, according to Imami doctrine, the knowledge of the Imams was passed down through an uninterrupted chain, from God to the Prophet to the Imams. Thus, any suggestion of "external influence" from the Mu'tazili school effectively undermined the fundamental tenet of divinely designated and continual guidance. But, regardless of what one makes of Ibn Taymiyya's claim of Mu'tazili influence over Shi'i exegesis and the varied affirmative or critical responses to that claim, it does open up the potentially productive question of how one should interrogate, evaluate, and assess the very concept of influence between and across different exegetical traditions. This question of influence, in relation to the encounter between Mu'tazili and Shi'i Imami exegetical traditions, forms the focus of this chapter. The question or problem I want to address is this: How might we be able to complicate generalized narratives of influence while thinking about the relationship between Shi'i and Mu'tazili exegesis, without completely dismissing often-visible forms of such influence, either?

The "Rationalization Thesis" in Contemporary Euro-American Scholarship

The competing claims of Ibn Taymiyya and al-Shaykh al-Mufid outlined above do not fall outside the bounds of characteristically polemical exchanges between different schools of thought in early Islam. Yet, a peculiar similarity exists between writings of traditional premodern scholars like Ibn Taymiyya and al-Shaykh al-Mufid and some works in current Euro-American scholarship on the history of early Imami Shi'ism. More specifically, the language used in recent works to describe the relationship between Imami Shi'is and Mu'tazilis echoes Ibn Taymiyya's early contention that Imami scholars in the tenth and eleventh centuries were subject to Mu'tazili influence. Martin McDermott's remarks on al-Shaykh al-Mufid represent a case in point:

> When the full history of Imamite theology comes to be written, it will be a story of growth in successive dialogue and contact with a

variety of voices from inside and outside the Shi'ite community. For a brief moment in its development, Imamite *kalam* was strongly influenced by Baghdadi Mu'tazili thought. That was during the few years when the leading Imamite thinker was Abu 'Abd Allah Muhammad b. Muhammad Ibn al-Nu'man, al-Shaykh al-Mufid (d. 1022).[4]

McDermott's view reflects a prevailing assumption that governs studies on early Shi'i history. This assumption can be termed as the "rationalization thesis." Central to this thesis is the view that Imami Shi'i scholars borrowed ideas and ways of reasoning from the Mu'tazilis and supplemented them with what constituted an "original," or "pre-Mu'tazili-influenced," Shi'i theology. According to this narrative, the turning point in the tradition of Shi'i thought allegedly occurred in the tenth century and signified an enduring paradigm shift in the school's overarching epistemology. Scholars of this period are accordingly acknowledged as the chief architects of what was to become the normative Shi'i stance on theological, hermeneutical, and juridical issues. The critical shift in their approach, namely that of explaining key Imami precepts through rational inquiry is characterized in contemporary scholarship as the "rationalization of Imami Shi'i thought" under the "influence" of the Mu'tazilites.[5] Robert Gleave, in his overview of studies on early Shi'ism, explains that the authors he surveys generally agree that there is a *disjuncture* between the theological system of the early Shi'is and of their later counterparts. He points out that this acceptance "pre-supposes the notion of doctrinal development between the time of the Imams and the so-called rationalization of Imami Shi'ism, which is often dated to the mid to late tenth century in Baghdad."[6]

Objects of Rationalization

Before delving into the arguments of specific proponents of the rationalization thesis, it is instructive to note what the *objects* were, which, according to the scholars Gleave surveys, underwent rationalization in Shi'i thought. The first such object was the Shi'i conception of the Imams and the nature of their religious authority. On this point, scholars argue that the Imams were first imagined as millennial figures with chiliastic themes, but then later rationalized or emasculated into more human characters.[7] The second *object* of rationalization is the Imami-Shi'i hermeneutic, or the extent to which 'aql (reason) was given equal or superior status to al-sam' (revelation) as a source of knowledge. According to the rationalization thesis, this method of deriving meaning stood in contrast to an earlier tradition that privileged the transmitted tradition of the Qur'an and sayings of the Prophets and Imams (naql) as the only authoritative sources of knowledge.[8]

These two objects of rationalization, namely the Twelver school's view of the Imams and their overarching epistemology, were closely connected. From early on, the Imams were synonymously referred to as the "speaking Qur'an," a title that affirmed their pivotal role as interpreters of what was otherwise a "silent" Qur'anic text.[9] The underlying idea here was that the lives of the Imams mirrored the teachings of the textual canon. What the rationalization of a previous Shi'i epistemology and hermeneutic hence entailed was a shift in the way to *access* Imami knowledge. Whereas the earlier approach had been to only cite the sayings of the Imams and let them speak for themselves, now their sayings had to be legitimized through human rational inquiry. Most importantly, according to the banner-bearers of the rationalization thesis, this emphasis on rational inquiry was a product of the Mu'tazili influence on Shi'i thought, an assumption that I question and interrogate further in the discussion that follows.[10]

Interrogating the Hyphen in the Descriptor "Mu'tazili-Shi'i"

The rationalization thesis is not limited to a small circle of scholars, but rather finds echoes in the work of multiple authors who otherwise take different positions on the history of early Shi'i history. Two influential voices in this field are Etan Kohlberg and Wilferd Madelung. It is helpful to note how the rationalization thesis is reinforced in each of their works, despite variations in their broader arguments.

In the study of early Imami history, the scholar whose theory of Mu'tazili influence on Shi'ism has arguably been the most influential is Etan Kohlberg.[11] As Robert Gleave has pointed out, the various writings of Kohlberg involve a definitive examination of the doctrinal development between the time of the Imams and the so-called rationalization of Imami Shi'ism, dated mid-to-late tenth-century Baghdad.[12] Kohlberg's writings on this question of rationalization focus on two main themes: the doctrine of occultation (of the twelfth Imam)[13] and the conception of the Imams as it evolved from viewing them as superhuman figures to ultra-rational guides. Kohlberg's chief goal is to demonstrate that the Imamite doctrine on the occultation of the twelfth Imam was a later development, one that was not present in early Shi'i writings. It is in trying to trace the genealogy of this doctrine that Kohlberg argued that the eleventh century marked the onset of a large-scale rationalization movement that swept through the Imami scholarly community and culminated in the formulation of rational explanations for doctrines such as the occultation of the twelfth Imam.

Limits of Social Constructionism

My objective in bringing attention to the framework of Kohlberg's study is not to deny an overall shift in the tone of Imami writings on certain doctrines like the occultation. Neither do I intend to undermine the value of studies that examine the sociopolitical context in which specific doctrinal elements emerged. Yet, I argue that the very task and ambition of unmasking the social underpinnings of religious dogma by revealing its chain of "influences" is conceptually unsound. As Ian Hacking points out in his provocative interrogation of "social constructionism," the exercise of demonstrating the construction of a certain idea is highly selective, thereby according certain ideas positions of importance—even if the objective is to illustrate how the same ideas are essentially social constructs.[14]

Kohlberg's study of the early history of Imami thought adopts precisely such a social constructionist approach that reinforces a conceptual history of select concepts without critically examining the value and politics of that selection.[15] For example, Kohlberg's theory of the rationalist turn in Imami thought hinges on the objectification of concepts like "occultation" and "Imamology" so that their origins could be documented and traced. Apart from its uncritical historicism, Kohlberg's narrative of influence is also problematic in the way it is informed by a heresiographical framework. The very concepts he chooses to interrogate are ones that might distinguish Shi'ism from its Sunni "other." Thus, Kohlberg's genealogical approach to mapping the history of these doctrines betrays an underlying attitude toward Imami thought as a phenomenon that stands external to the boundaries of a predetermined "orthodoxy." His approach is symptomatic of a larger tendency in the study of early Islamic history to assume that the categories of orthodoxy and heterodoxy are readily available for disciplinary canonization. As a corollary, such studies perpetuate the unsound assumption that religious identities represent distinct, predetermined, and closed-off entities. In the study of Shiʿism, this approach takes the form of replicating characteristically heresiographical framings of religious identities and their relationships, much like that of Ibn Taymiyyaʾs theory of Muʿtazili "influence" on the Imami Shiʿi school.

An attempt to modify Kohlbergʾs theory of Muʿtazili influence is found in the work of Wilferd Madelung, who, despite claiming a bumpier start to the Muʿtazili-Imami relationship, continued to maintain the view that, eventually, their relations stabilized and Muʿtazili influence prevailed. In making his case, Madelung invoked the work of Shiʿis who had objected to the incorporation of Muʿtazili doctrines and to the Muʿtazili principle of championing reason above transmitted reports (*hadith*). Madelung argued that this initial resistance to Muʿtazilite thought on the part of Shiʿi scholars shows that the "rationalization of Imami Shiʿism" was not a smooth and seamless process.[16] However, Madelungʾs revisionary thesis did nonetheless embrace the fundamental assumption that Muʿtazili ideas held considerable sway over those Imami Shiʿi scholars whose position would eventually come to represent the "orthodox" Shiʿi view. In assembling this argument, Madelung presented what might be termed as an "origin story" for Muʿtazili influence over Shiʿism. He observed that it was two members of the prestigious Imami Nawbakht family, Abu Sahl Ismaʿil (d. 923) and his nephew al-Hasan ibn Musa (d. between 912 and 922), who emerged as the founders of the first doctrinal school that truly amalgamated Muʿtazili theology with Imamite doctrine.[17] He further argued that evidence of this rationalizing trend confirms the early origins of the traditionist/rationalist (*akhbari/usuli*) divide among Imami scholars, a divide that resurfaces much later under the Safavid dynasty in the late sixteenth century. Implicit in this narrative is the assumption that religious doctrines and the identities invested in those doctrines represent objects whose origins and movement in time can be readily discovered, mapped, and empirically situated in a linear fashion. Therefore, following this logic, the rationalization of Shiʿi thought that began in the tenth century seamlessly resurfaced in sixteenth-century Safavid Iran. While their specific arguments were varied, both Kohlberg and Madelung shared a common conceptual apparatus that viewed the development and maturation of Shiʿi doctrine through the prism of Muʿtazili influence.[18]

Rethinking Religious Identity

The approach of Kohlberg and Madelung to early Shi'i history brings attention to the persistence of the "Mu'tazili influence" thesis in contemporary scholarship. I have sought to argue that what is neglected in such approaches to the study of Imami Shi'i history is a critical examination of the underlying theory of religious identity on which they rest. As we have seen, both contemporary and premodern scholars have made competing claims about the continuity and coherence of Imami Shi'i thought. Ibn Taymiyya, Kohlberg, and Madelung, for example, all argue for a rupture in the history of Imami thought and emphasize how fundamental Imami doctrines changed over time, especially under the influence of Mu'tazili scholars. On the other hand, al-Shaykh al-Mufid, and traditional Imami scholars today argue for a steady continuity in Imami thought that traces a firm and unbroken chain to its origin in the teachings of the Prophet and the Imams.

Yet, there is an important difference between these temporally distant discourses despite the similar rhetoric they employ in their arguments. The earlier characterization of Imami Shi'i thought as "borrowed" sprung from a need to discredit the authenticity of the Imami school by exposing the limitations of Imami teachings. Crucial here is that the object borrowed, that is, "a rationalizing tendency," was not in itself privileged as epistemologically superior in these polemical exchanges. Rather, al-Shaykh al-Mufid's motivation was to argue for the completeness, coherence, and autonomy of Imami theology, such that it had no need or demand for inspiration from outside the tradition of its own authorities. By contrast, I argue that what frames the Mu'tazili influence thesis of contemporary scholars today are the twin binaries of orthodoxy/heterodoxy and rational/irrational. In other words, the impulse to give credit to the more reasoned and rationalized elements of Imami Shi'i thought to an external "other" that eventually subdued the more erratic and supernaturally inclined tendencies inherent to an "original" Imami-Shi'ism perpetuates the orthodoxy/heterodoxy binary. In the process, it also reinforces a post-Enlightenment equation of orthodox or authentic religion with rationalism and the eclipse of the supernatural. This approach is problematic not least because it assumes a seamless correlation between the Mu'tazili emphasis on speculative reason and post-Enlightenment concerns for a moderated religiosity, erroneously assuming that the genealogies of "reason" in Mu'tazili theology perfectly correspond with modern understandings of this concept.[19]

My concern in this discussion is not to argue for a particular *direction* or *chronology* of influence (from the Muʻtazilis to the Shiʻis or vice versa). Moreover, I am also not arguing that crucial intellectual linkages between the Muʻtazili and Imami scholars in the tenth and eleventh centuries did not exist. My contention, rather, is that contemporary narratives of Imami-Muʻtazili relations are shaped by and indeed rooted in early debates surrounding the authenticity (or lack thereof) of the Imami-Shiʻi sect. In what follows, I move away from the stifling horizons of a theory that posits relations of "influence" and instead probe the possibilities of how to interpret the hyphen that simultaneously connects yet disconnects the Muʻtazili and Shiʻi schools of thought. In doing so, I seek to excavate those aspects of the relationship that the placement of a neat hyphen might conceal.

Let me first offer some preliminary words having to do with the very conceptual labor of examining the question of influence between two separate but overlapping intellectual and sectarian discursive fields. In other words, what are the avenues of inquiry or sorts of questions that one should pose to render such a task productive? First, it is useful as a point of departure to conceive of these cross-sectarian and cross-intellectual relationships as more nuanced and complex than the kind of picture of these relationships that the assumption of self-contained identities might generate. Put differently, one ought to rethink and ideally disturb the often-assumed distinction and neat separation between the self and other by approaching these entities as interlocked in an unpredictable dynamic of exchange and encounter. Second, how should we account for the internal heterogeneity of individual traditions while embarked on the project of comparison and evaluation of impact and influence? For instance, to be more specific, which Muʻtazili thinkers does one consider as the yardstick for measuring Muʻtazili thought and why? How does one demarcate and differentiate the center of a tradition from its periphery when such distinctions are ever fluid and often variable over time? And third, while examining the impact of an exegetical tradition or set of scholars over another tradition, what measures or yardsticks of impact does one privilege? Is it the presence of shared interpretive frameworks and arguments? Is it shared references and proof texts? Or will it be the presence of common teachers and intellectual lineage? I will take up these questions by examining the connections between al-Radi's *Haqa'iq* and its relationship to select works authored by Muʻtazili scholars.

Heterological Classifications of al-Radi and the *Haqa'iq*

Having demonstrated the pervasiveness of the theory that posits an inextricable link between the Mu'tazili and Imami scholars in the tenth and eleventh
centuries, it is not surprising to note that current studies classify a scholar of
al-Radi's stripe as a "Mu'tazili-Shi'i" figure. Although there exists to date no
sustained analysis of al-Radi's exegetical work, the *Haqa'iq* has received mention in a few recent studies in English.

Andrew Rippin, in an encyclopedia entry on *tafsir* (exegesis), briefly lists
al-Radi's *Haqa'iq* under the group of works that take a "theological approach
to the Qur'an." He states that al-Radi's work provides "a thorough-going
emphasis on a certain theological perspective."[20] In this short entry, Rippin
does not explain if his assessment comes from the fact that al-Radi's work
was an isolated study of the *mutashabih al-Qur'an* (ambiguous verses)—an
exegetical approach characteristic of Mu'tazili scholars—or if it was based on
the theological nature of the topics that concerned al-Radi in his work, such
as the preservation of God's justice and unity. It seems that by "theological"
Rippin is referring to a concern for the fundamental principles of a formal
theological school like that of the Mu'tazilis or Imami Shi'is. It is useful to
clarify what the term *kalam* comprises in this context, in terms of the topics
and themes it encompasses. This is particularly important, because the term
kalam and its most usual English translation "dialectical theology" are not
equivalent. In a recent analysis of the cosmological framework of the Basran Mu'tazili school, Alnoor Dhanani explains that "*kalam* does differ from
theology (at least as theology is commonly understood) in several respects.
One of these is its subject matter, which includes several topics, for example
logic, epistemology, cosmology, and anthropology, which properly belong to
philosophy (in its classic and broadly construed sense)." Moreover, he argues
that because the *mutakallimun* (theologians) regarded their discipline to be a
philosophical metaphysics, they were the intellectual rivals of the *falasifa* or
representatives of the Neoplatonized Aristotelian tradition. Dhanani argues
that the disdain with which the *falasifa* saw the *mutakallimun*, as apologet-
ics in the service of Islam, has unfortunately been adopted by several modern students of Islamic intellectual history. Dhanani is critical of this narrow
understanding of the role and concern of the *mutakallimun*, as, according to
him, it "fails to take into account the actual historical context within which
kalam was pursued. Moreover, it disregards the perspective of *mutakallimun*

themselves and ignores the non-theological aspects of their writings, which, in the early period were significant."[21] It is unclear whether Rippin's characterization of al-Radi's work as a "theological approach" has taken into account this expanded definition of theology.

Similarly, in his chapter-length study of al-Radi's Qur'anic hermeneutic, Mahmoud Ayoub concludes by referring to al-Radi as a "Mu'tazili-Shi'i" scholar.[22] There is, however, nothing in Ayoub's preceding discussion on al-Radi's exegetical style and literary overtures that sufficiently explains what Ayoub intends by the classification "Mu'tazili-Shi'i." The reader is left to infer that the link between these two schools of thought was but a natural one.

Both authors (Rippin and Ayoub) situate al-Radi and the *Haqa'iq* within an intellectual tradition linked to the Mu'tazili school of thought while still maintaining his distinct identity as an Imami Shi'i scholar. Let us examine more carefully possible reasons that would justify classifying al-Radi as a Mu'tazili-Shi'i scholar.

Al-Radi's Mu'tazili Links: Qadi 'Abd al-Jabbar

According to the biographical sources, al-Radi's main teachers for Mu'tazili ideas included the leading Imami theologian al-Shaykh al-Mufid, with whom al-Radi's mother entrusted both her sons for their education at an early age, after the death of their father. Also among al-Radi's most important teachers was the leading eleventh century Shafi'i Mu'tazili theologian Qadi 'Abd al-Jabbar. Al-Mufid himself studied with the Baghdadi line of Mu'tazili scholars and 'Abd al-Jabbar with the Basran.[23] The main difference between these two schools is the degree to which scholars accorded "reason" a prominent place in the hermeneutical exercise.[24] Although there were still some cases where the Baghdad school upheld the necessary recourse to revelation, the Basran school accorded reason a much more autonomous and decisive role. So al-Mufid, for example, "rejected the cardinal Mu'tazili position that the basic truths of religion can and must be discovered by reason alone, and he insisted that transmitted revelation (*sam'*) is indispensable for reason to gain religious knowledge."[25] In al-Radi's discussions in the *Haqa'iq*, there is no explicit mention of his teacher al-Mufid; 'Abd al-Jabbar, on the other hand, is cited frequently, as one among a host of scholarly sources on any particular issue.

It is not only al-Radi's teachers that connect him to the Mu'tazili school of thought. The very task of focusing on the ambiguous verses for the purpose of explication has been described as a characteristically Mu'tazili enterprise motivated by the need to offer alternate explanations for Qur'anic statements that, when read literally, carried anthropomorphic connotations. While the Mu'tazilites were not the first group to argue for a softening of the anthropomorphic expressions of God's person, they were the first to develop a hermeneutic on the basis of that premise by applying it to all verses of the Qur'an.[26] As a result, this style developed into a genre where, instead of explaining each and every verse in the Qur'an, it was common to elucidate only those verses that required clarification. As attested in the *Fihrist* (catalogue) of Ibn Nadim, several Mu'tazili scholars had titles under the name *mutashabih al-Qur'an*.[27] Most notably, al-Radi's teacher Qadi 'Abd al-Jabbar also composed a Qur'an commentary focused on the task of clarifying the ambiguous verses in the text. It bears the simple name *Mutashabih al-Qur'an*.[28]

It is due to the shared features and lineages of al-Radi and 'Abd al-Jabbar that I have chosen to compare their commentaries on the *mutashabihat*. This is to say that I have chosen two scholars whose works would be most susceptible to being explained through a relationship of "influence," precisely in order to question the conceptual purchase of such an explanation. Al-Radi and 'Abd al-Jabbar were connected through the intellectual bond of a teacher-disciple relationship and also by virtue of their individual attempts to identify and explain the ambiguous verses of the Qur'an. Moreover, the very impetus for the specialized genre of commentaries dedicated to the *mutashabihat* is, as mentioned above, often hailed as a Mu'tazili enterprise. Thus, al-Radi's very contribution to this genre might be reason enough to describe his work as markedly Mu'tazili.

I argue that, on the contrary, it remains problematic to characterize al-Radi's work simply as a product of "Mu'tazili influence." I instead posit that the presence of certain Mu'tazili figures in his intellectual genealogy does not translate into a relationship of unfiltered influence from Mu'tazili thought. While acknowledging the cross-pollination of Shi'i and Mu'tazili thought, it is critical to carefully unpack important points of commonality and disjuncture between these schools in relation to Qur'an exegesis. The objective of such an exercise should be neither to establish Mu'tazili influence over Shi'i exegesis nor to uncover an authentic Shi'ism cleansed from external influences. Rather, what is required is a careful reading of how Shi'i exegetes engaged and wrestled with important themes and questions brought into view by Mu'tazili thought. That is precisely what I attempt in the following section, by undertaking a comparative analysis of al-Radi's Qur'an hermeneutics in the *Haqa'iq* with that of his Mu'tazili teacher Qadi 'Abd al-Jabbar. The juxtaposition of these two important works reveals important moments of overlap and dissonance between Shi'i and Mu'tazili traditions of Qur'an exegesis in early Islam.

There is a further point that should be made here. Al-Radi was certainly not the only Shi'i scholar in early Islam and, of course, 'Abd al-Jabbar and the Bahshamiyya branch[29] of Mu'tazili thought reflected in his writings are certainly not representative of the entire Mu'tazili tradition. So, what if we were to bring other Mu'tazili thinkers and exegetes perhaps lesser known than 'Abd al-Jabbar but who yet serve as critical nodes of the Mu'tazili exegetical tradition into the conversation regarding this central question of Shi'i-Mu'tazili intellectual encounters on the issue of the Qur'an's ambiguous moments? What we find is the presence of different but equally striking and unpredictable forms of overlap as well as divergence. For instance, al-Radi's signature recourse to language, namely the literary canon (which to him was constituted by the authoritative sources of Qur'anic speech, Bedouin speech, and Arabic poetry) is found in strikingly similar forms in the works of other Mu'tazili figures writing on the *Mutashabih al-Qur'an* like the tenth-century thinker Ibn al-Khallal al-Basri (d. after 988), who was a student of Ibn al-Ikhshid (d. 938),[30] or al-Turaythithi (d. tenth century), a contemporary of 'Abd al-Jabbar. At times, the way al-Radi and these Mu'tazili thinkers discuss the semiotic potential of a particular term is directed toward the same interpretive or theological argument that is also advanced in the context of the same verse. But, yet, on other occasions, a similar linguistic assumption or argument is mobilized to assemble an altogether different exegetical point. Examples of this conflicting tendency are numerous; let me highlight just a couple.

For instance, in their interpretation of verse 3:178, one observes a remarkable resemblance between al-Radi's and Ibn al-Khallal's exegetical writings.[31] One finds in their works noticeable convergence in the forms of evidence and reasoning they marshal to buttress their linguistic arguments such as their mobilization of the same fragments of poetry and their recourse to linguistic concepts like prepositions as the key to the resolution of the ambiguity in verse 3:178 that I had discussed in some detail in Chapter 3.

Similar convergences of focus on linguistic qualities of individual words and explicit investment in resolving or addressing Qur'anic ambiguities through language can be discerned if one juxtaposes al-Radi's exegesis with the more thematic (rather than verse-by-verse exegetical) text of al-Turaythihi, also titled *Mutashabih al-Qur'an*.[32] For example, in al-Turaythithi's chapter on those Qur'anic verses that raise the question of whether it is possible for humans to "see" God, he argues for the distinction between the terms *ru'ya* and *nazar* and defends his views by turning to examples from what he regarded were the authoritative sources of Arabic poetry, Bedouin speech, and the Qur'an, the same sources that al-Radi also considered most authoritative and constitutive of the literary canon. In fact, al-Radi shared important interpretive strategies with al-Turaythihi in his own efforts to unpack the *ru'ya/nazar* distinction in the context of a different Qur'anic verse (verse 3:143). But the specific ambiguity that al-Radi set out to resolve was quite different: whether it was possible for Muslims fighting in battle to "see" their deaths. But, moreover and more fundamentally, what the very category of *mutashabih* meant to al-Turaythithi also differed significantly from what it did to al-Radi or, for that matter, 'Abd al-Jabbar. For al-Turaythithi, the source of ambiguity enwrapping *mutashabih* verses lay not so much in the multiplicity of meanings connected to those verses but rather the inconclusive nature of the purpose or wisdom inhering in them (*gharad wa hikma*). So, for him, examples of verses belonging to the category of *mutashabih* include verses that, for instance, discuss the final hour or the nature of God's promises, etc. This leads him to the position that the people referenced as *al-rasikhun fi al-'ilm*, or the firm in knowledge in the iconic verse 3:7 are not privy to *ta'wil* of the *mutashabih*. *Ta'wil* here for him of course refers not to meaning in general, but to the underlying purpose or intent of a given verse. This section in al-Turaythithi contrasts significantly with the same passages in al-Radi and the tenth-century Mu'tazili thinker al-Hakim al-Jishumi (d. 1101), for example, both of whom take this verse as a divine affirmation for the privileged interpretive authority of the *'ulama'*. Again, the patterns of overlap or divergence are neither predictable nor predetermined so as to render amenable generalized narratives or theories of influence.

Now, on examining the thought of other scholars from the Imami Shi'i and Mu'tazili schools beyond those I have touched on here, one may find significantly more or less overlap in their works. But, again, this possibility does not mean that such appropriation must reflect a process of influence and absorption. My larger argument, thus, is that the category of influence makes it seem as if intellectual exchange is always stable and predictable, so that the instance, magnitude, and direction of that influence might be readily identified and measured. But, as we have seen, the act of drawing on the thought of another scholar tends to be a process far too dynamic and elastic to be captured through the prism of the category of influence. Moreover, the language of influence operates under a problematic assumption about the constitution of religious identities. Namely, that the religious identities of both the subject and object of influence are already fully constituted and demarcated and, hence, readily available to "influence" and "be influenced." I would like to suggest that curbing the desire to locate agents and recipients of influence might open more productive avenues of engaging the topic of Qur'anic ambiguity in early Islam. For instance, instead of determining relations of influence, it might be more profitable to explore the multivalent intellectual as well as political conditions and currents that generate and make possible particular forms of discourse at particular historical conjunctures.

Structural Differences Between al-Radi's
Haqa'iq and 'Abd al-Jabbar's *Mutashabih*

While only a single volume of al-Radi's commentary, *Ḥaqa'iq al-ta'wil*, has survived, in it he devoted three hundred pages to the third sura of the Qur'an, *Al 'Imran*. 'Abd al-Jabbar's work, *Mutashabih al-Qur'an*, consists of two volumes, of which he devotes thirty-eight pages to *Al 'Imran*. For each verse examined, 'Abd al-Jabbar offers approximately three lines of discussion and al-Radi close to ten pages. To be sure, these numbers are in no way absolute, not only because there is often cross-referencing within a single text but also because their discussions on the same verses spill over into their other writings, as well.[33]

Structurally, a major difference between 'Abd al-Jabbar and al-Radi's discussions is that 'Abd al-Jabbar singles out verses that fulfill two different conditions: ambiguous verses that raise questions or dilemmas (*masa'il* sing. *mas'ala*) and verses that serve as doctrinal proofs (*dala'il* sing. *dalala*). Of the two hundred verses in *Al 'Imran*, 'Abd al-Jabbar identifies eighteen as proof verses and thirty-two as ambiguous. On the other hand, al-Radi only discusses ambiguous verses, of which he identifies thirty-one. Between the thirty-two ambiguous verses in *Al 'Imran* that 'Abd al-Jabbar selects and the thirty-one that al-Radi selects, only eleven are shared between them. In Figure 3, below, I have identified and described the ambiguities and doctrinal proofs discussed by al-Radi and 'Abd al-Jabbar in their respective texts. The shaded areas represent the common ambiguous verses engaged by them. Readers interested in attaining a better grasp of the ambiguities and doctrinal proofs presented here will benefit from visiting the precise Qur'anic verses in question.

Figure 3. Convergences and Divergences between al-Radi and 'Abd al-Jabbar

A List of Sura Al 'Imran's Ambiguous Verses (*masa'il*) and Doctrinal Proof Verses (*dala'il*) in:	
Al-Radi's *Haqa'iq al-Tawil fi Mutashabih al-Tanzil*	**'Abd al-Jabbar's** *Mutashabih al-Qura'n*
	Q.3.3-3.4 - The term descent points to the Qur'an as created (*dalala*)
Q. 3.7 - Use of singular noun "mother" (*umm*) to describe plural noun "verses" (*ayat*) (*Haqa'iq 3.1*)	Q.3.7 - Should ambiguous verses be adhered to only with faith and not with knowledge? (*mas'ala*)
Q. 3.8 - God as cause of human deviation? (*Haqa'iq 3.2*)	Q. 3.8 - Verse suggests that God is the cause for human deviation? (*mas'ala*)
Q. 3.13 - God reduced the number of believers in the eyes of the polytheists (*Haqa'iq 3.3*)	Q. 3.13 - Verse suggests that God gives victory to whom He wills? (*mas'ala*)
Q. 3.14 - God as beautifier of desires (*Haqa'iq 3.4*)	Q.3.14 - Verse suggests that God is the cause for the beautification of desires? (*mas'ala*)
Q. 3.18 - God testifies on Himself? (*Haqa'iq 3.5*)	Q.3.18 - Testification that God does not commit evil (*dalala*)
	Q.3.19 - God as hastener of accounting points to humans as agents (*dalala*)
Q. 3.26 - God gives power to the unjust? (*Haqa'iq 3.6*)	Q. 3.26 - Verse suggests that God gives power to the unjust? (*mas'ala*)
Q. 3.28 - Taking unbelievers as allies? (*Haqa'iq 3.7*)	
	Q. 3.33 - Verse suggests in "choosing" the prophets, God made them superior? (*mas'ala*)
Q. 3.36 - The man is not like the woman (*Haqa'iq 3.8*)	
Q. 3.40 - Zachariah's doubt on having a son (*Haqa'iq 3.9*)	
	Q. 3.42 - Verse suggests that by choosing Mary, God made her superior? (*mas'ala*)
Q. 3.45 - Jesus as the word of God, mismatched gender of pronoun (*Haqa'iq 3.10*)	
	Q. 3.47 - Verse suggests that God's speech is eternal? (*mas'ala*)
	Q. 3.54 - Verse posits God as plotter? (*mas'ala*)

(continues)

Figure 3. (*Continued*)

Al-Radi's *Haqa'iq al-Tawil fi Mutashabih al-Tanzil*	'Abd al-Jabbar's *Mutashabih al-Qur'an*
	Q. 3.55 - Verse suggests that God is locatable, and in a "place" where all things return? (*mas'ala*)
	Q. 3.55 - God exalts Jesus and raises him above others? (*mas'ala*)
	Q. 3.55 - God raises the followers of Jesus above the unbelievers? (*mas'ala*)
Q. 3.60 - Prophetic doubt (*Haqa'iq* 3.11)	
Q. 3.61 - Mubahala verse; how can the Prophet invite himself? (*Haqa'iq* 3.12)	
Q. 3.64 - People of the Book taking other gods? (*Haqa'iq* 3.13)	
	Q. 3.71 - God cloaks truth with falsehood? (*mas'ala*)
	Q. 3.73 - [True] guidance is God's guidance (*dalala*) and all bounty is in God's hand (*dalala*)
Q. 3.75 - Unreliable cheaters from the People of the Book (*Haqa'iq* 3.14)	
	Q. 3.78 - Verse states "people make false claims about the Bible"; this points to human agency (*dalala*)
Q. 3.81 - Prophets must recognize earlier prophets? (*Haqa'iq* 3.15)	
Q. 3.83 - Forced submission? (*Haqa'iq* 3.16)	Q. 3.83 - Compulsion in submission? (*mas'ala*)
	Q. 3.85 - *Din* (religion) is *iman*, it is *iman* and Islam (*dalala*)
	Q. 3.86 - God "prefers" the believers over the unjust? (*mas'ala*)
Q. 3.90 - Repentance of the unbelievers not accepted? (*Haqa'iq* 3.17)	Q. 3.90 - Repentance of unbelievers not accepted? (*mas'ala*)
Q. 3.91 - Superfluous letter 'waw' (*Haqa'iq* 3.18)	Q. 3.91 - those who die as unbelievers will have no forgiveness? (*mas'ala*)
Q. 3.96 - Mecca as the first house? (*Haqa'iq* 3.19)	
Q. 3.97 - Equating unbelievers with believers unable to perform Hajj (*Haqa'iq* 3.20)	Q. 3.97 - Pilgrimage is duty to God owed by all capable people; points to human ability preceding human action (*dalala*)

Al-Radi's *Haqa'iq al-Tawil fi Mutashabih al-Tanzil*	'Abd al-Jabbar's *Mutashabih al-Qura'n*
Q. 3.102 - Obeying God as He ought to be obeyed (*Haqa'iq* 3.21)	
	Q. 3.106 - Verse suggests that those who are not unbelievers will not go to the fire (*mas'ala*)
	Q. 3.108 - God does not wish any wrong for His creation (*dalala*)
Q. 3.109 - All actions must return to God - were they ever detached? (*Haqa'iq* 3.22)	
Q. 3.110 - Repetition of God's name (in discussion section) (*Haqa'iq* 3.23)	
Q. 3.111 - It won't hurt you except it will pain (*Haqa'iq* 3.24)	
	Q. 3.117 - It is not God that wrongs them but they wrong themselves (*dalala*)
	Q. 3.123 - God's aid in the battle of Badr? (*mas'ala*)
	Q. 3.126 - No victory except from God (*dalala*)
Q. 3.128 - No actions are from you (*Haqa'iq* 3.25)	Q. 3.128 - No actions are from humans? (*mas'ala*)
	Q. 3.131 - Fire is only for the unbelievers? (*mas'ala*)
Q. 3.133 - Breadth of paradise equal to heaven and earth (*Haqa'iq* 3.26)	Q. 3.133 - Verses states to "Hasten towards your Lord's forgiveness . . ."; Proof of human capability (*dalala*)
	Q. 3.134 - Verse praises those who suppress their anger and pardon others; Proof of human capability (*dalala*)
	Q. 3.135 - Verse refers to those who repent as recipients of His reward; Proof of human capability (*dalala*)
	Q. 3.138 - Proof for everyone, guidance for God conscious (*dalala*)
	Q. 3.140 - God as the agent of Muslims' defeat at Battle of Uhud? (*mas'ala*)
Q. 3:143 - Vision of death? (*Haqa'iq* 3.27)	
Q. 3.145 - Equivalence of reward seekers of this life and the Hereafter (*Haqa'iq* 3.28)	Q. 3.145 - Verse suggests no sin on the killer (*mas'ala*)

(continues)

Figure 3. (*Continued*)

Al-Radi's *Haqa'iq al-Tawil fi Mutashabih al-Tanzil*	'Abd al-Jabbar's *Mutashabih al-Qura'n*
	Q. 3.152 - Verse suggests that events of Uhud were from God (*mas'ala*)
	Q. 3.153 - God as agent of defeat at Uhud (*mas'ala*)
Q. 3.154 - What has been written down will happen (*Haqa'iq* 3.29)	Q. 3.154 - Humans are not agents of their own actions? (*mas'ala*)
	Q. 3.159 - Verse points to how the Prophet was affected by the actions of his community; proof of human capability (*dalala*)
	Q. 3.160 - Does God's "help" support the argument for predestination? (*mas'ala*)
	Q. 3.165 - Humans are the agents of their own actions (*dalala*)
	Q. 3.166 - God's permission for and commanding of the disobedience of Muslims at Uhud? (*mas'ala*)
	Q. 3.169 - Verse suggests that God is locatable, and in a "place" wherein the martyrs reside? (*mas'ala*)
Q. 3.175 - Satan fears his allies? (*Haqa'iq* 3.30)	
	Q. 3.176 - God wants the unbelievers to sin and not to have faith? (*mas'ala*)
Q. 3.178 - Respite for unbelievers so they increase in sin (*Haqa'iq* 3.31)	Q. 3.178 - God wants unbelievers to increase in sin? (*mas'ala*)
	Q. 3.179 - God as the granter of salutary/odious qualities in people? (*mas'ala*)
	Q. 3.182 - God is never unjust to his servants (*dalala*)
	Q. 3.192 - The wrongdoer will not receive the Prophet's intercession and will not escape the fire if he dies a wrongdoer (*dalala*)

*Note: Shaded areas represent the common ambiguous verses engaged by both al-Radi and 'Abd al-Jabbar

**Two numbering schemes are used in this figure. The first refers to the sura and verse numbers in the Qur'an. For example, "Q. 3.8" refers to verse 8 in Sura 3.

The second scheme reflects the Sura and issue number (*mas'ala*) in the *Haqa'iq*. For example, *Haqa'iq* 3.2 refers to issue number two in al-Radi's discussion of Sura 3.

As you can see from Figure 3, in most cases, even when al-Radi and 'Abd al-Jabbar consider a common verse ambiguous, they can hold very different views on the *type* of ambiguity that makes that verse ambiguous. A telling example of such diverging approaches to their conceptions of the source of ambiguity in Qur'anic verses in their works is found in their discussion of Q. 3:91:

Those who disbelieve and die disbelievers will not be saved even if they offer enough gold to fill the entire earth (*fa lan yuqbala min ahadihim mil'ul-ardi dhahaban wa-law iftada bihi*).[34]

For 'Abd al-Jabbar, the ambiguity of this verse lies in the theological conundrum it raises; it suggests that the repentance of a disbeliever will not be accepted.[35] This meaning had serious ramifications for the foremost principle of Mu'tazili theology: God's justice.[36] By contrast, for al-Radi, as I discuss in detail in chapter 5, the ambiguity in this verse gives rise to an entirely different dilemma; he is puzzled by the seeming redundancy of the Arabic letter *waw* between the two clauses of this verse. Al-Radi found it important to defend the authority of the Qur'an as a purposeful guidance from God by removing all possibilities of superfluity within it.[37] With these different interests in mind, 'Abd al-Jabbar sought to explain that it is only under certain conditions that repentance is not accepted, while al-Radi presented a detailed analysis of the subtle operations of the letter *waw*.

Another moment where al-Radi and 'Abd al-Jabbar diverge on the very nature of the ambiguity is in their discussion of Q. 3:133, "Hurry towards your Lord's forgiveness and a Garden as wide as the heavens and earth prepared for the righteous."[38] For al-Radi, the verse poses a logical problem: Why is the width of the heavens the unit of measure and not its length? This raises a theological problem: How can the Qur'an be illogical? Framing the ambiguity in this way leads al-Radi to address questions about time and space. Hypothetical interlocutors in al-Radi's discussion raise the following questions: "If Paradise is as wide as the heavens and the earth, then where is the space for hell?" and "Do heaven and hell already exist or will they be brought into existence after this world comes to an end?" In my discussion of this verse in chapter 5, I show how al-Radi presents his own views in response to each of these questions, providing evidence from the lexical canon, including the Qur'an, *hadith*, poetry, and the speech of the Arabs.[39] 'Abd al-Jabbar's discussion, in contrast, is concerned with the categorical assertion in the clause "heaven is prepared for the righteous" and its opposite, which appears in verse 131: "hell is prepared for the disbelievers." How, he asks, can the inhabitants of hell be limited to the category of "disbelievers" when there are many degrees of disbelief? He argues that the fate of the grave sinners, who do not fall under the category "disbelievers," cannot be left unexplained.[40] In order to account for this ambiguity, 'Abd al-Jabbar applies the logic of inference. He explains that, since we know that there are not only believers in Paradise but also children and the wide-eyed virgins, we can infer that hell can also include the grave sinner.[41]

These examples clearly demonstrate that, on several occasions, not only did al-Radi and 'Abd al-Jabbar differ from one another on the question of which verses count as ambiguous in the Qur'an, they also held distinct views on why any given verse was labelled ambiguous. On the basis of the two examples presented above, one might assume that 'Abd al-Jabbar's explanations address theological questions and al-Radi's do not. This would be a misleading assumption. For, on the contrary, many of the ambiguous verses that al-Radi identifies do pertain to theological conundrums, in that they threaten fundamental theological principles that al-Radi seeks to preserve, much like 'Abd al-Jabbar. But how does he preserve them? What discursive and hermeneutical strategies did he mobilize and how were these strategies different from or similar to 'Abd al-Jabbar's? In the remainder of this chapter, I pursue these questions by studying al-Radi and 'Abd al-Jabbar's discussions on three theological themes: (1) the agency of human beings, (2) the sovereignty of God, and (3) prophetic intercession and infallibility. I have selected these themes and the Qur'anic verses in which they are most explicitly discussed because, according to the existing narrative of "Mu'tazili influence," it is in this context that the interpretations and positions of Imami and Mu'tazili scholars ought to clearly converge (agency of human beings, sovereignty of God) or diverge (prophetic intercession and infallibility). However, a close examination of al-Radi and 'Abd al-Jabbar's individual concerns tells a different story. Their arguments and the normative sources on which those arguments were based alert us to moments that are difficult to plot onto a neatly demarcated map of distinct theological/sectarian identities. Let us begin our analysis by considering al-Radi's and 'Abd al-Jabbar's discussion on the theme of the interaction of human agency and submission to the divine sovereign.

Theme I: Agency of Human Beings

Ambiguity: Unwilling submission to God?

Do they seek anything other than God's religion [*din Allah*]? Everyone in the heavens and earth submits [*aslama*] to Him, willingly [*taw'an*] or unwillingly [*karhan*]; they will all be returned to Him (Q. 3:83).[42]

This verse raises some pressing theological questions. How, asks the questioner in al-Radi's text, can the verse imply that submitting (*islam*) is achieved through obedience (*taw'*) and force (*karh*)? What does an unwilling or "forced" submission to God mean, particularly when read together with verse 2:256, which states "there is no compulsion in religion"? What implications does "forced submission" have for free will and individual human agency? And, if submission is forced, then how can human beings be rewarded for their obedience or punished for their disobedience to the will of God?[43] In other words, does this not undermine the very foundation of the human condition as morally responsible agents (*mukallafun*)?[44] These are some of the questions that arise in both al-Radi's and 'Abd al-Jabbar's discussions of this verse, due to the ambiguity apparently inherent in Q. 3:83. In their effort to respond to the ambiguity, both al-Radi and 'Abd al-Jabbar proffer different explanations.

Moral Responsibility (*Taklif*) as an Exegetical Framework: 'Abd al-Jabbar's Commentary on Q. 3:83

In his *Mutashabih al-Qur'an*, 'Abd al-Jabbar addresses this ambiguity in a precise yet pointed fashion. His clarification is brief and to the point. The term *islam* here, he argues, is used in the meaning of surrender (*istislam, khudu'*). He notes:[45]

When the term *islam* is predicated to God, it does not convey the meaning of absolute submission [*al-islam al-mutlaq*]. Similarly, when faith [*al-iman*] is used in the expression "faith in God and His Prophet," here, too, it is the linguistic meaning of belief (even if its application suggests otherwise). What God means by this verse is that a person is not able to resist what God carries out in regard to his affairs. This kind of unwilling surrender is not entitled to reward.

Critical to note here is 'Abd al-Jabbar's distinction between the different *types* of submission to the divine. His classification suggests that submission occurs in the form of a necessary state or condition (*istislam*), or it is a choice that a morally responsible individual (*mukallaf*) actively makes and receives reward for (*islam*). He argues that the meaning of *islam* in Q. 3:83 is that of *istislam*, which does not incur any reward.

'Abd al-Jabbar reinforces the reading of *islam* as *istislam* in his treatment of Q. 3:85, also in his *Mutashabih al-Qur'an*. The verse reads, "If anyone seeks a *din* other than *islam*, it will not be accepted from him: he will be one of the losers in the Hereafter."[46] 'Abd al-Jabbar argues the following:

> This verse indicates that *din* and *islam* are synonymous, much like *islam* and faith [*iman*] are synonymous. This is because it is necessary to say that a person's faith [*iman*] is accepted. And if *din* and *iman* were other than *islam*, they would refer to that which is not accepted. For this rea- son, they must be the same as *islam*, which includes all obligations and obedience, from actions of the limbs and the hearts. Thus, the term *islam* on this occasion is invoked in its normative meaning [*shar'i*], not linguistic [*lughawi*]. This is because if its meaning was *istislam* and *khudu'* [generic surrender], it could [still] refer to [a person whose] actions include things that must be accepted like prayer,[47] etc.[48]

Here, 'Abd al-Jabbar makes a critical distinction: the term *islam*, he argues, can be interpreted according to its linguistic (*lughawi*) meaning or accord- ing to its normative (*shar'i*) meaning.[49] The linguistic meaning of *islam* is equivalent to the term *istislam*, and the normative meaning of *islam* is syn- onymous with the terms *iman* and *din*. In this verse, he contends, the norma- tive meaning is invoked. 'Abd al-Jabbar assembled his argument for reading the term *islam* with its normative meaning by making two critical points. First, *iman*, *islam*, and *din* carry the same meaning; if they did not, the verse would (inaccurately) state that *iman* is not accepted. Second, the use of *islam* and *din* in this verse is in their normative meaning because, if it was not, then the verse would (inaccurately) state that normative acts like the prayer of a person in a state of *istislam* will not be accepted.

Another aspect of 'Abd al-Jabbar's discussion of Q. 3:83 is found in the *Haqa'iq*. Al-Radi informs us that, while discussing this verse, 'Abd al- Jabbar's objective was not only to offer his own interpretation but to also chal- lenge existing interpretations of this verse.[50] 'Abd al-Jabbar identified and then critiqued the dominant view on the meaning of forced submission held by his contemporaneous scholars. The logic of their argument, as described by 'Abd al-Jabbar (according to al-Radi), was as follows:

1. All human beings possess an awareness of God's sovereignty.
2. People who attest to this awareness through their actions submit in obedience.
3. People who do not attest to this awareness through their actions submit by force.

'Abd al-Jabbar rejects this logic, since its very foundation, he argues, rests on a dubious premise: namely that all human beings possess knowledge of God's sovereignty, a priori. He explains that this cannot be the case, since, among the morally responsible humans, there are those who do not have any faith in God whatsoever. Here, 'Abd al-Jabbar sought to reinforce the central tenet of Mu'tazili thought, namely that knowledge of God is not a given; it is acquired. 'Abd al-Jabbar did not want to reduce the supreme moral act of submission to a stark binary of acceptance/rejection, since this model of divine-human relations left no room for the critical importance of acquiring knowledge. Thus, he explained that the unreflective form of submission referred to in this verse carries the linguistic meaning of *istislam* or "surrender," as opposed to the normative meaning of the term, "submission." As seen from this discussion, for 'Abd al-Jabbar, the level of submission implied by the normative meaning of *islam* could only be achieved through sustained rational inquiry.

By arguing that *islam* in its normative meaning of active submission was only possible through sustained rational inquiry, 'Abd al-Jabbar was invoking the Mu'tazili view that acquiring knowledge is a *means* for gaining proximity to God. 'Abd al-Jabbar employed the same line of reasoning to explain the presence of ambiguous verses in the Qur'an.[51] Had the Qur'an been completely straightforward, he argued, it would have denied its readers the privilege of struggling to acquire its meaning.[52] The responsibility of acquiring knowledge is thus a critical aspect of the Mu'tazili *taklif* (moral responsibility) framework, which determines how the godhead, creation, and the conditions of the relationship by which they are connected are imagined. By positing knowledge and its logical conclusion of submission as acquired acts, 'Abd al-Jabbar rejects the view that the fundamental relationship between God and creation is inevitably one of duress or force. As for Q. 3:83 and its reference to "forced submission," 'Abd al-Jabbar notes that it refers to the final moments before a person's death, when they are on the brink of leaving the state of moral responsibility (*taklif*).[53]

To sum up what has been argued thus far, according to 'Abd al-Jabbar's *taklif* framework, *islam* mandates the freedom to choose. The phrasing of Q. 3:83 obscures the cohesiveness of the *taklif* framework by threatening human agency. Therefore, it represents an ambiguity that must be resolved. For 'Abd al-Jabbar that resolution need not be derived from the text of the Qur'an itself but rather through the exertion of human inquiry. In what follows, I turn to al-Radi's treatment of this verse.

Language as the Site of Ambiguity: al-Radi's Commentary on Q. 3:83

As a prelude to a discussion of al-Radi's approach toward this verse, it is helpful to highlight some important points of similarity and those of contrast between al-Radi's and 'Abd al-Jabbar's hermeneutical procedures. The first thing that immediately grabs the reader's attention is the considerably lengthier discussion that al-Radi devotes to this topic as compared to 'Abd al-Jabbar. This is so because, in the *Haqa'iq*, al-Radi routinely prefaces his explanation of a Qur'anic verse with an overview of his predecessors' positions. An important benefit of this strategy, adopted by several exegetes, was that it allowed the author to hone in on how his own perspective was distinctive and novel. Most commonly, al-Radi only enumerates and describes multiple previous interpretations of a given verse, rather than engaging or stating clear positions on those interpretations. He neither accepts nor denies them but simply adds his own reading at the end of the list. However, his procedure of enumeration is in itself instructive, for it alerts us to the multiple discursive currents operative in al-Radi's intellectual milieu and to the intellectual resources and conceptual architecture on which al-Radi's own position rested. The varied intellectual resources that informed al-Radi's hermeneutical attitude, I would insist, cannot be reduced to or predicted through his apparent sectarian identity as a 'Shi'i' exegete.

In his discussion of Q. 3:83, al-Radi lists eight different scholarly opinions, including that of 'Abd al-Jabbar, which I have already analyzed. Curiously, in al-Radi's discussion of this verse and other verses in the *Haqa'iq*, the majority of opinions that he lists remain anonymous, *except* when they refer back to 'Abd al-Jabbar. This practice shows the importance al-Radi assigned to authoritatively connecting his arguments with those of his teacher. At the same time, al-Radi's discussion alerts us to other intellectual currents

to which his arguments were tied. As I will show, the conceptual apparatus of al-Radi's literary hermeneutic, as well as the lexical sources on which
he draws to make his arguments, indicate that the philological tradition of
approaching the Qur'an's difficult passages (*mushkil al-Qur'an*) represents a
critical discursive tradition in which al-Radi's commentary on the *mutashabih* verses is embedded.

Much like 'Abd al-Jabbar, al-Radi tackles the ambiguity surrounding the
notion of "forced submission" by reading the term *islam* in this verse as *istislam* (surrendering). However, he departs from 'Abd al-Jabbar by offering an
alternate view of what qualifies as *istislam karhan* or "forced surrender." In
addition, and here is the most crucial difference, in meeting this objective,
al-Radi relied almost exclusively on the linguistic canon to support his views.

To begin, al-Radi explains that "they submit unwillingly" (*aslamu karhan*) here is only applicable to beings of this world because the angels, or
inhabitants of the heavens, cannot be attributed with forced submission. Second, al-Radi seeks to clarify who or what would fit this description. Unlike
'Abd al-Jabbar, who held that it applied to those in the throes of death, since
it is at this time that they must submit out of necessity, al-Radi presents a
different scheme. He argues that "it is possible [to argue] that submission
[*islam*] of earthly beings—if it [submission] is read here as surrender [*istislam*]—refers to [the surrender of] nonrational beings from among children
and beasts."[54] According to al-Radi, it is the surrender of these nonrational
beings that counts as "unwilling surrender." He further explains that this
is so because nonrational beings are incapable of avoiding the pain, severity, and tribulations that God brings down upon them, despite the fact that
these are for them a cause of affliction. This condition, which renders them
incapable of resisting these affairs, is what warrants describing them as surrendering unwillingly.

However, another *grammatical* ambiguity is still left to be answered. In
order to ensure that his interpretation of "unwilling surrender" as a reference
to nonrational beings can apply, al-Radi must also explain why the verse uses
a certain form of the pronoun "those" (*man*) in this verse, which typically
only applies to intelligent or rational beings. Al-Radi devotes the majority of
his discussion to defending this point of linguistic detail. He furnishes lines
of poetry by the renowned Arab poets Farazdaq and Labid, as well as other
verses from the Qur'an, as primary evidence to bolster his argument.[55]

To recap, the ambiguity in Q. 3:83, which in its apparent meaning threatens the concept of human free will by its reference to "forced submission,"

is resolved by al-Radi by means of two critical clarifications. Al-Radi's first clarification is that *islam* here is not used in its normative meaning of active adherence to the teachings of the Qur'an and the Prophet. Rather, it is used in the meaning of *istislam* or *sallama*—both of which imply "the surrendering of oneself over to." Al-Radi's second clarification is that, since the linguistic meaning of "surrendering oneself over to" includes both rational and nonrational beings, the term "unwilling surrender" (*karhan*) in this verse can be attributed to nonrational beings.

According to al-Radi, for some (unnamed) scholars, the meaning of *islam* as *istislam* is illustrated through reference to Q. 15:36, in which the satanic figure Iblis states, "My Lord, give me respite until the Day when they are raised from the dead."[56] According to this view, the verse shows that Iblis's request for respite is indicative of his essential condition of surrendering to God's will and the acknowledgment that he is a slave ruled by God whose order he cannot escape. So, despite his deviance from the straight path, Iblis is counted as among those who surrender (*mustaslimun*).[57] This novel construal of Iblis is significant in the way it situates the transgression of the ultimate source of human error (that of Iblis)[58] within a larger scheme of natural and necessary submission. In addition, by counting Iblis from among the *mustaslimum*, this position highlights the critical difference between the linguistic meaning of *islam* or *istislam*, which even a figure like Iblis participates in, and the normative meaning of *islam*, which is the active surrender to God's will and the exclusive result of human deliberation and each individual's choosing.

A second example that al-Radi cites (from among the scholarly opinions he enumerates) to justify the use of the verb *aslama* in the meaning of *istislam* is a commentary on another Qur'anic verse, Q. 49:14,[59] that reads as follows:

> The desert Arabs say, 'We have faith [*amanna*].' [Prophet], tell them, 'You do not have faith [*lam tu'minu*]. What you should say instead is, "We have submitted [*aslamna*]," for faith has not yet entered your hearts.'[60]

The apparent meaning of this verse suggests that there is a difference between the condition of possessing faith and the condition of submission, such that the state of submission is understood to *precede* faith. It is for this reason that the Bedouins are corrected, or even scolded, and told not to presume that they have already attained the stage of attaining faith. According to the above reading, the human potential for spiritual growth is an important

message relayed in this verse. It conjures for the reader the image of an underlying hierarchy of spiritual conditions whereby an individual moves or pro-
gresses from one stage to the next. This idea was emphasized and further
developed in later mystical commentaries that sought to describe the journey of the human soul in its quest to know God. Many of al-Radi's predecessors and contemporaries, such as al-Tabari (d. 923), al-Qushayri (d. 1072),
and al-Tha'labi, also invoke this meaning.[61] What is instructive to note here is
that al-Radi's unnamed scholar presented a noteworthy exegesis of this verse,
according to which the distinction between "faith" (*iman*) and "submission"
(*islam*), which was posited in the above-mentioned works, is overturned.
According to this view, belief and submission are one and the same, and the
way to understand this verse is to grasp that there are multiple applications
of the term *islam*, "to submit." Specifically, according to this view, *aslama* was
read here as *istaslama* or "to surrender," so that the verse insinuates that the
Bedouins had not attained a state of active submission such that praise was
due to them. Rather, they remained in the necessary condition of surrendering to the will of God. Once faith entered their hearts, only then could
they claim active submission and/or belief. One of al-Radi's sources for this
argument for the interchangeability of *islam* and *iman* may have been 'Abd al-
Jabbar, although al-Radi does not refer to him in his discussion.[62]

In sum, even as al-Radi and 'Abd al-Jabbar sought to guarantee human
agency and freedom of choice by arguing for different levels of submission, their reading of Q. 3:83 ("everyone in the heavens and earth surrenders [*aslama*] to Him, willingly or unwillingly; they will all be returned to
Him") differed in critical ways. For instance, whereas 'Abd al-Jabbar turned
to external sources, namely the logic of Mu'tazili theological principles, al-
Radi pointed to the internal Qur'anic evidence of linguistic form. By "linguistic form," I mean to say that al-Radi's explanations are supported by multiple
etymologies and discussions of the connotation of specific terms. In turn, the
etymologies he uncovers are themselves bolstered by proof texts (*shawahid*)
drawn from the Qur'an, the poetic tradition, and everyday expressions of the
Arabs. The point is this: language and its underlying normative authority
were at the centerpiece of al-Radi's analytical apparatus.

Most crucially, what must be noted here is that al-Radi's attempt to argue
for the rationality of theological principles rested precisely on the authority of
language. Thus, on the one hand, al-Radi's explanations of the Qur'anic text
moved away from a characteristically logocentric approach that privileges
the *hadith*, or sayings of the Prophet and the Imams, as the only authoritative

source for interpretation. On the other hand, his deferral of meaning to the rules of a linguistic canon reinscribed a logocentrism even as it ultimately sought to defend the inherently "rational" principles shared between the Mu'tazili and the Shi'i Imami schools. Careful consideration of these differences between 'Abd al-Jabbar and al-Radi's reasoning—in particular, the varied projects for which they employed rational principles—is critical for the task of rethinking a narrative of "influence" that currently dominates academic discussions of Mu'tazili-Shi'i interactions in the realm of Qur'anic exegesis. Moving away from an identity-centered reading of these works allows us to approach the ambivalent relationship to authoritative sources of an author like al-Radi—associated at times with rational principles while at other times with the linguistic canon—not as a deviation from a predetermined template of what a Shi'i hermeneutic looks like but rather as the construction of what was effectively a literary hermeneutic inflected by a variety of prevailing intellectual currents.

As I have shown, al-Radi and 'Abd al-Jabbar's varied interpretive strategies point to a much more dynamic relationship of convergence and divergence than the predictable outcomes of reproduction suggested by the reductive language of "influence." In further illustrating an alternative conceptual approach that closely navigates the hermeneutical moves and logics on pressing theological and moral questions, I now turn to an analysis of al-Radi and 'Abd al-Jabbar's discussions on the theme of divine sovereignty and justice.

Theme II: God's Sovereignty

Ambiguity: God gives dominion to the unjust?

Say, 'God, holder of all control [*malik al-mulk*], You give control/ dominion [*mulk*] to whoever You will and remove it from whoever You will; You exalt whoever You will and humble whoever You will. All that is good lies in Your hand: You have power over everything' (Q. 3:26).[63]

The apparent meaning of this verse suggests that God is all-powerful, and it is within His power to elevate anyone (just or unjust) and to humble anyone (just or unjust). In al-Radi's discussion, a hypothetical interlocutor thus raises the following question: "Your school claims that the dominion of the oppressor is acquired unjustly and counts as an act of usurpation. So, how is it that this verse states that God gives dominion, which means that the oppressor's dominion is granted by God?"[64] Theologically, the ambiguity this verse raises is that it proposes a relationship between God and His creation that is not governed by the fundamental principle of God's justice. Instead, it could be said to depict an impulsive God who acts indiscriminately toward His creatures. Moreover, it challenges the view that human actions determine what God will decree for them. Both 'Abd al-Jabbar and al-Radi identify this verse as ambiguous because of the challenge it poses to the unconditional applicability of God's justice. However, al-Radi's interpretive strategy in tackling this verse operates on a different conceptual register from that of 'Abd al-Jabbar.

Al-Radi proposes a meaning of dominion (*mulk*) as "capacity" (*qudra*) and, in doing so, he shifts the discussion of *mulk* from a meta-theory of Muslim political power to one of individual capacity.[65] Most crucially, al-Radi's position is premised on an argument based on etymological nuance. 'Abd al-Jabbar, on the other hand, dissects the possible meanings of this verse by raising a theological question: What are the *terms* of a divine gift like *mulk*? Thus, unlike al-Radi's turn to the linguistic canon, 'Abd al-Jabbar draws extensively from the legal tradition to frame and provide proofs of his explanations. Let us consider each of these lines of argument in greater detail.

Defining Dominion (*Mulk*) as Capacity (*Qudra*): al-Radi's Commentary on Q. 3:26

As I have shown in the previous example, al-Radi deemed it necessary to include the views of other scholars on the same question. His own position was often woven into those opinions. Yet he adopted a distinctly subtle tone, quite unlike the disputatious style of typical theological treatises, in which the author leads the reader through the inadequacies of multiple perspectives, only to eventually champion his own view. Instead, al-Radi walks his reader through a series of opinions on a given question before presenting his own view. His language is not confrontational: he gently adds his two cents to an issue without attempting to negate or overturn the views of his colleagues. For the purposes of this discussion, what is most noteworthy about the spectrum of opinions that al-Radi mobilizes in this discussion is that the main source of difference between the various authors is not solely or even primarily premised on theological or sectarian "beliefs."

For example, in his discussion of Q. 3:26, al-Radi lists eight different views before presenting his own. Among these is the view that the term *mulk* or dominion in this verse invokes a meaning of dominion as a kind of "entitled power" that may not be visible in this world but can become manifest in the hereafter. This kind of power cannot be measured through the finite lens of the temporal world. Since the reach of this dominion extends to the realm of the hereafter, its temporal appearances do not reflect "true" dominion. Seen from this light, power that is currently not in the hands of the Muslim community is still rightfully theirs, even if it currently lies in someone else's possession. So, the dominion of believers can take the quality of a condition whereby unbelievers possess temporal power and push Muslims away from their possessions and believers continue to demand this power until they are successful in obtaining it. Put differently, according to this reading, *mulk* is understood as a condition in which religion/normative practice (*al-din*) and conquest/subjugation (*al-ghalaba*) are manifest. What is crucial to note here is that this interpretation comes close to making a case for Muslim political power and can therefore more appropriately be understood as a discourse on political theology and the sovereignty of the Muslim community at large.

Al-Radi does not indicate his agreement or disagreement with this position, but he does clarify the point further, in what one may speculate is his own additional explanation. He notes that the meaning of *mulk* is understood when it is situated as a necessary rule/decree (*hukm*) in God's normative arrangement of the world:

God made *mulk* His decree [*hukm*], in the same way that He made the Sunna of His Prophet for those who are firm in their religion, who fulfil the commandments of religion, and who are steadfast in their obedience to the prophets. And in the same way God decreed [*ahkama*] that the male be apportioned double the wealth to that of a female, and that the guardian of the deceased be given authority over the killer. However, the unjust refute this, and exceed it, and give to the women the same they give to the man and do not accord retribution to the killer. So, those on whom God has bestowed *mulk* and those He has elevated are the believers, even as they are dominated. And those who have not been given a share in *mulk* and are disgraced are the unjust, even as they dominate. This is so because the elevation of the unbeliever over the believers is not an elevation in religion [*din*], and not the fruit of their actions, which is ultimately disgrace and calamity. So, the subjugation of believers at the hands of unbelievers is not subjugation in reality because it [this apparent subjugation] will turn into the necessary exaltation and permanent merit [of the believers over the unbelievers]. And how can this be called disgrace when God has commanded it for His prophets, who were attacked by the unbelievers?[66]

Critical to note here are the various kinds of normative rules (*ahkam*) that this perspective provides as being put in place by God. According to this reasoning, the tradition of the Prophet as guidance for human beings is a normative rule (*hukm*) in much the same way that apportioning half of one's wealth to women is. Al-Radi further justifies this reading by means of a distinction between two kinds of divine statements: a normative rule (*hukm*) and an imperative command/description (*amr/khabar*).[67] According to this position, when a statement is a rule, it expresses a meta-reality or normative ideal. In contrast to normative rules or *ahkam*, the objects of imperative commands/descriptions or *umur* are necessarily reflected in the temporal world. Al-Radi substantiates this claim by referring to Q. 3:97, which states *he who enters it will be in peace*. The verse refers to the Ka'ba and he argues that this statement must carry the weight of a rule or ideal (*hukm*) since it is well known that many people took refuge in the Ka'ba and were subsequently killed.

Another position that al-Radi mentions transfers the relevance of Q. 3:26 to the hereafter by arguing that it refers to God's granting entry to heaven to whomever He pleases and withholding entry from whomever He desires.[68] In a rare moment of intervention, al-Radi critiques this position and characterizes it as highly unsatisfactory and regretful. Why? Because, according to al-Radi, the next verse clearly indicates that the reference of Q. 3:26 is to this world, since it points to a series of events relevant to this world (the night being extended into the day and so on). I argued above that it is characteristic of al-Radi to withhold comment on the opinions he lists, such that, to the reader, they appear in the form of an ongoing conversation between multiple scholars. Therefore, this particular instance, in which al-Radi interjects, raises the question of whether al-Radi's silence in other places can be interpreted as his tacit approval of different views as *possible*, but not preferable, readings. Whatever the case may be, juxtaposing al-Radi's approach with the other perspectives he lists allows us to better understand the possible hermeneutical objectives behind his interpretation, a task to which I now turn.

Power and Capacity

The first thing that captures our attention when reading al-Radi's position on this verse (which appears at the end of his discussion) is that he seeks to refute the view that Q. 3:26 legitimizes Muslim political power, such that those whom God elevates could be understood to refer to the present ruling dynasty. The way in which al-Radi moves away from this reading is by interpreting *mulk* in a new way: for al-Radi, *mulk* does not refer to dominion or the subjugation of an external object, but rather means *qudra* or "capacity."[69] Crucial to this alternate reading is a distinction he draws between the *possibility* of dominion and its *realization*. As a way to authorize his reading of this verse, al-Radi invokes the iconic verse from the opening chapter of the Qur'an: *malik yawm al-din* (Q. 1:4). Although this verse has typically been read as "Master of the Day of Judgment," al-Radi reads it as "God is the one who is capable of *bringing about* the Day of Judgement."[70] Al-Radi explains that *mulk* in the meaning of dominion refers to existing things, whereas *qudra* or capacity is not limited in this way. Since the day of judgement does not yet exist, he argues, the meaning here is that of capacity (*qudra*). By showing that the same meaning is invoked in Q. 3:26, al-Radi argues that it reads as "God is capable of giving dominion to whomever He wills, and of taking it away from whomever He wills." For al-Radi, then, the realization of the divine promise could be deferred to a different (possibly later) historical moment.

Now, one should note in passing that al-Radi's hermeneutical program was intimately connected to the political context in which he wrote. His interpretive framework aligned well with his individual efforts to gain political prestige under the Buyids. This is because al-Radi's interpretation of *mulk* as "capacity" left open the possibility that *real* power did not necessarily correspond to power in the temporal world. This view can be connected to his own aspirations for the seat of the caliphate, aspirations that were never realized during his life but which had explicitly been aired in his writings. As I have shown, in Chapter 2, al-Radi's poetic writings in the *Diwan* convey his frustrations under 'Abbasid caliphal rule and illustrate his own hope of receiving the recognition and position that he felt his talent and 'Alid lineage entitled him to.[71] Of course, it is also possible to interpret al-Radi's reading of Q. 3:26 as an implicit defense of the Imamate, which would align well with the Shi'i discourse of denouncing any leadership other than that of the Imams as illegitimate. While this may well be one of the implications of his interpretation, there is little in al-Radi's discussion that would support such a claim. Thus, insisting on such a sectarian reading would equate to interpreting al-Radi's hermeneutical decisions according to a fixed template of what he, as a Shi'i scholar, *ought to do*. The critical point I wish to emphasize is that, rather than reducing al-Radi's viewpoint to a representation of the typically 'Imami-Shi'i' or 'Mu'tazili-Shi'i' response, it is important to consider the ways in which al-Radi's arguments were embedded in his individual struggle for power in the complex imperial network of the Buyid dynasty.

Al-Radi's positing of this overarching normative outlook was only the beginning of his discussion. His main objective was to present a semiotic map of the term *mulk*—one that could demonstrate how the normative arrangement he described corresponded to, and was affirmed by, the language of the Qur'an. Thus, he drew on the linguistic canon to authorize his reading of *mulk* as "capacity." He argued that the metaphorical link between the two terms, "dominion" and "capacity" (*mulk* and *qudra*), is in the form of a relationship. Each person has power over the thing in which she or he is capable of affecting change. Thus, the term for God as "Possessor of Dominion" (*malik al-mulk*) implies that only in God does the ultimate power for making and changing things reside. In assembling his point, al-Radi mobilized two aphorisms, "well-being (*'afiyya*) is a hidden power" and "endurance is an immediate strength." Both these statements, he argues, refer to faculties (well-being, endurance) over which we have control and power, and the statements imply that effecting change in them is a form of strength or power.[72]

Al-Radi further reinforced his argument by interrogating the etymology of the term. He maintains that the term *mulk* also carries the meaning of "severity" (*shidda*) and "connection" (*rabt*), as in the saying "to knead with strength" (*mallaka al-'ajin*). Similarly, the verbal noun of the fourth grammatical form of the tri-letter root (*m-l-k*) from which *mulk* is derived, *imlak*, carries the meaning of "marriage," since a covenant requires a strong bond. So, al-Radi argues, the term *imlak* is used, since it is as if the woman were attached to the man.[73] A similar pattern, al-Radi continues, is found in the following verse of poetry:

[The bow] was strengthened [*mallaka*] by the bark that lay below it.
The egg was concealed by the lining that was above it.[74]

Al-Radi argues that this verse illustrates the subtle meaning of *m-l-k* as "strong attachment." This meaning is evoked through the imagery of a bow, which—contrary to a typical bow—had not had its skin removed. However, al-Radi explains that the presence of the skin has the positive effect of strengthening the bow. Similarly, the poet describes the lining or membrane above the egg as a protection for it. Al-Radi's analysis of this poetic verse serves to support the meaning of *mulk* as strength and the power to effect change, and further bolsters his argument that *mulk* is to be interpreted as "capability" (*qudra*) or "unrealized power."

In passing, al-Radi also addressed another hypothetical challenge.[75] Namely, how can God take away *mulk*, as that would equate to the taking away of a gift? Would that not be unjust? In responding to this possible objection, al-Radi explains that ownership (*tamlik*) can be of two kinds: permanent or temporary. The gift of *mulk* that God extends to humanity is of the second variety; it is temporary. Hence, it is perfectly just for God to give power for a specific purpose and time, al-Radi argued. When that time expires, the *mulk* is taken away, much like the manner in which a lender deals with a borrower. Also, al-Radi pointed out, if God made good the revocation of a gift, it could be for the sake of a greater compensation (in the hereafter). And finally, it is also possible that God expropriates *mulk* from a person, knowing that it will harm his religion (*din*) should it stay with him. Again, in his signature style, al-Radi assembled his case and through that his authority by unraveling an ambiguous puzzle that he himself had staged.

Ambiguity and the Language of Law: 'Abd al-Jabbar's Commentary on Q. 3:26

Turning to 'Abd al-Jabbar, his discussion of Q. 3:26 occurs in three different sources: in his treatise on ambiguous verses of the Qur'an (*Mutashabih al-Qur'an*); in his monograph on the transcendence of the Qur'an from error (*Tanzih al-Qur'an min al-Mata'in*); and in al-Radi's report of 'Abd al-Jabbar's views in the *Haqa'iq al-ta'wil*. Among the notable differences between the methods of 'Abd al-Jabbar and al-Radi is that, while the former drew support for his explanation of this verse from legal discourse, the latter relied indefatigably on the linguistic canon. But their differences are not limited to the sources that supported their arguments.

'Abd al-Jabbar's primary concern in his discussions of Q. 3:26 was to offer a classification of the different types of ownership, as well as the terms of the relationship between human and divine dominion. His underlying goal was to preserve the notion of independent human agency, while at the same time upholding God's ultimate dominion over all things. There are two ambiguous elements in Q. 3:26 that raised questions around which he framed his discussion, the first being "How can God give dominion to the unjust?" and the second being "How can God take away dominion from the just?" Both questions raise pressing concerns about divine justice, and the relationship between human actions and their outcomes. In response to the first ambiguity, or the question of how God can give dominion to the unjust, 'Abd al-Jabbar pointed out that dominion, when it pertains to God, is starkly different from when it pertains to human beings. Real dominion, he argued, only belongs to God.[76] The conditions of dominion and exaltation (*'izza*), however, he argues, do extend to just and unjust individuals, but the critical difference is that dominion that can be ascribed to an unjust person is not real dominion, since it is tied to the condition of disbelief (*kufr*). In this way, 'Abd al-Jabbar posits a clear distinction between real dominion, which only belongs to God, and the dominion of humans, who can be just or unjust. The upshot of 'Abd al-Jabbar's point, it seems, is that dominion as granted by God can only be salutary. It is then up to humans what they do with it. They can use dominion for just or unjust purposes.

'Abd al-Jabbar's response to the second ambiguity, or the question of how God could take away dominion from the unjust, is most clearly articulated in his discussion in the *Mutashabih al-Qur'an*. Here we see that 'Abd al-Jabbar's explanation is the same as al-Radi's own final discussion point in the *Haqa-'iq*. He argues that ownership of any kind is either perpetual and absolute or temporary, as jurists have explicated in the case of gifts, loans, donations in perpetuity, and temporary donations. Thus, it is perfectly just for God to take back a gift in the same fashion as lenders and donors.[77] But, crucially, unlike al-Radi, 'Abd al-Jabbar directs this explanation as a challenge to those who seek to respond to the same question by relying solely on the revealed tradition (*al-sam'*). He argues that they refer to the revealed sources of knowledge (Qur'an and *hadith*) to show that they permit the revocation of a gift from a stranger or a father. He critiques this explanation as insufficient from a rational point of view since the gift becomes like all the other possessions of a person and it is not permissible to take those without mutual consent.[78] Although 'Abd al-Jabbar does not say so explicitly, with this direct rejoinder to the tradition-centered exegetical explanation, he makes the case for a hermeneutical framework that corresponds to rational normative expectations.

Interestingly, al-Radi cites an entirely different facet of 'Abd al-Jabbar's explanation in the *Haqa'iq*, which is not found in 'Abd al-Jabbar's commentary on this verse in the *Mutashabih* or *Tanzih*. In this excerpt, 'Abd al-Jabbar explains that the dominion that God grants is divided into dominion in religion, such as prophethood and Imamate, as well as what branches out from them, and what one may call forms of ownership in the world, which God bestows from among the permissibles (*mubahat*), such as abundant wealth, sublime gifts, resoluteness, strength, and endurance. All these possessions are attributed to God because they are permissible.[79] Thus, he reiterates his position that real *mulk*, which can only be beneficial, is from God alone.

He then turns to a different but related topic, by raising the following question: "Is it possible for there to be a form of ownership that God does not grant its possessor?" It is here that 'Abd al-Jabbar again unleashes his juridical outlook and discourse. He begins his answer with the general premise that God creates things for the benefit of others. He goes on to argue that if *mulk* is such that it is beneficial only when bestowed to a person, then God necessarily bestows it. But if *mulk* does not lose its benefit when not granted to a specific person, then it is possible that God does not grant it to someone specific. This can occur in two ways: either God makes *mulk* a permissible public good that anyone can benefit from (*mubahat*),[80] or He distributes it among humanity such that no one individual can be called its sole possessor.[81] It is evident here, and of little surprise given his role as a judge (*qadi*), that 'Abd al-Jabbar organizes his discussion and draws his examples from legal categories. For this verse, he uses the legal division of goods into two categories—*mubahat* and *mulk*—as a way to bolster his underlying premise, which is that real *mulk* belongs to God alone, yet its worldly manifestations are varied. It can be distributed among creation in such a way that it does not count as ownership per se, or there must be several conditions in place for a single individual to have ownership or dominion over a thing.

In sum, 'Abd al-Jabbar's discussion of this ambiguous verse relies on legal distinctions, like owned goods versus publicly accessible goods and gifts versus loans to argue that the overarching category *mulk* must not be understood to mean a single homogenous entity, even as it originates in God. This provides 'Abd al-Jabbar with the hermeneutical leverage to balance God's ultimate sovereignty and justice and human agency and responsibility.

In his insightful study of 'Abd al-Jabbar's hermeneutics, David Vishanoff has shown that law represented the centerpiece of 'Abd al-Jabbar's intellectual project. According to Vishanoff, for 'Abd al-Jabbar, all Qur'anic statements possess legal value.[82] This characterization is critical for contrasting his approach with al-Radi's language-based approach. As I have shown throughout this chapter, al-Radi's attempt to argue for the rationality of theological principles rests primarily on the authority of language. In al-Radi's thought, theology and language are mutually entangled. Thus, on the one hand, his commentary employed the structural technique of focusing on the ambiguous verses, a technique widespread among Mu'tazili scholarly circles that focused on verses presenting theological or linguistic challenges. On the other hand, al-Radi's emphasis on literary arguments, derived from the canonical Arabic lexicon, resonated with other congruent genres of writing from the philological tradition that dealt with Qur'anic ambiguities. These included specific works on the *mushkil al-Qur'an* (difficulties in the Qur'an) as well as works that expounded on the problem of homonymous or polysemous verbal forms.

Let me end this thread by briefly discussing some of the larger conceptual arguments in relation to questions of religious identity and difference that I wish to make through the preceding comparative analysis of al-Radi and 'Abd al-Jabbar's hermeneutical programs. I have argued that the presence of certain Mu'tazili figures in al-Radi's intellectual genealogy does not translate into a relationship of unfiltered influence from Mu'tazili thought. Classifications of al-Radi's *Haqa'iq* as "Shi'i" or "Mu'tazili-influenced" endorses and advances a heresiographical narrative and attitude toward the boundaries of religious identity in early Islam. Governed as it is by highly reified notions of religious identity, the uncritical embrace of heresiographical literature is at once problematic and misleading. As I have labored to show in this chapter, such neatly demarcated categories are less than helpful in conceptualizing hermeneutical moves and maneuvers that populate early Muslim texts like al-Radi's *Haqa'iq*. Let me further cement and close this argument with the help of one final example.

Theme III: Prophetic Intercession and Infallibility

Ambiguity: The Prophet has no authority?

A crucial doctrine, on which the Mu'tazili theologians differed from Imami and Sunni Ash'ari scholars, was prophethood. Specifically, the Mu'tazili scholars had a distinct conception of the extent and limits of prophetic power. In the tenth and eleventh centuries, discussions about prophets were also the precursor to discussions about the Qur'an. This is so because according to the Qur'an, past prophets were attributed with a miracle, which led scholars to assert that the Qur'an was Muhammad's miracle. Yet, even as Mu'tazili theologians argued in favor of prophetic miracles, they stopped short of attributing prophets with any intercessory powers. This unwillingness to grant prophets the power to intercede on behalf of their followers was tied to the *taklif* framework, which privileged the principle of God's justice above all other principles. The notion of intercession disrupted the logic of how justice was accorded and, for this reason, was ruled out. The issue was not so much about granting a prophet "supernatural" powers as it was about ensuring the robustness and cohesiveness of their justice-centered theological system.

One of the verses al-Radi and 'Abd al-Jabbar use to discuss their views on this thorny issue of prophetic power is 3:128:

> Whether God relents toward them or punishes them, you [Muhammad] have no authority [al-amr] in the matter: they are wrongdoers.[83]

Al-Radi's hypothetical interlocutor highlights a specific phrase within this verse as objectionable: specifically, "You have no authority [al-amr] in the matter [al-shay']." The interlocutor assumes that the verse refers to the Prophet having no say in *any* matter. Consequently, he argues, the verse points to God as the ultimate agent of all human affairs and actions. Challenging al-Radi, he adds that this is clearly not in line with what al-Radi's school (*madhhab*) has claimed. In reply, al-Radi presents a scholarly opinion (unnamed) that lashes out against what is characterized as the interlocutor's inane suggestion that this verse undermines the all-important and well-supported principle of human free will. He asserts that the questioner is well aware that God commanded His prophet to invite the unbelievers to God, to repeatedly urge them to listen to his invitation, to be a guide on the path of belief and illumination, to be a warner and informer, and to be a protection for them from the torments of fire. So, when God has designated these tasks for the Prophet, how can the questioner assert that this verse robs the Prophet of his authority? Al-Radi further elaborates on this position, explaining that the meaning of this verse should be understood as follows:[84]

> The Prophet has no power over the salvation of the people, or over their reward, destruction, or reform. He does not possess the capacity to manage their affairs at designated times, or to hasten or delay their end. He also has no knowledge of what will improve their conditions

in God's normative order [*din*], or of the decay of their subsistence due to disbelief.

When the Prophet witnessed the grave extremity of people's disbelief in him, and their exaggerated attempts to extinguish his light, he asked God for permission to pray for their destruction and for the hastening of their end just like the prophets had done in the past. To this request, God replied with this verse to pacify the Prophet, and to fortify his heart and explain to him that God is all-Knowing of their affairs and their consequences. It is for this reason that God does not give the Prophet permission to pray against them, due to His Knowledge of who among them repents and believes. . . .

God is aware of the place where trees are planted, the point of the ascent of fruits, the beginnings of cross-pollination and fertilization, and of the results of births and ends. Thus, God oversees the order for improvement and the rules of this order. He has provided proofs of recompense and witnesses of it. And it is according to this order that God has established the resource of prophets and contiguous alternations of fortune, and made the happiness of a people be followed by misery, and the misery of a people unveil as happiness, on the basis of their betterment and decay, and the knowledge of outcomes.

What reaffirms this is what God says before this statement [you have no authority in the matter]: "Whether God relents toward them or punishes them." This clarifies that the consequence for him who disbelieves is one of two things: either he repents and God accepts his repentance and forgives his error, or he dies persisting [in disbelief]. God's punishment for him in the Afterlife is greater than His punishment for him in this world. Hence, the Prophet is not given permission to pray against them, as it would break off repentance with the punishment of destruction, and cut off the appointed duration of time.[85]

Critical to note from this discussion is that, according to this view, the reason the Prophet ought not to intercede or pray for the destruction of the disbeliever was not because the Prophet was not capable of doing so, but rather because it would interrupt the divine plan. In other words, the argument that the Prophet has not been given permission to pray for the destruction of disbelievers was based on the assumption that the Prophet's prayers would necessarily be answered by God.

Following this perspective, al-Radi highlighted how other exegetes, among them the Mu'tazili Abu Muslim ibn Bahr (d. 934), the early exegete Muqatil ibn Sulayman, and the grammarian al-Zajjaj (d. 922), approached the ambiguity in verse 3:128. The main question that occupied the attention of the exegetes he lists was this: "What was the context that occasioned this revelation?" Some argued that this verse was revealed after the Battle of Uhud—a regrettable event for the early Muslim community since, on this day, the Prophet sustained several injuries due to the ineptitude of his own followers. The disgracefulness of the event led the Prophet to exclaim, "How can a community that treats its Messenger this way, while he invites them to worship their Lord, ever succeed?" And it was in response to this statement that the verse "You have no say in the matter" was revealed. A different occasion of revelation cited by exegetes for this verse is the moment when the Prophet prayed against his enemies for forty days when they killed one of his envoys from the early community of helpers (al-ansar), who had been sent to teach them the Qur'an. Other exegetes argue that the verse indicates that the Prophet had power over smaller affairs of his community but not over larger issues such as whether they would be forgiven or punished on the day of judgment.

After laying out the views of different scholars (except 'Abd al-Jabbar's, whom he lists at the very end), al-Radi proposes his own reading of the verse, so as to shift the issue away from the debate over its occasion of revelation. He does this by locating the "solution" to the ambiguity in another meaning of the term al-amr (authority). He explains that al-amr is used in the meaning of "sovereignty" (al-sultan), and sovereignty in its real meaning is only for God, even if the Prophet does have some power over the affairs of his community. With this explanation, al-Radi suggests that the Qur'an is making a claim about power in its absolute sense, which cannot be ascribed to anyone other than God. In this way he divests the verse from meaning that the Prophet has no authority over his community and devotes the rest of his discussion to linguistic evidence for using the term al-amr in this meaning. He refers to the Qur'anic verse 27:33 in which the people of Bilquis, Queen of Sheba, answered her request for advice on how to respond to Solomon's invitation to submit. They replied, "You are in command [al-amr], so consider what orders to give us." Al-Radi explained that this means "authority is with you so command what you will; your command will be followed." He then turns to another source for the same use of *al-amr* in its absolute meaning. In the speech of Arabs, it is said, "this happened after so-and-so took power [*taqallada al-amr*] as caliph or so-and-so as amir." Al-Radi argued that this expression means "after he commanded power [*malaka al-sultan*] and regulated the affairs of time [*dabbara al-zaman*]." Similar to this is their saying, "the power [*al-amr*] shifted from so-and-so to so-and-so." In al-Radi's view, here too *al-amr* is used in the meaning of authority and direction. With these three examples from the Qur'an and speech of the Arabs, al-Radi concluded:

> The meaning of the verse is that you [Prophet] have no power or dominion over anything; indeed this is only for God and no one else from His creation, even if the Prophet has authority over the managing of the community in categories other than real dominion and power, both of which cannot be ascribed to anyone except God. And whoever describes human beings with these traits, employs them metaphorically [*majazan*] and by extension [*bi al-ittisa'*].[86]

In sum, in his discussion of verse 3:128, al-Radi made two critical points. First, according to al-Radi, the Prophet is denied permission to ask for a community's destruction because he does not possess knowledge of their possible change of heart in the future. Second, the verse does not pose a challenge to prophetic authority because in this context the term *al-amr* refers to sovereignty in the more absolute sense. Noteworthy here is how al-Radi puts on display the flexible semantic potential of the Qur'an and the Arabic language more generally. In addition, he remains chiefly concerned with preserving the authority of prophetic power rather than entertaining what he deems as a ludicrous assertion by his interlocutor: that this verse could in any way detract from the authority and charisma of the Prophet.

Turning to ʿAbd al-Jabbar, again, his interpretation of this verse can be found in three different sources: in his treatise on ambiguous verses of the Qur'an (*Mutashabih al-Qur'an*), in his monograph on the transcendence of the Qur'an from error (*al-Tanzih al-Qur'an min al-Mata'in*), and through al-Radi's report of ʿAbd al-Jabbar's view in the *Haqa'iq*. The first source, ʿAbd al-Jabbar's exposition in his work on ambiguous verses, reads very similar to al-Radi's position:

The apparent meaning of this verse points to what no Muslim would say because God has firmly established that he designated the Prophet for the task of warning and preaching and inviting [people] to the path of God with wisdom. And God says in 39:65: "If you ascribe any partner to God, all your work will come to nothing," and all of this necessitates that he [the Prophet] had many powers, for if it were not for this he would not be deserving of elevation, and would not be distinguished with virtue, and it would not be obligatory to follow what he commands and forbids. So, the apparent meaning [of the verse] does not give weight to the community's relationship to him.

So, the meaning of the verse is that the welfare of the followers and the betterment of their conditions in God's normative order is not the Prophet's responsibility because he, peace and blessings upon him, does not know these things. So when he saw someone from among the unbelievers being severe in their disbelief and rejection of him, he asked God to give him permission to pray for that person's destruction, as all the prophets before him had done. Hence with this verse God fortifies him and explains that He is the All-Knowing when it concerns their welfare. It is for this reason that God said after [the verse "you have no authority in the matter"], "whether God relents toward them or punishes them, they are wrongdoers." In this way, God explained that either He would relent toward them and they would be among the believers, or he punishes them in the Hereafter with what is greater than the punishment of this world.

If the Prophet did not have any authority, then why would he deserve elevation and praise? And why has he been exclusively selected for the jurisdiction of mandatory obedience? And why has it been required that he be followed? If he could exert no authority over his actions, then why would he be given this exclusive status as the most exceptional object of praise? If in reality al-amr is as if one were to say, "do this," then the apparent meaning of the verse is that the Prophet did not have the authority to command or forbid, and this is something no Muslim would say![87]

From this discussion, it is possible to note that al-Radi agreed with 'Abd al-Jabbar on the purpose and intention behind this verse. The kernel of both their explanations lies in a rejection of the view that this verse points to God as the sole determiner of human actions. Also central to both authors' concern is to preserve the notion of prophetic authority over the community of followers. At the same time, both al-Radi and 'Abd al-Jabbar seek to define what responsibilities come under the jurisdiction of the Prophet. What should be noted is that their discussion shifts the question from "What are the *powers* of the Prophet?" to "What are the prophetic *responsibilities*?" This point is made most clearly in their emphasis on the Prophet's asking for divine permission before making his supplication, since it suggests that the Prophet, too, was aware that his supplication would necessarily be answered if he were to make it. 'Abd al-Jabbar presents this very point in the excerpt of his view as stated in al-Radi's *Haqa'iq*. He states:

The apparent meaning of God's words, "you have no authority in the matter," determines that these words were a response to and prohibition of something the Prophet did. Therefore, there is difference [among exegetes] over the occasion of its revelation. Whatever the Prophet did in this instance has to have been good: the supplication against a specific people deserving of punishment. But the supplication of prophets for hastened destruction and the meting out of punishment necessitates an answer [from God] in the affirmative. If it did not, it would result in the condition of God turning away from his prophets. So, the Prophet [Muhammad], on him be peace, is not prevented from intending this supplication, and setting his mind to it, and asking permission for it. Hence God revealed this verse to explain that the right thing to do would be to withhold this supplication due to the outcome of an action through reform, and that is something God knows about: the repentance by some of them. This is the reason for their being rescued; their subsistence in the world is due to the possibility of betterment.[88]

These additional comments of 'Abd al-Jabbar underscore the fundamental principle at play in his discussion on prophetic power, namely, that supplication of the prophets must be answered. Implicit here is the idea that if prophets' prayers were not answered, this would undermine God's justice. In addition, 'Abd al-Jabbar asserts that the prophetic act of requesting divine permission is not in itself bad. Thus, God's justice is preserved, since the possibility of repentance of individual humans at any time is maintained, and prophetic authority is preserved because the matter from which the Prophet is excluded falls outside the bounds of his responsibilities (not outside his power). The crucial point here is that, in trying to understand the operations of a reason-centered logic in Mu'tazili thought, it must be noted that the goal of authorizing a justice-based system was not tied to the *devaluation* of prophetic power.

'Abd al-Jabbar's discussion makes another important point on this issue in the work *Transcendence of the Qur'an from Errors*:

God's saying afterward, "whether God relents toward them or punishes them," proves that the meaning of this is what we have said, because this makes it clear that their betterment is attained by their repentance, not by their love of the Prophet.[89]

In this note, 'Abd al-Jabbar shifts the significance of the verse from prophetic authority and responsibility to the community's *relationship* with the Prophet. Seeking to underscore individual human action as the determiner of reward or punishment as opposed to intercession of any kind, he reiterates that hope for salvation does not lie in the people's love for the Prophet, but rather in their repentance to God.

At this juncture, let us return to the question of how al-Radi and 'Abd al-Jabbar's independent approaches to verse 3:128 on prophetic authority converge, as well as how they differ. The underlying principle that guides both their arguments is a belief in the necessity of divine response to prophetic supplication. It is for this reason, they argued, that the Prophet seeks God's permission before making his request. Since this verse stands in for a response, and in it God does not grant permission to the Prophet, the purpose of this verse is to define the limits of prophetic responsibility. More importantly, according to this reading, what this verse does not do is limit the realm of prophetic power, and on this point both al-Radi and 'Abd al-Jabbar agreed.

However, the hermeneutical roots and routes of their respective arguments varied in important ways. Al-Radi defended his argument by positing an overarching normative arrangement of the world governed by God's knowledge of cause and effect, and the operations of time. Hence, a prophetic demand for retribution would alter the natural order of this normative arrangement. However, al-Radi's positing of this outlook was only the beginning of his discussion. His main objective was to present a semiotic map of the term *al-amr*, one that could demonstrate how the normative arrangement he described corresponds to and was affirmed by the language of the Qur'an. In contrast, 'Abd al-Jabbar steered the discussion to a different conclusion. He used the reasoning of this verse to argue against the idea that a person's love for the Prophet has any salvific value.

In the first section of this chapter, I noted that current scholars justify the "rationalization thesis" by pointing to a shift in the Imami community's understanding of the Imam as it evolved from seeing the Imam as a super-natural hero to an ultra-rational guide. What becomes increasingly evident when the rationalizing tendency in Imami thought is examined together with Mu'tazili arguments for God's justice is that "rationalization" did not neces-sarily equate to a puncturing of the prophet's extraordinary qualities. For Imami and Mu'tazili scholars writing in the eleventh century, a more "ratio-nal" outlook was not necessarily opposed to religious excess. The category of rationality (*'aql*) was not hostage to modern binaries such as "rational/mystical" or "religion/reason."

In sum, we have to remind ourselves that "rationalization" as it operated during this time was not bound to a modern conceptual grammar. There-fore, it is at once anachronistic and conceptually wanting to assume that the supposed "emasculation" of the Imams resulted from the efflorescence of a rational theology in Shi'ism. Instead, I would argue that, rather than search for a Mu'tazili inspired rationalization of prophetic and Imami authority in Shi'i thought, it would be more profitable to think carefully about the general episteme that dominated the social and intellectual currents at this time. This task is even more crucial when we consider the possibility that not all Imami scholars who moved in Mu'tazili circles during this era had a more rational stance toward the figure of the Imam. A case in point is al-Shaykh al-Mufid, al-Radi's main teacher of Imami theology. On this issue, Martin McDermott makes some arresting observations:

> Eccentric exaggerations aside, the supernatural stature of the Imams seems to have been steadily growing during the fourth century. Thus while the Nawbakhtis had denied that the Imams worked miracles and that their bodies were transported to the Garden after death, al-Mufid affirmed both these theses. And whereas Ibn Babuya in com-mon with the traditionist school of Qumm allowed the possibility of the Prophet—and a fortiori the Imams—making mistakes through distraction during religious duties, al-Mufid chided them for mini-mizing and lack of respect.[90]

McDermott's observations do not come as a surprise, despite the fact that, in current scholarship, al-Shaykh al-Mufid is regarded as the founder of a rational Imami theology. The significance of McDermott's statement, I would argue, lies in the very fact that it seems to be an aberration to the claims of the "rationalization thesis." This shows the conceptual dominance that the rationalization thesis has come to have over studies on Shi'i thought in early Islam. Even attempts to undermine it invariably tend to be organized through binaries such as rational/supernatural that form the foundational logic of this thesis.

Conclusion

In this chapter I have argued that any attempt to understand al-Radi's *Haqa'iq* demands a critical rethinking of our approach to religious identity and the categories of analysis that our approach employs. I have shown that conventional classifications of al-Radi's *Haqa'iq* as "Shi'i" or "Mu'tazili-influenced" betray a reliance on heresiographical literature and attitudes toward the boundaries of religious identity in early Islam. Indeed, the very genre of heresiography is governed by the construction of reified notions of identity. As a result, the use of such categories in our inquiry of al-Radi's *Haqa'iq* does little to capture and conceptualize al-Radi's hermeneutical moves and maneuvers in the *Haqa'iq*. By engaging al-Radi's arguments contrapuntally with those of 'Abd al-Jabbar, I have argued that the kinds of questions that animated al-Radi's examination of what would otherwise be characterized as "theological" issues participate in a host of varying and at times overlapping discourses, irreducible to any rigidly defined genre, that populated the discursive forcefield of tenth- and eleventh-century Baghdad. Crucially, such discourses were not limited to the scholastic exchanges of the *mutakallimun* (theologians, in the broader meaning of the term). Julie Scott Meisami, who has studied the shifting of attitudes in this period through developments in scholarly approaches to history, notes the following:

> The tenth and eleventh centuries saw the development of a new attitude towards history, predominantly ethical and rhetorical, reflecting the interests and culture of the secretaries and court officials to whom the writing of history was more and more entrusted.[91]

I would argue that a similar tone and ambition, one that combined ethics and rhetoric, can be discerned in al-Radi's treatment of ostensibly theological questions that arise from the Qur'an's ambiguous verses. This shift is most evident in his discussion of those verses that touch on sensitive political questions, such as 3:26, which asks how God can grant dominion to the unjust. Al-Radi's attempt to turn attention away from dynastic authority to individual agency by referring to the rhetorical features of the verse is significant. In addition, al-Radi's citations of early Islamic poetry and everyday speech to demonstrate grammatical nuance often play the crucial function of directing meaning toward a particular ideological trajectory. In other words, al-Radi mobilized the idiom of literary expression to invoke important ethical norms and values. Similarly, Meisami brings to our attention the close relationship between rhetoric and ethics in the medieval Persian historian al-Bayhaqi's work. She argued:

> The rhetorical approach to the writing of history cannot, therefore, be dismissed merely as a literarization of historical topics, but must be understood in its broader context. [Abu Bakr] Bayhaqi's [d.1066] history of Mas'ud, in which we witness a deliberate effort to marry history with ethics and with rhetoric, represents the culmination of this tendency in Arabo-Persian historiography.[92]

The marrying of history with rhetoric and ethics as a development of the tenth and eleventh centuries therefore presents a helpful avenue through which to examine al-Radi's Qur'an commentary and its literarization of exegetical topics.

Conceptually, in this chapter I have sought to question an approach toward the study of early Shi'i and Mu'tazili thought that uncritically accepts a narrative of influence and external borrowing. The problem with such an approach is that it replicates sectarian divisions and boundaries that are a product of heresiographical discursive frameworks and contexts. Moreover, a narrative of Mu'tazili influence over Shi'ism perpetuates an essentialist attitude toward religion that views religious identities as if they were like "billiard balls, bouncing off each other on a table, but remaining indivisible wholes all the while."[93] In moving away from such an essentialist reading of Shi'i identity, in this chapter I have tried to present a detailed account of the hermeneutical strategies and logics through which two prominent early Muslim scholars, al-Radi and 'Abd al-Jabbar, articulated and presented their religious authority. Through a close navigation of their exegetical approaches toward certain important questions of theological and ethical significance, I have

presented one example of the commonalities and departures between Shiʻi
and Muʻtazili approaches to Qurʾan exegesis in early Islam. What emerges is
a picture of Shiʻi-Muʻtazili relations whereby the hyphen in this construction
signifies an encounter of dynamic and often unpredictable intellectual cross-
pollination rather than a static and predetermined relationship of influence
and borrowing.

Conclusion

Rethinking "Shi'i Studies"

In these concluding remarks, I reiterate the key arguments and themes of this book, while also describing the larger theoretical implications of my argument about the interaction of sect, hermeneutics, and religious identity for the study of religion, Islam, Shi'ism, and the wider humanities. I begin, though, with a brief word on the reception and material history of the *Haqa'iq*, which will also provide me with an entry point into some broader discussions on theory, method, and politics.

The only surviving volume of the *Haqa'iq* is the same volume that includes al-Radi's treatment of Q. 3:7, the iconic verse announcing the division of the text into clear and ambiguous parts. Might this explain why this is the one volume that survived? Or is this a mere coincidence? Another dominant theme of the third sura relates to the relationship between Muslims and Jews and Christians. Might this account for the text's increased relevance, circulation, and eventual survival? While we can only speculate an answer here, shifting our attention to the materiality of the *Haqa'iq* manuscript and its preservation does raise the critical question regarding its reception. This is not to suggest that knowledge about a manuscript's circulation alone can serve as a measure for determining the text's salience or significance. Yet, it can shed light on the question of the communities and intellectual circles in which al-Radi's work may have enjoyed favor, readership, and patronage. Another way to gauge the reception of the *Haqa'iq* is that of attending to how it was cited by other scholars of his time. To this measure we must add the caveat, of course, that citational practices then were markedly different from our own. Thus, the absence of explicit references to a text does not necessarily negate the possibility of its readership nor that of its importance. That said, I have not come across any direct references to the *Haqa'iq* in later exe-geses or in lexicographical and theological writings. But the question of the *Haqa'iq*'s reception cannot yet be answered definitively. It is a matter of open and ongoing inquiry, especially given the number of Islamic manuscripts that have yet to be made accessible and carefully studied.[1]

Typically, the publishing patterns and, by extension, the accessibility of a text are regarded as the default measures of its significance. However, religion scholar Ahmed El Shamsy's path-breaking study, *Rediscovering the Islamic Classics*, has convincingly shown some of the glaring problems with such an approach. According to El Shamsy, patterns of publishing are hardly neutral indicators for the popularity or canonicity of a particular text or field in the Islamic intellectual tradition that could be assumed to be enclosed in some space "out there."[2] Rather, decisions on how often, when, where, and which texts get published are borne out of deeply polemical debates about what Islam is and through which authoritative voices it can be represented. Thus, the point being that when we broach the question of reception and explore the multiple means of arriving at an answer to that question—from the physical circulation of a text in its material form as manuscript or printed book, or the intellectual circula-tion of a text through citation and representation—we must remain vigilant to the ways in which these indicators work at once to sketch and skew our picture of Islam as a contested discursive tradition. Also, on a connected note, it is no longer tenable to take Orientalist writings and pronouncements on the influ-ence of particular Islamic texts or Muslim actors at face value without attending to those Orientalist authors' biases, desires, and notions of "authentic religion and Islam." Deep-seated Orientalist biases often explicitly or implicitly continue to haunt current scholarship. Let me offer just one among many possible exam-ples of this phenomenon most relevant to the context of this book, whereby the prevalent use of Orientalist categories for understanding traditional Muslim sects is often replayed in contemporary Euro-American scholarship.

In the opening pages of the widely used and circulated English-language resource for classical Arabic today, titled *Arabic-English Lexicon: Derived from the Best and Most Copious Eastern Sources*, the author, Edward Lane (d.1876), lists the main authorities he consulted in order to compile this mon-umental work. Lane's lexicon, which was published in 1863, is still among the most important and authoritative tools for serious students, researchers, and anyone who wishes to understand the etymological basis of Arabic words in their classical meaning. Through Lane's meticulous and detailed discussions, we are given a rare glimpse of how the sociopolitical and cultural milieus of the early centuries of Islam, during which lexical works were compiled, had a constituting effect on the meaning and application of words. But aside from tracing the outlines of how language developed, and the multitude of inter-related polysemous meanings that words possess, what Lane's work offers to the reader is a canon of Arabic lexicology.

It is this function of the book that accords immense value to the opening pages, in which Lane lists the figures from the Muslim scholarly traditions that constitute his authorities for the Arabic language. The list Lane compiles includes many who would have been familiar to al-Radi, featuring as it does not only the latter's contemporaries but also some of his teachers, including Ibn Jinni, al-Farisi, and al-Sirafi. Al-Radi himself, however, is not included in Lane's list of selected authorities. This is an unfortunate omission, since, as I have shown over the course of this book, al-Radi's discussion in the *Haqa'iq* is highly relevant to the discipline of determining the etymological basis of words and their homonymous properties through examples from the speech of Arabs, pre-Islamic Arabic poetry, and the revelatory sources. Indeed, not only did al-Radi draw on these sources in his work, he also played a critical role in their subsequent canonization. Perhaps it is the classification of the *Haqa'iq* as a Qur'anic exegesis that led Lane to overlook its critical contribution to the canonization and constitution of the Arabic language. Yet, in light of the heav-ily Sunni bent of Lane's chosen figures, I would speculate that al-Radi's label as a Shi'i scholar may in itself have cautioned Lane against including his name or views. But my concern here is not primarily with Lane's choices nor with the calculus of the decision-making process that might have gone into that process. I want to instead point to a critical issue that Lane's work brings to light: the extensive reach and tentacles of sectarian understandings of differ-ence that are derived from heresiological writings within the tradition but that permeate, often in unnoticeable ways, not only the conceptual frameworks we employ but also the very language we employ to build our arguments.

Inspecting Sectarian Assumptions

An apt analogy for what I am describing here is found in the vignette with which Jewish studies scholar Daniel Boyarin begins his now classic mono-graph *Border Lines*, a book that centers on the artificial but immensely con-sequential and powerful nature of the borders separating Judaism and early Christianity:

Every day for thirty years a man drove a wheelbarrow full of sand over the Tijuana border crossing. The customs inspector dug through the sand each morning but could not discover any contraband. He remained, of course, convinced that he was dealing with a smuggler. On the day of his retirement from the service, he asked the smuggler to reveal what it was that he was smuggling and how he had been doing so. "Wheelbarrows; I've been smuggling wheelbarrows, of course."

The customs inspectors, in their zeal to prevent any contraband from crossing the borders that they sought to enforce by fiat, were, themselves, the agents of illicit interchange of some of the most important contraband, the wheelbarrows. Similarly, and this is Boyarin's main argument, in the drive to separate Judaism from early Christianity, one must not lose sight of the wheelbarrow, the very discourse of heresiology itself, that posits such religious borderlines as innate and fixed rather than contingent.[3] Similarly, the example of Lane's lexicon highlights how we, as users of a canonical Arabic language authorized by a nineteenth-century British Orientalist philologist, might also unwittingly partake in the persistence of heresiological frameworks which imagine sectarian identities as stable, unchanging entities that differ from their competing "others" in neatly defined and identifiable ways.

At the crux of this book has been the attempt to highlight such unsuspecting places where our vigilance, like that of the customs inspectors in Boyarin's humorous anecdote, escapes us, and we become complicit, through the language and methodologies we employ, in facilitating the continuation of the very categories we may set out to carefully scrutinize and critique—in this case, the perpetuation of frameworks that privilege self-ascribed sectarian orthodoxies. I have questioned the pervasive assumption in Euro-American studies on Qur'anic exegesis that there exists a neat correspondence between an author's sectarian identity and his hermeneutical aesthetic.

Through al-Radi's example, I have sought to demonstrate that approaching Qur'an commentaries, especially those emanating from Twelver Shiʿi exegeses, as works in which authors make claims on the text's meaning primarily on the basis of their sectarian identity casts a severely narrowing effect on the kinds of questions that get asked of the Muslim commentarial tradition. Moreover, I have argued that, in addition to diminishing the very scope of our analysis, exclusively sectarian readings of Qur'an commentaries reinforce a conceptually unsound understanding of the formations and operations of religious identity.

Under a sectarian-driven conceptual schema, religious identities are conceived as predetermined bounded entities—a view that does not account for the specific historical conditions in which identities are constituted, nor the processes through which they are constantly reinvented. Consequently, an uncritical emphasis on sectarian identity as the key to exegetical choices perpetuates explanations for an author's hermeneutical decisions, language philosophy, political theory, and other intellectual arguments and dispositions that hinge on such binary categories as assimilation and resistance, borrowing and influence, and majority and minority. In lieu of such a binary framing, in the preceding pages, I have argued for a conceptual approach that resists a reified approach to identity formation, as reflected in works of Qur'an exegesis. I have done so by showcasing a template for what a nonsectarian reading of a Shi'i Qur'an commentator's exegetical exercise might look like, through a focus on analyzing the multivalent intellectual and political currents that informed al-Radi's Qur'an hermeneutic.

A Brief Recap

I went about this task by taking as my point of departure a set of competing narratives about al-Radi in the biographical and historical literature within the tradition. I argued that he was most consistently remembered as a gifted poet with an exceptional command over the Arabic language and that the significance of his poetic leanings in the discipline of Qur'anic exegesis was dual. First, central to his hermeneutic was the view that language was the fundamental source of authority for interpreting the Qur'anic text. Second, as a renowned poet, he belonged to an influential and emergent class of scholars who saw themselves as the custodians of a pure Arabic language.

In Chapter 2, I illustrated the political context of al-Radi's hermeneutical temperament and choices, a view that further interrupts the viability of a sectarian framework of analysis. This context was defined by the following major features: the fragmentation of political authority under the Buyids, the diminishing role of the caliph, and the resultant opening of multiple networks of patronage that paved the way for the articulation of new forms of religious authority, like that of the guardians of a pure Arabic language. Al-Radi was a powerful player and stakeholder in these debates surrounding the authority of language over logic. He interpreted his own position as a descendent of the Prophet (*sayyid*) and a leader of the Shi'i community as a testament to

his linguistic authority. Further, he saw his sacred lineage as intimately connected to his knowledge of a pure Arabic language. For him, language and
lineage were mutually entwined. Further still, exclusive access to a pure lineage and pure language authorized al-Radi to lay claim to the highest political
office: that of the caliphate. The logic of power on which al-Radi's claim to
the caliphate relied was one that linked rhetorical might to imperial might,
or one whereby linguistic and political authority were conjoined. Crucially,
such a logic of political, religious, and linguistic authority was part and parcel
of the intellectual and political climate in which he lived, wrote, and participated, and not a product or remainder of a determinative sectarian identity as
a Shi'i Qur'an exegete. A Shi'i poet and Qur'an exegete he certainly was, but
that identity cannot serve as a definitive variable of explanation for his multifaceted intellectual output or for his political aspirations; this is a point I have
made throughout this book.

Al-Radi's *Haqa'iq* and the linguistic achievement it put on display through
an argument for, and mastery of, ambiguity, was part of his ongoing appeal to
save the community from a linguistic cum political crisis. The predominant
sentiment that pulsates through his discourse is that of disappointment. He
laments the professionalization of poetry and its contribution to the tradition's overall decline; he bemoans how individuals other than an exclusively
aristocratic Arab class (like his own) have come to populate and dominate
this art. At the same time, he also decries the status quo in which political
power has been wrested from the rightful rulers (like himself and his father)
and led to a decline of the caliphal office. The *Haqa'iq*, and his broader literary oeuvre, presents his description of and answer to this sorry state of
affairs. A poetics of lament and the sentiment of disappointment hovers over
the question-and-answer space, or the problem space of the *Haqa'iq*.

In the second part of this book (Chapters 3 to 5), I presented select
examples from the *Haqa'iq* to show that al-Radi's Qur'an commentary is the
site through which he most vividly *performs* language and constructs for his
readers and audience a language archive: a set of ideas, thoughts, narratives,
images, and impressions about what language represents. The literary device
of ambiguity is central to this archive. I argue that al-Radi celebrates ambiguity for its ability to evoke wonder. He shows how ambiguity multiplies the
range of meanings available to a word, and how it effectively sets words "free"
from their habitual referents and, in doing so, creatively dismantles conventional readings with which the reader might be overly familiar. This act of
defamiliarization or "making strange" evokes a sense of wonder in the reader

and works to inculcate a fresh, new, meaning. Throughout this process, al-Radi emerges as the enabler of that new meaning or vision, which, he would argue, is the very meaning that the Qur'an intends. It is no exaggeration to state that in the *Haqa'iq* al-Radi evinces a distinct literary swagger, all the while giving the reader an insight into an array of pertinent questions that captured the imagination of the scholars of his period.

In his quest to decipher the puzzle of Qur'anic ambiguities, al-Radi combed the literary canon to identify authoritative proofs. Citing examples from Qur'anic verses, Arabic poetry, and the Arabic oral speech tradition performed for him two interconnected purposes. First, that of cementing his own authority as a Qur'an exegete and expert of the Arabic language. And second, it fulfilled the purpose of curating a distinct literary canon of the Arabic language through the labor of Qur'an exegesis. In this way, al-Radi's Qur'an commentary was situated in an intellectual environment whereby the critical relationship between language and revelation was at once formulated and hotly debated. The demands and pressures placed by the theological premise of the Qur'an's absolute clarity, and the exegetical striving to resolve the Qur'an's ambiguities as a way to meet that demand, played a determining role in the theorization of literary tools like ambiguity and metaphor. This is among my key arguments in this book.

In the final chapter, I reinforced the larger argument of this book through a comparison of al-Radi's and his teacher, the leading Mu'tazili theologian, 'Abd al-Jabbar's treatment of the Qur'an's ambiguous verses. Specifically, I demonstrated the overlapping yet divergent ways they applied a reason-oriented approach to exegesis on issues of theological importance, such as prophetic infallibility, God's sovereignty, and human agency. My purpose in staging this discussion was to challenge a narrative of early Shi'i exegesis as the product of Mu'tazili influence. Rather than casting al-Radi's hermeneutic as having come under the "influence" of 'Abd al-Jabbar's Mu'tazili teachings, I instead sought to argue for an approach focused on specifying the particular points of convergence and divergence found in their respective exegetical missions and programs. Unearthing specificity is the key to overcoming predictable generalizations; this is the conceptual principle I tried to put in motion in this final segment of the book. My aim in this discussion was not to dismiss visible forms of influence. Rather, the question I sought to explore was this: What do we gain by approaching relationships of cross-intellectual and inter-sectarian encounter in ways that are more nuanced than assuming self-contained intellectual and sectarian identities that emerge as objects or subjects of external influence or appropriation? My argument has been that casting a healthy dose of doubt and suspicion on the assumption of enclosed predetermined hermeneutical or sectarian identities allows us to view such identities not as fully furnished but as contingently authorized in a specific set of historical and political conditions. This conceptual argument is among the central contributions of this book to the academic study of religion.

Rethinking "Shiʻi Studies"

Taken together, through these illustrations and arguments, I have strived to make centrally visible a discursive archive that had thus far largely escaped the interpretive canopy of Western scholarship on Shiʻism and early Islam. In building a hermeneutical space for al-Radi's Qurʾan commentary, I have also pushed for a conceptual approach that closely navigates and describes the internal logics and interpretive moves that govern a particular exegetical project.

The trans-sectarian approach that I have sought to implement in this book makes the case for two important directions that I propose are critical for future projects in Shiʻi studies and in Islamic studies more broadly. First, too often, scholarly explorations of general Islamicate themes and topics such as exegesis, legal theory, and *hadith*, to name a few, have refrained from extending the scope of their analysis to the "Shiʻi" context. The justification for this neglect is couched in the language of humility, where the author admits his or her own limits as a scholar and argues that she or he must draw the line somewhere. But this strategy of epistemological humility has important implications that are often left unexamined.

It promotes the view that the study of Shiʻi subjects, be they texts, individuals, themes, or theories, quite naturally fall outside the scope of the otherwise separate field of Sunni Islam. Ironically, this same luxury of epistemological humility as an excuse for ignoring a vast and critical archive of Islamic thought is seldom available for scholars who focus on the religious thought of thinkers of a minority community, such as the Twelver Shiʻi, among others. A sectarian-driven paradigm of the study of Shiʻi Qurʾan exegesis, thus, is not only a conceptually wanting exercise but, among its implications and outcomes is also the perpetuation of a majoritarian understanding of Islam and Muslim identity that, in turn, transposes thoroughly modern notions of "majority" and "minority" onto premodern texts and actors.[4] As I have tried to show throughout this book, not only is this view historically

inaccurate, it also yields a limited understanding of the overarching episteme within which ideas and identities are constituted. As anthropologist
and religion theorist Talal Asad has succinctly argued, "If the adherents of
a religion enter the public sphere, can their entry leave the pre-existing discursive structure intact? The public sphere is not an empty space for carry-
ing out debates. It is constituted by the sensibilities—memories, aspirations,
fears and hopes—of speakers and listeners."[5] Building on Asad's point, one
may argue that relegating "Shi'i studies" as a separate field altogether is to
reinforce the view that the rituals, practices, texts, and sensibilities of Shi'i
Muslims can be carved out for individual study without causing a dent on the
conclusions about the discourse from which they have been taken.

The same can be argued for studies that come under the classification of
"Shi'ism," which devote an exclusive focus to what are uncritically taken to
represent characteristically Shi'i themes. What is most troubling about this
approach is the analytical foreclosure it effects on the study of topics that are
embedded in multiple intellectual traditions. While this book has examined
only one genre, that of Qur'anic exegesis, the conceptual commitment to disentangle religious thought and sectarian identity can be productively applied
to a number of different intellectual fields. Again, to repeat yet again, my point
has never been that sectarian identity is always unimportant to the intellectual
work of Muslim scholars or that it bears no consequence to their thought, be
that in whichever field of knowledge. My plea, rather, is that when sectarian
identity, especially in the case of a minoritized identity such as the Twelver
Shi'i, is privileged as the primary determiner of a scholar like al-Sharif al-
Radi's hermeneutical and religious imaginary, such a move invariably thwarts
the possibility of a number of potentially productive pathways of analysis and
inquiry. This book has represented an exercise in documenting a less traversed
discursive archive and pointing to conceptual avenues through which such
alternative analytical pathways could be navigated and explored.

NOTES

INTRODUCTION

1. Al-Sharif al-Radi, *Khasa'is al-A'imma 'alayhim al-salam: Khasa'is Amir al-Mu'minin 'alayhi al-salam*, ed. Muhammad Hadi al-Amini (Mashhad: Majma' al-Buhuth al-Islamiyya, 1985), 37.

2. At the time of al-Radi's writing, the term "Imami" or "Imami Shi'i" referred to one of the two major divisions within Islam, the other being the majority Sunni tradition. One of the main points of disagreement between the Sunni and Shi'a is over what count as authoritative sources of religion after the Qur'an and the normative practice of Prophet Muhammad. For the Imami Shi'i, the authority of the hereditary successors (Imams) is binding, whereas Sunnis instead privilege the consensus arrived on decisions of the scholars of the community. Moreover, al-Radi's reference to the term "Imami" in this quote identifies with a specific group that emerged (among several others) from the early Imami Shi'a: the Twelvers. The number twelve points to the group's eventual consolidation around the doctrinal belief in and argument for the authority of a specific line of twelve hereditary successors after Muhammad, the last of whom is believed to be in a state of occultation where God has hidden him from sight and will make him return at the end of time as the awaited messianic savior. The Twelver Shi'i position was articulated at the same time that other groups made competing arguments about the number, names, nature, authority, and status of the Imams. Like the Twelver Shi'a, some of these positions persisted and developed their own consolidated identities (Zaydi, Isma'ili, etc.), while others did not gain any ground. See Adam Gaiser, *Sectarianism in Islam: The Umma Divided* (Cambridge University Press, 2022), 86–125.

3. Al-Sharif al-Radi, *Haqa'iq al-Tawil fi Mutashabih al-Tanzil*, edited by Muhammad Rida Kashif al-Ghita. Beirut: Dar al-Adwa', 1986. The edition includes "Biography of the author (Tarjuma al-Mu'allif)" by 'Abd al-Husayn al-Hilli, and an introduction by a team of the printing press (al-Muntadi al-Nashr).

4. Even as I have translated it as such for the sake of brevity, the term "*Haqa'iq*" in the title of al-Radi's commentary, or "*Haqa'iq al-Ta'wil*," more specifically, conveys not just the sense of "hermeneutical realities" but also a specific understanding of how to arrive at those realities. As I will show later in the book, al-Radi's project is more congruent with a definition of *haqiqa* captured in the work of his contemporary lexicographer and literary critic, Abu Hilal al-'Askari (d. 1010). Abu Hilal defines *haqiqa* as "a speech act lexically placed according to its assigned place in the lexicon." See Alexander Key,

Language Between God and the Poets (Berkeley: University of California Press, 2018), 39. Accordingly, al-Radi's work might best be described as an interpretation of Qur'anic ambiguities arrived at through the art of identifying their rightful or accurate place in the lexicon (*fi al-lugha*).

5. Gaiser, *Sectarianism in Islam*, 12.

6. Ussama Makdisi, *Age of Coexistence: The Ecumenical Frame and the Making of the Modern Arab World* (Oakland: University of California Press, 2019), 4.

7. One reference that illustrates the diversity of approaches that constitutes the tradition of Shi'i exegesis is the entry on *"tafsir"* in the encyclopedic compendium *Da'iratul Ma'arif-i Buzurg-i Islami*, which lists the variety of methods and styles associated with Qur'an commentaries composed by Shi'i scholars in different time periods.

8. Makdisi, *Age of Coexistence*, 4.

9. Devin Stewart, *Islamic Legal Orthodoxy: Twelver Shiite Responses to the Sunni Legal System* (Salt Lake City: University of Utah Press, 1998), 6.

10. See Meir Bar-Asher, *Scripture and Exegesis in Early Imami-Shi'ism* (Leiden: Brill, 1999); Bar-Asher, "The Qur'an Commentary Ascribed to Imam Hasan al-Askari," *Jerusalem Studies in Arabic and Islam* 24 (2000): 358–79; Diane Steigerwald, "Twelver Shi'i Ta'wil" in *The Blackwell Companion to the Qur'an*, ed. Andrew Rippin (Malden, 2006), 373–85; Mahmoud Ayoub, "The Speaking Qur'an and the Silent Qur'an: A Study of the Principles and Development of Imami Shi'i tafsir," in *Approaches to the History of the Interpretation of the Qur'an*, ed. Andrew Rippin (Oxford, 1988), 177–98.

11. Meir Bar-Asher, "Exegesis II. In Shi'ism," in *Encyclopedia Iranica*, vol. 9 (New York: Bibliotheca Persica Press, 1999), 116–19.

12. Ayoub (drawing from Allama Tabataba'i) states: "The main principle of Shi'i exegesis is supported by the Prophetic saying that 'the Qur'an has an outer dimension and an inner dimension which has up to seven inner dimensions' (Ayoub, "The Speaking Qur'an and the Silent Qur'an," 187; Sayyid Muhammad Husayn al-Tabataba'i, *al-Qur'an fi al-Islam*, tr. Sayyid Muhammad al-Husayni (Beirut, Dar al-Zahra, 1973), 28).

13. See Tomoko Masuzawa, *The Invention of World Religions: Or, How European Universalism Was Preserved in the Language of Pluralism* (Chicago: University of Chicago Press, 2005).

14. The relationship between identity, memory, and accountability is eloquently argued in Ananda Abeysekara's *The Politics of Postsecular Religion: Mourning Secular Futures* (New York: Columbia University Press, 2008), 84–100. Within Western Islamic Studies, Adam Gaiser's excellent work dissects the categories of "sect" and "sectarianism" and details the problems they raise in the study of Islam. See Gaiser, "A Narrative Identity Approach to Islamic Sectarianism," in *Sectarianization: Mapping the Politics of the New Middle East*, ed. Nader Hashemi and Danny Postel, 61–75 (London: Hurst, 2017); and, more recently, Gaiser, *Sectarianism in Islam*, 2022.

15. Abeysekara, *The Politics of Postsecular Religion*; and Abeysekara, "Identity for and against Itself: Religion, Criticism, and Pluralization," *Journal of the American*

Academy of Religion 72, no. 4 (2004), 973–1001. I want to thank SherAli Tareen for alerting me to these sources.

16. Or what the anthropologist David Scott has called a "problem-space." See David Scott, *Refashioning Futures: Criticism after Postcoloniality* (Princeton, N.J.: Princeton University Press, 1999).

17. Two representative examples of this translation include: Eric Chaumont, "Ambiguity" in *Encyclopaedia of Islam*, 3rd ed., vol. 4 (Leiden: Brill, 2013), 50–54; Andrew Rippin, "Lexicographical Texts and the Qur'an," in *Approaches to the History of the Interpretation of the Qur'an* (Oxford: Oxford University Press, 2019), 171.

18. The most common Arabic definition for *majaz*, as Heinrichs shows, is "a word (or utterance) used for something other than that for which it was originally instituted." As for a translation of *majaz* into English, Heinrichs argues that although *majaz* has a larger compass, the idea of the 'non-literal' is paramount in it, and thus the use of the terms 'figurative'/'trope' can be justified." See Wolfhart P. Heinrichs, "On the figurative (*majaz*) in Muslim interpretation and legal hermeneutics" in *Interpreting Scriptures in Judaism, Christianity, and Islam: Overlapping Inquiries*, ed. Mordechai Z. Cohen and Adele Berlin (Cambridge University Press, 2016), 254.

19. The critical clause in this verse is the explicit warning for those who falsely claim to have knowledge of the *mutashabihat*. The verse clearly states that the authority to interpret is limited to a privileged few. Yet, this stern warning notwithstanding, the vague syntactic structure of the final part of the verse accommodates two possible answers to the question of to whom authority is limited. The first reading, which is reflected in the translation provided in the main text, states that God and those elevated in knowledge can interpret the *mutashabihat*. By contrast, a second reading holds that God alone can interpret the *mutashabihat*. In this case, the final sentences reads as follows: "But none knows its interpretation except God. Those who are rooted in knowledge say, 'We believe in it, all is from our Lord.' But only those who understand take notice." Translations from Carl W. Ernst, *How to Read the Qur'an: A New Guide, with Select Translations* (Chapel Hill: University of North Carolina Press, 2011), 175–76.

20. Mohammadreza Ardehali, *The Formation of Classical Imami Exegesis: Rawd al-jinan wa-rawh al-janan fi tafsir al-Qur'an of Abu al-Futuh Razi (d. in or after 552/1157)* (Toronto: University of Toronto ProQuest Dissertations Publishing, 2018), 7–126.

21. George Warner's recent work on al-Shaykh al-Saduq (d. 991) makes the important point of nuancing this narrative, arguing that, "Told a certain way, history casts the Imami Shi'a as going to sleep one night in a world in which all their questions could be answered by God's infallible representative on earth, only to wake up the next morning in a world from which that representative was catastrophically absent." Instead, he argues that we temper this "dramatic picture with an understanding of the historical and social realities of how the imamate had been working in the earlier ninth century, and how it initially continued to function in substantially the same way after al-'Askari's

death." See Warner, *The Words of the Imams, al-Shaykh al-Saduq and the Develop-ment of Twelver Shiʻi Hadith Literature* (London: I. B. Tauris, 2022), 38. He also raises the important question of "how ongoing, occultation-inspired changes to the imam's authority in theory effected how authority was exercised in practice in the Imami com-munity—authority of texts, of scholars and of legal and theological rulings. Even if the scholarly elites of the community remained in charge through the period of occultation's solidification as a doctrine, at the very least they had a new set of questions to answer" (Warner, *The Words of the Imams*, 40).

22. For instance, two articles on al-Radi's exegetical works brought attention to the distinctly literary taste and aesthetic of al-Radi, but no attempt was made to sit-uate his intellectual ambitions in the broader context of scholarly and imperial life in tenth-century Baghdad. See Mahmoud Ayoub, "Literary Exegesis of the Qur'an: The Case of Sharif al-Radi," in *Literary Structures of Religious Meaning in the Qur'an*, ed. Issa J. Boullata, 292–309 (Richmond: Curzon, 2000); and Kamal Abu-Deeb, "Studies in the Majaz and Metaphorical Language of the Qur'an: Abu ʻUbayda and al-Sharif al-Radi," in *Literary Structures of Religious Meaning in the Qur'an*, ed. Issa J. Boullata, 310–53 (Richmond: Curzon, 2000). Moreover, Abu-Deeb assumes that al-Radi's foray into the topic of the Qur'an's ambiguous elements reflects his Shiʻi background and the supposed familiarity of any Shiʻi scholar with the Qur'an's hidden (*batini*) meanings (Abu-Deeb, "Studies in the Majaz," 316). The value of Ayoub and Abu-Deeb's articles is not in question here. Their work has been vital for extending the discourse on the various modes and styles of Qur'anic exegesis beyond a narrow selection of majority Sunni writings. However, their work also alerts us to the way in which a lack of proper attention to the discursive palimpsest that layers a Qur'an commentary, like al-Radi's, leads to a markedly reified understanding not only of this work but of the larger milieu of which he was a part.

23. The Buyid Empire, founded by Shiʻite military leaders of Iranian origin, stretched from the southern and western parts of Iran to Iraq and lasted from 945–1055.

24. "I was confronted by an empty place, like the confrontation of a pony to its rope, a confrontation where my killing doesn't move [away] for me" (*taʻaradtu li bimakanin hallu, taʻaradu al-mahratu fi al-tuli, taʻarrudan lam taʻli ʻan qatlan li*), Haqa'iq, 4; "The wind weeps in affliction, as the lightning flashes in the clouds." (*Fa al-rihu tabki shuju-han, wa al-barqu yalmaʻu fi al-ghamamati*)," Haqa'iq, 12.

25. Lara Harb, *Arabic Poetics: Aesthetic Experience in Classical Arabic Literature* (Cambridge: Cambridge University Press, 2021). I discuss this more fully in Chapter 3 of this book, "Ambiguity, Hermeneutics, and Power."

26. Mary-Jane Rubenstein, *Strange Wonder: The Closure of Metaphysics and the Opening of Awe* (New York: Columbia University Press, 2011), 10.

27. Rubenstein, *Strange Wonder*, 4.

28. For a different articulation of this argument regarding the centrality of ambi-guity to the larger Islamic tradition, see Thomas Bauer, *A Culture of Ambiguity*, trans. Hinrich Biesterfeldt and Tricia Tunstall (Columbia University Press, 2021), 20–29.

29. For a discussion on how these seemingly opposed objectives were, in fact, harmoniously conjoined in the writings of other medieval Muslim authors, see Travis Zadeh's essay on Zakariyya al-Qazwini's (d. 1283) *Marvels of Creation ('Aja'ib al-makhluqat)*. Zadeh persuasively shows how al-Qazwini's work on worldly marvels (fictive) went hand in hand with the author's deep concern for veracity. He states: "The aesthetic logic that informs writings on the wonders of the world is one which is in constant dialectic with questions of veracity and mendacity." See Zadeh, "The Wiles of Creation: Philosophy, Fiction, and the 'Aja'ib Tradition," *Middle Eastern Literatures* 13, no. 1 (2010): 31.

30. Again, Zadeh's insights on al-Qazwini's investment in wonder resonate with al-Radi's approach to ambiguity. Zadeh shows that for al-Qazwini, while wonder functioned as a catalyst for knowledge, it was also an end, in and of itself. As such, "pleasure" forms a key element in al-Qazwini's justification for his subject matter (Zadeh, "The Wiles of Creation," 30–31).

31. In his overview of Shi'i hermeneutics, Lawson divides the works and their main features chronologically, recognizing that "methods of interpretation in Shi'ite exegesis themselves vary considerably, often according to the socio-political fortunes of the community." See Todd Lawson, "Hermeneutics," in *Encyclopedia Iranica*, vol. 12 (New York: Bibliotheca Persica Press, 2004): 235–39.

32. For a reiteration of this position through a different genre, that of Muslim historiography, see Najam Haider, *The Rebel and the Imam in Early Islam: Explorations in Muslim Historiography* (Cambridge: Cambridge University Press, 2020). Other individual examples can also demonstrate the futility of this "functional" relationship. A figure like Husayn Va'iz Kashifi (d. 1504), for example, was a preacher, scholar, Naqshbandi shaykh, astrologer, lettrist, and classic polymath. The sheer diversity of genres that his writings cover would make it a grave error to classify his work titled *Rawdat al-shuhada'* as a "Shi'i" text. This is in spite of the fact that this same text became a crucial work for the lived Shi'i tradition. See M. E . Subtelny, "Kashifi, Kamal Al-Din Hosayn Wa'ez," in *Encyclopaedia Iranica*, vol. 15 (New York: Bibliotheca Persica Press, 2011), 658–61.

33. See Kambiz GhaneaBassiri, *A Window on Islam in Buyid Society: Justice and Its Epistemological Foundation in the Religious Thought of 'Abd Al-Jabbar, Ibn Al-Baqillani, and Miskawayh* (PhD diss., Harvard University, 2003); Richard W. Bulliet, *Islam: The View from the Edge* (New York: Columbia University Press, 1993); and Omid Safi, *Politics of Knowledge in Premodern Islam* (Chapel Hill: University of North Carolina Press, 2006).

34. See Carl W. Ernst, *Following Muhammad, Rethinking Islam in the Contemporary World* (Chapel Hill: University of North Carolina Press, 2003), 156.

35. Lawson, "Hermeneutics."

36. This is a broader term than that of "linguistic philosophy," which the contemporary philosopher of language, John R. Searle, described as "the attempt to solve particular philosophical problems by attending to the ordinary use of particular words or other elements in a particular language. See Shukri Abed, *Aristotelian Logic and the Arabic Language in Alfarabi* (Albany: State University of New York Press, 1991), 173.

CHAPTER 1

1. ʿAli ibn al-Yusuf al-Qifti (d. 1248), *Inbah al-Ruwat*, vol. 3 (Cairo: Dar al-Kutub al-Misriyya, 1955), 114–15; Ibn al-ʿImad (d. 1679), *Shadharat al-dhahab fi akhbar man dhahab*, vol. 3 (Cairo: Maktabat al-Qudsi, 1931–32), 182–84; Yusuf Ibn Ahmad al-Bahrani (d. 1772), *Luʾluʾat al-Bahrayn* (Najaf: Matbaʿat al-Nuʿman, 1966), 322–29.

2. For a translation of ʿAli ibn Abi Talibʾs words, see Tahera Qutbuddin, *A Treasury of Virtues: Sayings, Sermons, and Teachings of ʿAli, with the One Hundred Proverbs attributed to al-Jahiz* (New York: New York University Press, 2013), 201–4.

3. A. J. Wensinck, "ʿAmr," in *Encyclopaedia of Islam, First Edition (1913–1936)*, vol. 1 (Leiden: Brill, 1987), 334–35.

4. Joel L. Kraemer, *Humanism in the Renaissance of Islam: The Cultural Revival during the Buyid Age* (Leiden: E. J. Brill, 1992); Lenn Evan Goodman, *Islamic Humanism* (New York: Oxford University Press, 2003).

5. Ibn Jinni was also on good terms with the esteemed poet al-Mutanabbi and authored two commentaries on his *Diwan*. See J. Pedersen, "Ibn Djinni" in *Encyclopaedia of Islam*, 2nd ed., vol. 2 (Leiden: Brill, 1991), 754.

6. "Sabian" here refers to his association to the Sabians of Harran, a community that followed an old Semitic polytheistic religion but had a strongly Hellenized elite. They adopted the Qurʾanic name Sabiʾa during the third/ninth century so as to be able to claim the status of *ahl al-kitab* and thus avoid persecution. See F. C. de Blois, "Sabiʾ," in *Encyclopaedia of Islam*, 2nd ed., vol. 8, 672–75.

7. For biographical overviews on al-Sharif al-Radi, see ʿAbd al-Ghani Hasan, *al-Sharif al-Radi* (Cairo: Dar al-Maʿarif, 1970); Muhammad Sayyid al-Kilani, *al-Sharif al-Radi* (Cairo: Matbaʿat al-Ahram, 1937); Mahfuz, *al-Sharif al-Radi* (Beirut: Maktabat Beirut, 1944); Ihsan ʿAbbas, *Al-Sharif al-Radi* (Beirut: Dar Beirut, 1959); ʿAbd al-Fattah Muhammad al-Hulw, *Al-Sharif al-Radi: hiyatuhu wa-dirasat shiʿrihi* (Cairo: Hajr li al-Tibaʿa wa al-Nashr, 1986); Muhammad Hadi al-Amini, *Al-Sharif al-Radi, Muhammad ibn al-Husayn ibn Musa al-Musawi* (Tehran: Muʾassasat Nahj al-Balagha, 1987); and Islam Abu ʿAli, *Al-Sharif Al-Radi: His Life and Poetry* (PhD diss., Durham University, 1974).

8. Hasan Amin, "Nahj ul-Balagha," in *Daʾirat al-Maʿarif al-Islamiyya al-Shiʿiyya* (Beirut: Muʾassasat ʿAbd al-Hafiz al-Bisat, 1972), 355–63. It remains to be established whether the Imami Shiʿi position on the *Nahj al-Balagha* as second in status to the Qurʾan is a modern reflection or a historical position amongst the Imami Shiʿa.

9. Suzanne Stetkevych traces these links across al-Radiʾs poetry and the *Nahj al-Balagha* in "Al-Sharif al-Radi and *Nahj al-balaghah*: Rhetoric, Dispossession, and the Lyric Sensibility." *Journal of Arabic Literature*, no. 3/4 (2019): 211–50.

10. The relationship between al-Maʿarri and al-Radiʾs brother al-Murtada, however, was not cordial. Reports exist about al-Maʿarri being expelled (literally "dragged by the foot") from al-Murtadaʾs literary salon on account of his critique of al-Murtadaʾs lack of appreciation of the poet al-Mutannabi. See P. Smoor, "al-Maʿarri," in *Encyclopaedia of Islam*, 2nd ed., vol. 5 (Leiden: Brill, 1986), 927–35.

11. J. S. Nielsen explains that the "jurisdiction of *mazalim* tended to be very wide. Receiving and processing petitions against official and unofficial abuse of power was an important part of its activity, but it also on occasion functioned as a court of appeal against the decisions of *qadis*." See Nielsen, "Mazalim," in *Encyclopaedia of Islam*, 2nd ed., vol. 6 (Leiden: Brill, 1991), 933–35.

12. Members of the Banu Hashim clan were the ancestral relatives of the Prophet. They were divided into two groups, the 'Alids and 'Abbasids, on the basis of their specific genealogical link. Both groups received a salary from the government due to this prestigious lineage. They also had their own court, headed by their own religious leader called the *naqib*. It was under the Buyid ruler Mu'izz al-Dawla (d. 967) that the 'Alids were first separated from the jurisdiction of the 'Abbasid *naqib*. See A. Havemann, "Naqib al-Ashraf," in *Encyclopaedia of Islam*, 2nd ed., vol. 7 (Leiden: Brill, 1993), 926–27.

13. Havemann, "Naqib al-Ashraf." For a more extensive study on the office of the *niqaba*, see Teresa Bernheimer, *The 'Alids: The First Family of Islam, 750–1200* (Edinburgh: Edinburgh University Press, 2013), 52–70.

14. Shainool Jiwa, "The Baghdad Manifesto (402/1011): A Re-Examination of Fatimid-Abbasid Rivalry," in *The Fatimid Caliphate, Diversity of Traditions*, ed. Farhad Daftary and Shainool Jiwa (London: I. B. Tauris, 2018), 40.

15. Jiwa, "The Baghdad Manifesto," 38.

16. Tahera Qutbuddin, "Al-Sharif al-Radi," *Encyclopaedia of Islam*, 3rd ed., vol. 1 (Leiden: Brill, 2023), 147–51; Muhammad Mahdi Jafri, *Sayyid Radi* (Iran: Tarhe Naw, 1959), 138.

17. See Qasim Samarra'i, *Niqabat al-ashraf fi al-Mashriq al-islami hatta nihayat fatrat hukm al-usra al-Jala'iriyya: muntasaf al-qarn al-thalith al-hijri hatta awa'il al-qarn al-tasi' al-hijri* (Beirut: Dar al-Kutub al-'Ilmiyya, 2013), 147.

18. Abu al-Mahasin Yusuf Ibn Taghribirdi (d. 1412), *Nujum al-Zahra* (Cairo: Mat-ba'at Dar al-Kutub al-Misriyya, 1952), 223, 240.

19. Islam Abu 'Ali, *Al-Sharif Al-Radi*, 9.

20. I return to this issue in detail in Chapter 2.

21. Adam Mez, for example, has argued that al-Radi was the first 'Alid aristocrat who publicly abandoned resistance to authority. Mez supports this position by referring to an incident where al-Radi exchanged the white dress, which his father had worn, for the black uniform of the 'Abbasid courtier and official. See Adam S. Mez, *The Renaissance of Islam*, trans. Khuda Bukhsh and D. S. Margoliouth (Patna: Jubilee Print and Publishing, 1937), 153, 272.

22. See Wilferd Madelung, "A Treatise of the Sharif al-Murtada on the Legality of Working for the Government (*Mas'ala fi al-'Amal Ma'a al-Sultan*)," *Bulletin of the School of Oriental and African Studies, University of London* 43, no. 1 (1980): 18–31.

23. Madelung, "A Treatise of the Sharif al-Murtada," 24–31.

24. Suzanne Stetkevych, "Al-Sharif al-Radi and the Poetics of 'Alid Legitimacy: Elegy for al-Husayn ibn 'Ali on 'Ashura', 391 A.H.," in *Arabic Literary Thresholds: Sites*

of Rhetorical Turn in Contemporary Scholarship, ed. Muhsin Jasim Musawi and Jaroslav Stetkevych (Leiden: Brill, 2009), 56.

25. Abu al-Faraj Ibn al-Jawzi, *al-Muntazam fi Tarikh al-Muluk wa al-Umam* (Beirut: Dar al-Kutub al-ʿIlmiyya, 1992), 115–19.

26. Ihsan ʿAbbas, *al-Sharif al-Radi* (Beirut: Dar Beirut, 1959), 106.

27. For this version of the account, see Tamima Bayhom-Daou, *Shaykh Mufid* (Oxford: Oneworld, 2005), 27. In an excellent more recent study of these events, and especially al-Qadir's issuing of the "Baghdad Manifesto," Shainool Jiwa has analyzed the sources that document these two incidents, namely, al-Radi's composition of the pro-Fatimid verses and his signing of the Baghdad Manifesto denouncing the Fatimids (a year after his father's death). She concludes that the differences in the accounts with regard to their chronology and details leave open the question of whether al-Radi actually signed the Manifesto of 1011, and whether he wrote the pro-Fatimid verses (this second conclusion is less persuasive). See Jiwa, "The Baghdad Manifesto," 38–43.

28. Jiwa, "The Baghdad Manifesto," 38.

29. *Haqaʾiq*, 16.

30. ʿAbbas, *al-Sharif al-Radi*, 103–7.

31. ʿAbbas, *al-Sharif al-Radi*, 104–5.

32. Al-Radi, *Diwan*, annotated by Yusuf Shukri Farhat, vol. 2 (Beirut: Dar al-Jil, 1995), 216. Translation is mine.

33. Abu Mansur ʿAbd al-Malik al-Thaʿlibi, *Yatimat al-dahr*, vol. 3 (Beirut: Dar al-Kutub al-ʿIlmiyya, 1983), 131–51.

34. Al-Khatib al-Baghdadi (d. 1071), *Tarikh Baghdad* (Cairo: Maktabat al-Khanji, 1931), 246–47. It is cited with its full chain of transmission in Ibn al-Qifti, *Inbah al-Ruwat*, 114–15; and Ibn al-ʿImad, *Shadharat*, 182–84.

35. Martin J. McDermott, *The Theology of Al-Shaikh Al-Mufid (d. 413/1022)* (Beirut: Dar el-Machreq éditeurs, 1978), 8.

36. Perhaps a telling detail to note is that in Ibn ʿInaba's (d. 1424) *ʿUmdat al-Talib*, whose main authority is the Shiʿi genealogist ʿUmari, the author compares al-Radi to the finest poets from the Quraysh tribe, including Yazid ibn Muʿawiya, the archenemy of Islam in the Shiʿi imagination and the tyrant who was responsible for the massacre at Karbala in 680. See Ibn ʿInaba (Ahmad ibn ʿAli Dawudi al-Hasani), *ʿUmdat al-Talib fi ansab Al Abi Talib* (Beirut: Manshurat Dar Maktabat al-Hayat, 1980), 167–73.

37. Carl Brockelmann, *Geschichte der Arabischen Litteratur* (Leiden: E. J. Brill, 1943), I, 81, S I, 131–32).

38. Ibrahim Nijad, *Al-Sharif al-Radi: The Compiler of Nahj al-Balagha*, tr. Husayn ʿAlamdar (Qum: Ansariyan, 1996), 32–35; Muhammad ibn Ismaʿil al-Mazandarani (d. 1800), *Muntaha al-maqal fi ahwal al-rijal* (Beirut: al-Muʾassasat Al al-Bayt, 1998), 28–29; Vahid (Waheed) Akhtar, *Early Shiʿite Imamiyyah Thinkers* (Delhi: Ashish Publication House, 1988), 127; Abdul Husayn Ahmad Amini Najafi, *al-Ghadir* (Beirut: Dar al-Kitab al-ʿArabi, 1967), 184.

39. Abu Hamid ibn Hibat Allah Ibn Abi al-Hadid, *Sharh Nahj ul Balagha*, vol. 1 (Beirut: Dar Ihya' al-Kutub al-'Arabiyya, 1975), 31–41.

40. Fatima's own predilection for theological discourse is also mentioned and further affirmed in a report according to which al-Shaykh al-Mufid dedicated one of his treatises on theology to her. See Muhammad Agha Buzurg Tehrani, *al-Dhari'a ila Tasanif al-Shi'a*, vol. 1 (Najaf: Matba'at al-Ghari, 1936), 302.

41. Kazuo Morimoto, *Sayyids and Sharifs in Muslim Societies: The Living Links to the Prophet* (London: Routledge, 2012), 18; Louise Marlow, *Dreaming Across Boundaries: The Interpretation of Dreams in Islamic Lands* (Boston: Ilex Foundation, 2008), 1–11.

42. Amira Mittermaier, *Dreams That Matter: Egyptian Landscapes of the Imagination* (Berkeley: University of California Press, 2011), 2–3.

43. Morimoto, *Sayyids*, 17–19.

44. Morimoto, *Sayyids*, 17–19.

45. Leah Kinberg, "Literal Dreams and Prophetic Hadith in Classical Islam: A Comparison of Two Ways of Legitimation," *Der Islam* 70 (1993): 279–300.

46. Morimoto, *Sayyids*, 18–19.

47. Morimoto, *Sayyids*, 26.

48. Morimoto, *Sayyids*, 19.

49. Robert Gleave, *Islam and Literalism* (Edinburgh: Edinburgh University Press, 2011), 131; Mohammad Ali Amir Moezzi, *The Divine Guide in Early Shi'ism: The Sources of Esotericism in Islam* (Albany: State University of New York Press, 1994), 207 n427.

50. *Diwan al-Radi*, vol. 2, 724. Cited in Islam 'Abu 'Ali, *Al-Sharif Al-Radi* (PhD diss., Durham University, 1974), 39.

51. Ibn al-Jawzi, *al-Muntazam*, vol. 15, 115–19; Ibn 'Inaba, *'Umdat al-Talib*, 170–73. It is interesting to note that in some sources (Ibn al-Jawzi and Ibn 'Inaba), this story is presented as part of a longer anecdote, which compares al-Radi to his brother al-Murtada. In it, the vizier Fakhr al-Mulk gives al-Radi a more welcoming reception than his brother and is asked about this by his companion. Embedded in the questioner's inquiry is the assumption that al-Radi would rank lower due to his fame as a poet, as opposed to al-Murtada who had achieved recognition as a scholar of religious disciplines. In his reply, Fakhr al-Mulk narrates an incident where he had to charge al-Murtada a sum for administrative purposes and al-Murtada had made a request for a discount on this charge. He then compares this incident with the event of his gifting al-Radi one thousand dinars on the birth of a son and receiving the reply that he did.

52. Ibn al-Jawzi, *al-Muntazam*, vol. 15, 115–19; Ibn Abi al-Hadid, *Sharh Nahj ul Balagha*, vol. 1, 31–41.

53. Others included the vizier, Sabur ibn Ardeshir.

54. Ibn Khallikan, *Wafayat al-A'yan*, vol. 4, ed. Ihsan 'Abbas (Beirut: Dar al-Thaqafa, 1968), 414–20; 'Abd al-Ghani Hasan, *al-Sharif al-Radi* (Cairo: Dar al-Ma'arif, 1970), 18; 'Abd al-Husayn al-Hilli, "Author's biography," in *Haqa'iq al-Ta'wil fi Mutashabih al-Tanzil* (Beirut: Dar al-Adwa', 1986), 85.

55. Muhammad Mahdi Jafri, "Sharif Radi," in *Danishnama-yi Jahan-i Islam (Encyclopaedia of the World of Islam)*, vol. 27 (Tehran: Bunyad-i Da'irat al-Ma'arif-i Islami, 1996), 152–57.

56. Al-Radi, *Talkhis al-Bayan fi Majazat al-Qur'an*, ed. Makki al-Sayyid Jasim (Beirut: 'Alam al-Kutub), 2011.

57. Al-Radi, *Al-Majazat al-Nabawiyya* (Beirut: Dar al-Kutub al-'Ilmiyya, 2007), 9–10.

58. This work is not extant. See 'Abd al-Husayn al-Hilli in his biography of the author (*tarjuma al-mu'allif*) that prefaces the text of the *Haqa'iq* in the edition published by Dar al-Adwa', 1986, 92.

59. Qutbuddin, "Al-Sharif al-Radi." For a more extensive study of these sermons, see Tahera Qutbuddin, "The Sermons of 'Ali ibn Abi Talib: At the Confluence of the Core Islamic Teachings of the Qur'an and the Oral, Nature-Based Cultural Ethos of Seventh Century Arabia," *Anuario de Estudios Medievales* 42, no. 1 (2012): 201–28.

60. Qutbuddin, "Al-Sharif al-Radi."

61. Stetkevych, "Al-Sharif al-Radi and Nahj al-balaghah," 220.

62. Islam Abu 'Ali, *Al-Sharif Al-Radi*, 58.

63. Another critic said of al-Radi's dirges that in them he is like a mother mourning her own son. See Islam Abu 'Ali, *Al-Sharif Al-Radi*, 214.

64. Jafri, "Sharif Radi,"156.

65. Jafri, "Sharif Radi,"156.

66. Stetkevych, "Al-Sharif al-Radi and Nahj al-balaghah"; Stetkevych, "Al-Sharif al-Radi and the Poetics of 'Alid Legitimacy."

67. Stetkevych, "Al-Sharif al-Radi and Nahj al-balaghah," 250.

68. Stetkevych, "Al-Sharif al-Radi and Nahj al-balaghah," 220.

69. Al-Hilli, "Author's biography," 92.

70. These works are not extant. See al-Hilli, "Author's biography," 92.

71. Jafri mentions the publication of a few additional letters in "Sharif Radi," 154.

72. This work is not extant, but it is possible that this was a commentary on his teacher al-Farisi's book. Mentioned in al-Najashi, *Kitab al-Rijal* (Tehran: Manshurat-i Markaz-i Nashr-i Kitab, 1965), 310–11; and Ibn 'Inaba, *'Umdat al-Talib*, 170–73.

73. These works are not extant. See al-Hilli, "Author's biography," 92.

74. Qutbuddin, "Al-Sharif al-Radi."

75. See Walid Saleh, *The Formation of the Classical Tafsir Tradition: The Qur'an Commentary of Al-Tha'labi (d. 427/1035)* (Boston: Brill, 2004), 203; Tariq Jaffer, *Razi: Master of Qur'anic Interpretation and Theological Reasoning* (Oxford: Oxford University Press, 2015), 27–28.

76. In his work on 'Abd al-Jabbar, Gabriel Reynolds points out that this method of presenting one's argument developed as a tool through which a scholar would demonstrate his position rather than inductively deriving it. Other such tactics employed to achieve this goal included, for instance, the positing of questions by hypothetical opponents and then driving those hypothetical interlocutors to a logically untenable

position. See Reynolds, *A Muslim Theologian in a Sectarian Milieu: 'Abd al-Jabbar and the Critique of Christian Origins* (Leiden: Brill, 2004), 26.

77. There are two main manuscript sources for the current edition of volume five of the *Haqa'iq*. The first, composed around the year 1137, approximately one hundred twenty-five years after al-Radi's death, is located in the Imam Rida shrine library in Mashhad, Iran. It was collated with the help of another copy, which had been read to al-Radi. The renowned Shi'i scholar Mirza Husayn Nuri Tabrisi (d. 1902) played a critical role in making this manuscript available by copying it during his visit to the library and by circulating it among scholars. The second main manuscript source is located in a private library in Isfahan. However, as the editor of the *Haqa'iq*, al-Hilli bemoans "this manuscript is replete with errors, indicating the copyists' lack of knowledge and linguistic expertise." See the introduction to the *Haqa'iq* by 'Abd al-Husayn al-Hilli, p. 10–12.

78. References to the figure 'Imran in the Qur'an generally point to the father of Mary, the mother of Jesus. The "Household of 'Imran," as per the title of the third sura, refers to the family that God chose, along with Adam, Noah, and the family of Abraham. According to the dominant exegetical tradition, the family of 'Imran is an allusion to Mary and Jesus. A variant exegetical trend adopted by one of the early exegetes, Muqatil ibn Sulayman (d. 767), is that "Household of 'Imran" refers to the family of Moses and Aaron. This is so because the name 'Imran also refers to the father of Moses and Aaron, the biblical 'Amraam. See Roberto Tottoli, "'Imran," *Encyclopedia of the Qur'an*, ed. Jane McAuliffe, vol. 2 (Leiden: Brill, 2001): 509.

79. Shawkat M. Toorawa, *Ibn Abi Tahir Tayfur and Arabic Writerly Culture: A Ninth-Century Bookman in Baghdad* (London: Routledge Curzon, 2005). According to Toorawa, the emergence of the writerly culture in ninth-century Baghdad witnessed the expansion of manuscript markets and transformed learned and literary life.

CHAPTER 2

1. Mez, *The Renaissance of Islam*; Kraemer, *Humanism in the Renaissance of Islam*; Goodman, *Islamic Humanism*.

2. See, for example, Claude Cahen, "Buwayhids or Buyids," *Encyclopaedia of Islam*, 2nd ed., vol. 1 (Leiden: Brill, 1986), 1350–57; Kraemer, *Humanism in the Renaissance of Islam*; Muhammad Ismail Marcinkowski, "Twelver Shiite Scholarship and Buyid Domination: A glance on the life and times of Ibn Babawayh Al-Shaykh Al-Saduq (D-381/991)," *The Islamic quarterly* 45 (2001): 199; Meir Bar-Asher, *Scripture and Exegesis in Early Imami- Shi'ism*; Kabir Mafizullah, *The Buwayhid Dynasty of Baghdad, 334/946–447/1055* (Calcutta: Iran Society, 1964); John Donohue, *The Buwayhid Dynasty in Iraq 334 H./945 to 403 H./1012: Shaping Institutions for the Future* (Leiden: Brill, 2003).

3. Cahen, "Buwayhids or Buyids."

4. Bar-Asher, *Scripture and Exegesis in Early Imami-Shi'ism*, 9.

5. See, for example, M. G. Carter, "Review of *Humanism in the Renaissance of Islam: The Cultural Revival During the Buyid Age*," *Journal of the American Oriental Society* 109, no. 2 (1989): 304–5; Ira M. Lapidus, "Review of *Humanism in the Renaissance of*

Islam: The Cultural Revival During the Buyid Age," *American Historical Review* 93, no. 1 (1988): 199; GhaneaBassiri, "A window on Islam in Buyid society."

6. Samuel England, *Medieval Empires and the Culture of Competition* (Edinburgh: Edinburgh University Press, 2017).

7. England, *Medieval Empires*, 6–11.

8. GhaneaBassiri, *A Window on Islam in Buyid Society*, 1.

9. Similar arguments against a dynastic approach to history have been made in Bulliet, *Islam: The View from the Edge* (New York: Columbia University Press, 1993); and Omid Safi, *Politics of Knowledge in Premodern Islam* (Chapel Hill: University of North Carolina Press, 2006).

10. GhaneaBassiri, *Window on Islam in Buyid Society*, 1.

11. Alexandre M. Roberts, "Being a Sabian at Court in Tenth-Century Baghdad," *Journal of the American Oriental Society* 137, no. 2 (2017), 254.

12. Roberts, "Being a Sabian," 260. Roberts cites this exchange from al-Thaʻlibi's anthology of tenth-century poetry, *Yatimat al-dahr fi mahasin ahl al-ʻasr*.

13. *Ahl al-dhimma*, lit. "people with whom a covenant has been made," referred to non-Muslims living under sovereign Muslim dynasties; in exchange for the special tax they paid (*jizya*), they were granted freedom and protection by the rulers.

14. Roberts, "Being a Sabian," 262–63.

15. Cahen, "Buwayhids or Buyids."

16. Warner, *The Words of the Imams*, 34.

17. I treat this issue of the "rationalist turn" in Shiʻi thought more fully in Chapter 6, "Is the *Haqaʼiq* a Muʻtazili-Shiʻi Exegesis?"

18. Cahen, "Buwayhids or Buyids."

19. Cahen, "Buwayhids or Buyids."

20. Marshall G. S. Hodgson, *The Venture of Islam: Conscience and History in a World Civilization*, vol. 2 (Chicago: University of Chicago Press, 1974), 36.

21. Safi, *Politics of Knowledge in Premodern Islam*; Bulliet, *Islam: The View from the Edge*.

22. Cahen, "Buwayhids or Buyids"; Kraemer, *Humanism in the Renaissance of Islam*.

23. Roy P. Mottahedeh, *Loyalty and Leadership in an Early Islamic Society* (London: I. B. Tauris, 2001), 98–104.

24. Erez Namaan, *Literature and the Islamic Court* (London: Routledge, 2019), p. 10. "Court," the author stresses, refers not so much to a particular physical space but rather to a social configuration.

25. Namaan, *Literature and the Islamic Court*, 41.

26. Namaan, 28–29.

27. Wen-chin Ouyang, *Literary Criticism in Medieval Arabic-Islamic Culture: The Making of a Tradition* (Edinburgh: Edinburgh University Press, 1997), chapter titled "Functions of Poetry in Medieval Arabic-Islamic Society," 55–83.

28. Ibn Khalikan, *Wafayat al-Aʻyan*, tr. De Slane, vol. 2 (Beirut: Librairie du Liban, 1970) 167.

29. Fuller discussions on the intellectual and literary climate during the Buyid period can be found in: Nuha A. Alshaar, *Ethics in Islam: Friendship in the Political Thought of al-Tawhidi and his Contemporaries* (New York: Routledge, 2015), 27–58; Erez Naaman, *Literature and the Islamic Court* (Abingdon, 2016); Donohue, *The Buwayhid Dynasty in Iraq*; Kraemer, *Humanism*; Mafizullah, *The Buwayhid Dynasty of Baghdad*.

30. David Scott, *Conscripts of Modernity: The Tragedy of Colonial Enlightenment* (Durham, N.C.: Duke University Press, 2004), in which he draws on Reinhart Koselleck, *Futures Past: On the Semantics of Historical Time* (Cambridge, Mass.: MIT, 1985), 44.

31. Al-Khatib al-Baghdadi, *Tarikh Baghdad*, vol. 2 (Cairo: Maktabat al-Khanji, 1931), 246–47.

32. Stetkevych, "Al-Sharif al-Radi and the Poetics of 'Alid Legitimacy," 53.

33. Stetkevych, "Al-Sharif al-Radi and *Nahj al-balaghah*," 217.

34. Stetkevych attributes this valorization to modern 'Abbasid poets; their intense innovation was displayed and competed in courts, which enabled the tying together of rhetorical might with Islamic (imperial/sovereign) might.

35. Stetkevych, "Al-Sharif al-Radi and the Poetics of 'Alid Legitimacy," 56.

36. Al-Radi, *Diwan*, 2:39.

37. Wilferd Madelung, "The Assumption of the Title Shahanshah by the Buyids and 'The Reign of the Daylam (Dawlat Al-Daylam),'" *Journal of Near Eastern Studies* 28, no. 3 (1969): 168–83.

38. Abu Ishaq Ibrahim al-Sabi served as the secretary to the Buyid Mu'izz al-Dawla and to the 'Abbasid caliphs al-Muti' and al-Ta'i'. He is also the author of a history of the Buyid dynasty, *al-Kitab al-Taji fi akhbar al-dawla al-Daylamiyya*. The book was commissioned by 'Adud al-Dawla as a price of al-Sabi's release when he, along with a few others, including al-Radi's father, were imprisoned by 'Adud al-Dawla. These conditions are provided as the reason for reports about al-Sabi's assertion that the history was nothing but a pack of lies (the veracity of this report has been questioned). See Wilferd Madelung, "Abu Ishaq al-Sabi on the 'Alids of Tabaristan and Gilan," *Journal of Near Eastern Studies* 26, no. 1 (1967): 17–57.

39. Biographers like 'Abd al-Ghani Hasan have interpreted their friendship as proof of al-Radi's open-mindedness in light of their differences in age and religion. See 'Abd al-Ghani Hasan, *al-Sharif al-Radi*.

40. Adapted from the translation in Islam Abu 'Ali, *Al-Sharif Al-Radi*, 123.

41. As I alluded to in the introduction of this chapter, Alexandre M. Roberts's article nicely highlights the contradictions and complexities that being a Sabian in these times entailed, and the rhetorical strategies by which one could both assert difference and argue for proximity. See Roberts, "Being a Sabian," 253–77.

42. 'Abd al-Ghani Hasan, *al-Sharif al-Radi*, 23.

43. The writings of al-Radi's teacher, al-Shaykh al-Mufid, and his brother, al-Sharif al-Murtada, are central to this body of literature. As for al-Radi, his name is remembered

not so much for his writings on the Qur'an or the Imams but mostly for his contribution as the compiler of the *Nahj al-Balagha*.

44. See Muhammad Baqir Khwansari, *Rawdat al-Jannat fi Ahwal al-'Ulama' wa al-Sadat* (Tehran: Maktabat Isma'iliyan, 1970). Ibn 'Inaba mentions this move on the part of some biographers, without making clear his own position. See Ibn 'Inaba, *'Umdat al-Talib*, 172.

45. Hanadi Za'al Mas'ud al-Hindawi, "Al-Sharif al-Radi wa Tumuhihi nahw al-Khilafa zaman al-Khalifa al-Qadir billah (r. 969–1015)," *Dirasat al-'Ulum al-Insaniyya wa al-Ijtima'iyya* 46, no. 2 (2019): 147.

46. Islam, *Al-Sharif Al-Radi*, 259.

47. Cahen, "Buwayhids or Buyids."

CHAPTER 3

1. For a discussion on introductions to *tafsir* works, see Karen Bauer, "Justifying the Genre: A Study of Introductions to Classical Works of Tafsir," in *Aims, Methods and Contexts of Qur'anic Exegesis (2nd/8th–9th/15th Centuries)* (Oxford University Press, 2013), 39–68.

2. Lara Harb, *Arabic Poetics*, 10n30.

3. Heinrichs opts for "figurative/trope" as the closest English translations for the term *majaz* to convey its key meaning of the non-literal. See Heinrichs, "On the Figurative (*majaz*) in Muslim Interpretation and Legal Hermeneutics," 254.

4. On the specific connotation of the term "*Haqa'iq*" in the title of al-Radi's commentary on the Qur'an's ambiguous verses, *Haqa'iq al-Ta'wil fi Mutashabih al-Tanzil*, I refer to Alexander Key's excellent mapping of this concept, including its significance in the context immediately concerned with al-Radi. Key helpfully highlights how the lexicographer and literary critic Abu Hilal al-'Askari explains usage of this term in his book of lexical definitions, *al-Furuq al-Lughawiyya* (a work that sought to clarify the subtle differences between terms close in meaning and thereby dismantle the idea that there was such a thing as synonyms). In his entry on *haqa'iq*, al-'Askari maintained that it referred to speech acts that were lexically placed according to their assigned place in the lexicon (Key, *Language Between God and the Poets*, 39). The significance of this definition, as Key explains, is that the notion of vocal forms used according to their "original lexical placement" referred to a specific kind of accuracy, one that relied entirely on the lexicon. By invoking the lexicon as its authoritative guide, the term *haqiqa* laid claim to a consensus of meaning (Key, *Language Between God and the Poets*, 101). These insights are critically useful as we approach al-Radi's arguments in the *Haqa'iq*, guided as they are by the principle of identifying the proper lexical arrangement of speech in order to unravel the Qur'an's ambiguities. We will also see the significant place the lexicon held throughout al-Radi's exegesis. Accordingly, the term *haqa'iq* in the title of al-Radi's work could also be rendered as "accurate accounts." As Key points out, this was also the usage intended by al-Raghib al-Isfahani and several other scholars of the Qur'an and the Arabic language. (Key, *Language Between God and the Poets*, 43).

5. Stetkevych, "Al-Sharif al-Radi and *Nahj al-balaghah*," 217.

6. Harb, *Arabic Poetics*, 4.

7. As noted in the Introduction, in a recent article, Abu-Deeb draws a connection between al-Radi's Shi'i background and his focus on Qur'anic metaphors. See Abu-Deeb, "Studies in the Majaz and Metaphorical Language of the Qur'an," 316.

8. For a brief survey on the varied understandings of the term *mutashabihat*, see Leah Kinberg, "Muhkamat and Mutashabihat (Koran 3/7): Implications of a Koranic Pair of Terms in Medieval Exegesis," *Arabica* 35, no. 2 (July 1988): 143–72.

9. Nabia Abbott, *Studies in Arabic Literary Papyri* (Chicago: University of Chicago Press, 1957), 99.

10. David Vishanoff, *The Formation of Islamic Hermeneutics: How Sunni Legal Theorists Imagined a Revealed Law* (New Haven, Conn.: American Oriental Society, 2011), 17.

11. According to al-Farra', for example, the *muhkamat* are verses that clarify what is allowed (*halal*) and what is prohibited (*haram*)—that is, verses that are not abrogated. See Abu Zakariyya al-Farra', *Ma'ani al-Qur'an*, ed. Ahmad Yusuf Najati and Muhammad 'Ali Najjar, vol. 1 (Cairo: al-Hay'ah al-Misriyya al-'Amma li al-Kitab, 1980), 190.

12. Al-Farra' and al-Tabari are two exegetes, among others, who discuss the opening letters (*fawatih*) within the framework of the *mutashabihat*. Cited in Kinberg, "Muhkamat and mutashabihat," 156.

13. See Abu al-Hasan al-Ash'ari, *Maqalat*, ed. Muhammad Muhyi al-Din 'Abd al-Hamid (Cairo: Maktabat al-Nahda al-Misriyya, 1969), 293–94; Abu Ja'far Muhammad Ibn Jarir al-Tabari *Jami' al-bayan 'an ta'wil 'an al-Qur'an*, ed. Sidqi Jamil al-'Attar (Beirut: Dar al-Fikr, 2009), 211–15, cited in Vishanoff, *The Formation of Islamic Hermeneutics*, 17.

14. See the Introduction in this volume.

15. Vishanoff, *The Formation of Islamic Hermeneutics*, 17.

16. Vishanoff, *The Formation of Islamic Hermeneutics*, 17.

17. For example, see Ibn Qutayba, *Mushkil al-Qur'an* (Medina: Al-Maktaba al-'Ilmiyya, 1981); al-Farra', *Ma'ani al-Qur'an*.

18. Vishanoff, *The Formation of Islamic Hermeneutics*, 16.

19. The *Fihrist* of Ibn Nadim, for example, lists the works of scholars under three relevant genres: *Ma'ani al-Qur'an*, *Gharib al-Qur'an*, and *Mutashabih al-Qur'an*. See Muhammad ibn Ishaq ibn al-Nadim, *al-Fihrist*, ed. Yusuf 'Ali Tawil and Ahmad Shams al-Din (Beirut: Dar al-Kutub al-'Ilmiyya, 1996), 52–57. Also see John E. Wansbrough, *Qur'anic Studies: Sources and Methods of Scriptural Interpretation* (Oxford: Oxford University Press, 1977), 208–26.

20. Abu 'Ubayda authored the *Majaz al-Qur'an* (Frankfurt: Institute for the History of Arabic-Islamic Science at the Johann Wolfgang Goethe University, 2010), and is credited with works on *Gharib al-Qur'an* and *Ma'ani al-Qur'an*. Al-Farra' is credited with works on *Ma'ani al-Qur'an*.

21. Abu 'Ubayd al-Qasim ibn Sallam, *Gharib al-Hadith* (Beirut: Dar al-Kutub al-'Ilmiyya, 2011), and Ibn Qutayba, *Gharib al-Hadith* 2 vols. (Beirut: Dar al-Kutub al-'Ilmiyah), 1988.

22. Sahiron Syamsuddin, "*Muhkam* and *Mutashabih*: An Analytical Study of Al-Tabari's and Al-Zamakhshari's Interpretations of Q.3:7," *Journal of Qur'anic Studies* 1, no. 1 (1999): 68.

23. Muqatil ibn Sulayman, *Tafsir Muqatil ibn Sulayman*, ed. 'Abd Allah Mahmud Shihatah (Cairo: Mu'assasat al-Halabi, 1969), 1:5.

24. *Al-Ashbah wa al-naza'ir*, also called *al-wujuh wa al-naza'ir*. Vishanoff notes that meanings were called *wujuh*, occurrences with different meanings were called *ashbah*, and occurrences with the same meaning were called *naza'ir*. See Vishanoff, *The Formation of Islamic Hermeneutics*, 18. Muqatil ibn Sulayman also has a work titled *Mutashabih al-Qur'an*, but Nabia Abbott suggests that references to it may be mistitled copies of the same *al-Wujuh wa al-Naza'ir*. See Abbott, *Studies in Arabic Literary Papyri*, 2:96.

25. Abbott, *Studies in Arabic Literary Papyri*, 2:100.

26. Vishanoff notes that appeals to Arabic poetry are characteristic of the works of Abu 'Ubayda and al-Farra', but not of commentaries from the early eighth century, such as Muqatil ibn Sulayman's. See Vishanoff, *The Formation of Islamic Hermeneutics*, 20; Wansbrough, *Qur'anic Studies*, 216–17.

27. Yasir Suleiman, *The Arabic Grammatical Tradition: A Study in Ta'lil* (Edinburgh: Edinburgh University Press, 1999), 2; Jonathan Owens, *The Foundations of Grammar: An Introduction to Medieval Arabic Grammatical Theory* (Amsterdam: Benjamins, 1988), 4.

28. Vishanoff, *The Formation of Islamic Hermeneutics*, 20; Versteegh, *Arabic Grammar*, 39.

29. Suleiman, *The Arabic Grammatical Tradition*, 45, 64.

30. John Wansbrough, who in "Majaz al-Qur'an: Periphrastic Exegesis," *Bulletin of the School of Oriental and African Studies, University of London* 33, no. 2 (1970): 247–66, has closely examined Abu 'Ubayda's work, has also observed its parallels with what would later come to be called a discussion on the *mutashabih* verses. See Wansbrough, *Qur'anic Studies*, 220. Kamal Abu-Deeb also gestures toward the overlaps between al-Radi and Abu 'Ubayda in his comparative analysis of their works. See Abu-Deeb, "Studies in the Majaz and Metaphorical Language of the Qur'an."

31. I borrow this translation of *majaz* from David Vishanoff. As he explains, "*majaz* is often translated 'figurative' or 'metaphorical,' but this suggests a much narrower concept than is usually in view, so I will most often translate the word in its most basic sense of crossing over or passing beyond, using the terms 'transgression' and 'transgressive,' which should be understood without the strong negative connotation they have in English." See Vishanoff, *The Formation of Islamic Hermeneutics*, 21.

32. Abu 'Ubayda's work on the Qur'an and grammar is regarded by some to be a turning point in its philological analysis and departing from a previous tradition of "naive" exegesis. See Claude Gilliot, "Les debuts de l'exegese coranique," *Revue des mondes musulmans et de la Méditerranée* 58 (1990): 82–100, cited in Versteegh, *Arabic Grammar and Qur'anic Exegesis in Early Islam* (Leiden: E. J. Brill, 1993), 47.

33. Heinrichs, "On the figurative," 255.

34. Recent studies have argued for a clear distinction between the work of al-Radi and that of Abu 'Ubayda, with regard to their respective uses of the term *majaz*: al-Radi's two treatises on *majaz* represent specific treatments of metaphors in the Qur'an and the hadith, as compared to the work of Abu 'Ubayda, which, although also working with the term *majaz*, was intended for a much broader meaning of "interpretation." See Muhammad 'Abd al-Ghani Hasan, *Al-Sharif Al-Radi* (Cairo: Dar al-Ma'arif, 1970), 79–80. To be clear, the similarity I wish to draw is that between al-Radi's use of *mutashabih* (ambiguity) and Abu 'Ubayda use of *majaz* (interpretation).

35. Heinrichs interprets Abu 'Ubayda's use of *majaz* as "explanatory reading." See Wolfhart Heinrichs, "On the Genesis of the *Haqiqa-Majaz* Dichotomy," *Studia Islamica*, no. 59 (1984): 129.

36. Earlier works on this topic sought to highlight not just metaphors but a range of linguistic transgressions. These works came under titles like *Gharib al-Hadith* (*Strange [Language] in the Hadith*) and sought to address the problematic passages in the hadith literature, such as Ibn Qutayba's *Gharib fi al-Hadith*. By contrast, al-Radi's work on the *majazat* was concerned exclusively with metaphors in the Prophetic statements, not with all linguistic transgressions.

37. Al-Radi employed the Arabic terms *majaz* (to transgress) and *isti'ara* (to borrow) interchangeably to mean metaphor. It was only later, in the theoretical treatment by 'Abdul Qahir al-Jurjani (d. 1078 CE), that an effort was made to systematically differentiate between simile (*tashbih*), analogy (*tamthil*), metaphor (*isti'ara*), and trope (*majaz*).

38. Heinrichs, "On the Genesis of the *Haqiqa-Majaz* Dichotomy," 134–35, 138–39. Heinrichs traces the narrowing of *majaz* to the specific meaning of metaphor to the Mu'tazili scholars particularly the works of al-Jahiz.

39. Heinrichs, "On the Genesis of the *Haqiqa-Majaz* Dichotomy," 134–35, 138–39.

40. Heinrichs, "On the Genesis of the *Haqiqa-Majaz* Dichotomy," 135–37. Heinrichs associates the *majaz/haqiqa* pairing with more theologically inclined (Mu'tazili) writings, where the terms were used to solve not linguistic but theological quandaries. Heinrichs argues that in the discussions of the theologians, it is not always clear whether the pair of terms are used ontologically or linguistically.

41. Nasr Hamid Abu Zayd, *Al-Ittijah al-'Aqli fi al-Tafsir: Dirasa fi Qadiyat al-Majaz fi al-Qur'an 'inda al-Mu'tazila* (Beirut: al-Markaz al-Thaqafi al-'Arabi, 1982), 184.

42. This was characteristic in the work of Ibn Qutayba, who also states that he begins his discussion with *isti'ara* because it is the most common type of *majaz*. See Heinrichs, "On the Genesis of the Haqiqa-Majaz Dichotomy," 131. Heinrichs regards Ibn Qutayba's (d. 885) work as marking a critical turning point in the understanding and application of *majaz*. He argues that Ibn Qutayba's distinct dual position as both philologist and theologian led him to restrict the semantic compass of *majaz* from earlier conceptualizations like that of Abu 'Ubayda, for whom *majaz* could stand for all sorts of non-alignments between language and reality. Ibn Qutayba, in contrast, held a stricter and narrower conception of *majaz* that comes closer to the idea of the "trope,"

or non-literal meaning or function. See Heinrichs, "On the Genesis of the Haqiqa-Majaz Dichotomy," 255–57.

Al-Radi does not cite Ibn Qutayba in the *Haqa'iq*, so it is not clear if he was familiar with this work. However, another figure who uses *majaz* in the broader sense of linguistic transgression and *isti'ara* or metaphor as one specific type of *majaz* is al-Rummani (d. 994). For al-Rummani's use of metaphor, see Wolfhart Heinrichs, *The Hand of the Northwind: Opinions on Metaphor and the Early Meaning of Isti'ara in Arabic Poetics* (Mainz: Deutsche Morgenländische Ges., 1977). Some biographers list al-Rummani as al-Radi's teacher, hence it is safe to assume that al-Radi was at the very least aware of the different interpretations of *majaz*, and his decision to regard *majaz* as interchangeable with *isti'ara* was not due to his lack of awareness of alternate theories.

43. Al-Radi, *Talkhis*, 11–12.

44. For this translation, see Lidia Bettini, "Mushtarak," in *Encyclopedia of Arabic Language and Linguistics*, vol. 3 (Leiden: Brill, 2008), 320-23.

45. Mustafa Shah, "The Philological Endeavours of the Early Arabic Linguists: Theological Implications of the Tawqif-Istilah Antithesis and the Majaz Controversy – Part I," *Journal of Qur'anic Studies* 1, no. 1 (1999): 37–42.

46. A recent Beirut publication of al-Radi's *Haqa'iq* appears side by side with Muqatil ibn Sulayman's *Ashbah wa al-Naza'ir*, indicating the publisher's recognition of the relationship between the two works. Of course, the fact that another name under which Muqatil's text circulated was *Mutashabih al-Qur'an* may also account for, if not further explain, the choice of pairing the two works. For the thesis that textual references to Muqatil's *Mutashabih al-Qur'an* likely referred to mistitled copies of *al-Wujuh wa al-Naza'ir*, see Nabia Abbott, *Studies in Arabic Literary Papyri*, 2:96.

47. Al-Mubarrad is remembered for his famous debates with Tha'lab on points of grammar, and the different positions of these scholars are what are reported to have led to the division between the Kufan (Tha'lab) and Basran (al-Mubarrad) schools of grammar. Al-Mubarrad's commentary and criticism on Sibawayh's *al-Kitab* has also been recognized by scholars for playing an important role in securing *al-Kitab*'s acceptance as an authoritative source on the grammar of the Arabic language. See Monique Bernards, *Changing Traditions: Al-Mubarrad's Refutation of Sibawayh and the Subsequent Reception of the Kitab* (Leiden: Brill, 1996).

48. This phrase and its discussion were common in grammatical treatises and appeared in Sibawayh's *al-Kitab*. See Andrew Rippin, "Al-Mubarrad (d. 285/898) and Polysemy in the Qur'an," in *Books and Written Culture of the Islamic World Studies Presented to Claude Gilliot on the Occasion of his 75th birthday*, ed. Andrew Rippin and Roberto Tottoli (Leiden: Brill, 2015), 64.

49. Rippin, "Al-Mubarrad (d. 285/898) and Polysemy in the Qur'an," 56–69. Note that Rippin regards al-Mubarrad's work as a treatment of polysemy, not homonymy, even as the title of the work, *Ma Ittafaqa Lafzuhu wa Ikhtalafa Ma'nahu*, could apply to both.

50. Rippin, "Al-Mubarrad (d. 285/898) and Polysemy in the Qur'an," 59.

51. Rippin, "Al-Mubarrad (d. 285/898) and Polysemy in the Qur'an," 63.

52. Muqatil ibn Sulayman, *al-Wujuh wa al-Naza'ir fi al-Qur'an al-Karim*, ed. Ahmad Farid al-Mazidi (Beirut: Dar al-Kutub al-'Ilmiyya, 2008), 15–16.

53. Rippin, "Al-Mubarrad (d. 285/898) and Polysemy in the Qur'an," 65.

54. There is an example in the *Haqa'iq* of al-Radi challenging al-Sijistani, which suggests his familiarity with al-Sijistani's works.

55. Shah, "The Philological Endeavours," 40–41.

56. Muhammad ibn Yazid al-Mubarrad, *Kitab Ma Ittafaqa Lafzuhu wa Ikhtalafa Ma'nahu min al-Qur'an al-Majid* (Cairo: al-Matba'a al-Salafiyya, 1931), 8.

57. Gregor Schwarb, "Capturing the Meanings of God's Speech: The Relevance of *Usul al-fiqh* to an Understanding of *Usul al-tafsir* in Jewish and Muslim *Kalam*," in *A Word Fitly Spoken: Studies in Medieval Exegesis of the Hebrew Bible and the Qur'an Presented to Haggai Ben-Shammai* (Jerusalem: Ben-Zvi Institute, 2007), 132. Cited in Rippin, "Al-Mubarrad (d. 285/898) and Polysemy in the Qur'an," 67.

58. This was most systematically authorized by al-Shafi'i and his canonization of the Qur'an and Prophetic hadith as the fundamental sources of law.

59. In addition, both disciplines drew from the terminology and theories of the other. For example, Sibawayh found legal reasoning to be the most useful for his description of grammar. Although he may not have been making a case for the parity of language and law, his work was eventually used for this purpose. See Michael Carter, "Sibawayhi," in *Encyclopaedia of Islam*, 2nd ed., vol. 9 (Leiden: Brill, 1997), 524–31.

In another example, the very edifice of al-Shafi'i's effort to canonize the Prophetic hadith literature as a source for interpreting the Qur'an bore echoes with Muqatil ibn Sulayman's theories of polysemy. See Vishanoff, *The Formation of Islamic Hermeneutics*, 34–65.

60. See M. G. Carter, *Sibawayhi's Principles: Arabic Grammar and Law in Early Islamic Thought* (Atlanta, GA: Lockwood, 2016); Vishanoff, *The Formation of Islamic Hermeneutics*, 45–56.

61. This was not the only way to imagine revelation as a source of law, as is seen in al-Baqillani (d. 1013), 'Abd al-Jabbar's Ash'ari contemporary, who imagined the words of the Qur'an as "dim and partial expressions of God's inscrutable command," and Hanbali Abu Ya'ala ibn al-Farra' (d. 1066 CE), who "treated revelation as a single eternal speech act by which God brings about obligations performatively in the hearts of his servants." See Vishanoff, *The Formation of Islamic Hermeneutics*, 125.

62. Vishanoff, *The Formation of Islamic Hermeneutics*, 125.

63. Vishanoff, *The Formation of Islamic Hermeneutics*, 126.

64. This same view was held by the head of the Hanafis in Baghdad, Ahmad ibn 'Ali Abu Bakr al-Razi al-Jassas (d. 981), and was a central tenet in his work on legal theory, further reinforcing the important overlaps between the legal, exegetical, and philological traditions. See Wolfhart Heinrichs, "Contacts between Scriptural Hermeneutics and Literary Theory in Islam: The Case of Majaz," *Zeitschrift Für Geschichte Der Arabisch-Islamischen Wissenschaften* 7 (1991): 253–84.

65. Al-Tabari, *Jami' al-Bayan 'an Ta'wil al-Qur'an* (Cairo: Mustafa al-Babi al-Halabi, 1954), 173–74, 183, cited in and translated by Kristin Zahra Sands, *Sufi Commentaries of the Qur'an* (London: Routledge, 2008), 15, 19.

66. Suleiman, *The Arabic Grammatical Tradition*, 15. Suleiman examines the work of *ta'lil* (ratiocination) in the works of four key figures, including al-Radi's teacher and mentor Ibn Jinni. Suleiman argues that an interest in the *'illa* (rationale) as the means for articulating explanations in Arabic grammatical theory was at the heart of Ibn Jinni's work in his *Khasa'is*. See chapter 4 of his book, "Ibn Jinni and *Ta'lil* in the Arabic Grammatical Tradition," 64–105.

67. It should be noted that the question of whether these schools were historical realities or retrospective constructions of later grammarians is a subject of considerable debate amongst scholars. Aside from the question of their historical reality, the main principle of difference between these schools as pointed out by Yasir Suleiman: pivoted on the extent to which either school was invested in using certain data for generative purposes as opposed to simply using data for the sake of legitimization. As Suleiman writes, "the Kufans were more open to allowing rare features of the language (like variant readings of the Qur'an) to act as generative bases or models for producing novel data. This was unlike the qiyas-driven position of the Basran grammarians, who sought to restrict the generative power of the data." See Suleiman, *The Arabic Grammatical Tradition*, 19n10.

68. Suleiman, *The Arabic Grammatical Tradition*, 16.

69. Suleiman, *The Arabic Grammatical Tradition*, 16.

70. There were two ways in which a source like variant readings of the Qur'an could be invoked: as a means for generating novel data that would make up the authoritative corpus of language, or as an example of existing data whose authority had been established elsewhere. As Suleiman argues, however, "the Arab grammarians were reluctant to accept all the variant readings as equally generative bases or models for the analogical creation of novel data, arguing that only those readings which conform to the regular or productive norms of the language can serve in this capacity." See Suleiman, *The Arabic Grammatical Tradition*, 19.

71. Note that this is not to say that al-Radi or Ibn Jinni "belonged" to the Kufan school of grammar. In fact, Ibn Jinni occupied a middle position between the Kufan and Basran schools of grammar, and it is possible to identify elements of both schools in al-Radi's exegetical choices as well.

72. Vicente Cantarino, *Arabic Poetics in the Golden Age: Selection of Texts Accompanied by a Preliminary Study* (Leiden: Brill, 1975), 27–39.

73. Suleiman, *The Arabic Grammatical Tradition*, 20.

74. Initially, data was said to have been collected from Qurayshi speakers and from speakers who belonged to the tribes of Qays, Tamim, Asad, Hudayl, and branches of Kinana and Tayy. The data came from speakers who "adopted a pronounced, some would say deliberately exaggerated Bedouin lifestyle—especially shepherds, hunters, raiders—so much so that some informants who lived in, or on the edge of the urban centers used to conform to this mode of life in their appearance to enhance their own professional

credibility in the eyes of the grammarians." See Suleiman, *The Arabic Grammatical Tradition*, 23.

75. Suleiman, *The Arabic Grammatical Tradition*, 22.

76. Suleiman's historicist approach to this data leads him to describe it as "defective," due to multiple factors like fabrication, male gender bias, internal rivalries between grammarians, and an exclusive reliance on memory.

77. Suleiman, *The Arabic Grammatical Tradition*, 26.

78. Suleiman, *The Arabic Grammatical Tradition*, 31.

79. Part of verse 3:7 states: "The perverse at heart eagerly pursue the ambiguities in their attempt to make trouble and to pin down a specific meaning of their own." Rather than read this clause to imply a categorical ban on interpreting the *mutashabihat*, altogether, scholars like al-Jassas, al-Zamakhshari, and later Ibn Kathir (d. 1373) understood it to mean that the *mutashabihat* could only be interpreted by referring them back to their *muhkamat*. See Syamsuddin, "*Muhkam* and *Mutashabih*," 69. The same principle of returning the *mutashabihat* to the *muhkam* can also be found in the sayings of the Shi'i Imams. See Ayoub, "The Speaking Qur'an and the Silent Qur'an," 189; and al-Tabataba'i, *al-Qur'an fi al-Islam*, 38–40.

80. We might say that al-Radi's discussion did not focus on the question of authority here because the *Haqa'iq* is not a general *tafsir* that comments on all aspects of the verses under discussion. Rather, it is a specialized work that only treats the ambiguous aspects of the verses. Yet, commentaries on ambiguous verses have often been interpreted in secondary scholarship as opportunities for Mu'tazili scholars to present Qur'anic proof of their principles, determined a priori. Similarly, al-Radi's *Haqa'iq* has been described as an opportunity for him to justify and argue for Shi'i doctrinal principles (as if such a thing were fixed and unchanging). A closer reading of the *Haqa'iq*, however, reveals this not to be the case. At the same time, though, while al-Radi does not center the issue of interpretive authority as the focus of his discussion, he also does not leave it entirely unaddressed, either. In a separate discussion section at the end of the chapter, he does clarify his stance on questions of interpretive authority connected to verse 3:7. I discuss this section in detail in the next chapter, "The Politics of Language."

81. Al-Radi, *Haqa'iq*, 2.

82. On this, al-Radi is aligned with al-Tabari and brings forward the same supporting Qur'anic verse as him, as well (23:50). See Syamsuddin, "*Muhkam* and *Mutashabih*," 70.

83. Al-Radi, *Haqa'iq*, 166.

84. Kees Versteegh, *The Explanation of Linguistic Causes: Al-Zajjaji's Theory of Grammar; Introduction, Translation, Commentary* (Amsterdam: John Benjamins BV, 1995), 21n9. This aspect of the Arabic grammatical tradition, as Versteegh notes, is analyzed by Weil in a widely cited article on the methods of Arab grammarians. See Gotthold Weil, "Zum Verstandnis der Methode der moslemischen Grammatiker," *Festschrift E. Sachau gewidmet* (1915): 380–92.

85. Slightly modified translation of M. A. Abdel Haleem, *The Qur'an: English Translation and Parallel Arabic Text* (Oxford: Oxford University Press, 2010), 47.

86. Qur'an, 51:56.

87. Al-Radi, *Haqa'iq*, 277–78.

88. The gist of al-Radi's argument (including his textual proofs) in this section is very similar to the discussion of Ibn al-Khallal (d. after 988) in his *Kitab al-Radd*. This could mean two things: either Ibn al-Khallal is a direct source or there was a source they both shared and cited. Theoretically, al-Jubba'i is a common authority in both of these works and could be argued to be the main source. What complicates this theory (while not dismissing it entirely) is that al-Radi ascribes a different point about this verse to al-Jubba'i. See Suleiman Mourad, "The Mu'tazila and Their Tafsir Tradition: A Comparative study of five exegetical glosses on Qur'an 3.178," in *Tafsir Interpreting the Qur'an*, vol. 3, ed. Mustafa Shah (London: Routledge, 2013), 267–82. Further complicating the view that al-Jubba'i is the source is Rosalind Gwynne's observation that either he did not use poetry in his explanations, or that his poetic usages did not make it into the parts about him that later scholars cited. See Rosalind Gwynne, The *"Tafsir"* of Abu 'Ali al-Jubba'i (PhD diss., University of Washington, 1982), 68.

89. Gleave, *Islam and Literalism*, 138–39.

90. See Sudipta Kaviraj, "Modernity and Politics in India," *Daedalus* 129, no. 1 (2000): 137–62.

CHAPTER 4

1. Owens, *The Foundations of Grammar*, 4.

2. Cornelis H. M. Versteegh states: Guillaume's analysis "shows that in Baghdad grammarians no longer could be content with a language-internal explanation of the grammatical rules. In order to be able to compete with the new logical and philosophical fashions they had to show that their object of research, too, was explicable with non-circular arguments. In order to be able to do so, they had to take recourse to partly extra-linguistic arguments, 'objective' facts, that no longer were dependent on the language system but linked the phenomena with such arguments as the wisdom of the Arabs, the laws of nature, the physical reality of sound, the attitude of the speakers, etc." See *The Explanation of Linguistic Causes: Al-Zajjaji's Theory of Grammar: Introduction, Translation, Commentary* (Amsterdam: John Benjamins BV, 1995), 91.

3. See Damien Janos, "Al-Farabi," in: *Encyclopaedia of Islam*, 3rd ed., vol. 2 (Leiden: Brill, 2015), 108–26.

4. For example, Nadja Germann and Noel A. Rivera Calero argue that the basic setup of language for Ibn Jinni constitutes "a sphere almost on a par with (theological) ethics and metaphysics. It is, among other things, governed by first, self-evident principles that explain why certain (namely, the most fundamental) grammatical rules cannot be otherwise . . . precisely like the fundamental ethical and metaphysical principles applied in theology." See "The Causes of Grammar: Ibn Jinni on the Nature of Language" in *Philosophy and language in the Islamic world* (Berlin: Walter de Gruyter & Co, 2021), 59.

5. For a detailed account and analysis of this debate, see Muhsin Mahdi, "Language and Logic in Classical Islam," in *Logic in Classical Islamic Culture*, ed. G. E. von

Grunebaum (Wiesbaden: Otto Harrassowitz Verlag, 1970), 51–83. Also see Wen Chen Ouyang, "Literature and Thought: Re-reading al-Tawhidi's Transcription of the Debate between Grammar and Logic," in *The Heritage of Arabo-Islamic Learning: Studies Presented to Wadad Kadi*, ed. Maurice A. Pomerantz and Aram A. Shahin (Leiden: Brill, 2016), 444–60.

6. Mahdi, "Language and Logic in Classical Islam," 60. Mahdi also succinctly explains,

Matta's original thesis was based on the assumption that logic builds a bridge or forms an intermediate stage between language and science or knowledge of the intelligible meanings, between conventional opinions and scientific knowledge. Al-Sirafi denies this place to logic. The necessary condition for attaining intelligible meanings is language, and logic does not provide a necessary bridge between the two. Logic does not transcend language and its conventional character, but merely reflects a particular linguistic convention or the rules and characteristic ways that a particular linguistic group agrees upon in speaking its language. To call upon non-Greeks to learn Greek logic is not to provide them with a universal instrument of thought, but with the characteristic structure of the Greek language, which is of no use unless one plans to learn that language (66).

7. Shukri Abed, *Aristotelian Logic and the Arabic Language in al-Farabi* (Albany: State University of New York Press, 1991), 167.

8. Abed, *Aristotelian Logic and the Arabic Language in al-Farabi*, 167–68.

9. Scholars have noted that the Christian-Arabic Aristotelian teaching in tenth-century Baghdad is the immediate background of al-Farabi's thought and for the reception of the *Organon*—that is, the logical portion of the Aristotelian corpus. Most crucial is how the Arabic canonization of Aristotle's *Rhetoric* and *Poetics*, as parts of the *Organon*, drew these fields into the domain of the syllogism. This led scholars like al-Farabi to explain the logical, ethical, and political implications of the poetic syllogism. See Janos, "al-Farabi"; Abed, *Aristotelian Logic and the Arabic Language in al-Farabi*; and Deborah Black, *Logic and Aristotle's Rhetoric and Poetics in Medieval Arabic Philosophy* (Leiden: Brill, 1990).

Also directly relevant here is Lara Harb's argument that "an aesthetic of wonder also forms the basis of poetic theories developed by the philosophers (also starting in the fifth/eleventh century) in their treatment of Aristotle's Poetics" (*Arabic Poetics*, 29). And:

Like their predecessors writing commentaries on the Aristotelian corpus in Greek and Syriac, philosophers writing in Arabic tried to explain poetry and rhetoric as forms of syllogistic reasoning. As a result, they had their own unique concerns (and vocabulary) when it came to describing what renders speech poetic. Nevertheless, their solution to the problem of fitting poetic speech into the logical sciences echoes developments in Arabic literary criticism at the time. Early solutions to the philosophical problem distinguished poetic speech from other forms of syllogistic reasoning based on a truth scale in which the poetic was defined by its falsehood, paralleling debates in the old school of criticism that evaluated poetry based on its truthfulness or falsehood. However, like in the nonphilosophical critical tradition, this framework was soon replaced by another, which defined the poetic by its ability to evoke wonder (Harb, *Arabic Poetics*, 29).

10. This living, creative dimension of lexicography as a field is well-highlighted in Alexander Key's recent study. For example, he states:

Scholars in the eleventh century could look to the books on their shelves to find out what words meant, and therefore to understand what people and God intended. But their activity was more than just passive recourse; it was an active drive to produce more of the lexical reference that they were using, and thereby improve the stock of lexicography. . . . It is important to remember how active this lexical drive to create meaning was, because the lexicon can appear static, and the rhetoric around its historical status stressed the conservative approach that lexicographers took to its modification. But when Arabic scholars were looking for meaning, they were creating meaning. . . . The primary way to do this was through statements about the origins of words and their morphological construction. The Arabic word here was *asl*, a root or root principle" (Key, *Language between God and the Poets*, 90).

11. Thomas Bauer, *A Culture of Ambiguity*, 7–8 (emphasis added).

12. Bauer, *A Culture of Ambiguity*, 12.

13. See, for instance, Etan Kohlberg, "From Imamiyya to Ithna-'ashariyya," *Bulletin of the School of Oriental and African Studies, University of London* 39, no. 3 (1976): 521–34; Kohlberg, "Some Notes on the Imamite Attitude to the Qur'an," *Oriental Studies* (1972), 209–24.

14. Robert Gleave, "Recent Research into the History of Early Shi'ism," *History Compass* 7, no. 6 (2009): 1600.

15. Paul Luft and Colin Turner, eds., *Shi'ism: Critical Concepts in Islamic Studies*, volumes 1–4 (London: Routledge, 2008).

16. *Haqa'iq*, 7.

17. Al-Radi was not the first or only Shi'i scholar to hold this view. Meir Bar Asher has pointed out how al-Tusi and al-Murtada also refrained from identifying the "firm in knowledge" exclusively with the Imams. See Bar-Asher, *Scripture and Exegesis*, 100.

18. *Haqa'iq*, 8.

19. Critical in the above statement is that, according to this view, not all of the *mutashabihat* are polysemous verses. Rather, he states that *many of them* have multiple meanings. If we take these words to be phrased precisely, then this alerts us to the fact that there is something even more generic that makes a verse *mutashabih*. From the previous chapter we can infer that the most basic criterion of a *mutashabih* verse for al-Radi is a verse that cannot be read in its apparent meaning.

20. The move of regarding this verse as the justification for practicing *ta'wil* of the *mutashabihat* is associated with the Mu'tazili scholars, in particular. See Abu Zayd, *al-Ittijah*, 164, 180.

21. *Haqa'iq*, 9.

22. This view is also supported by al-Jassas. See Syamsuddin, *"Muhkam* and *Mutashabih,"* 73.

23. That is, when the particle *waw* is understood to *join* the two parts of the verse.

24. The second predicate *(khabar)* for the exception *(illa)*.

25. Describing the state *(hal)* of the subject *rasikhun*.

26. For more on al-Jubbai's argument that speech can carry multiple meanings, see Rosalind W. Gwynne, *The "Tafsir" of Abu 'Ali al-Jubba'i*, 47.

27. Tarif Khalidi, *The Qur'an* (New York: Penguin Group), 239.

28. *Haqa'iq*, 10–11.

29. This equalizing effect of language extends even further for some other scholars like, for instance, Ibn Qutayba. The same authoritative canon of language is seen as the tool through which to interpret the content of dreams. It is the material aspect of dreams, constituting language content, that makes them interpretable via the same linguistic canon. Differences in textual authority are flattened, and borders between the temporal and imaginal realms are made porous through the linguistic canon. See M. J. Kister, "The Interpretation of Dreams: An Unknown Manuscript of Ibn Qutayba's *'Ibarat al-Ru'ya," Israel Oriental Studies* 4 (1974): 67–103.

30. *Haqa'iq*, 249.

31. *Haqa'iq*, 250.

32. *Haqa'iq*, 250.

33. Haleem, *The Qur'an*, 287.

34. *"Taqlid al-hadaqa al-sahiha fi jihat al-mar'i iltimasan li-ru'yatihi."* See *Haqa'iq*, 253.

35. *Haqa'iq*, 109.

36. W. Schmucker, "Mubahala," in *Encyclopaedia of Islam*, 2nd ed., vol. 7 (Leiden: Brill, 1993), 276–77.

37. Qur'an 3:61, translation by Haleem, in *The Qur'an*, 39.

38. For example, the *mubahala* is depicted in a fourteenth-century Ilkhanid illustrated manuscript of a text by the eleventh-century Persian Muslim polymath al-Biruni, *Al-Athar al-Baqiya 'an al-Qurun al-Khaliya (The Chronology of Ancient Nations)*, Tabriz or Maragha, Iran, 1307, Edinburgh University Library, Arab Ms. 161, folio 160r, cited in Christiane Gruber, "In Defense and Devotion: Affective Practices in Early Modern Turco-Persian Manuscript Paintings," in *Affect, Emotion, and Subjectivity in Early Modern Muslim Empires*, ed. Kishwar Rizvi (Leiden: Brill, 2018), 102.

39. Louis Massignon, *La Mubahala de Medine* (Paris: Libr. orientale et américaine, 1955); R. Mikati, "Cross My Heart and Hope to Die: A Diachronic Examination of the Mutual Self-Cursing *(Mubahala)* in Islam," *Journal of the American Oriental Society* 139, no. 2 (2019): 317–31.

40. Louis Massignon, trans. Herbert Mason, *The passion of al-Hallaj: mystic and martyr of Islam* (Princeton, N.J.: Princeton University Press, 1982), 153.

41. John Victor Tolan, *Saint Francis and the Sultan: The Curious History of a Christian-Muslim Encounter* (Oxford: Oxford University Press, 2009), 296.

42. Muhammad ibn Muhammad al-Mufid, *Kitab al-Irshad*, trans. I. K. Howard (Elmhurst, NY: Tahrike Tarsile Qur'an, 1981), 119.

43. Ibn Tawus, *Iqbal al-A'mal* (Beirut: Mu'assasat al-A'lami li al-Matbu'at, 1996), 842.

44. Ali Mamouri, "Bar Rasi-i Tarikhi-i Ayah-i Mubahala wa Baz Tabha-yi Kalami-i An," *Fasalnamah-i Shi'a Shanasi* 5, no 19 (1964): 85–100; Qawam al-Din Muhammad Washnawi, *Ahl Bayt wa Aya-i Mubahala* (Qom: Dar al-Nashir); Muhammad Rada Ansari, *Asrar-i Mubahala* (Tehran: Dalil-i Ma, 1963).

45. Haleem, *The Qur'an*, 268.

46. A similar logic was mobilized in the famous debate between al-Sirafi and Matta, where al-Sirafi asked Matta to distinguish between two phrases: "Zayd is the best of the brothers" and "Zayd is the best of his brothers." The argument he gave for the correctness of the first construction "the brothers" was that the term "his brothers" could not include Zayd himself. Similarly, in this verse, al-Radi marshals his knowledge of Arabic grammar (acquired under the tutelage of none other than al-Sirafi, among others) in order to defend the view that the command giver cannot be included in the act of fulfilling the command. See Mahdi, "Language and Logic in Classical Islam," 76.

47. A similar report is cited in the work of al-Mufid, al-Radi's teacher of Shi'i theology, with some differences. First, al-Nushjani is omitted from the exchange, and the conversation occurs directly between Imam al-Rida and al-Ma'mun. Second, al-Ma'mun asks al-Rida to cite for him the best praise of 'Ali that is found in the Qur'an. Third, al-Ma'mun is said to have challenged al-Rida's position by presenting the argument that the term "sons" is plural, as it refers to Hasan and Husayn, and the term "daughters" is in the plural, even as it refers to Fatima alone, so it is possible that the term "ourselves" refers to the Prophet. To this challenge, al-Rida is quoted to have provided the rule that one who invites is like the one who commands, where both cannot be the subject of their own invitation/command. Finally, al-Ma'mun's expression of satisfaction at al-Rida's reasoning is also slightly modified, where he is quoted to have exclaimed: "When the answer is reached, the question falls away!" See Muhammad ibn Muhammad al-Mufid, *al-Fusul al-Mukhtara min al-'Uyun wa al-Mahasin* (Najaf: Manshurat al-Matba'a al-Haydariyya wa Maktabatiha, 1962), 16.

48. *Haqa'iq*, 113. The translation is from *The Study Qur'an: A New Translation and Commentary*, ed. Seyyed Hossein Nasr (New York: HarperCollins, 2015), 1261.

49. *Haqa'iq*, 113. Al-'Adwani was a poet and warrior from the late sixth century, who mourned the past glories of his tribe al-'Adwan.

50. *Haqa'iq*, 114. Slightly modified translation of Haleem, *The Qur'an*, 225.

51. *Haqa'iq*, 114.

52. The editor points out that al-Radi's brother, al-Murtada, whose works include theological and legal treatises from the Imami perspective, used this rule to justify the levying of the *khums* tax. See *Haqa'iq*, 115.

53. Al-Khwarazmi was an Imami Shi'i scholar and celebrated author of epistles in artistic prose, as well as poetry.

54. Most likely a reference to Abu Hanifa's other pupil and transmitter, Muhammad ibn al-Hasan ibn Farqad al-Shaybani (d. 805).

55. Muhammad Rida Kashif al-Ghita (d. 1947) hailed from Iraq and was part of the well-respected Kashif al-Ghita family. A scholar of jurisprudence and a poet, some of his other published works include a biography of al-Sharif al-Radi: *Hayat al-Sharif al-Radi* (Najaf: Dar al-Nashr wa al-Ta'lif, 1941) and *al-Ghayb wa al-shahada* (Najaf: Matba'a al-Haydariyya, 1928). Some of his poems were published in *Shu'ara' al-ghira* Ed. Ali Khaqani, (Qom: Maktaba Ayatullah al-'Uzma al-Mar'ashi al-Najafi, 1987), vol. 8, 418–430.

56. *Haqa'iq*, 115–16.

57. See Hossein Modarressi, *Crisis and Consolidation in the Formative Period of Shi'ite Islam: Abu Ja'far Ibn Qiba Al-Razi and His Contribution to Imamite Shi'ite Thought* (Princeton, N.J.: Darwin Press, 1993).

58. *Haqa'iq*, 116.

59. *Haqa'iq*, 116.

60. Kraemer, *Humanism in the Renaissance of Islam*, 11–15.

61. *Haqa'iq*, 15.

62. Haleem, *The Qur'an*, 34–35.

63. *Haqa'iq*, 15 (emphasis added).

64. *Haqa'iq*, 15.

65. *Haqa'iq*, 17–18

66. *The Study Qur'an*, 1240.

67. *Haqa'iq*, 20.

68. I have not included it here, but al-Radi's discussion of this position continues, where the unnamed author spends some time arguing for the privileged place of the heart in relation to other body parts in order to explain its being singled out in this verse. See *Haqa'iq*, 21–22.

69. *Haqa'iq*, 22.

70. *Haqa'iq*, 22.

71. The privileging of rational meaning according to the principles of justice in al-Radi's exegesis aligns with the hermeneutical system adopted by other Mu'tazili scholars of his time. See Mourad, "The Mu'tazila and Their *Tafsir* Tradition," 273–75.

72. Claude Gilliot, "Exegesis of the Qur'an: Classical and Medieval: Etymology and significance of the Arabic words *tafsir, ta'wil,* and related terms," in *Encyclopaedia of the Qur'an*, vol. 2, ed. Jane McAuliffe (Leiden: Brill, 2002), 99–101.

73. This is in line with the terminology used by grammarians of this time, as well. For example, al-Zajjaji describes his work on language as follows: "This book was

composed by us primarily about the causes of grammar, the argumentation about it, the revelation of its secrets and the disclosure of its most hidden subtleties and nuances, though not about the principles [of grammar]" (Versteegh, *The Explanation of Linguistic Causes*, 17). Zajjaji also refers to this book by a different title in the introduction as *Kitab al 'idah li asrar al-nahw* instead of *Kitab al-idah fi 'ilal al-nahw*. See Versteegh, *The Explanation of Linguistic Causes*, 21n9.

74. The language of classifying actions as inherently good or bad emerges from a markedly Mu'tazili position. See Kambiz Ghaneabassiri, "The Epistemological Foundation of Conceptions of Justice in Classical 'Kalam': A Study of 'Abd al-Jabbar's *al-Mughni* and al-Baqillani's *al-Tamhid*," *Journal of Islamic Studies* 19, no. 1 (2008): 71–96. Ghaneabassiri directs the reader to George Hourani, *Islamic Rationalism: The Ethics of 'Abd al-Jabbar* (Oxford: Clarendon Press, 1971), 37–128, for a fuller discussion of 'Abd al-Jabbar's treatment of the goodness and badness of acts.

75. *Haqa'iq*, 24.

76. *Haqa'iq*, 24–25.

77. The term *ittisa'*, literally "extension" or "wideness," in this context refers to free choice or flexibility. In grammatical literature, it means deviation from the rules enabling the speaker to adapt language to her own needs. For example, placing elements at the end of sentences when they ought to be at beginning (*taqdim/ta'khir*). See Versteegh, *The Explanation of Linguistic Causes*, 108.

78. *Haqa'iq*, 26.

79. Slightly modified translation of Haleem, *The Qur'an*, 219.

80. Haleem, *The Qur'an*, 160–61.

81. *Haqa'iq*, 27.

82. *Haqa'iq*, 28–29 (emphasis added).

83. Haleem, *The Qur'an*, 80.

84. Michael Carter, "Language Control as People Control in Medieval Islam: The Aims of the Grammarians in Their Cultural Context," *al-Abhath* 31 (1983): 65–84.

85. David Scott, *Conscripts of Modernity*, 53.

86. In his study of al-Qazwini's work on the wonders of creation, Travis Zadeh argues that authors of this genre, like Abu Hamid al-Gharnati and al-Qazwini, used *saj'* as a common literary feature. Accordingly, he points out that their legitimacy is based not only on scientific merit but also on account of their aesthetic value. See Travis Zadeh, "The Wiles of Creation," 34.

CHAPTER 5

1. Alexander Stern, *The Fall of Language: Benjamin and Wittgenstein on Meaning* (Cambridge, Mass.: Harvard University Press, 2019), 1.

2. Charles Taylor, *The Language Animal: The Full Shape of the Human Linguistic Capacity* (Cambridge, Mass.: The Belknap Press of Harvard University Press, 2016), 1.

3. Travis Zadeh, "Fire Cannot Harm It: Mediation, Temptation and the Charismatic Power of the Qur'an," *Journal of Qur'anic Studies* 10, no 2 (2008): 57.

4. Taylor, *The Language Animal*, 3.

5. Taylor, *The Language Animal*, 4.

6. Stern, *The Fall of Language*, 3.

7. Versteegh, *The Explanation of Linguistic Causes*.

8. M. G. Carter, *Sibawayhi's Principles: Arabic Grammar and Law in Early Islamic Thought* (Atlanta, Ga.: Lockwood Press, 2016), 116–17.

9. Versteegh, *The Explanation of Linguistic Causes*, 36–37, note 20.

10. A key figure on the interaction of God's essence/names and reality/language is al-Jubba'i, as shown by Rosalind Gwynn in her dissertation on al-Jubba'i's Qur'an exegesis, *The "Tafsir" of Abu 'Ali al-Jubba'i*.

11. Mustafa Shah, "Classical Islamic Discourse on the Origins of Language: Cultural Memory and the Defense of Orthodoxy," *Numen* 58, no. 2/3 (2011): 324.

12. Key, *Language between God and the Poets*, 100.

13. Alexander Key has pointed out that another discursive arena in which the question of the relationship between language and reality unfolded with particular interest was that of the *basmala*, or the canonical statement with which almost every chapter in the Qur'an begins: "in the name of God; the full of mercy, ever compassionate." This statement, which also holds paramount ritual significance in Islam, of course makes reference to God's "name." In addition, the Qur'anic reference to Adam being taught all the "names" also serves as an important point of discussion in this broader conversation over the interaction of language and reality. As Key argues, where one stood on these questions held serious theological implications. In fact, the debate about the named and the name and whether they were the same or different served as a pivotal battleground for much larger theological conundrums and contestations. See Key, *Language between God and the Poets*, 96.

14. Shah, "Classical Islamic Discourse on the Origins of Language," 320.

15. Shah explains: "If language had been established initially via *tawqif*, with God's inventing language and establishing the relationship between words and meanings, then he would have had to reveal necessarily the design and intention behind the use of language. This would entail disclosing to humans knowledge of God before the actual imposition of religious obligation. . . . The reasoning is that knowledge of the attribute of an entity, in this case God's imposition of language, would *a fortiori* necessitate knowledge of the essence of that entity, namely God" (Shah, "Classical Islamic Discourse on the Origins of Language," 321).

16. J. R. T. M. Peters, *God's Created Speech: A Study in the Speculative Theology of the Mu'tazili Qadi al-Qudat Abul-Hasan 'Abd al-Jabbar Ibn Ahmad al-Hamadani* (Leiden: Brill, 1976), 327–29.

17. J. R. T. M. Peters, *God's Created Speech*, 329. Peters is citing *Mughni* VII, 53, lines 1–3, and *Muhit* I, 320 for this.

18. According to Versteegh, original lists of categories of speech contained four: predication, command, question, wish (for example, in Ibn Qutayba and Tha'lab), but later versions expanded the number. Versteegh explains that, in the formalization of semantic syntax by authors such as Sakkaki (d. 1229), the basic distinction became

between truth/non-truth utterances (*khabar*) on the one hand, and utterances that don't involve a judgment (*talab*) on the other, where the latter is divided into *tamanni* (unrealizable wish), *istifham* (question), *amr* (command), *nahy* (prohibition), and *nida'* (invocation). From the thirteenth century onward, the term to indicate the latter category became *insha'*. See Versteegh, *The Explanation of Linguistic Causes*, 35.

19. Talal Asad, "Thinking About Religion through Wittgenstein," *Critical Times: Interventions in Global Critical Theory* 3, no. 3 (2020): 405.

20. Asad, "Thinking About Religion through Wittgenstein," 406.

21. Asad, "Thinking About Religion through Wittgenstein," 406.

22. From Key, *Language Between God and the Poets*, 89: "The Arabic word for 'lexicon' was *al-lugah*, often translated as 'language' (and usually in modern Arabic used to mean just that). For eleventh-century Arabic, a translation of *al-lugah* as 'language' doesn't quite work. 'Language' in English has to include the use human beings make of it. But the Arabic lexicon is the part of language that does not move during a conversation: humans refer to it for explanation and are limited by it when it comes to choice of expression; it is where one goes to determine meaning."

23. Alexander Key helpfully translates this term as "lexical placing" and describes it as such: "Arabic lexicography understood any connection between mental content and vocal form, between cognition and the physical existence of voice or writing, as a moment of 'placing' (*wad'*). This is the act of name giving or reference setting that is sometimes called 'imposition' in Anglophone philosophy of language" (Key, *Language Between God and the Poets*, 89).

24. A. Haj-Salah, "Lugha," in *Encyclopaedia of Islam*, 2nd ed., vol. 5 (Leiden: Brill, 1986), 803–5.

25. Key, *Language Between God and the Poets*, 89.

26. For a detailed discussion of Ibn Taymiyya's position, including his fascinating rationale rejecting the *wad'* position, see Abdul Rahman Mustafa, "Ibn Taymiyyah & Wittgenstein on Language," *The Muslim World* 108, no. 3 (2018): 472–73, 475–78.

27. Abdul Rahman Mustafa, "Ibn Taymiyyah & Wittgenstein on Language," 474.

28. Asad, "Thinking About Religion through Wittgenstein," 425.

29. Asad, "Thinking About Religion through Wittgenstein," 424.

30. Bernard Weiss, "Wad' al-Lugha," in *Encyclopaedia of Islam*, 2nd ed., vol. 11 (Leiden: Brill, 2002), 7.

31. Abu Hashim was al-Jubba'i's son.

32. Bernard Weiss, "Medieval Muslim Discussions of the Origin of Language," *Zeitschrift der Deutschen Morgenländischen Gesellschaft* 124 (1974): 33–41.

33. Ibn Taymiyya, in an attempt to discredit this theory, holds that no one before Abu Hashim ever held the conventionalist theory. However, we do not have any evidence of the debate apart from Ibn Taymiyya's reference to it. See Weiss, "Medieval Muslim Discussions of the Origin of Language," 34.

34. Margaret Larkin, *The Theology of Meaning: 'Abd al-Qahir al-Jurjani's Theory of Discourse* (New Haven, Conn.: American Oriental Society, 1995), 31–38.

35. Weiss, "Medieval Muslim Discussions of the Origin of Language," 39.

36. In addition to the pioneering discussion of etymology (*ishtiqaq*) in his *al-Munsif*, Ibn Jinni argued that prepositions, nouns, and verbs have more than one meaning. See Abu al-Fath Ibn Jinni, *Khasa'is*, vol. 3 (Beirut: Dar al-Huda li-al-Tiba'a wa al-Nashr, 1952), 110–11.

37. There are conflicting views about Ibn Jinni's position on the origin of language. While Shah presents him as upholding the view of language as divinely determined, J. Pedersen has argued that Ibn Jinni held a position midway between the Kufan and Basran schools. Meanwhile, according to Versteegh, Ibn Jinni did not take a definitive position on the origin of language question and remained conflicted. But the point I have tried to impress through this discussion is that reducing Ibn Jinni's authorship of works on *ishtiqaq* to him basing language on convention is untenable.

38. Bruce Fudge, *Qur'anic Hermeneutics: al-Tabrisi and the Craft of Commentary* (London: Routledge, 2011), 73.

39. Ibn Jinni is said to have been among the leading inspirations for al-Radi to become a poet. See Moktar Jebli, "Al-Sharif al-Radi," in *Encyclopaedia of Islam*, 2nd ed., vol. 9 (Leiden: Brill, 1997), 340–43.

40. Haleem, *The Qur'an*, 41 (emphasis added).

41. *Haqa'iq*, 165.

42. This rule is tied to that of "ellipsis" where "nothing can be deleted unless there is something which refers to it in the context, and unless there is an awareness of it in its absence" (Ibn Jinni, *Khasa'is* II: 360) quoted in Owens, *Foundations of Grammar*, 1988, p. 186.

43. Haleem, *The Qur'an*, 300.

44. *Haqa'iq*, 169.

45. *Haqa'iq*, 172.

46. Kinberg, "Muhkamat and mutashabihat," 162–63.

47. Vishanoff, *The Formation of Islamic Hermeneutics*, 20; Heinrichs "On the Genesis of the *Ḥaqiqa-Majaz* Dichotomy," 122–23.

48. Heinrichs, "On the Genesis of the *Ḥaqiqa-Majaz* Dichotomy," 129–40.

49. Haleem, *The Qur'an*, 37.

50. *Haqa'iq*, 84.

51. *Haqa'iq*, 84.

52. *Haqa'iq*, 86.

53. *Haqa'iq* 86–87

54. Aisha Geissinger, *Gender and Muslim Constructions of Exegetical Authority: A Rereading of the Classical Genre of Qur'an Commentary* (Leiden: Brill, 2015), 35.

55. Al-Hakim al-Tirmidhi M. A., *Al-Furuq wa Man' al-Taraduf*, ed. Muhammad Ibrahim Juyushi (Cairo: al-Nahar li-al-Tab' wa al-Nashr wa al-Tawzi', 1998).

56. al-Tirmidhi M. A., *Al-Furuq wa Man' al-Taraduf*.

57. Although I previously rendered *majaz* as linguistic transgression, when used in opposition with the term *haqiqa*, *majaz* carries the narrower sense of "metaphor."

58. Vishanoff, *The Formation of Islamic Hermeneutics*, 22; Heinrichs, "On the Genesis of the *Haqiqa-Majaz* Dichotomy," 136.

59. See Heinrichs, "On the Genesis of the *Haqiqa-Majaz* Dichotomy," 136.

60. Haleem, *The Qur'an*, 54.

61. *Haqa'iq*, 323.

62. *Haqa'iq*, 324.

63. *Study Qur'an*, 347.

64. *Study Qur'an*, 348.

65. *Haqa'iq*, 324–25.

66. Haleem, *The Qur'an*, 319. "Malik" here is often understood as the name of the angel Malik, the keeper of Hell.

67. *Haqa'iq*, 331.

68. Slightly modified from Haleem, *The Qur'an*, 56.

69. *Haqa'iq*, 332.

70. Haleem, *The Qur'an*, 44.

71. *Haqa'iq*, 238.

72. *Haqa'iq*, 239.

73. A. J. Arberry, *The Koran Interpreted* (New York: Simon & Schuster, 1996), 253.

74. *Haqa'iq*, 240.

75. *Haqa'iq*, p. 240–1. Haleem, *The Qur'an*, 310.

76. *Haqa'iq*, 241.

77. Haleem, *The Qur'an*, 284.

78. *Haqa'iq*, 242–3.

CHAPTER 6

1. Ibn Taymiyya, *Kitab minhaj al-sunna al-nabawiyya fi naqd kalam al-Shi'a wa al-Qadariyya*, vol. 1 (Bulaq: al-Matba'a al-Kubra al-Amiriyya, 1904), 16.

2. Ibn Taymiyya, *Kitab*, 31.

3. Wilferd Madelung, "Imamism and Mu'tazilite Theology," in *Religious schools and sects in medieval Islam* (London: Variorum Reprints, 1985), 18n2. Also, Madelung notes that al-Mufid wrote a book on "the agreement of the Baghdadis of the Mu'tazila with what is related from the Imams." See Madelung, "al-Mufid," in *Encyclopaedia of Islam*, 2nd ed., vol. 7 (Leiden: Brill, 1993), 312–13.

4. McDermott, *The Theology of Al-Shaikh Al-Mufid*, 397.

5. Gleave, "Recent Research into the History of Early Shi'ism," 1600.

6. Gleave, "Recent Research into the History of Early Shi'ism," 1600.

7. Gleave, "Recent Research into the History of Early Shi'ism," 1602. Author's reference is to the work of S. A. Arjomand, "The Consolation of Theology: The Shi'ite Doctrine of Occultation and the Transition from Chiliasm to Law," *The Journal of Religion* 76, no. 4 (1996): 548–71; Arjomand, "Crisis of the Imamate and the Institution of Occultation in Twelver Shi'ism: A Sociohistorical Perspective," *International Journal of Middle East Studies* 28, no. 4 (1996): 491–15; and Arjomand, "*Imam absconditus* and the

Beginnings of a Theology of Occultation: Imami Shi'ism circa 280–90 A.H. /900A.D.," *Journal of the American Oriental Society* 117, no. i (1997): 1–12.

8. Gleave, "Recent Research into the History of Early Shi'ism," 1600.

9. Ayoub, "The Speaking Qur'an and the Silent Qur'an."

10. Hussein Abdulsater, in his recent study on al-Murtada's theological writings, brings attention to the limits of using the term "influence" to describe or understand the role and relationship of Mu'tazili ideas to al-Murtada's thought. Abdulsater's push to theorize and complicate the category of "influence" is an essential intervention. *Shi'i Doctrine, Mu'tazili Theology: al-Sharif al-Murtada and Imami Discourse* (Edinburgh: Edinburgh University Press, 2017), 5–6.

11. Etan Kohlberg, *Belief and Law in Imami Shi'ism* (Aldershot: Variorum, 1991).

12. Gleave, "Recent Research into the History of Early Shi'ism," 1600.

13. According to Imami Shi'i theology as it came to be canonized after the eleventh century, the twelfth Imam was not dead but in a state of occultation. This logic has secured the belief in God's continuous guidance for His community and the spiritual dominion of the Imams.

14. Ian Hacking, *The Social Construction of What?* (Cambridge, Mass: Harvard University Press, 1999), 19–20.

15. See Kohlberg's articles dedicated to terms *taqiyya* (forced dissimulation), *ithna 'ashariyya* (twelver), and *ghayba*: Kohlberg, "Taqiyya in Shi'i Theology and Religion," in *Secrecy and Concealment: Studies in the History of Mediterranean and Near Eastern Religions*, ed. Hans G. Kippenberg and Guy G. Stroumsa (Leiden: Brill, 1995), 345–80; Kohlberg, "Early attestations of the term 'ithna 'ashariyya,'" *Jerusalem Studies in Arabic and Islam* 24 (2000): 343–57; Kohlberg, "From Imamiyya to Ithna-'ashariyya."

16. See Wilferd Madelung, "Imamism and Mu'tazilite Theology" in *Le Shi'isme Imamite: colloque de Strasbourg*, ed. Toufic Fahd (Paris: Presses Universitaires de France, 1970), 13–30, 17; reprinted in *Religious Schools and Sects in Medieval Islam* (London: Variorum Reprints, 1985), article VII.

17. Although none of their dogmatic works have been preserved, their views have been fragmentarily established from statements of al-Mufid and the titles of their books. See Madelung, "Imamism and Mu'tazilite Theology," 15.

18. Some studies, captured, for example, in the work of Paul Sander, have questioned the credibility of the "rationalist turn" narrative. Sander refers to early *hadith* collections to assert that the Imams supported the chief principles of rational theology, such as the justice of God and freewill. Therefore, he argues, they provide us with ample evidence that Mu'tazili ideas were thriving in an Imami environment well before the more sophisticated justifications of Imami doctrine put forward in the eleventh century. Sander's argument thus lends weight to the view that the so-called rationalist turn in Twelver Shi'ism was not a dramatic shift from an earlier Imami conservatism but that it was one of many possible theologies that continued to persist long after their origins. See Gleave, "Recent Research into the History of Early Shi'ism," 1601; Tamima Bayhom-Daou, Review of *Zwischen Charisma und Ratio: Entwicklungen in der frühen*

imamitischen Theologie by Paul Sander, *Bulletin of the School of Oriental and African Studies* 60, no. 1 (1997): 128–29. More recently, George Warner has highlighted the limits of the traditionalist/rationalist divide in his examination of the important place and scholarly contribution of Shaykh al-Saduq. See his *Words of the Imams.*

19. David Vishanoff presents a compelling critique of the characterization of the Mu'tazila as "the free thinkers of Islam" as part of his treatment of 'Abd al-Jabbar's theory of revelation. See David R. Vishanoff, *The Formation of Islamic Hermeneutics*, 149.

20. Andrew Rippin, "Tafsir," in *Encyclopaedia of Islam*, 2nd ed., vol. 10 (Leiden: Brill, 1998), 83–88.

21. Alnoor Dhanani, *The Physical Theory of Kalam: Atoms, Space, and Void in Basrian Mu'tazili Cosmology* (Leiden: E. J. Brill, 1994), 2–3.

22. Ayoub, "Literary Exegesis of the Qur'an," 296.

23. Abu al-Qasim al-Balkhi al-Ka'bi (d. after 962), the head of the Baghdad school of the Mu'tazila, was al-Shaykh al-Mufid's main teacher in Mu'tazili theology. See Wilferd Madelung, "al-Mufid." 'Abd al-Jabbar's main teacher was Abu 'Abd Allah al-Basri (d. 980). See J. van Ess, "Abu 'Abd Allah al-Basri," in *Encyclopaedia of Islam*, 2nd ed., vol. 12 (Leiden: Brill, 2004), 12–14.

24. McDermott, *The Theology of Al-Shaikh Al-Mufid*, 396.

25. Madelung, "al-Mufid."

26. Fudge, *Qur'anic Hermeneutics*, 115.

27. Muhammad ibn Ishaq ibn al-Nadim, *al-Fihrist*, ed. Yusuf 'Ali Tawil, and Ahmad Shams al-Din (Beirut: Dar al-Kutub al-'Ilmiyya, 1996), 52–57.

28. 'Abd al-Jabbar, *Mutashabih al-Qur'an*, ed. 'Adnan Muhammad Zarzur (Cairo: Dar al-Turath, 1969).

29. The Bahshamiyya school reflects followers of Abu Hashim al-Jubba'i (son of al-Jubba'i).

30. The Ikhshidiyya (followers of Ikhshid) represent another branch of the Mu'tazili school, rivaling the Bahshamiyya. Essentially, the split was between al-Jubba'i's students: al-Ikhshid and al-Samyari and Abu Hashim al-Jubba'i. For more on this intra-Mu'tazili conflict, see Margaretha Heemskerk, *Suffering in the Mu'tazilite Theology: 'Abd al-Jabbar's Teaching on Pain and Divine Justice* (Leiden: Brill, 2000), 21–28.

31. Suleiman Mourad, "The Mu'tazila and Their Tafsir Tradition: A Comparative Study of Five Exegetical Glosses on Qur'an 3.178," in *Tafsir: Interpreting the Qur'an*, vol. 3, ed. Mustafa Shah (London: Routledge, 2013), 267–75.

32. Rukn al-Din Abu Tahir Turaythithi, *Mutashabih al-Qur'an*, ed. Abdulrahman al-Salimi (Cairo: Ma'had al-Makhtutat al-'Arabiyya, 2015), 277.

33. 'Abd al-Jabbar also provides his interpretations of specific Qur'anic verses in *Tanzih al-Qur'an 'an al-Mata'in* (Beirut: Dar al-Nahda al-Haditha, 1966), as does al-Radi, in *Talkhis al-bayan.*

34. Haleem, *The Qur'an*, 41.

35. 'Abd al-Jabbar, *Mutashabih al-Qur'an*, 151–52; 'Abd al-Jabbar, *Tanzih*, 71.

36. U. Rudolph, "*al-Wa'd wa 'l-Wa'id*" [The Promise and the Threat], *Encyclopaedia of Islam*, 2nd ed., vol. 11 (Leiden: Brill, 2002): 6–7.

37. *Haqa'iq*, 165.

38. Haleem, *The Qur'an*, 44.

39. *Haqa'iq*, 238–45.

40. The fate of the grave sinner was a contentious question and eventually became one of the doctrines by which the Mu'tazili school distinguished themselves from others (including the Imami Shi'i school). Through the slogan "the Promise and the Threat," one of the "Five Principles" considered characteristic of Mu'tazili theology, the Mu'tazila expressed their conviction that not only the unbelievers had to face damnation on the day of judgment, but that Muslims who had committed a grave sin without repentance were also threatened by eternal hellfire. See Rudolph, "*al-Wa'd wa 'l-Wa'id*."

41. 'Abd al-Jabbar, *Mutashabih al-Qur'an*, 160–61.

42. Slightly modified translation from Haleem, *The Qur'an*, 40 (emphasis added).

43. *Haqa'iq*, 148–49.

44. According to the Mu'tazili framework of *taklif* (moral responsibility), justice works both ways. It is due to God's justice that humans are held accountable because they are responsible for their actions and possess the ability to act. It is also due to God's justice that it is incumbent on God to accept human repentance and prayer. Any beliefs that fell outside the rules of this justice-centered system were rejected, including intercession. See Rudolph, "*al-Wa'd wa 'l-Wa'id*."

45. 'Abd al-Jabbar, *Mutashabih al-Qur'an*, 147–48.

46. Apart from the terms *din* and *islam*, which I have left in their original Arabic, the translation is from Haleem, *The Qur'an*, 40–41.

47. 'Abd al-Jabbar's use of the term *salat* (prayer) here is in its general linguistic meaning, not the technical meaning of prayer as prescribed by Muhammad.

48. 'Abd al-Jabbar, *Mutashabih al-Qur'an*, 149–50.

49. The earliest work where this division has been noted is in the famous lexicographer Ibn Faris's (d. 1004) *Sahibi*. The idea of the evolution of terms into a technical meaning was perhaps first brought up by al-Zajjaji, but Ibn Faris introduced the categories of *ism lughawi* (linguistic meaning) and *ism shar'i* (normative legal epithet), and argued that it was normal for terms to carry both literal and technical (*sina'i*) meanings. Thus, it is possible to trace through 'Abd al-Jabbar's invocation of the *islam/istislam* distinction a multitude of theological and literary conversations taking place in Baghdad's scholarly circles at the time. See Michael Carter, "Language Control as People Control in Medieval Islam," 69.

50. *Haqa'iq*, 156–57.

51. 'Abd al-Jabbar, *Mutashabih al-Qur'an*, 23–25.

52. Abu Zayd, *Al-Ittijah*, 180–90.

53. *Haqa'iq*, 156–57.

54. *Haqa'iq*, 153–54.

55. *Haqa'iq*, 154–55.

56. Haleem, *The Qur'an*, 163.

57. *Haqa'iq*, 149.

58. Q. 15:39–40: Iblis said to God, "Because You have put me in the wrong, I will lure mankind on earth and put them in the wrong, all except your devoted servants."

59. *Haqa'iq*, 149.

60. Haleem, *The Qur'an*, 339.

61. For example, al-Qushayri argues that *islam* is *istislam* or "external surrender," and not everyone who surrenders on the outside is pure (*mukhlis*) inside (*sirran*). See Abu al-Qasim al-Qushayri, *Tafsir al-Qushayri*, vol. 3 (Beirut: Dar al-Kutub al-'Ilmiyya, 2015), 223. Similarly, al-Tha'labi explains that *islam* is *istislam*: "As for *al-iman*, it is affirmation with the heart. Attestations of the tongue and body do not count as *iman* without purity [*ikhlas*], which occurs in the heart." See al-Tha'labi's discussion of Qur'an verse 49:14 in *al-Kashf wa al-bayan*, vol. 9, ed. Abi Muhammad Ibn 'Ashur (Beirut: Dar Ihya' al-Turath al-'Arabi, 2002), 89–90. Al-Tabari also maintains a qualitative distinction between the states of *islam* and *iman*, where *islam* refers to the utterance of submission (in speech), and *iman* to the confirmation of the utterance through action. See al-Tabari, *Tafsir al-Tabari*, vol. 11 (Beirut: Dar al-Kutub al-'Ilmiyya, 2014), 399–402.

62. 'Abd al-Jabbar, *Mutashabih al-Qur'an*, 149–50.

63. Slightly modified translation from Haleem, *The Qur'an*, 36.

64. *Haqa'iq*, 61.

65. The semantic field occupied by the term *mulk* is expansive. It can be translated as "dominion," "ownership," "possession," or "control." In the analysis that follows, especially when I turn to 'Abd al-Jabbar, I will render *mulk* however it best fits the particular context of discussion.

66. *Haqa'iq*, 61.

67. *Haqa'iq*, 65.

68. *Haqa'iq*, 65.

69. *Haqa'iq*, 69–72.

70. He gives credit for this reading of *malik yawm al-din* to an earlier Mu'tazili teacher, Abu 'Ali al-Jubba'i. See *Haqa'iq*, 69.

71. al-Radi, *Diwan*, vol. 2, 39.

72. *Haqa'iq*, 70.

73. *Haqa'iq*, 70.

74. The editor, Muhammad Rida Kashif al-Ghita', identifies the poet as Aws b. Hajar (d. 600s).

75. 'Abd al-Jabbar advances the same argument in the *Mutashabih al-Qur'an*. While al-Radi does not mention 'Abd al-Jabbar by name here, it is plausible that the latter represented a major source of inspiration for this particular line of inquiry.

76. 'Abd al-Jabbar, *Tanzih*, 62–63.

77. 'Abd al-Jabbar, *Mutashabih al-Qur'an*, 142–43.

78. 'Abd al-Jabbar, *Mutashabih al-Qur'an*, 144.

79. *Haqa'iq*, 68–69.

80. *Mubahat* refers to that which is permissible to everyone but is not owned by anyone (such as a river).

81. *Haqa'iq*, 68–69.

82. Vishanoff, *The Formation of Islamic Hermeneutics*, 109–51.

83. Haleem, *The Qur'an,* 43–44.

84. From the text it is not entirely clear whether al-Radi is still citing the opinion of the unnamed scholar or whether he is now providing his own commentary on the position. Based on the lyrical style, rhyme, and poetic language, it seems that it is al-Radi's commentary on the commentary.

85. *Haqa'iq*, 233–34.

86. *Haqa'iq*, 234.

87. 'Abd al-Jabbar, *Mutashabih al-Qur'an*, 159–60.

88. *Haqa'iq*, 234.

89. 'Abd al-Jabbar, *Tanzih al-Qur'an*, 77–78.

90. McDermott, *The Theology of Al-Shaikh Al-Mufid*, 396.

91. Julie Scott Meisami, "Dynastic History and Ideals of Kingship in Bayhaqi's *Tarikh-i Mas'udi*," *Edebiyat*, n.s. 3 (1989): 71.

92. Meisami, "Dynastic History and Ideals of Kingship," 72.

93. Adeeb Khalid, *Islam after Communism: Religion and Politics in Central Asia* (Berkeley: University of California Press, 2007), 7.

CONCLUSION

1. Walid Saleh, "Qur'an Commentaries," in *The Study Qur'an*, 1646.

2. Ahmed El Shamsy, *Rediscovering the Islamic Classics: How Editors and Print Culture Transformed an Intellectual Tradition* (Princeton, N.J.: Princeton University Press, 2020).

3. Daniel Boyarin, *Border Lines: The Partition of Judaeo-Christianity* (Philadelphia: University of Pennsylvania Press, 2004), 1–2.

4. Ussama Makdisi, *The Culture of Sectarianism: Community, History, and Violence in Nineteenth-Century Ottoman Lebanon* (Berkeley: University of California Press, 2000).

5. Talal Asad, *Formations of the Secular: Christianity, Islam, Modernity* (Stanford, Calif.: Stanford University Press, 2003), 185.

BIBLIOGRAPHY

Sources in Islamicate Languages

Note: Most of the sources below are in Arabic. The remainder in Persian have been identified as such with the label (Pr.).

'Abbas, Ihsan. *Al-Sharif al-Radi.* Beirut: Dar Beirut, 1959.

'Abd al-Hamid, Muhammad Muhyi al-Din. *Sharh Diwan al-Sharif al Radi.* Beirut: Dar Ihya' al-Kutub al-Arabiyya, 1949.

'Abd al-Jabbar, Abu al-Hasan. *Mutashabih al-Qur'an.* Edited by 'Adnan Muhammad Zarzur. Cairo: Dar al-Turath, 1969.

———. *Tanzih al-Qur'an 'an al-Mata'in.* Beirut: Dar al-Nahda al-Haditha, 1966.

———. *Tathbit Dala'il al-Nubuwwa.* Cairo: Dar al-Mustafa, 2006.

Abu Shari'ah, Ziyad Ahmad. *Aghrad al-Shi'r wa Khasa'isuhu fi al-Tafsir.* Amman: Jadara lil-Kitab al-'Alami; 'Alam al-Kutub al-Hadith, 2008.

Abu 'Ubaydah. *Majaz al-Qur'an.* Frankfurt: Institute for the History of Arabic-Islamic Science at the Johann Wolfgang Goethe University, 2010.

Abu Zayd, Nasr Hamid. *Al-Ittijah al-'Aqli fi al-Tafsir: Dirasa fi Qadiyat al-Majaz fi al-Qur'an 'inda al-Mu'tazila.* Beirut: al-Markaz al-Thaqafi al-'Arabi, 1982.

Ahmad, Muhammad Khalaf Allah. *Thalath Rasa'il fi I'jaz al-Quran.* Cairo: Dar al-Ma'arif, 1968.

Amin, Hasan. *Da'irat al-Ma'arif al-Islamiyya al-Shi'iyya.* Beirut: Mu'assasat 'Abd al-Hafiz al-Bisat, 1972.

Amin, Muhsin ibn 'Abd-al-Karim. *A'yan al-Shi'a.* Beirut: Dar al-Ta'aruf, 1986.

al-Amini, Muhammad Hadi. *al-Sharif al-Radi: Muhammad ibn al-Husayn ibn Musa al-Musawi.* Tehran: Mu'assasat Nahj al Balagha, 1987.

al-'Amiri, Muhammad ibn Yusuf. *al-I'lam bi Manaqib al-Islam.* Cairo: Dar al-Katib al-'Arabi, 1967.

Ansari, Muhammad Rada. *Asrar-i Mubahala.* Tehran: Dalil-i Ma, 1963. (Pr.)

al-Ash'ari, Abu al-Hasan. *Maqalat.* Edited by Muhammad Muhyi al-Din 'Abd al-Hamid. Cairo: Maktabat al-Nahda al-Misriyya, 1969.

Ayyazi, Sayyid Muhammad 'Ali. *Sayr-i Tatavvur-i Tafasir-i Shi'ah.* Tehran: Intisharat-i vizarat-i farhang va irshad-i islami, 1994. (Pr.)

'Aziz al-Sayyid, Jasim. *al-Ightirab fi Hayat wa Shi'r al-Sharif al-Radi*, vol. 1. Beirut: Dar al-Andalus, 1986.

al-Baghdadi, Khatib Abu Bakr Ahmad ibn 'Ali. *Tarikh Baghdad aw Madinat al-Salam*, 14 vols. Cairo: Maktabat al-Khanji, 1931.

al-Bahrani, Yusuf Ibn Ahmad. *Lu'lu'at al-Bahrayn*. Najaf: Matba'at al-Nu'man, 1966.

al-Farra', Abu Zakariyya. *Ma'ani al-Qur'an*. Edited by Ahmad Yusuf Najati and Muhammad 'Ali Najjar. 3 vols. Cairo: al-Hay'ah al-Misriyya al-'Amma li al-Kitab, 1980.

al-Hamawi, Yaqut ibn 'Abd Allah, and 'Abbas, Ihsan. *Mu'jam al-Udaba': Irshad al-Arib ila Ma'rifat al-Adib*. Beirut: Dar al-Gharb al-Islami, 1993.

Hasan, Muhammad 'Abd al-Ghani. *Al-Sharif al-Radi*. Cairo: Dar al-Ma'arif, 1970.

Hasani, Hashim Ma'ruf. *al-Shi'ah bayna al-Asha'irah wa al-Mu'tazilah*. Beirut: Dar al-Nashr lil-Jami'yin, 1964.

al-Hindawi, Hanadi Za'al Mas'ud. "Al-Sharif al-Radi wa Tumuhihi nahw al-Khilafa zaman al-Khalifa al-Qadir billah (r. 969–1015)." *Dirasat al-'Ulum al-Insaniyya wa al-Ijtima'iyya* 46, no. 2 (2019): 141-155.

al-Hilli, 'Abd al-Husayn. "Author's biography." In *Haqa'iq al-Ta'wil fi Mutashabih al-Tanzil*. Beirut: Dar al-Adwa', 1986.

al-Hulw, 'Abd al-Fattah Muhammad. *Al-Sharif al-Radi: Hiyatuhu wa dirasat shi'rihi*. Cairo: Hajr lil-Tiba'ah wa al-Nashr, 1986.

Ibn Abi al-Hadid, 'Abd al-Hamid ibn Hibat Allah. *Sharh Nahj al-Balagha*. Beirut: Dar Ihya' al-Kutub al-'Arabiyya, 1975.

Ibn al-'Imad. *Shadharat al-Dhahab fi Akhbar Man Dhahab*. Cairo: Maktabat al-Qudsi, 1931-32.

Ibn 'Inaba (Ahmad ibn 'Ali Dawudi al-Hasani). *'Umdat al-Talib fi Ansab Al Abi Talib*. Beirut: Manshurat Dar Maktabat al-Hayat, 1980.

Ibn al-Jawzi, Abu al-Faraj. *al-Muntazam fi Tarikh al-Muluk wa al-Umam*. Beirut: Dar al-Kutub al-'Ilmiyya, 1992.

Ibn Jinni, Abu al-Fath. *Khasa'is*. Beirut: Dar al-Huda li-al-Tiba'a wa al-Nashr, 1952.

Ibn Khallikan, Abu al-'Abbas Ahmad ibn Muhammad. *Wafayat al-A'yan wa Anba' Abna' al-Zaman*. 8 vols. Edited by Ihsan 'Abbas. Beirut: Dar al-Thaqafa, 1968–1972.

———. *Wafayat al-A'yan wa Anba' Abna' al-Zaman*. Translated by De Slane, 4 vols. Beirut: Librairie du Liban, 1970.

Ibn al-Nadim, Muhammad ibn Ishaq. *al-Fihrist*. Edited by Yusuf 'Ali Tawil and Ahmad Shams al-Din. Beirut: Dar al-Kutub al-'Ilmiyya, 1996.

Ibn Qutayba. *Ta'wil Mushkil Al-Qur'an*. Medina: Al-Maktaba al-'Ilmiyya, 1981.

———. *Gharib al-Hadith*. 2 vols. Beirut: Dar al-Kutub al-'Ilmiyya, 1988.

Ibn Sallam, Abu 'Ubayd al-Qasim. *Gharib al-Hadith*. Beirut: Dar al-Kutub al-'Ilmiyya, 2011.

Ibn Shahrashub, Muhammad ibn 'Ali. *Ma'alim al-'Ulama'*. Beirut: Dar al-Mahajjah al-Bayda', 2012.

———. *Mutashabih al-Qur'an wa al-Mukhtalaf fihi*. Edited by Hamid al-Mu'min. Beirut: Mu'assasat al-'Arif li al-Matbu'at, 2008.

Ibn Sulayman, Muqatil. *Tafsir Muqatil ibn Sulayman*. Edited by 'Abd Allah Mahmud Shihatah. Cairo: Mu'assasat al-Halabi, 1969.

———. *Al-Wujuh wa al-Naza'ir fi al-Qur'an al-Karim.* Edited by Ahmad Farid al-Mazidi. Beirut: Dar al-Kutub al-'Ilmiyya, 2008.

Ibn Taghribirdi, Abu al-Mahasin Yusuf. *Nujum al-Zahra.* Cairo: Matba'at Dar al-Kutub al-Misriyya, 1952.

Ibn Taymiyya, Ahmad Ibn 'Abd al-Halim. *Kitab Minhaj al-Sunna al-Nabawiyya fi Naqd Kalam al-Shi'a wa al-Qadariyya.* Bulaq: al-Matba'a al-Kubra al-Amiriyya, 1904.

Ibn Tawus, Radi al-Din 'Ali ibn Musa. *Iqbal al-A'mal.* Beirut: Mu'assasat al-A'lami li al-Matbu'at, 1996.

Jafri, Muhammad Mahdi. *Sayyid Radi.* Iran: Tarhe Naw, 1959. (Pr.)

———. "Sharif Radi." In *Danishnama-yi Jahan-i Islam (Encyclopaedia of the World of Islam).* Edited by Ghulam 'Ali Haddad Adil, Hasan Tarimirad, vol. 27, 152–57. Tehran: Bunyad-i Da'irat al-Ma'arif-i Islami, 1996. (Pr.)

Khurramshahi, Baha al-Din. *Tafsir va Tafasir-i Jadid.* Tehran: Sazman-i Intisharat-i Kayhan, 1985. (Pr.)

Khwansari, Al-Mirza Muhammad Baqir al-Musawi. *Rawdat al-Jannat fi Ahwal al-'Ulama' wa al-Sadat.* Tehran: Maktabat Isma'iliyan, 1970.

al-Kilani, Muhammad Sayyid. *al-Sharif al-Radi.* Matba'at al-Ahram: Cairo, 1937.

Mahdavi Rad, Muhammad 'Ali. *Afaq-i Tafsir: Maqalat va Maqulati dar Tafsir Pizhuhi.* Tehran: Hasti nama, 2003. (Pr.)

Mamouri, Ali. "Bar rasi-i Tarikhi-i Ayah-i Mubahala wa Baz Tabha-yi Kalami-i an." *Fasalnamah-i Shi'a Shanasi* 5, no. 19 (1964): 85–100. (Pr.)

Mahfuz. *Al-Sharif al-Radi.* Beirut: Maktabat Beirut, 1944.

Ma'rifat, Muhammad Hadi. *al-Tafsir wa al-Mufassirun: fi Thawbihi al-Qashib.* Mashhad: al-Jami'a al-Radawiyya li al-'Ulum al-Islamiyya, 1997.

Matrudi, Muhammad I. *Al-Sharif Al-Radi: Hayatuhu wa Shi'ruhu.* Riyadh: al-Nadi al-Adabi, 1984.

al-Mazandarani, Muhammad ibn Isma'il. *Muntaha al-Maqal fi Ahwal al-Rijal.* Beirut: al-Mu'assasat Al al-Bayt, 1998.

al-Mubarrad, Muhammad ibn Yazid. *Kitab Ma Ittafaqa Lafzuhu wa Ikhtalafa Ma'nahu min al-Qur'an al-Majid.* Cairo: al-Matba'a al-Salafiyya, 1931.

Mubarak, Zaki. *'Abqariyat Al-Sharif Al-Radi.* Cairo: Matba'a Hijazi, 1952.

———. *al-Mada'ih al-Nabawiyya fi al-Adab al-'Arabi.* Cairo: Dar al-Kitab al-'Arabi, 1967.

al-Najashi, Ahmad ibn 'Ali. *Kitab al-Rijal.* Tehran: Manshurat-i Markaz-i Nashr-i Kitab, 1965.

Najafi, Abdul Husayn Ahmad Amini. *al-Ghadir.* Beirut: Dar al-Kitab al-'Arabi, 1967.

Nassar, Husayn. *al-Mutashabih.* Cairo: Maktabat al-Khanji bi al-Qahira, 2003.

al-Qifti, 'Ali ibn al-Yusuf. *Inbah al-Ruwat.* Cairo: Dar al-Kutub al-Misriyya, 1955.

Qubbanji, Sadr al-Din. *Muqaddimat fi 'Ilm al-Tafsir.* Al-Najaf: Mu'assasat Ihya' al-Turath al-Shi'i, 2006.

al-Qushayri, Abu al-Qasim. *Tafsir al-Qushayri.* 3 vols. Beirut: Dar al-Kutub al-'Ilmiyya, 2015.

al-Sabi, Ibrahim ibn Hilal, and Muhammad ibn al-Husayn al-Sharif al-Radi. *Rasa'il al-Sabi wa al-Sharif al-Radi*. Kuwait: Da'irat al-Matbu'at wa al-Nashr, 1961.

Safadi, Khalil ibn Aybak. *Kitab al-Wafi bi al-Wafayat*. Leipzig: Deutsche Morgenländische Gesellschaft, in Kommission bei F.A. Brockhaus, 1931.

Samarra'i, Qasim. *Niqabat al-ashraf fi al-Mashriq al-islami hatta nihayat fatrat hukm al-usra al-Jala'iriyya: muntasaf al-qarn al-thalith al-hijri hatta awa'il al-qarn al-tasi' al-hijri*. Beirut: Dar al-Kutub al-'Ilmiyya, 2013.

al-Sharif al-Radi, Muhammad ibn al-Husayn. *Diwan*. Annotated by Yusuf Shukri Farhat. 2 vols. Beirut: Dar al-Jil, 1995.

———. *Haqa'iq al-Ta'wil fi Mutashabih al-Tanzil*, vol. 5. Edited by Muhammad Rida Kashif al-Ghita. Beirut: Dar al-Adwa', 1986.

———. *Khasa'is al-A'imma 'alayhim al-salam: Khasa'is Amir al-Mu'minin 'alayhim al-salam*. Edited by Muhammad Hadi al-Amini. Mashhad: Majma' al-Buhuth al-Islamiyya, 1985.

———. *Al-Majazat al-Nabawiyya*. Beirut: Dar al-Kutub al-'Ilmiyya, 2007.

———. *Nahj Al-Balagha*. Beirut: Anwar al-Hadi, 2006.

———. *Talkhis al-Bayan fi Majazat al-Qur'an*. Edited by Makki al-Sayyid Jasim. Beirut: 'Alam al-Kutub, 2011.

Al-Sharif al-Murtada, Abu al-Qasim. *Amali al-Sayyid al-Murtada fi al-Tafsir wa al-Hadith wa al-Adab*. Qum: Mabsurat Maktabat, 1983.

———. *al-Dhakhira fi 'Ilm al-Kalam*. Qum: Mu'assasat al-Nashr al-Islami, 1990.

———. *al-Mudih 'an Jihat I'jaz al-Quran: wa huwa al-Kitab al-Ma'ruf bi al-Sarfa*. Mashhad: Majma' al-Buhuth al-Islamiyya, 2003.

Sharshar, Muhammad Hasan. *al-Balagha al-Qur'aniyya wa al-Nabawiyya fi Athar al-Sharifayn*. Cairo: Zahra al-Sharq, 2006.

al-Shaykh al-Mufid, Abu 'Abd Allah. *al-Fusul al-Mukhtara min al-'Uyun wa al-Mahasin*. Najaf: Manshurat al-Matba'a al-Haydariyya wa Maktabatiha, 1962.

———. *Kitab al-Irshad*. Translated by I. K. Howard. Elmhurst, NY: Tahrike Tarsile Qur'an, 1981.

al-Tabari, Abu Ja'far Muhammad ibn Jarir. *Jami' al-Bayan 'an Ta'wil al-Qur'an*. 15 vols. Edited by Sidqi Jamil al-'Attar. Beirut: Dar al-Fikr, 2009.

———. *Jami' al-Bayan 'an Ta'wil al-Qur'an*. 30 vols. Cairo: Mustafa al-Babi al-Halabi, 1954.

———. *Tafsir al-Tabari*. 13 vols. Beirut: Dar al-Kutub al-'Ilmiyya, 2014.

al-Tabataba'i, Sayyid Muhammad Husayn. *al-Qur'an fi al-Islam*. Translated by Sayyid Muhammad al-Husayni. Beirut: Dar al-Zahra, 1973.

al-Tha'libi, Abu Mansur 'Abd al-Malik. *Yatimat al-Dahr*. 5 vols. Beirut: Dar al-Kutub al-'Ilmiyya, 1983.

———. *al-Kashf wa al-Bayan*. 10 vols. Edited by Abi Muhammad ibn 'Ashur. Beirut: Dar Ihya' al-Turath al-'Arabi, 2002.

Tawhidi, 'Ali ibn Muhammad. *Kitab al-Imta' wa al-Mu'anasa*. Beirut: Dar al-Kutub al-'Ilmiyya, 1997.

Tehrani, Muhammad Agha Buzurg. *Al-Dhari'a ila Tasanif al-Shi'a*. Najaf: Matba'at al-Ghari, 1936.

al-Tirmidhi, al-Hakim. *Al-Furuq wa Man' al-Taraduf.* ed. Muhammad Ibrahim Juyushi. Cairo: al-Nahar li al-Tab' wa al-Nashr wa al-Tawzi', 1998.

Turaythithi, Rukn al-Din Abu Tahir. *Mutashabih al-Qur'an.* Edited by Abdulrahman al-Salimi. Cairo: Ma'had al-Makhtutat al-'Arabiyya, 2015.

Washnawi, Qawam al-Din Muhammad. *Ahl Bayt wa Aya-i Mubahala.* Qom: Dar al-Nashir, 1972. (Pr.)

al-Zirikli, Khayr al-Din ibn Mahmud. *Al-A'lam.* 5 Volumes. Beirut: Dar al-'Ilm li-al-Malayin, 1990.

Sources in English

Abbott, Nabia. *Studies in Arabic Literary Papyri.* Chicago: University of Chicago Press, 1957.

Abdel Haleem, M. A. *The Qur'an: English Translation and Parallel Arabic Text.* Oxford: Oxford University Press, 2010.

Abdulsater, Hussein Ali. Shi'i Doctrine, Mu'tazili Theology: al-Sharif al-Murtada and Imami Discourse. Edinburgh: Edinburgh University Press, 2017.

Abed, Shukri. *Aristotelian Logic and the Arabic Language in Alfarabi.* Albany: State University of New York Press, 1991.

Abeysekara, Ananda. "Identity for and against Itself: Religion, Criticism, and Pluralization." *Journal of the American Academy of Religion* 72, no. 4 (2004): 973–1001.

———. *The Politics of Postsecular Religion: Mourning Secular Futures.* New York: Columbia University Press, 2008.

Abu 'Ali, Islam. *Al-Sharif Al-Radi: His Life and Poetry.* PhD diss., Durham University, 1974.

Abu-Deeb, Kamal. "Al-Jurjani's Classification of Isti'ara with Special Reference to Aristotle's Classification of Metaphor." *Journal of Arabic Literature* 2 (1971): 48–75.

———. "Studies in the Majaz and Metaphorical Language of the Qur'an: Abu 'Ubayda and al-Sharif al-Radi." In *Literary structures of religious meaning in the Qur'an.* Edited by Issa J. Boullata, 310–53. Richmond: Curzon, 2000.

Adang, Camilla, Sabine Schmidtke, and David Eric Sklare, eds. *A Common Rationality: Mu'tazilism in Islam and Judaism.* Würzburg: Ergon Verlag in Kommission, 2007.

Akhtar, Vahid. *Early Shi'ite Imamiyyah Thinkers.* New Delhi: Ashish Publication House, 1988.

Alshaar, Nuha A. *Ethics in Islam: Friendship in the Political Thought of al-Tawhidi and His Contemporaries.* New York: Routledge, 2015.

Arberry, A. J. *The Koran Interpreted.* New York: Simon & Schuster, 1996.

Ardehali, Mohammadreza. "The Formation of Classical Imami Exegesis: Rawd al-jinan wa-rawh al-janan fi tafsir al-Qur'an of Abu al-Futuh Razi (d. in or after 552/1157)." Toronto: University of Toronto ProQuest Dissertations Publishing, 2018.

Arjomand, S. A. "The Consolation of Theology: The Shi'ite Doctrine of Occultation and the Transition from Chiliasm to Law." *Journal of Religion* 76, no. 4 (1996): 548–71.

———. "Crisis of the Imamate and the Institution of Occultation in Twelver Shi'ism: A Sociohistorical Perspective." *International Journal of Middle East Studies* 28, no. 4 (1996): 491–515.

———. "*Imam absconditus* and the Beginnings of a Theology of Occultation: Imami Shi'ism circa 280–90 A.H./900 A.D." *Journal of the American Oriental Society* 117, no. 1 (1997): 1–12.

Arkoun, M., and Joel L Kraemer. "Review of *Humanism in the Renaissance of Islam: The Cultural Revival during the Buyid Age.*" *Arabica* 34, no. 3 (1987): 392.

Asad, Talal. *Formations of the Secular: Christianity, Islam, Modernity.* Stanford, Calif: Stanford University Press, 2003.

———. "Thinking About Religion through Wittgenstein." *Critical Times: Interventions in Global Critical Theory* 3, no. 3 (2020): 403–42.

Austin, J. L. *How to Do Things with Words.* Cambridge, Mass.: Harvard University Press, 1962.

Ayoub, Mahmoud. "Literary Exegesis of the Qur'an: The Case of Sharif al-Radi." In *Literary Structures of Religious Meaning in the Qur'an*, ed. Issa J. Boullata, 292–309. Richmond, UK: Curzon, 2000.

———. *The Qur'an and Its Interpreters.* Vols. 1 and 2. Albany: State University of New York Press, 1984.

———. "The Speaking Qur'an and the Silent Qur'an: A Study of the Principles and Development of Imami Shi'i tafsir." In *Approaches to the History of the Interpretation of the Qur'an*, ed. Andrew Rippin, 177–98. Oxford, UK: Clarendon Press, 1988.

Bar-Asher, Meir Mikha'el. "Exegesis II. In Shi'ism." In *Encyclopaedia Iranica*, ed. Ehsan Yarshater, vol. 9, 116–19. New York: Bibliotheca Persicas 1999.

———. "The Qur'an commentary ascribed to Imam Hasan al-Askari." *Jerusalem Studies in Arabica and Islam* 24 (2000): 358–79.

———. *Scripture and Exegesis in Early Imami-Shi'ism.* Leiden: Brill, 1999.

Bauer, Karen. "Justifying the Genre: A Study of Introductions to Classical Works of Tafsir." In *Aims, Methods and Contexts of Qur'anic Exegesis (2nd/8th–9th/15th Centuries)*, 39–68. Oxford: Oxford University Press, 2013.

Bauer, Thomas. *A Culture of Ambiguity: An Alternative History of Islam.* Translated by Hinrich Biesterfeldt and Tricia Tunstall. New York: Columbia University Press, 2021.

Bayhom-Daou, Tamima. "The Imam's Knowledge and the Quran According to al-Fadl B. Shadhan al-Nisaburi (d. 260 A.H./874 A.D.)." *Bulletin of the School of Oriental and African Studies, University of London* 64, no. 2 (2001): 188–207.

———. "Review of *Zwischen Charisma und Ratio: Entwicklungen in der frühen imamitischen Theologie.*" *Bulletin of the School of Oriental and African Studies* 60, no. 1 (1997): 128–29.

———. *Shaykh Mufid.* Oxford, UK: Oneworld, 2005.

Berkey, Jonathan Porter. *The Formation of Islam: Religion and Society in the Near East, 600–1800.* New York: Cambridge University Press, 2003.

Bernards, Monique. *Changing Traditions: Al-Mubarrad's Refutation of Sibawayh and the Subsequent Reception of the Kitab.* Leiden: Brill, 1996.

Bernheimer, Teresa. *The 'Alids: The First Family of Islam, 750–1200.* Edinburgh, UK: Edinburgh University Press, 2013.

Bettini, Lidia. "Mushtarak." In *Encyclopedia of Arabic Language and Linguistics,* vol. 3, ed. Kees Versteegh, 320–23. Leiden: Brill, 2008.

Black, Deborah. *Logic and Aristotle's Rhetoric and Poetics in Medieval Arabic Philosophy.* Leiden: Brill, 1990.

Boullata, Issa J., ed. *Literary Structures of Religious Meaning in the Qur'an.* Richmond, Va.: Curzon, 2000.

Boyarin, Daniel. *Border Lines: The Partition of Judaeo-Christianity.* Philadelphia: University of Pennsylvania Press, 2004.

Bray, Julia. *Writing and Representation in Medieval Islam: Muslim Horizons.* London: Routledge, 2006.

Brockelmann, Carl. *Geschichte der Arabischen Litteratur.* Leiden: E. J. Brill, 1943.

Bulliet, Richard W. *Islam: The View from the Edge.* New York: Columbia University Press, 1993.

———. *The Patricians of Nishapur: A Study in Medieval Islamic Social History.* Harvard Middle Eastern Studies, 16. Cambridge, Mass.: Harvard University Press, 1972.

Cahen, Claude. "Buwayhids or Buyids." In *Encyclopaedia of Islam,* 2nd ed., vol. 1, ed. H. A. R. Gibb et al., 1350–57. Leiden: Brill, 1986.

Calder, Norman, J. A. Mojaddedi, and Andrew Rippin. *Interpretation and Jurisprudence in Medieval Islam.* Aldershot: Ashgate/Variorum, 2006.

Cantarino, Vicente. *Arabic Poetics in the Golden Age: Selection of Texts Accompanied by a Preliminary Study.* Leiden: Brill, 1975.

Carter, Michael. "Language Control as People Control in Medieval Islam: The Aims of the Grammarians in Their Cultural Context." *Al-Abhath* 31 (1983): 65–84.

———. "Review of *Humanism in the Renaissance of Islam: The Cultural Revival During the Buyid Age.*" *Journal of the American Oriental Society* 109, no. 2 (1989): 304–5.

———. "Sibawayhi." In *Encyclopaedia of Islam,* 2nd ed., vol. 9, ed. C. E. Bosworth et al., 524–31. Leiden: Brill, 1997.

———. *Sibawayhi's Principles: Arabic Grammar and Law in Early Islamic Thought.* Atlanta: GA: Lockwood, 2016.

Chaumont, Eric. "Ambiguity." In *Encyclopaedia of Islam,* 3rd ed., vol. 4., ed. Kate Fleet et al., 50–54. Leiden: Brill, 2013.

Cole, Juan. *Sacred Space and Holy War: The Politics, Culture and History of Shi'ite Islam.* London: I. B. Tauris, 2002.

Copeland, Rita. *Rhetoric, Hermeneutics, and Translation in the Middle Ages: Academic Traditions and Vernacular Texts.* Cambridge: Cambridge University Press, 1991.

Clark, Elizabeth A. *History, Theory, Text: Historians and the Linguistic Turn.* Cambridge, Mass: Harvard University Press, 2004.

Clarke, Lynda, ed. *Shi'ite Heritage: Essays on Classical and Modern Traditions*. Bingham-ton, N.Y.: Global Publications, 2001.

Dakake, Maria M. *The Charismatic Community: Shi'ite Identity in Early Islam*. Albany: State University of New York Press, 2007.

De Blois, F. C. "Sabi." In *Encyclopedia of Islam*, 2nd ed., vol. 8, 672–75. Leiden: Brill, 1986.

Dhanani, Alnoor. *The Physical Theory of Kalam: Atoms, Space, and Void in Basrian Mu'tazili Cosmology*. Leiden: E. J. Brill, 1994.

Donohue, John. *The Buwayhid Dynasty in Iraq 334 H./945 to 403 H./1012: Shaping Insti-tutions for the Future*. Leiden: Brill, 2003.

Elias, Jamal. *Key Themes for the Study of Islam*. Oxford: Oneworld, 2010.

Elmi, M. J. "The Views of Tabataba'i on Traditions (*ahadith*) and Occasions of Revela-tion (*asbab al-nuzul*) in Interpreting the Qur'an." *Journal of Shi'ite Islamic Studies* 1, no. 1 (2006): 57–84.

El-Rouayheb, Khaled. *Relational Syllogisms and the History of Arabic Logic, 900–1900*. Leiden: Brill, 2010.

El Shamsy, Ahmed. *Rediscovering the Islamic Classics: How Editors and Print Culture Transformed an Intellectual Tradition*. Princeton, N.J.: Princeton University Press, 2020.

England, Samuel. *Medieval Empires and the Culture of Competition*. Edinburgh: Edin-burgh University Press, 2017.

Ernst, Carl W. *Eternal Garden: Mysticism, History, and Politics at a South Asian Sufi Center*. Albany: State University of New York Press, 1992.

———. *Following Muhammad, Rethinking Islam in the Contemporary World*. Chapel Hill: University of North Carolina Press, 2003.

———. *How to Read the Qur'an: A New Guide, with Select Translations*. Chapel Hill: University of North Carolina Press, 2011.

Ernst, Carl W., and Richard C. Martin, eds. *Rethinking Islamic Studies: From Orientalism to Cosmopolitanism*. Columbia: University of South Carolina Press, 2010.

Fudge, Bruce. "Qur'anic Exegesis in Medieval Islam and Modern Orientalism." *Die Welt Des Islams* 46, no. 2 (2006): 115–47.

——— *Qur'anic Hermeneutics: Al-Tabrisi and the Craft of Commentary*. London: Rout-ledge, 2011.

Gaiser, Adam. "A Narrative Identity Approach to Islamic Sectarianism." In *Sectarianiza-tion: Mapping the Politics of the New Middle East*, ed. Nader Hashemi and Danny Postel, 61–75. London: Hurst, 2017.

———. *Sectarianism in Islam: The Umma Divided*. Cambridge: Cambridge University Press, 2022.

Geissinger, Aisha. *Gender and Muslim Constructions of Exegetical Authority: A Reread-ing of the Classical Genre of Qur'an Commentary*. Leiden: Brill, 2015.

Germann, Nadja, and Noel A. Rivera Calero. "The Causes of Grammar: Ibn Jinni on the Nature of Language." In *Philosophy and Language in the Islamic World*, vol. 2, 49–76. Berlin: Walter de Gruyter, 2020.

Gerrit, Jan van der. *The Truth (and Untruth) of Language: Heidegger, Ricoeur, and Derrida on Disclosure and Displacement*. Pittsburgh, Pa.: Duquesne University Press, 2010.

GhaneaBassiri, Kambiz. "The Epistemological Foundation of Conceptions of Justice in Classical *Kalam*: A Study of 'Abd al-Jabbar's *al-Mughni* and al-Baqillani's *al-Tamhid*." *Journal of Islamic Studies* 19, no. 1 (2008): 71–96.

———. "A Window on Islam in Buyid Society: Justice and Its Epistemological Foundation in the Religious Thought of `Abd al-Jabbar, Ibn al-Baqillani, and Miskawayh," Phd diss., Harvard University, 2003.

Gibbs, Raymond W., ed. *The Cambridge Handbook of Metaphor and Thought*. Cambridge: Cambridge University Press, 2008.

Gilliot, Claude. "Exegesis of the Qur'an: Classical and Medieval; Etymology and Significance of the Arabic Words *Tafsir, Ta'wil*, and Related Terms." In *Encyclopaedia of the Qur'an*, vol. 2, ed. Jane McAuliffe, 99–101. Leiden: Brill, 2002.

———. "Les debuts de l'exegese coranique." *Revue des mondes musulmans et de la Méditerranée* 58 (1990): 82–100.

Gleave, Robert. *Islam and Literalism: Literal Meaning and Interpretation in Islamic Legal Theory*. Edinburgh: Edinburgh University Press, 2012.

———. "Recent Research into the History of Early Shi'ism." *History Compass* 7, no. 6 (2009): 1593–1605.

———. *Scripturalist Islam the History and Doctrines of the Akhbari Shi'i School*. Leiden: Brill, 2007.

Goldziher, Ignác. *On the History of Grammar among the Arabs: An Essay in Literary History*. Amsterdam: Benjamins, 1994.

———. *Schools of Koranic Commentators*. Wiesbaden: Harrassowitz, 2006.

Goodman, Lenn Evan. *Islamic Humanism*. New York: Oxford University Press, 2003.

Green, Nile. "Idiom, Genre and the Politics of Self-Description on the Peripheries of Persian." In *Religion, Language and Power*, ed. Nile Green and Mary Searle-Chatterjee, 202–19. New York: Routledge, 2008.

———. *Sufism: A Global History*. Chichester: Wiley-Blackwell, 2012.

Gruber, Christiane. "In Defense and Devotion: Affective Practices in Early Modern Turco-Persian Manuscript Paintings." In *Affect, Emotion, and Subjectivity in Early Modern Muslim Empires*, ed. Kishwar Rizvi, 95–123. Leiden: Brill, 2018.

Grunebaum, G. E. Von. *Logic in Classical Islamic Culture*. Wiesbaden: Otto Harrassouitz, 1970.

———. *A Tenth-century Document of Arabic Literary Theory and Criticism*. Chicago: University of Chicago Press, 1950.

Günther, Sebastian. "Assessing the Sources of Classical Arabic Compilations: The Issue of Categories and Methodologies." *British Journal of Middle Eastern Studies* 32, no. 1 (2005): 75–98.

Gwynne, Rosalind. *The "Tafsir" of Abu 'Ali al-Jubba'i*. PhD diss., University of Washington, 1982.

Hachmeier, K. U. "Private Letters, Official Correspondence: Buyid Insha' as a Historical Source." *Journal of Islamic Studies* 13, no. 2 (2002): 125–54.

Hacking, Ian. *The Social Construction of What?* Cambridge, Mass: Harvard University Press, 1999.

Haider, Najam Iftikhar. *The Origins of the Shi'a: Identity, Ritual, and Sacred Space in Eighth-Century Kufa.* New York: Cambridge University Press, 2011.

———. *The Rebel and the Imam in Early Islam: Explorations in Muslim Historiography.* Cambridge: Cambridge University Press, 2020.

Haj-Salah, A. "Lugha." In *Encyclopaedia of Islam*, 2nd ed., vol. 5, ed. C. E. Bosworth et al., 803–5. Leiden: Brill, 1986.

Hamza, Feras, Sajjad Rizvi, and Farhana Mayer, eds. *An Anthology of Qur'anic Commentaries.* Oxford: Oxford University Press, 2008.

Hanne, Eric J. *The Caliphate Revisited: the Abbasids of 11th and 12th Century Baghdad.* Ann Arbor: University of Michigan Press, 1998.

———. *Putting the Caliph in His Place: Power, Authority, and the Late Abbasid Caliphate.* Madison, N.J.: Fairleigh Dickinson University Press, 2007.

Harb, Lara. *Arabic Poetics: Aesthetic Experience in Classical Arabic Literature.* Cambridge: Cambridge University Press, 2020.

Hasan, Saeed. *The Early History of the Buwaihids.* Allahabad: Senate House, 1948.

Havemann, A. "Naqib al-Ashraf." In *Encyclopaedia of Islam*, 2nd ed., vol. 7, ed. C. E. Bosworth et al., 926–27. Leiden: Brill, 1993.

Heemskerk, Margaretha. *Suffering in the Mu'tazilite Theology: 'Abd al-Jabbar's Teaching on Pain and Divine Justice.* Leiden: Brill, 2000.

Heinrichs, Wolfhart. "Contacts between Scriptural Hermeneutics and Literary Theory in Islam: The Case of Majaz." *Zeitschrift Für Geschichte Der Arabisch-Islamischen Wissenschaften* 7 (1991): 253–84.

———. *The Hand of the Northwind: Opinions on Metaphor and the Early Meaning of Isti'ara in Arabic Poetics.* Mainz: Deutsche Morgenländische Ges.: 1977.

———. "On the Figurative (*majaz*) in Muslim Interpretation and Legal Hermeneutics." In *Interpreting Scriptures in Judaism, Christianity, and Islam: Overlapping Inquiries*, ed. Mordechai Z. Cohen and Adele Berlin, 249–65. Cambridge: Cambridge University Press, 2016.

———. "On the Genesis of the Haqiqa-Majaz Dichotomy." *Studia Islamica*, no. 59 (1984): 111–40.

Hirschler, Konrad. *Medieval Arabic Historiography Authors as Actors.* Abingdon: Routledge, 2006.

Hodgson, Marshall G. S. "How Did the Early Shi'a Become Sectarian?" *Journal of the American Oriental Society* 75, no. 1 (1955): 1–13.

———. *The Venture of Islam: Conscience and History in a World Civilization*, vol. 2. Chicago: University of Chicago Press, 1974.

Hourani, George. *Islamic Rationalism: The Ethics of 'Abd al-Jabbar.* Oxford: Clarendon Press, 1971.

Al-Jamil, Tariq. "Cooperation and Contestation in Medieval Baghdad (656/1258–786/1384): Relationships between Shi'i and Sunni Scholars in the Madinat al-Salam." PhD diss., Princeton University, 2004.

Jaffer, Tariq. *Razi: Master of Qur'anic Interpretation and Theological Reasoning.* Oxford: Oxford University Press, 2015.

Janos, Damien. "Al-Farabi." In *Encyclopaedia of Islam*, 3rd ed., vol. 2, ed. Kate Fleet, 108–26. Leiden: Brill, 2015.

Jebli, Moktar. "Al-Sharif al-Radi." In *Encyclopaedia of Islam*, 2nd ed., vol. 9, ed. C. E. Bosworth et al., 340–43. Leiden: Brill, 1997.

———. "Nahdj al-Balagha." In *Encyclopaedia of Islam*, 2nd ed., vol. 7, ed. C. E. Bosworth et al., 903–4. Leiden: Brill, 1993.

Jiwa, Shainool. "The Baghdad Manifesto (402/1011): A Re-Examination of Fatimid-Abbasid Rivalry." In *The Fatimid Caliphate, Diversity of Traditions*, ed. Farhad Daftary and Shainool Jiwa, 22–79. I. B. Tauris, 2018.

Kabir, Mafizullah. *The Buwayhid Dynasty of Baghdad, 334/946–447/1055.* Calcutta: Iran Society, 1964.

Kadhim, Abbas K. "Politics and Theology of Imami Shi'a in Baghdad in the 5th/11th Century." PhD diss., University of California, Berkeley, 2006.

Kaviraj, Sudipta. "Modernity and Politics in India." *Daedalus* 129, no. 1 (2000): 137–62.

Kemal, Salim. "Philosophy and Theory in Arabic Poetics." *Journal of Arabic Literature* 20, no. 2 (1989): 128–47.

Kennedy, Hugh. *When Baghdad Ruled the Muslim World: the Rise and Fall of Islam's Greatest Dynasty.* Cambridge, Mass.: Da Capo Press, 2005.

Key, Alexander. *Language Between God and the Poets.* Berkeley: University of California Press, 2018.

Khalid, Adeeb. *Islam after Communism: Religion and Politics in Central Asia.* Berkeley: University of California Press, 2005.

Khalidi, Tarif. *The Qur'an.* New York: Penguin Group, 239.

Al-Khu'i, Abu al-Qasim. *Al-Bayan fi Tafsir al-Qur'an, The Prolegomena to the Qur'an.* Translated by Abdulaziz Sachedina. New York: Oxford University Press, 1998.

Kinberg, Leah. "Literal Dreams and Prophetic Hadith in Classical Islam: A Comparison of Two Ways of Legitimation." *Der Islam* 70 (1993): 279–300.

———. "Muhkamat and Mutashabihat (Koran 3/7): Implications of a Koranic Pair of Terms in Medieval Exegesis." *Arabica* 35, no. 2 (July 1988): 143–72.

Kippenberg, Hans G., and Guy G. Stroumsa, eds. *Secrecy and Concealment: Studies in the History of Mediterranean and Near Eastern Religions.* Leiden: Brill, 1995.

Kister, M. J. "The Interpretation of Dreams: An Unknown Manuscript of Ibn Qutayba's 'Ibarat al-Ru'ya." *Israel Oriental Studies* 4 (1974): 67–103.

Kohlberg, Etan. *Belief and Law in Imami Shi'ism.* Aldershot: Variorum, 1991.

———. "Early attestations of the term 'ithna 'ashariyya.'" *Jerusalem Studies in Arabic and Islam* 24 (2000): 343–57.

———. "From Imamiyya to Ithna-'ashariyya." *Bulletin of the School of Oriental and African Studies, University of London* 39, no. 3 (1976): 521–34.

———. "Some Notes on the Imamite Attitude to the Qur'an." *Oriental Studies* (1972): 209–24.

———. "Taqiyya in Shi'i Theology and Religion." In *Secrecy and Concealment: Studies in the History of Mediterranean and Near Eastern Religions*, ed. Hans G. Kippenberg and Guy G. Stroumsa, 345–80. Leiden: Brill, 1995.

Kohlberg, Etan, ed. *Shi'ism*. The Formation of the Classical Islamic World, vol. 33. Burlington, Vt.: Ashgate, 2003.

Kohlberg, Etan, and Mohammad Ali Amir-Moezzi. *Revelation and Falsification: The Kitab al-Qira'at of Ahmad B. Muhammad al-Sayyari*. Leiden: Brill, 2009.

Koselleck, Reinhart. *Futures Past: On the Semantics of Historical Time*. Translated by Keith Tribe. Cambridge, Mass.: MIT, 1985.

Kraemer, Joel L. *Humanism in the Renaissance of Islam: The Cultural Revival during the Buyid Age*. Leiden: E. J. Brill, 1992.

Lapidus, Ira M. "Review of *Humanism in the Renaissance of Islam: The Cultural Revival during the Buyid Age*." *The American Historical Review* 93, no. 1 (1988): 199.

Larkin, Margaret. "The Inimitability of the Qur'an: Two Perspectives." *Religion & Literature* 20, no. 1 (1988): 31–47.

———. *The Theology of Meaning: 'Abd al-Qahir al-Jurjani's Theory of Discourse*. New Haven, Conn.: American Oriental Society, 1995.

Lassner, Jacob. *The Topography of Baghdad in the Early Middle Ages; Text and Studies*. Detroit: Wayne State University Press, 1970.

Lawson, Todd. "Akhbari Shi'i approaches to tafsir," in *Approaches to the Qur'an*. Edited by Hawting, G. R., and Abdul-Kader A. Shareef, 173–210. London: Routledge, 1993.

———. "Exegesis vi. In Akbari and Post-Safavid Esoteric Shi'ism." In *Encyclopaedia Iranica*, vol. 9, ed. Ehsan Yarshater, 123–25. New York: Bibliotheca Persica, 1999.

———. "Hermeneutics." In *Encyclopedia Iranica*, vol. 12, ed. Ehsan Yarshater, 235–39. New York: Bibliotheca Persica, 2004.

Leitch, Vincent B. *The Norton Anthology of Theory and Criticism*. New York: Norton, 2001.

Le Strange, G. *Baghdad during the Abbasid Caliphate from Contemporary Arabic and Persian Sources*. London: Oxford University Press, 1924.

Luft, Paul, and Colin Turner, eds. *Shi'ism: Critical Concepts in Islamic Studies*. Volume 1–4, Theology and Philosophy. London: Routledge, 2008.

Madelung, Wilferd. "Abu Ishaq al-Sabi on the 'Alids of Tabaristan and Gilan." *Journal of Near Eastern Studies* 26, no. 1 (1967): 17–57.

———. "The Assumption of the Title Shahanshah by the Buyids and 'The Reign of the Daylam (Dawlat Al-Daylam).'" *Journal of Near Eastern Studies* 28, no. 3 (1969): 168–83.

———. *Authority in Twelver Shiism in the Absence of the Imam in La Notion D'autorite Au Moyen Age: Islam, Byzance, Occident. Colloques Internationaux De La Napoule.* Paris: Presses Universitaires de France, 1982.

———. "Imamism and Mu'tazilite Theology." In *Religious Schools and Sects in Medieval Islam*, article VII. London: Variorum Reprints, 1985.

———. "al-Mufid." In *Encyclopaedia of Islam*, 2nd ed., vol. 7., C. E. Bosworth et al., 312–13. Leiden: Brill, 1993.

———. "A Treatise of the Sharif al-Murtada on the Legality of Working for the Government (*Mas'ala fi al-'Amal Ma'a al-Sultan*)." *Bulletin of the School of Oriental and African Studies* 43, no. 1 (1980): 18–31.

Mahdi, Muhsin. "Language and Logic in Classical Islam." In *Logic in Classical Islamic Culture*, ed. G. E. von Grunebaum, 51–83. Wiesbaden: Otto Harrassowitz Verlag, 1970.

Makdisi, Ussama. *Age of Coexistence: The Ecumenical Frame and the Making of the Modern Arab World*. Oakland: University of California Press, 2019.

Marcinkowski, Muhammad Ismail. "Twelver Shiite Scholarship and Buyid Domination: A Glance on the Life and Times of Ibn Babawayh Al-Shaykh Al-Saduq (D-381/991)." *Islamic Quarterly* 45, no. 3 (2001): 199–222.

Margoliouth, D. S. *The eclipse of the Abbasid Caliphate*. London: I. B. Tauris, 2012.

Marlow, Louise. *Dreaming Across Boundaries: The Interpretation of Dreams in Islamic Lands*. Boston: Ilex Foundation, 2008.

Martin, Richard C., Dwi Atmaja Surya, and Mark R. Woodward, eds. *Defenders of Reason in Islam: Mu'tazilism from Medieval School to Modern Symbol*. Oxford: Oneworld, 1997.

Massignon, Louis. *La Mubâhala de Médine et l'Hyperdulie de Fatima*. Paris: Librairie orientale et américaine, 1955.

———. *The Passion of al-Hallaj: Mystic and Martyr of Islam*. Translated by Herbert Mason. Princeton, N.J.: Princeton University Press, 1982.

Masuzawa, Tomoko. *The Invention of World Religions: Or, How European Universalism Was Preserved in the Language of Pluralism*. Chicago: University of Chicago Press, 2005.

McAuliffe, Jane Dammen, ed. *Encyclopaedia of the Qur'an*. Leiden: Brill, 2001.

———. *Quranic Christians: An Analysis of Classical and Modern Exegesis*. Cambridge: Cambridge University Press, 1991.

McAuliffe, Jane D., Barry Walfish, and Joseph W. Goering, eds. *With Reverence for the Word: Medieval Scriptural Exegesis in Judaism, Christianity, and Islam*. Oxford: Oxford University Press, 2003.

McDermott, Martin J. *The Theology of al-Shaikh al-Mufid (d. 413/1022)*. Beirut: Dar el-Machreq, 1978.

Meisami, Julie Scott. "Arabic Poetics Revisited." *Journal of the American Oriental Society* 112, no. 2 (1992): 254–68.

———. "Dynastic History and Ideals of Kingship in Bayhaqi's *Tarikh-i Mas'udi*." *Edebiyat*, n.s. 3 (1989): 57–77.

Meisami, Julie Scott, and Paul Starkey, eds. *Encyclopedia of Arabic Literature*. London: Routledge, 1998.

Messick, Brinkley Morris. *The Calligraphic State Textual Domination and History in a Muslim Society.* Berkeley: University of California Press, 1993.

Mez, Adam. *The Renaissance of Islam.* Translated by Khuda Bukhsh, and D. S. Margoliouth. Patna: Jubilee Print and Publishing, 1937.

Mikati, R. "Cross My Heart and Hope to Die: A Diachronic Examination of the Mutual Self-Cursing (*Mubahala*) in Islam." *Journal of the American Oriental Society* 139, no. 2 (2019): 317–31.

Mittermaier, Amira. *Dreams That Matter: Egyptian Landscapes of the Imagination.* Berkeley: University of California Press, 2011.

Modarressi, Hossein. *Crisis and Consolidation in the Formative Period of Shi'ite Islam: Abu Ja'far Ibn Qiba Al-Razi and His Contribution to Imamite Shi'ite Thought.* Princeton, N.J.: Darwin Press, 1993.

———. "Early Debates on the Integrity of the Qur'an: A Brief Survey." *Studia Islamica,* no. 77 (1993): 5–39.

———. "Rationalism and Traditionalism in Shi'i Jurisprudence: A Preliminary Survey." *Studia Islamica,* no. 59 (1984): 141–58.

———. "Some Recent Analyses of the Concept of Majaz in Islamic Jurisprudence." *Journal of the American Oriental Society* 106, no. 4 (1986): 787–91.

Moezzi, Mohammad Ali Amir. *The Divine Guide in Early Shi'ism: The Sources of Esotericism in Islam.* Albany: State University of New York Press, 1994.

Momen, Moojan. *An Introduction to Shi'i Islam: The History and Doctrines of Twelver Shi'ism.* New Haven, Conn.: Yale University Press, 1985.

Moosa, Ebrahim. *Ghazali and the poetics of imagination.* Chapel Hill: University of North Carolina Press, 2005.

Morimoto, Kazuo. *Sayyids and Sharifs in Muslim Societies: the Living Links to the Prophet.* London: Routledge, 2012.

Morrison, Robert G. *Islam and Science: The Intellectual Career of Nizam al-Din al-Nisaburi.* New York: Routledge, 2007.

Mottahedeh, Roy P. *Loyalty and Leadership in an Early Islamic Society.* London: I. B. Tauris, 2001.

Mourad, Suleiman A. "The Mu'tazila and Their Tafsir Tradition: A Comparative Study of Five Exegetical Glosses on Qur'an 3.178." In *Tafsir: Interpreting the Qur'an,* vol. 3, ed. Mustafa Shah, 267–82. London: Routledge, 2013.

———. "The Survival of the Mu'tazila Tradition of Qur'anic Exegesis in Shi'i and Sunni tafasir." *Journal of Qur'anic Studies* 12 (2010): 83–108.

Musawi, Muhsin Jasim, and Jaroslav Stetkevych. *Arabic Literary Thresholds Sites of Rhetorical Turn in Contemporary Scholarship.* Leiden: Brill, 2009.

Mustafa, Abdul Rahman. "Ibn Taymiyyah & Wittgenstein on Language." *The Muslim World* 108, no. 3 (2018): 465–91.

Namaan, Erez. *Literature and the Islamic Court.* London: Routledge, 2019.

Nasr, Seyyed H., and Oliver Leaman. *History of Islamic Philosophy.* London: Routledge, 1996.

Nielsen, J. S. "Mazalim." In *Encyclopaedia of Islam*, 2nd ed., vol. 6, ed. C. E. Bosworth et al., 933–35. Leiden: Brill, 1991.

Nijad, Ibrahim. *Al-Sharif al-Radi: The Compiler of Nahj al-Balaghah (The path of Eloquence)*. Translated by Husayn 'Alamdar. Qum: Ansariyan, 1996.

Neurwith, Angelika. "Qur'an and History." *Journal of Qur'anic Studies* 5, no. 1 (2003): 1–18.

Neuwirth, Angelika, Nicolai Sinai, and Michael Marx, eds. *The Qur'an in Context: Historical and Literary Investigations into the Qur'anic Milieu*. Leiden: Brill, 2010.

Newman, Andrew J. *The Formative Period of Twelver Shi'ism : Hadith as Discourse Between Qum and Baghdad*. Richmond: Curzon, 2000.

Nicholson, Andrew J. *Unifying Hinduism: Philosophy and Identity in Indian Intellectual History*. New York: Columbia University Press, 2010.

Oberoi, Harjot. *The Construction of Religious Boundaries: Culture, Identity, and Diversity in the Sikh Tradition*. Chicago: University of Chicago Press, 1994.

Ouyang, Wen-chin. *Literary Criticism in Medieval Arabic-Islamic Culture: The Making of a Tradition*. Edinburgh: Edinburgh University Press, 1997.

———. "Literature and Thought: Re-reading al-Tawhidi's Transcription of the Debate between Grammar and Logic." In *The Heritage of Arabo-Islamic Learning: Studies Presented to Wadad Kadi*, ed. Maurice A. Pomerantz and Aram A. Shahin, 444–60. Leiden: Brill, 2016.

Owens, Jonathan. *The Foundations of Grammar: An Introduction to Medieval Arabic Grammatical Theory*. Amsterdam: Benjamins, 1988.

Pedersen, Johannes, and Robert Hillenbrand. *The Arabic Book*. Princeton, N.J.: Princeton University Press, 1984.

———. "Ibn Djinni." In *Encyclopaedia of Islam*, 2nd ed., vol. 2, ed. B. Lewis et al., 754. Leiden, Brill, 1991.

Pemberton, Kelly, and Michael Nijhawan, eds. *Shared Idioms, Sacred Symbols, and the Articulation of Identities in South Asia*. New York: Routledge, 2009.

Peters, J. R. T. M. *God's Created Speech: A Study in the Speculative Theology of the Mu'tazili Qadi l-Qudat Abul-Hasan 'Abd al-Jabbar Ibn Ahmad al-Hamadani*. Leiden: Brill, 1976.

Pomerantz, Maurice A. *Licit Magic: The Life and Letters of Al-Sahib B. 'Abbad (D. 385/995)*. Leiden: Brill, 2018.

Punter, David. *Metaphor*. London: Routledge, 2007.

Qutbuddin, Tahera. "Al-Sharif al-Radi." In *Encyclopaedia of Islam*, 3rd ed., vol. 1, ed. Kate Fleet et al., 147–51. Leiden: Brill, 2023.

———. *A Treasury of Virtues: Sayings, Sermons, and Teachings of 'Ali, with the One Hundred Proverbs Attributed to al-Jahiz*. New York: New York University Press, 2013.

Reynolds, Gabriel Said, ed. *A Muslim Theologian in a Sectarian Milieu: 'Abd al-Jabbar and the Critique of Christian Origins*. Leiden: Brill, 2004.

———. *The Qur'an in Its Historical Context*. Routledge Studies in the Qur'an. London: Routledge, 2008.

Rippin, Andrew, ed. *Approaches to the History of the Interpretation of the Qur'an.* Oxford: Oxford University Press, 1988.

——. "Lexicographical Texts and the Qur'an." In *Approaches to the History of the Interpretation of the Qur'an*, 158–76. Oxford: Oxford University Press, 2019.

——. "Al-Mubarrad (d. 285/898) and Polysemy in the Qur'an." In *Books and Written Culture of the Islamic World Studies Presented to Claude Gilliot on the Occasion of his 75th Birthday*, ed. Andrew Rippin and Roberto Tottoli, 56–69. Leiden: Brill, 2015.

——. *The Qur'an and Its Interpretive Tradition.* Aldershot: Ashgate, 2001.

——. *The Qur'an, Style and Contents. The Formation of the Classical Islamic World*, vol. 24. Aldershot: Ashgate, 2001.

——. "Tafsir." In *Encyclopaedia of Islam*, 2nd ed., vol. 10, ed. C. E. Bosworth et al., 83–88. Leiden: Brill, 1998.

Roberts, Alexandre M. "Being a Sabian at Court in Tenth-Century Baghdad." *Journal of the American Oriental Society* 137, no. 2 (2017): 253–77.

Rudolph, U. "*al-Wa'd wa 'l-Wa'id*" [The Promise and the Threat]. In *Encyclopaedia of Islam*, 2nd ed., vol. 11, ed. P. J. Bearman et al., 6–7. Leiden: Brill, 2002.

Rüsen, Jörn, and Henner Laass. *Humanism in Intercultural Perspective: Experiences and Expectations.* Bielefeld: Transcript, 2009.

Sadr al-Din Shirazi, Muhammad ibn Ibrahim. *On the Hermeneutics of the Light-Verse of the Qur'an: Tafsir Ayat Al-Nur.* Translated, introduced, and annotated by Latimah-Parvin Peerwani. London: ICAS Press, 2004.

Safi, Omid. *The Politics of Knowledge in Premodern Islam: Negotiating Ideology and Religious Inquiry.* Chapel Hill: University of North Carolina Press, 2006.

Saleh, Walid. *The Formation of the Classical Tafsir Tradition: The Qur'an Commentary of Al-Tha'labi (d. 427/1035).* Boston: Brill, 2004.

——. "Marginalia and Peripheries: A Tunisian Historian and the History of Quranic Exegesis." *Numen* 58, no. 2/3 (2011): 284–313.

——. "Qur'an Commentaries." In *The Study Qur'an: A New Translation and Commentary*, ed. Seyyed Hossein Nasr, 1645–1658. New York: Harper Collins, 2015.

Sands, Kristin Zahra. *Sufi Commentaries of the Qur'an.* London: Routledge, 2008.

Schmucker, W. "Mubahala." In *Encyclopaedia of Islam*, 2nd ed., vol. 7, ed. C. E. Bosworth et al., 276–77. Leiden: Brill, 1993.

Schoeler, Gregor. *The Genesis of Literature in Islam: From the Aural to the Read.* Translated by Shawkat M. Toorawa. Edinburgh: Edinburgh University Press, 2009.

——. *The Oral and the Written in Early Islam.* Edited by James E. Montgomery. Translated by Uwe Vagelpohl. London: Routledge, 2006.

Schwarb, Gregor. "Capturing the Meanings of God's Speech: The Relevance of *Usul al-fiqh* to an Understanding of *Usul al-tafsir* in Jewish and Muslim *kalam*." In *A Word Fitly Spoken: Studies in Medieval Exegesis of the Hebrew Bible and the Qur'an presented to Haggai Ben-Shammai*, 111–56. Jerusalem: Ben-Zvi Institute, 2007.

Scott, David. *Conscripts of Modernity: The Tragedy of Colonial Enlightenment.* Durham, N.C.: Duke University Press, 2004.

———. *Refashioning Futures: Criticism after Postcoloniality*. Princeton, N.J.: Princeton University Press, 1999.

Shah, Mustafa. "Classical Islamic Discourse on the Origins of Language: Cultural Memory and the Defense of Orthodoxy." *Numen* 58, no. 2/3 (2011): 314–43.

———. "The Philological Endeavours of the Early Arabic Linguists: Theological Implications of the Tawqif-Istilah Antithesis and the Majaz Controversy—Part I." *Journal of Qur'anic Studies* 1, no. 1 (1999): 27–46.

Smoor, P. "al-Ma'arri." In *Encyclopaedia of Islam*, 2nd ed., vol. 5, ed. C. E. Bosworth et al., 927–35. Leiden: Brill, 1986.

Steigerwald, Diane. "Twelver Shi'i Ta'wil." In *The Blackwell Companion to the Qur'an*, ed. Andrew Rippin, 373–85. Malden, Mass: Blackwell Publishing, 2006.

Stellardi, Giuseppe. *Heidegger and Derrida on Philosophy and Metaphor: Imperfect Thought*. Amherst, N.Y.: Humanity Books, 2000.

Stern, Alexander. *The Fall of Language: Benjamin and Wittgenstein on Meaning*. Cambridge, Mass.: Harvard University Press, 2019.

Stetkevych, Suzanne Pinckney. "Al-Sharif al-Radi and *Nahj al-balaghah*: Rhetoric, Dispossession, and the Lyric Sensibility." *Journal of Arabic Literature*, no. 3/4 (2019): 211–50.

———. "Al-Sharif al-Radi and the Poetics of 'Alid Legitimacy: Elegy for al-Husayn ibn 'Ali on 'Ashura', 391 A.H." In *Arabic Literary Thresholds: Sites of Rhetorical Turn in Contemporary Scholarship*, ed. Muhsin Jasim Musawi and Jaroslav Stetkevych, 53–84. Leiden: Brill, 2009.

Stewart, Devin. *Islamic Legal Orthodoxy: Twelver Shiite Responses to the Sunni Legal System*. Salt Lake City: University of Utah Press, 1998.

Subtelny, M. E. "Kashifi, Kamal Al-Din Hosayn Wa'ez." In *Encyclopaedia Iranica*, vol. 15, ed. Ehsan Yarshater, 658–61. New York: Bibliotheca Persica Press, 2011.

Sugirtharajah, R. S. *Exploring Postcolonial Biblical Criticism: History, Method, Practice*. Chichester: Wiley-Blackwell, 2012.

———. *Postcolonial Criticism and Biblical Interpretation*. Oxford: Oxford University Press, 2002.

Suleiman, Yasir. *The Arabic Grammatical Tradition: A Study in Ta'lil*. Edinburgh: Edinburgh University Press, 1999.

Swinburne, Richard. *Revelation: from Metaphor to Analogy*. 2nd ed. Oxford: Clarendon, 2007.

Syamsuddin Sahiron. "*Muhkam* and *Mutashabih*: An Analytical Study of Al-Tabari's and Al-Zamakhshari's Interpretations of Q.3:7." *Journal of Qur'anic Studies* 1, no. 1 (1999): 63–79.

Tabari, Abu Ja'far Muhammad ibn Jarir, and George Saliba. *The History of al-Tabari -Ta'rikh Al-rusul Wa al-muluk. Vol. 35: The Crisis of the Abbasid Caliphate*. Albany: State University of New York Press, 1985.

Tabatabai, Muhammad Husayn. *The Qur'an in Islam: Its Impact and Influence on the Life of Muslims*. Karachi: Zahra Publishing, 1987.

————. *Shiʿite Islam*. Albany: State University of New York Press, 1975.

Taylor, Charles. *The Language Animal: The Full Shape of the Human Linguistic Capacity*. Cambridge, Mass.: Harvard University Press, 2016.

Tehrani, Agha Buzurg. *Bibliography of Shiʿiteʾs Literary Works*. Tehran: Al-Dhariʾa Ila Tasanif Al-Shiʿa, 1960.

Tolan, John Victor. *Saint Francis and the Sultan: The Curious History of a Christian-Muslim Encounter*. Oxford: Oxford University Press, 2009.

Toorawa, Shawkat M. *Ibn Abi Tahir Tayfur and Arabic Writerly Culture: A Ninth-Century Bookman in Baghdad*. London: Routledge Curzon, 2005.

Tottoli, Roberto. "ʿImran." In *Encyclopedia of the Qurʾan*, vol. 2, ed. Jane McAuliffe, 509. Leiden: Brill, 2001.

Thaver, Tehseen. "Encountering Ambiguity: Muʿtazili and Twelver Shiʿi Approaches to the Qurʾanʾs Ambiguous Verses." *Journal of Qurʾanic Studies* 18, no. 3 (2016): 91–115.

————. "Twelver Shiʿi Tafsir." Oxford Bibliographies. https://www.oxfordbibliographies .com/display/document/obo-9780195390155/obo-9780195390155-0144.xml.

Van Ess, J. "Abu ʿAbd Allah al-Basri." In *Encyclopaedia of Islam*, 2nd ed., vol. 12, ed. P. J. Bearman et al., 12–14. Leiden: Brill, 2004.

Versteegh, C. H. M. *Arabic Grammar and Qurʾanic Exegesis in Early Islam*. Leiden: E. J. Brill, 1993.

————. *The Explanation of Linguistic Causes: Al-Zajjajiʾs Theory of Grammar: Introduction, Translation, Commentary*. Amsterdam: John Benjamins BV, 1995.

Vishanoff, David R. *The Formation of Islamic Hermeneutics: How Sunni Legal Theorists Imagined a Revealed Law*. New Haven, Conn.: American Oriental Society, 2011.

Viswanathan, Gauri. *Outside the Fold: Conversion, Modernity, and Belief*. Princeton, N.J.: Princeton University Press, 1998.

Waldman, Marilyn Robinson. *Toward a Theory of Historical Narrative: A Case Study in Perso-Islamicate Historiography*. Columbus: Ohio State University Press, 1980.

Wansbrough, John E. "Majaz Al-Qurʾan": Periphrastic Exegesis." In *Bulletin of the School of Oriental and African Studies* 33, no. 2 (1970): 247–66.

————. *Quranic Studies: Sources and Methods of Scriptural Interpretation*. Oxford: Oxford University Press, 1977.

Warner, George. *The Words of the Imams: al-Shaykh al-Saduq and the Development of Twelver Shiʿi Hadith Literature*. London: I. B. Tauris, 2022.

Weil, Gotthold. "Zum Verständnis der Methode der moslemischen Grammatiker." In *Festschrift E. Sachau gewidmet* (1915): 380–92.

Weiss, Bernard. "Medieval Muslim Discussions of the Origin of Language." *Zeitschrift der Deutschen Morgenländischen Gesellschaft* 124 (1974): 33–41.

————. "Wadʿ al-Lugha." In *Encyclopaedia of Islam*, 2nd ed., vol. 11, ed. P. J. Bearman et al., 7. Leiden: Brill, 2002.

Wensinck, A. J., "ʿAmr." In *Encyclopaedia of Islam*, 1st. ed. (1913–1936), ed. M. Th. Houtsma et al., 334–35. Leiden: Brill, 1987.

White, Hayden V. *The Content of the Form: Narrative Discourse and Historical Representation*. Baltimore: Johns Hopkins University Press, 1987.

Wimbush, Vincent L., ed. *Theorizing Scriptures: New Critical Orientations to a Cultural Phenomenon*. New Brunswick, N.J.: Rutgers University Press, 2008.

Yücesoy, Hayrettin. *Messianic Beliefs and Imperial Politics in Medieval Islam: The 'Abbasid Caliphate in the Early Ninth Century*. Columbia: University of South Carolina Press, 2009.

Zadeh, Travis E. "'Fire Cannot Harm It': Mediation, Temptation and the Charismatic Power of the Qur'an." *Journal of Qur'anic Studies* 10, no. 2 (2008): 50–72.

———. *The Vernacular Qur'an: Translation and the Rise of Persian Exegesis*. Oxford: Oxford University Press, 2012.

———. "The Wiles of Creation: Philosophy, Fiction, and the 'Aja'ib Tradition." *Middle Eastern Literatures* 13, no. 1 (2010): 21–48.

Zysow, Aron. *The Economy of Certainty: An Introduction to the Typology of Islamic Legal Theory*. PhD diss., Harvard University, 1984.

INDEX

'Abbad ibn Sulayman, 152

'Abbasids: and Buyids, 50–51, 54; and political careers of al-Radi and his family, 23–24; al-Radi's argument for 'Alid authority over, 65; al-Radi's poetic denouncement of caliphs, 24–29, 61, 71, 206

'Abd al-Jabbar, Abu al-Hasan: on acquired knowledge, 149–50, 161; as al-Radi's teacher, 22, 184; cited in al-Radi's *Haqa'iq*, 110, 124–25, 131, 184, 198–99, 209–10, 217; on divine punishments, 124–25; on *majaz*, 78, 79; on principle of clarity, 87–88; Qur'an commentary, 185, 188–98, 201, 208–11, 215–19, 229; theory of language, 149–51, 153, 155–56, 157, 161; on verses with multiple meanings, 110; view of Qur'anic ambiguity, 87–88, 193–94, 196

Abraham, 113, 135, 243n78

Abu Ahmad al-Musawi: companion of al-Sabi, 62; imprisonment, 24, 54, 245n38; lineage, 31; political career, 23–24, 27, 29, 34, 54, 64; al-Radi's biography of, 35

Abu Hanifa, 123

Abu Muslim ibn Bahr, 214

Abu Tammam, 36, 38

Abu 'Ubayd al-Qasim ibn Sallam, 75–76

Abu 'Ubayda, 75, 77–78, 248n26

acquired knowledge, 149–50, 161

Adam, 155, 243n78, 261n13

'Adud al-Dawla, 24, 245n38

al-'Adwani, Dhu al-'Asba' Hurthan, 122

al-Akhfash, Abu al-Hasan, 163

'Ali ibn Abi Talib: accounts of battles, 20–21; linguistic traditions associated with, 36; al-Radi's biography of, 35; in readings of the *mubahala* verse, 116–19, 121, 122, 126; sayings collected in *Nahj al-Balagha*, 61, 63; al-Shaykh al-Mufid's biography of, 35–36, 117–18; usurpation of power from, 21–22

'Ali al-Rida, 121

'Alids: arguments for 'Alid authority, 60–61, 62, 65, 72, 245n43, 259n52; and the *mubahala*, 116; al-Radi's identification with, 22, 25–29, 37–38, 61, 206; al-Radi's position in Baghdad's 'Alid community, 23–24, 25, 28, 29, 87, 227; in tenth-century Baghdad, 23, 26, 52, 62

ambiguity: 'Abd al-Jabbar's view of, 87–88, 193–94; central to al-Radi's hermeneutic, 8–10, 67–69; *A Culture of Ambiguity* (Thomas Bauer), 105; epistemological purpose of, in the Qur'an, 87, 158, 159–65; evokes wonder, 12–13, 228–29; language as site of, for al-Radi, 186–87, 193–94; and *muhkam/mutashabih* interpretive dynamic, 79, 86, 87–89, 92–98, 103–4, 131–37; and polysemy, 83–87; and principle of clarity, 87–89; theological significance of, 99; and "transgressive" use of language, 74, 77–78, 87–88, 98; al-Turaythithi's view of, 187; types of, in *Haqa'iq*, 106. See also *mutashabihat* (ambiguous verses)

ACKNOWLEDGMENTS

In the course of completing this book, I have accumulated the debt of several esteemed colleagues and mentors. Foremost among them I would like to thank Carl Ernst, whose generous and always helpful comments pushed me—always just enough—to be more thoughtful in framing my questions and in thinking about and with my actors. His sound advice that the stakes of the project—for Islamic and religious studies—always be categorically stated has been invaluable for shaping how this book is written. My dear friend Omid Safi has been by my side to support, guide, and celebrate each step of this project and made every part of this intellectual journey more meaningful. Anna Bigelow nurtured and nourished my effort to read and think broadly in framing and executing this project. I could not have asked for a more brilliant interlocutor for such conversations. Randall Styers's and Julianne Hammer's insights on an early iteration of this book were profoundly helpful for developing its specific themes. Many thanks as well to the two anonymous reviewers of the University of Pennsylvania Press for their astute and very productive feedback and critiques.

I want to register my gratitude to the Department of Religion at Princeton University for generously supporting a workshop on the manuscript. Qasim Zaman's elegant and brilliant questions and interventions, Shaun Marmon's sharp observations and queries, and Suzanne Stetkevych's carefully crafted remarks were critical in sharpening the contours of this book. In addition to his feedback on this book, Qasim Zaman has served as a generous mentor and a true pillar of support. I am also much grateful to Shaun Marmon for her capacious intellectual collegiality beyond this project. In addition to Qasim and Shaun, I am indebted to each one of my colleagues at Princeton (in the Department of Religion and beyond) and previously at Bard College and Lehigh University. I must especially mention Judith Weisenfeld and Leora Batnitzky, who as chairs of the Princeton Department of Religion prioritized my research and made possible the timely completion of this book. I am also grateful to Kerry Smith, Mary-Kay Bodnar, Florian Fues, and Jeffrey

Guest for always making time to help with the administrative details and for making 1879 Hall such a pleasurable place to work.

Over the years I have had the opportunity to present various parts of this book at multiple venues, including the Berlin ZfL Center for Literature and Culture; the Research Institute of Culture, Art, and Communications in Tehran; the American University of Beirut; the American Academy of Religion meetings; the Middle East Studies Association meetings; the Hartford Seminary; and Princeton University. I am thankful to all organizers, discussants, and audience members at these venues. In writing this book, I have especially benefited from conversations with and comments from (in no order) Walid Saleh, Devin Stewart, Mohammad Rustom, Cyrus Zargar, Maurice Pomerantz, Nargis Virani, Kristin Zahra Sands, Alex Caeiro, Omar Ali-de-Unzaga, Rob Rozehnal, Khurram Hussain, Matthew Melvin Koushki, Lara Harb, Ebrahim Moosa, Hamed Fayezi, Mohsen Kadivar, Ghasem Kakaei, Sarab Rahmouni, and Annette Aronowicz. This project was supported by the pretenure sabbatical research leave at Princeton University, the American Academy of Religion Collaborative International Research Grant, the Bard College Research Fund, and the Lehigh University Mellon Postdoctoral Fellowship.

Parts of this book have appeared n previous publications. Specifically, sections of Chapters 4 and 6 appeared in the *Journal of Royal Asiatic Society* and the *Journal of Qur'anic Studies*. I thank the original publishers for their permission to use that material here. The editorial team at the University of Pennsylvania Press has been an absolute pleasure to work with at every step. Elisabeth Maselli has been a keen supporter of this project from the outset. I consider it my good fortune to have worked with her to publish this book and to have benefited from her astute and timely input throughout. I am also extremely thankful to Jeremy Lane, who was outstanding in his copyediting help, and Jon Dertien and Noreen O'Connor for their excellent guidance during the book's editing and production. My sincere thanks also to Erika Zabinsky, for her thorough and carefully detailed work in preparing the book's index. Farah Mohammad generously shared her stunning print for the book's cover, thus allowing her work to sit in the company of mine; for this I am deeply grateful. I am also indebted to the staff of Firestone Library at Princeton University, the British Library in London, and the Ganj Bakhsh Library in Islamabad, where research for this project was conducted.

Support comes in many forms. I would be remiss not to mention the warmth and care provided by the people inhabiting the many spaces in which I researched and wrote this book, namely for the many cups of chai, homemade food, and deep discussion that sustained me in Karachi, at the Bawa Muhayuddin Fellowship in Philadelphia, and at multiple research sites in Iran and the United Kingdom. I have been blessed with the company and support of numerous friends, family, and mentors in the multiple cities that have been "home" for me while working on this project. I owe them all a sincere thanks: Ismat and Atteqa apa, Fazilat, Kiran, Shama, Maheen, Zainab Khala, Mrs. Rizvi, Dr. G., Shobhana, Fareeha, Betsy, Isra, Gabriel, Seth, Canguzel, Shehryar, Mustafa, Subuhi, Mehnaz, Najeeba, Erum, Irum, Naveed, Seema, Maya, and Arifa.

A special thanks to SherAli Tareen, whose clarity of thought is a gift to all who know him; his comments on the manuscript significantly refined its arguments. Special thanks also go to Ajab Khan Tareen, supplier of much joy, wonder, and perplexity during the book's final stages.